Social Research Methods

Third Edition

David Dooley
*University of California
at Irvine*

Prentice Hall
Englewood Cliffs, New Jersey 07632

Library of Congress Cataloging-in-Publication Data

Dooley, David.
    Social research methods / David Dooley — 3rd ed.
        p.   cm.
    Includes bibliographical references (p.   ) and index.
    ISBN 0-13-126161-4
    1. Sociology—Research—Methodology. 2. Social sciences-
-Research—Methodology. I. Title.
HM48.D66 1995
300′.1—dc20   94-6044
                                      CIP

Production supervision
  and interior design: Keith Faivre
Acquisitions editors: Heidi Freund/Pete Janzow
Manufacturing buyer: Tricia Kenny
Cover design: Pat Woczyk

Printed in the United States of America
10 9 8 7 6 5 4 3 2

ISBN 0-13-126161-4

Prentice-Hall International (UK) Limited, *London*
Prentice-Hall of Australia Pty. Limited, *Sydney*
Prentice-Hall Canada Inc., *Toronto*
Prentice-Hall Hispanoamericana, S.A., *Mexico*
Prentice-Hall of India Private Limited, *New Delhi*
Prentice-Hall of Japan, Inc., *Tokyo*
Simon & Schuster Asia Pte. Ltd., *Singapore*
Editora Prentice-Hall do Brasil, Ltda., *Rio de Janeiro*

Table of Contents

Preface to the Third Edition

This text introduces social research methods. Although the chapter structure remains intact, this edition represents a major revision.

Rewritten to make the text easier to read without loss of substance. The standard measures of reading ease reflect average word length in syllables and average sentence length in words. On such measures, all chapters have improved readability, dropping on average more than one full grade level. This revision greatly shifted sentence construction from passive (33% passive sentences, second edition) to active voice (5%, this edition).

New material to keep the text current. The third edition has over 100 new citations, an average of about 7 per chapter. The basic tenets of research design and analysis have not changed since the last edition, but changes have occurred in such areas as ethics. For example, new statements of ethical principles have come from several professional associations. The federal government has become much more active in its oversight of research misconduct with its creation of the Office of Research Integrity. Some topics thought settled have resurfaced. For example, many texts, including earlier editions of this one, report that Cyril Burt faked his data. Recent biographies of Burt have challenged this view and require a new look at this scandal.

More examples to make the text clearer and more interesting. A methods text can all too easily read like a dry list of do's and don't's. Anecdotes can teach such principles better by avoiding the vagueness and generality of rule statements. Specific cases of research violations can make the principles clearer and more concrete. Stories about real researchers and subjects can make the material more personal and engaging. Topical or vivid examples can help make the principles more memorable. For example, I could write "Subject every research finding to rigorous criticism by yourself and others before making any claim of discovery." Or I could summarize the parable of cold fusion as detailed by Gary Taubes in his book *Bad Science* (1993). In this fascinating account, we learn about Pons and Fleischmann, two chemists who destroyed their good reputations by claiming test tube nuclear reactions. We learn how these two scientists called a press conference before they had submitted their findings to external review and how their mistaken claim led the scientific community to spend almost $100 million to disconfirm it. Anyone who has read this story will almost certainly think twice before rushing to stake a doubtful scientific claim.

None of these changes affect two core themes of this text. First, the approach remains interdisciplinary in that it introduces and respects a wide array of methods. Great social problems and knotty theoretical questions do not care about disciplinary boundaries, and serious social researchers should have access to all research methods. Second, the concept of validity organizes and integrates these diverse research methods—whether how to measure a construct, design an experiment, make a statistical inference, or generalize findings to other populations.

I owe a debt of gratitude to all of those who helped with the earlier editions, to my undergraduate students and graduate teaching assistants who keep trying to teach me how to teach, and to the following reviewers who gave constructive feedback on the second edition: James R. Haines, Indiana University at South Bend, and Steve A. Nida, Franklin University.

Partial listing of new or updated material by chapter:

Chapter 1. New introduction based on the debate about Needleman's work on effect of lead on IQ, illustrating the impact and conflict of social research.

Chapter 2. Updated ethical principles from three organizations and recent revision of the Cyril Burt story.

Chapter 3. New material on purposes of journals and on research writing style.

Chapter 4. New illustration of theory with a new diagram distinguishing constructs from operationalizations.

Chapter 5. New material on measuring reliability by kappa coefficient illustrated with new tables.

Chapter 6. Shifted material on scaling from Chapter 7 to consolidate with discussion of measures; recent measures such as MMPI-2 and PET.

Chapter 7. More on the Literary Digest Poll; illustrations of bias in telephone surveys (from answering machines) and in personal surveys (from item phrasing).

Chapter 8. New material on power and design sensitivity.

Chapter 9. New illustrations of experimental designs including effect of stress on people intentionally exposed to common cold.

Chapter 10. More material on the placebo effect; how pretesting (for HIV) can modify the effects of an intervention (AIDS education).

Chapter 11. New perspectives on evaluations of Head Start with substantially reduced wordage.

Chapter 12. New examples of inferential problems with correlational designs and a new figure summarizing the variety of causal links.

Chapter 13. Added material on qualitative methods and the ethics of unobtrusive research illustrated by Humphrey's *Tearoom Trade*.

Chapter 14. Expanded coverage of meta-analytic review. Retains overview of design types of by validity types.

Chapter 15. Updated material on evaluation methods and use of evaluations to influence law and social policy but in fewer words.

1

The Logic of Social Research
Ruling Out Rival Hypotheses

SCIENCE AS SYSTEMATIC DOUBTING

Skepticism and Integrity

Lead and Intelligence.   Health alerts about lead in drinking water and its threat to children have appeared with rising urgency. In 1991, the U.S. Centers for Disease Control (CDC) reduced the intervention level for lead exposure to 25 micrograms per deciliter of blood (µg/dl), the third such reduction since 1970. This action resulted from research connecting blood levels of as little as 10 µg/dl to intelligence deficits in children. Based in part on the same research, the Environmental Protection Agency (EPA) in 1991 adopted new rules for lead levels in community water systems. Dr. Herbert Needleman, one of the leading scholars in this field, has received much of the credit for raising concern about lead in the environment ("Is there lead in your water?", 1993). For example, he found lower IQ scores in children with higher levels of lead as measured from their baby teeth (Needleman, Gunnoe, Leviton, Reed, Peresie, Maher, & Barrett, 1979).

In the same year that the CDC and EPA were basing policy in part on Needleman's work, a third federal agency, the National Institutes of Health (NIH), received complaints about his work. By April 1992, Needleman faced an open hearing on charges that he had engaged in scientific misconduct in the 1979 study. Dr. Clare Ernhart and Dr. Sandra Scarr had raised doubts about his conduct and report of that earlier research. They testified against him as part of his university's inquiry, an inquiry by the Office of Scientific Integrity of NIH (Ernhart, Scarr, & Geneson, 1993). This episode teaches some important lessons about social research.

The Needleman Case.   The story begins in 1975 when Needleman's team began collecting baby teeth from 3329 first- and second-grade children and then measuring the lead content of these teeth. While trying to identify children with high and low lead levels, the team collected intelligence measures from 270 of the subjects most likely to be high or low in lead content. However, the researchers excluded some of those tested and compared just 58 children with high-lead levels with 100 children with low levels in the paper published in 1979. Needleman went on to conduct other studies that pointed to lead's adverse effects on human intelligence. Recognized as an expert and concerned about protecting children against the dangers of lead, he had a major impact on public policy.

In 1990, the Department of Justice asked Needleman to assist in a suit brought under the Superfund Act. Superfund bills the cost of cleaning up toxic waste to those who caused the pollution, and it often has to wage legal battles to extract these payments. In this case, the Justice Department wanted to force the cleanup of lead tailings from a mine in Midvale, Utah. The defense hired Ernhart and Scarr as witnesses. Knowing that Needleman's testimony for the government would rely in part on his 1979 study, Ernhart and Scarr sought access to his original data. To prepare for the trial, they spent two days in his lab checking his work. Before the trial could begin, the litigants settled the case with $63 million obtained for cleaning up the mine site.

Ernhart and Scarr's brief view of Needleman's data raised questions about his 1979 report. They wrote a complaint to the NIH Office of Scientific Integrity (OSI, since renamed the Office of Research Integrity or ORI and moved to the Public Health Service). Of their several concerns, one had to do with the way Needleman chose only some of the tested children for analysis. They suspected that he picked just the subjects whose pattern of lead levels and IQ scores fit his belief. The OSI instructed the University of Pittsburgh, Needleman's home institution, to explore the charges in October 1991.

The resulting hearings took on the bitterness of a legal trial complete with published rebuttals and charges about selfish motives. Needleman likened the hearing to witch trials (1992). He cast Ernhart and Scarr as paid defenders of a lead industry that wanted to protect its profits by casting doubt on his work (1993a, 1993b). For their part, his critics denied serving the lead industry and told of the human and professional costs of serving as honest whistle-blowers (Ernhart et al., 1993; Scarr & Ernhart, 1993).

This Pittsburgh inquiry resulted in a final report in May 1992 (Needleman Hearing Board, 1992). This report absolved Needleman of scientific misconduct, finding no evidence that he intentionally biased his data or methods. However, the hearing board did find that "Needleman deliberately misrepresented his procedures" in the 1979 study (Taylor, 1992, p. 44). The report said that "misrepresentations may have been done to make. . .the procedures appear more rigorous than they were, perhaps to ensure publication" (Taylor, 1992, p. 44). The hearing board judged that this behavior did not fit the definitions of misconduct that focus on faking data and plagiarism. But others wondered why such misreporting did not fall within another rule that forbids serious deviations from commonly accepted research practices.

The Moral of the Story.   Researchers often disagree about results, but they seldom take such differences before hearing boards. More often, the scientists argue with each other in published articles and let other researchers decide for themselves. Sometimes, a scholar will share the challenged data with critics for additional analysis, perhaps even working with them to produce a joint finding. In Needleman's case, the scientists had a history of distrust based on their conflict as expert witnesses in civil trials about lead exposure and toxic waste cleanup. Because the 1979 study had become a weapon in these disputes, the researchers chose not to work together to resolve their differences. Instead one side turned to the research integrity office of the government, which in turn handed the problem to a university. Charged with fighting research fraud, these offices had little experience with a case bordering on method differences. The procedures of this case pleased neither side. Needleman sued the federal government and the University of Pittsburgh, charging that they had denied him due process. Scarr and Ernhart hoped additional information would lead to a more severe judgment on later review. Whatever the final outcome of this dispute, we can draw some important conclusions from it.

First, social researchers can address very important matters. In this case the stakes involved the mental health of the nation's children, the economic well-being of a major industry, crucial federal policies on the environment, lawsuits for monetary damages, and the reputations of prominent scholars.

Second, this case shows how science works through the adversarial process. Researchers should doubt their own findings and those of other scholars. As consumers of research, we should not believe everything we read. Instead, we should assume a doubtful posture in the face of research claims. We call this posture **skepticism**. This term does not mean unyielding disbelief but rather the habit of checking the evidence. Skepticism requires us to distinguish poor research, unworthy of our belief, from good research, which deserves at least provisional acceptance. The dispute about Needleman's findings, although unusual in its form, represents a normal and accepted approach to getting at the truth. This episode highlights the importance of research methods as the focus for scientific debate and as the content of this text.

Third, this dispute forces us to view our research practice as an ethical duty. Scientific **integrity** consists of

> a kind of utter honesty—a kind of leaning over backwards. For example, if you're doing an experiment, you should report everything that you think might make it invalid—not only what you think is right about it. . . . You must do the best you can—if you know anything at all wrong, or possibly wrong—to explain it. If you make a theory, for example, and advertise it, or put it out, then you must also put down all the facts that disagree with it, as well as those that agree with it. (Feynman, 1985, p. 341, adapted from his commencement address at the California Institute of Technology in 1974).

This view of integrity challenges us to help our worst critics attack our most cherished conclusions. We will need a detachment from our theories if we are to value the credibility of our results more than victory in our disputes.

Finally, does lead affect IQ? Improved analyses of Needleman's original data gave evidence in support of his lead–IQ link that was even stronger than that reported in his 1979 article (Taylor, 1992, citing the Needleman Hearing Board's Final Report, 1992). However, these results come from only one small sample, and other research findings have given mixed results. The current EPA and CDC positions agree with Needleman's conclusion, but they could change should new data appear.

How Do We Come to Know?

Assertion, Authority, and Evidence.   Social research produces claims about causation for example, that *A* causes *B*. However, some causal claims appear without evidence. Anyone can assert a causal relation, but we need not accept it without support. If the causal claim has no evidence, why should anyone believe it or prefer it to a rival view that has support?

Sometimes claims draw their support not from evidence but rather from the authority, expertise, or rank of the source. If the authority refers to evidence, we expect to see the data in order to make our own judgment. We often hear assertions that some new treatment can cure a terrible disorder such as schizophrenia, cancer, or heroin addiction. Perhaps a few patients testify to the success of the new cure. Recruiting desperate, paying clients with the promise of a miracle drug may motivate such claims. However, neither the fame nor the academic degree of the source will substitute for evidence.

Some authorities base their assertions entirely on faith with no claims to scientific foundation. Clashes between claims based on faith and those based on evidence have made for some dramatic moments. One of the most famous came to a head in Galileo's heresy trial. The Copernican model of the solar system held that the earth moved around the sun rather than the sun around the earth. In 1616 a church court condemned this view as being contrary to the Bible. In 1632 Galileo published his *Dialogue on the Two Principal World Systems*, which seemed to favor the Copernican view. The Inquisition summoned him to Rome for trial in 1633, forced him to recant, and prohibited his book. He remained under house arrest for the last eight years of his life (Hummel, 1986).

Contrary to the popular view, this trial did not derive from a simple conflict of science versus religion. The matter involved complex personal jealousies and power struggles. Redondi (1983/1987) even suggests that Galileo's trial stemmed from theological disputes other than his support of Copernicanism.

Although we may never know the full story of the trial, Galileo gave an eloquent defense of science: "I do not feel obliged to believe that the same God who has endowed us with sense, reason, and intellect has intended us to forgo their use" (quoted by Durant & Durant, 1961, p. 607). The centuries have vindicated Galileo. In 1757 the Church took books teaching the mobility of the earth off the Index of Prohibited Books. In 1979, Pope John Paul II called for a reexamination of the Galileo case. Thirteen years later, the Church found him not guilty (Montalbano, 1992). The Vatican has published its secret archives on the Galileo case and admitted that the judges were wrong (Poupard, 1983).

One irony of this episode is that Galileo had many friends in the Church (including the Pope). They advised him not to claim proof for his theory in order to avoid confronting the Church. As it turned out, Galileo should not have claimed that his theory was proved since he had made some mistakes (for example, in his theory of tides). This episode shows that assertions based on good evidence prevail over those based on authority and, in their turn, yield to better ones based on better evidence. In the long run, the more truthful and useful explanation should emerge from this competition between rival ideas.

Philosophy of Science.   Our skepticism about social research goes beyond rare cases of data fraud or common disputes about methods. Philosophers of knowledge have long wondered how and even whether we can know about our world. The phrase "know about our world" implies that certain "facts" exist that we can learn. Science pursues these facts by **empirical** methods, that is, methods based on experience of the world. But philosophers disagree about how far we can trust our observations (for more on this debate, see Guba, 1990; Hughes, 1990; Little, 1991; Roth, 1987).

In the social sciences, empiricism sometimes goes by the name **positivism**. Positivism rejects speculation and instead emphasizes *positive* facts. In this regard, social science shares a unity of method with the natural sciences. That is, we can test theories by seeing how well they fit the facts that we observe. Although no consensus has formed around an alternate view, traditional positivism has many critics.

What we usually mean by the notion of observation is that we feel sensations within us that we attribute to external causes. When I say "I see a tree," I really mean that I have an inner visual sensation consistent with what I have learned is called a tree. But how can you or I be sure that a tree really exists? Perhaps I am hallucinating and my inner sensations come not from a tree at all but rather some malfunction of my nervous system. We "know" the world only indirectly: "We do not actually see physical objects, any more than we hear electromagnetic waves when we listen to the wireless" (Russell, 1948, p. 311). In short, the positive data that we had hoped to anchor our theories seem like constructions. Our scientific facts resemble collective judgments subject to disagreement and revision.

To speak of facts suggests that we can say what does or does not exist in the world. The branch of philosophy called **ontology** deals with this problem of the ultimate nature of things. Do external things really exist out there to serve as sources of our sensations? Belief that there are such real sources is called **realism**. We cannot demonstrate realism. We can never prove the reality of an external source with suspect perceptions. Most scientists and laypeople act and talk most of the time as though they believed in realism. Nevertheless, some philosphers have argued for another view called *fictionalism* or *instrumentalism*. This latter view regards the supposed external sources of our perceptions as fictions dependent on our observing instruments.

Supposing that real facts exist, we still have the problem of showing how we know them. The term **epistemology** applies to this concern with the relation between knower and known. Claiming that you know something implies that you can defend the methods by which you got your knowledge. The ever present rival to your claim is that you have misperceived.

Selective Perceptions.   Much evidence suggests that our observations are selective and subject to error. According to Thomas Kuhn (1970), normal science consists in solving puzzles within a framework of widely accepted beliefs, values, assumptions, and techniques. Scientists working on a problem share certain basic assumptions and research tools that shape their observation of reality. Kuhn called this shared framework a **paradigm** and considered it a lens through which we see the world.

Whole generations of researchers may engage in normal science within a paradigm before enough conflicting data force a **paradigm shift**. Such paradigm shifts or revolutions occur when existing theories can no longer adjust to handle discrepant findings. Paradigm shifts resemble gestalt perceptual shifts. Kuhn illustrates this by a psychology experiment in which subjects viewed cards from a deck. This deck had some peculiar cards, such as black hearts and red spades, but the subjects were not told about them in advance. Most subjects needed repeated viewings before noticing these odd cards. Seemingly, the subjects looked at black hearts and "saw" red hearts because they believed that only red hearts existed. When they grasped the idea that black hearts could exist, it was as though someone threw a switch in their minds. Suddenly they could "see" the cards as they existed rather than as imagined. We need to reflect on the framework in which we think and do research. Would we notice the black hearts and red spades if they appeared in our data?

Another major critique of scientific observation came from Karl Marx who challenged its neutrality and completeness. For Marx, sensation implied an active noticing based on motivation for some action (Russell, 1945). We only perceive a few out of the universe of possible stimuli. We select for attention those that affect our interests and disregard those that do not. Marx thus locates science in the context of politics and economics, driven by the self-interest of the researchers who themselves belong to economic classes.

Can We Discover Causal Laws?

Faith of Science. We face other problems beyond perceiving the world accurately. Positivism holds that the mission of science is to discover the timeless laws governing the world. This notion implies what Bertrand Russell (1948) called the "faith of science" (p. 314). By this phrase he meant that we assume that regularities exist in the connection of events and that these regularities or "laws" have a continuity over time and space. We cannot prove this covering law, but we must believe it if we expect to find stable regularities with our science. The great success of the physical sciences in the past two centuries lends credence to this faith. For example, our lunar astronauts confirmed that physical relationships discovered on earth hold on the moon as well.

However, the overthrow of Newtonian physics by Einstein early in this century shook the confidence in our capacity to discover timeless physical laws (Stove, 1982). Social scientists have long doubted their chances of matching the success of the natural sciences. In the social domain, some scientists reject the existence of objective laws knowable by observation. Rather, these critics hold, our understanding of the world is a social construction dependent on the "historically situated interchanges among people" (Gergen, 1985, p. 267).

Fallibilism. Suppose physical or social events do follow laws independent of the socially constructed perception of them. Philosophers of science warn us that such causal connections will resist discovery. One problem has to do with **induction**, finding an idea among observed events that might explain other, not yet observed events. Hume, writing in the 1700s, made a strong case against such an inductive leap (Stove, 1982). Repeated instances of an observation, no matter how many, cannot guarantee its future repetition. However, most people would say that such repetition does increase the chances of its occurring again. Nevertheless, we must remind ourselves that we run the risk of making inductive mistakes—that is, we are fallible in this regard. **Fallibilism** refers to the posture of suspecting our own inductions.

In sum, the tools of our knowing, both the procedures of measurement and the induction of lawful patterns, come from human experience and risk human error. We can assert a causal connection. But we do so only under warrant of (that is, limited by and no more valid than) our methods for perceiving such relations. This limited and cautious approach to research provides a continuing topic of debate about the philosophical foundations of social science (Gholson & Barker, 1985; Manicas & Secord, 1983).

The Strategy of Research

Theory as Testable Explanation. Social research tries to explain human events. What causes people to abuse their children, to become depressed, to remain homeless, to fail to learn to read and write, to commit crimes? Besides our natural curiosity about how things work, we have a strong practical motive to explain, predict, and shape certain human conditions.

Social research includes a great many activities, each falling in one of three main clusters: tentative explaining, observing, and testing rival views against data. We need all three to do social research. If all we did was imagine different explanations, we would never have a basis for choosing among them. On the other hand, proposing tentative explanations helps make sense out of diverse observations and guides us in making still better observations. Such tentative explanations constitute **theory**.

We can usually think of two or more different theories to explain many events. Collecting data helps us decide which theory best fits reality. In order to help us understand causation, our data must come into contact with theory. For example, we may observe and describe the incidence of death by cholera or suicide. But merely counting and sorting deaths, what we call **descriptive** research, does not explain them.

However, observing with a theory in mind becomes **causal** research by joining a cause to an effect. For example, John Snow suspected that fouled water caused cholera. In the period from 1848 to 1854, he linked the different rates of cholera deaths to the different companies supplying London houses with water (Lilienfeld, 1976, pp. 24–25). In the same way, Emile Durkheim linked changes over time in the rate of suicide with changing economic conditions (Durkheim, 1897/1951). These men could have looked at an enormous number of social and physical factors as possible causes of death. Their theories helped them to narrow their focus to water supply and economic conditions.

In the last step of the research cycle we compare our causal idea with our observations. Does our theory fit? Does another theory fit better? Science consists of seeing whether data confirm or disconfirm our explanations. Popper (1987) argued that we should not simply look for confirmations. Rather, he said, any "genuine test of a theory is an attempt to falsify it, or refute it. Testability is **falsifiability**" (p. 141). As an example of **pseudoscience**, he offered astrology "with its stupendous mass of empirical evidence based on observation—on horoscopes and on biographies" (p. 139) but without the quality of refutability.

Rules of Evidence.   In order to judge our theory's fit, we rely on standard decision rules. Our research reports make public both theories and data, so that anyone can look over our shoulder and second-guess us using these same guidelines. Researchers usually demand that we meet three criteria before claiming a causal link: (1) **covariation**; (2) cause prior to effect; and (3) absence of **plausible rival hypothesis** or explanation.

The first criterion seems simple enough. If *A* causes *B*, they should move together or co-vary. If polluted water causes cholera, we expect to find more cholera cases in houses supplied with bad water and fewer cases in ones with pure water. If rapidly changing economic conditions cause suicide, we should count more suicides in changing economic times and fewer in stable ones. Knowing that two things do not co-vary, on the other hand, casts doubt on the theory that they have a causal link. However, association alone does not tell us the type of causal link between *A* and *B*.

The philosopher Hume warned us of our habit of mind that tends to see causation in the association of events. When two events coincide again and again, we come to expect one when we notice the other. We often wrongly treat this "prediction" as "causation." However, we must separate these two notions in our minds. Russell (1948) illustrates this problem with the story of "Geulinex's two clocks." These perfect timepieces always move together such that when one points to the hour, the other chimes. They co-vary and allow us to make good predictions from the hands of one to the chimes of the other. But we would not make a causal claim. No one supposes that one clock causes the other to chime. In fact, a prior event causes both, namely the work of the clock maker. Thus we need more criteria beyond simple association to judge causation.

The second requirement deals only in part with this problem of telling covariation from causation. A cause should precede its effect. Economic change cannot cause suicide if the upturn in suicide rates comes before the change in the economy. Knowing the sequence of events can help us rule out one causal direction. But knowing that two events are correlated and that one comes before the other still does not settle the question. Recall Geulinex's two clocks, and suppose that one clock is set one second before the other so that its chimes always sound before the other. Would we argue that the former clock causes the latter's chimes just because it occurs first? Of course, we would not.

The third rule for causation also deals with the problem of Geulinex's two clocks. It says that we must be able to rule out any rival explanation as not plausible. By plausible we mean reasonable or believable. This test of causation can prove hard to pass. A rival explanation that seems unlikely to one researcher may later appear quite likely to others. Anything that can cause two events to appear linked serves as a plausible rival explanation.

Much of what social researchers do helps guard against such rival explanations. We grade social research largely on its success in ruling out rival explanations. Someone may think of a new and plausible rival years after a study is published. Thus, the social researcher must design studies in ways that minimize, as much as possible, present and future competing explanations. To the extent that a researcher shows covariation and temporal precedence and casts doubt on opposing rationales, we will accept his or her causal claim.

The threat of competing inferences shapes almost every aspect of data collection and research design. Whether as a consumer or producer of social research, you must learn to judge research on the basis of how well it limits and rejects rival interpretations. This text covers the major types of research threats. One threat arises when we collect measures. We cannot claim that A causes B if our measures fail to reflect both A and B (a problem explored in Chapter 5). Another threat has to do with the fact that much of social research comes from samples. We must take care not to claim that a finding holds true for a whole population when it occurs only in a small group drawn from that population (a topic dealt with in Chapter 8). A third problem concerns the many different ways we can design our studies. Designs differ in their control of third variables that might cause A and B to appear linked (the theme of Chapter 9). Finally, we must guard against the temptation to generalize findings to people, places, or times not actually represented in our study (a danger raised in Chapter 10). You must consider not just one of these threats in reading research, but rather remain alert to all of them. For a preview of all of these research hazards, you should scan the first part of Chapter 14.

Because of these threats, social research does not always reach conclusions agreed upon by all. Rather than providing laws of social behavior, it gives evidence for and against preliminary, would-be laws. This evidence requires interpretation. Almost weekly, we hear of results that, if believed, would change our behavior (for example, that lead causes intelligence loss in children) or raise fears in some of us (for example, that left-handers have a shorter life expectancy, Coren & Halpern, 1991). In the same announcements we may also hear that the conclusions could change pending further research, leaving us to decide how much faith to place in the claims.

Constantly weighing the conflicting findings of scientists can prove frustrating. Why is it that researchers cannot decide which scientists have the right answers and settle such debates once and for all? This conflict between opposing researchers becomes most urgent in court cases that rely on the expert testimony of scientists. When such experts give conflicting views, the courts must seek ways to choose the more credible scientist. State and federal courts have sometimes relied on the 1923 Frye rule, which allows "experts into court only if their testimony was founded on theories, methods, and procedures 'generally accepted' as valid among other scientists in the same field" (Huber, 1991, p.14). However, this principle of ignoring "junk science" has come under fire by those plaintiffs whose cases depend on the challenged experts. The Supreme Court took up this question in the case of *Daubert v. Merrell Dow*, which involved claims that the drug Bendectin caused birth defects. Lower courts, following the Frye rule, said that the plaintiff's experts could not give their views because their evidence was not accepted as reliable by most scientists. The Supreme Court, in its decision of June 28, 1993, reversed the lower courts and relaxed this rule. The courts can still screen out unreliable "experts." However, judges must now do so not on the basis of the witnesses' acceptance by other scientists but rather on the quality of their methods. Justice Harry Blackmun wrote that "Proposed testimony must be supported by appropriate validation—i.e. 'good grounds' . . ." (quoted by Houston, 1993, p. A14).

This decision comforts those scientists who distrust a rule that imposes certainty or publicly grades researchers. By freezing the research process at some fixed "truth" or annointing good and bad researchers, we might hinder future Galileos who point to new ways of seeing things. Later research may displace the currently most favored theory, and it will do so more quickly in a climate that tolerates conflicting ideas. Scientists draw the line at fraud and have set up ethical guidelines against making up or falsely reporting data (see Chapter 2). However, they worry about science courts that punish researchers for using improper research methods (as illustrated in the lead and IQ case cited at the beginning of this chapter). Instead, researchers compete in the marketplace of ideas, hoping to earn research support, publications, and promotions by convincing their peers of the excellence of their methods. In this spirit, the Supreme Court's decision in *Daubert* v. *Merrell* trusts judges and juries to sift good from bad science. This text aims to give you the power to judge for yourself the quality of research that will affect your life.

USES OF SOCIAL RESEARCH AND RIVAL EXPLANATIONS

Personal Use of Research

Causal assertions surround us. We hear advice on how to spend money on cars, toothpaste, cigarettes, political candidates, health habits, and a thousand other things based on brief references to data. For example, you may have heard a radio news brief reporting a study of running and heart attacks. Perhaps it claimed that running helps prevent heart attacks because of evidence that marathon runners have a lower than expected rate of heart attacks. Although running may help prevent heart attacks, this evidence does not prove it. Following our rules of evidence, can we think of a plausible rival explanation of these observations?

Assume that marathon runners do have a better record of heart attacks than nonrunners. Maybe marathon runners differ in some other respects from most people. A photo of a group of Olympic marathon runners lined up for the start of their event shows us a relatively young, lean, small-boned group of people. Certainly, we would not mistake a marathon runner for a sumo wrestler. Maybe marathon runners have different body types from birth. Maybe they have stronger hearts or more efficient circulatory systems than nonrunners do. Such physical advantages would help beginning runners succeed initially, thus encouraging them to become devoted long-distance runners. In short, the successful runners may have been selected for their healthy hearts and resistance to heart attack (not to mention their long stride and self-discipline).

The same evidence can support two quite different assertions: (1) Running prevents heart attacks; (2) people resistant to heart attacks become runners. Such dilemmas occur often in sorting out research claims. Frequently, the available evidence suggests one causal assertion but cannot rule out a plausible rival. Thinking of rival explanations can prove very useful in a personal way because we must make so many choices based on evidence. Get in the habit of checking the evidence to see if it permits a plausible rival explanation. If it does, we regard the evidence as weak. For important decisions, you may want to look for more convincing evidence, based on better research methods.

Most of us do not have the time or desire to check all causal claims. Perhaps a wrong decision involving choices about goods, services, or personal behavior has a small cost. For other kinds of choices, the evidence may prove too complicated for us to assess. In these cases, we pay experts to check the research and think about rival explanations for us. We may ask a physician about the safety of a new jogging regime before trying it. We trust that this doctor has been skeptical for us. In the same way, we trust clinical psychologists, educators, criminal justice workers, and other human service professionals to gauge the evidence in their areas of expertise. One characteristic that identifies professionals is their ability to make independent judgments of research reports. If you plan a professional social service or academic career, you will need to learn how to make the sort of evaluations of research evidence treated in this text.

Professional Use of Research

Just as a layperson checks a causal claim by looking for plausible rival explanations, in the same way professionals challenge published research in their areas. Writing to a critical and expert readership, professional researchers design their research to rule out rival explanations. But the best efforts of serious researchers may not prevent alternative ways of explaining their findings. A case of such conflicting interpretations comes from the mental health field.

Of the various mental disorders, schizophrenia poses the gravest challenge. It represents a major drain on the nation's health resources and wrecks havoc in the lives of both patients and their families. Every few years a news release raises our hopes that a researcher has found the chemical key to this disease. Sadly, such claims have always proved premature.

The tale of one of these "breakthroughs" shows how data from professional research can be explained in more than one way. Solomon Snyder (1974) relates the story that began with a theory by two psychiatrists. Osmond and Smythies (1952) argued that some toxic substance produced schizophrenic behavior. They supposed that this chemical occurred naturally in the bodies of schizophrenics but not in the bodies of normal people. They assumed that this unknown toxic substance would resemble chemicals (such as mescaline) known to produce hallucinations in normals. They noted a chemist's findings that adrenaline, which naturally occurs in human bodies, was structurally similar to mescaline. Perhaps some bodily malfunction produces a variant of adrenaline that could, in turn, produce the symptoms of schizophrenia.

This theory gained support from the research of Hoffer, Osmond, and Smythies (1954), who reported two new pieces of evidence. First, they found adrenochrome (a breakdown product of adrenaline) in the blood and urine of schizophrenics but not in most normal people. Second, when adrenochrome was given to normal people, they reported psychedelic experiences like those of people under the influence of LSD. As Snyder says, "It would seem that the millenium of psychiatry had arrived" (1974, p. 56). Adrenochrome appeared to cause schizophrenia. It remained only to find a control for this chemical before hundreds of thousands of schizophrenics could lead normal lives.

As with prior breakthroughs, Hoffer's two crucial findings did not reproduce in other researchers' labs. After many failures of **replication** (that is, an attempt to reproduce the studies with the same results), the search began to find other ways to explain this evidence. Why did Hoffer find more adrenochrome in schizophrenics than in normal people? Adrenaline, when exposed to air, breaks down into adrenochrome. Synder (1974) assumes that Hoffer's samples from schizophrenics and normals started out with the same low levels of adrenochrome. He believes that the schizophrenics' samples were left exposed to air longer before testing because they had to come to the lab from the mental hospital. As a result, they broke down to a greater extent into adrenochrome.

Why did Hoffer find that normal people given adrenochrome reported hallucinations? Snyder explains this observation by **suggestion**. The normal subjects knew that they were receiving a chemical thought to cause hallucinations and, in effect, obeyed this "suggestion." The effect of subject belief on behavior is well known in psychology and requires special controls (discussed in Chapter 10). Figure 1—1 compares the two causal links of the Osmond-Smythies theory with Snyder's rival explanations of Hoffer's findings.

To choose between these two rival theories, we needed more research. Later studies that exposed blood samples from schizophrenics and normals to air for the same

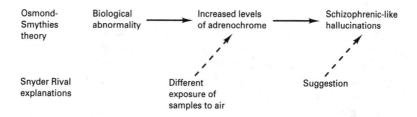

Figure 1

length of time found no adrenochrome differences. When subjects did not know whether they were receiving adrenochrome or some neutral substance, adrenochrome produced no hallucinations.

Although misleading at first, Hoffer's research had the useful effect of advancing the search for the cause of schizophrenia. As Snyder summarizes, "After the adrenochrome fiasco, psychiatrists became disillusioned and immensely skeptical about the drug-induced model psychosis approach to schizophrenia" (1974, p. 57). Researchers rechecked the nature of schizophrenic symptoms and concluded that the psychedelic drugs did not actually produce those symptoms. These findings revealed the psychedelic drug approach to schizophrenia as a dead end, and research resources moved to more promising methods. The search goes on for a new toxic substance or neural defect that might cause schizophrenic symptoms. Improved theories resulted from this episode and are, ironically, our legacy from Hoffer, Osmond, and Smythies.

Political Use of Research

One reward for studying social research will come as greater power to analyze the claims that affect your personal decisions. Moreover, you must learn about research in order to enter certain professions. Besides personal and career reasons, you need to understand social research in order to join fully in the civic process. Increasingly, significant social policy decisions derive from causal claims that depend on research evidence. Judges, members of Congress, and heads of health, education, and environmental agencies are all making decisions based in part on the data supplied by researchers. As a voting citizen, you will cast your ballot best only if you can make your own judgment of the social research that informs policy debates.

A dramatic example of social research affecting policy comes from the Coleman report (Coleman et al., 1966). Coleman and his colleagues surveyed the educational opportunities and achievements of a great many American students. They concluded, among other things, that black students did better in integrated than in racially isolated schools. The Coleman report seemed to support the causal claim that desegregation would help equalize achievement. This evidence became the most frequently cited scientific support for school integration by forced busing.

Jencks and his colleagues (1972) reanalyzed the same data but arrived at a rival explanation for the connection of integration and achievement. Coleman's study compared already integrated blacks with segregated blacks. Opponents of busing could "argue that the high test scores of blacks in naturally integrated schools reflect the greater motivation or resources of black parents who put their children in desegregated schools" (Jencks et al., 1972, p. 99). Thus the Coleman evidence may not apply to new desegregation by public policy. If learning stems more from parental motivation than school integration, busing would have little effect. Jencks found that busing can produce small achievement gains or losses depending on the specific conditions of the integration. He emphasizes how little school conditions affect attainment and how little both school conditions and achievement affect later income levels. Just as we are still searching for the cause of schizophrenia, so we continue to ponder the relationship of education to social justice.

This case shows how both sides of a major political question can cite high-quality research to support their views. You may have to decide at the polls which view you favor, if not on the question of busing, then some other divisive issue. If you have a closed mind on the question, you may find some social scientist with evidence that supports your view. But if you want to support the best possible policy, you must do some work. You will need to know how to judge competing explanations of the data for yourself.

SUMMARY

The battle over the effects of lead on intelligence shows the need for skepticism in using social research. Drawing causal inferences from social research can prove difficult and uncertain. Philosophers of knowledge even dispute the degree to which we can know the real world.

Social research proceeds by raising tentative explanations, making observations, and then seeing how well the proposed ideas fit the data. The claim that A causes B, for example, requires observations showing that (1) A and B co-vary; (2) A occurs before B; and (3) no rival explanation for the A-with-B association remains plausible. The last rule requires that we design research to prevent all possible alternative ways of explaining observed linkages. This text covers the various types of threats to research conclusions.

With these rules, we can assess causal claims in a public way. Assertions based on such evidence have proven more convincing than claims based on faith or authority. Social research can play an important role in making personal, professional, and public decisions. For these reasons, everyone can benefit by learning to read research critically.

EXERCISES

1. Find a newspaper or popular magazine article that claims a causal relationship. Check to see whether the causal link rests on evidence or on authority or faith. Does the evidence show an association of the two variables and that the cause comes before

the effect? Finally, see if you can think of a rival explanation for this association. Repeat this exercise several times until you can do it routinely for any causal claim that you hear (for example, via television or from professors).

2. For a handy collection of causal claims with alternative explanations, see the book *Rival Hypotheses* by Huck and Sandler (1979). Some of their 100 problems rely on common sense and a creative skepticism, and you can probably solve them now. Others assume knowledge of topics that appear in the following chapters. Try your hand at some of the problems now and again later after you have read this text.

KEY TERMS

Causal	**Paradigm**
Covariation	**Paradigm shift**
Descriptive	**Plausible rival hypothesis**
Empirical	**Positivism**
Epistemology	**Pseudoscience**
Fallibilism	**Realism**
Falsifiability	**Replication**
Induction	**Skepticism**
Integrity	**Suggestion**
Ontology	**Theory**

2

Ethics:
Protecting Human Subjects and Research Integrity

RESEARCH VALUES

The research enterprise includes many roles—those of scholar, subject, funder, and society to name just a few. The people who occupy these roles have needs and wants that sometimes converge and sometimes conflict. As a research consumer your curiosity about the way things work may agree with the researcher's desire for discovery. But if you should use the researcher's words as your own without credit, your desire to get a good grade conflicts with the author's copyright on the work. This chapter explores a variety of such value conflicts. The first part concerns the conflict between researchers and their subjects and places it in the context of ethical philosophy. The second reviews various ways of protecting human subjects. The final section takes up a variety of other conflicts that threaten research integrity.

Tuskegee Syphilis Study

On July 25, 1972, a news story by Jean Heller appeared in the *Washington Star*. Although overshadowed by a presidential election campaign, this revelation of the Tuskegee Syphilis Study led to government actions that halted the 40-year–long research study. Thus prompted, a U.S. Senate committee held hearings in 1973 that led in 1981 to guidelines for human research that were sponsored by the Department of Health and Human Services. These new ethical guidelines now govern most social research in the United States (Jones, 1981).

The Beginning.   Penicillin, the present treatment for syphilis, did not become widely available until the 1940s. In 1929, the U.S. Public Health Service and the private Rosenwald Fund jointly supported several demonstration programs for the control of syphilis. The Macon County, Alabama, project, one site in this series of syphilis control programs, ended in 1931. But as this project came to an end, an idea for further monitoring the effects of untreated syphilis emerged.

The Macon County project staff wanted to continue their involvement with this large, unsolved public health problem. They had discovered an incredible 36 percent rate of syphilis, much of it transmitted congenitally (that is, from an infected mother to her fetus), but with little treatment. They justified such extended monitoring with three objectives: (1) to study the untreated course of the disease in black people for comparison with an earlier study of a white population; (2) to raise the consciousness of the public to the problem of syphilis; and (3) to maintain the momentum of public health work in the area by sustaining the cooperative arrangements among state, local, and Tuskegee Institute medical personnel. This study of untreated syphilitics continued year after year into the 1970s. The research consisted of periodic checks of the subjects, including the painful and sometimes dangerous lumbar puncture method for diagnosing neural syphilis.

Prevention of Treatment.   By 1933, the project had studied 412 syphilitics and 204 controls (all black males), and the researchers actively worked to prevent their subjects from receiving treatment. To avoid "contaminating" the study with effective treatment, the researchers gave medicine with helpful but noncurative powers such as aspirin and iron tonic. Families of the subjects received burial stipends in exchange for permission to autopsy the deceased subjects.

A mobile Public Health Service unit came to Macon County in 1939, but a nurse working on both this new service and the research project kept study subjects from receiving treatment. In World War II, the military draft called some of the study's subjects in the registration process. The researchers broke both state and federal laws to keep such subjects from the treatment given to other men diagnosed by draft screening. Even when penicillin became available in several clinics in Macon County in the 1940s, the research team continued the study and their efforts to deny treatment to the subjects. The researchers judged that the penicillin treatment would prove ineffective in the late stages of their subjects' disease. They valued the scientific benefits of studying the elderly subjects more than the possible health benefits of treatment.

Aftermath.   How did the Tuskegee Study continue for four decades? One reason has to do with the powerlessness of the victims—impoverished, diseased blacks in the rural South at the mercy of the local and federal white medical power structures. In exchange for their participation, these subjects received some medicine and more attention in the form of regular medical checkups than they might otherwise have received.

However, reproaching the subjects for their passivity only blames the victims. How can we understand the actions of the researchers and the larger scientific community in condoning this project? These public health workers began as pioneers bringing medical care to a heretofore unattended medical problem. With little incentive other than altruism and scientific curiosity, they showed friendliness and affection in dealing with their subjects. The researchers took pride in their work, regularly published and discussed their findings, and welcomed visiting scholars and interns. Despite this openness, the first complaints about the project from the scientific community did not appear until the mid-1960s. These early complaints came as a surprise to the researchers who either ignored or rejected them as unfounded and ill informed. In retrospect, one must conclude that well-intentioned scholars can have too little objectivity about their own research. Informal peer review from outsiders may prove too little or come too late to prevent human subject abuse.

The 40-year Tuskegee Syphilis Study began as a moral crusade to help the diseased poor and ended as a symbol of research immorality. By 1981, the Public Health Service had still not made a public admission of wrongdoing, but an out-of-court settlement of a civil suit yielded $37,500 to each of the survivors. The study had little scientific value. Despite their efforts, the researchers had kept virtually none of the subjects from getting some treatment. Because of the widespread use of penicillin for infections other than syphilis, most of the syphilitics received this drug over the years. The effort to prevent treatment succeeded only in preventing systematic treatment adequate to care for the subjects. Sadly, the Tuskegee Study has contributed to the modern distrust by blacks of the public health system. This discontent appears in some conspiracy theories about the causes of AIDS. The history of the Tuskegee Syphilis Study seems to validate the worst fears of blacks about the intentions of the medical research establishment (Thomas & Quinn, 1991).

Philosophy and Practice

If the Tuskegee Syphilis Study were unique, we might have less concern about the ethics of human research. Sadly, many cases of such violations in medical (Beecher, 1970) and psychological (Ad Hoc Committee on Ethical Standards of Psychological Research, 1973) research have occurred. The review of human research guidelines, which led to the National Research Act of 1974, stemmed from other major scandals besides the Tuskegee Syphilis Study. In the 1960s, live cancer cells were injected into humans without their informed consent in the Brooklyn Jewish Chronic Disease Hospital. Drug research without subject consent had taken place, also in the 1960s, in the Milledgeville State Hospital in Georgia. Such incidents made it clear that human subjects needed more protection from researchers (Hershey & Miller, 1976).

Ethics. **Ethics** involves the study of right and wrong conduct. This branch of philosophy has produced numerous ethical theories throughout recorded history. For example, Plato held that proper conduct led to harmony. But we observe that the desires of people tend rather to conflict than to harmony. Thus the central ethical question asks how we are to reconcile two or more conflicting preferences.

This dilemma appears in a dialogue from the *Republic* between Socrates and Thrasymachus, in which the latter says that "justice is nothing else than the interest of the stronger" (Plato, quoted by Russell, 1945, p. 117). Later philosophers became unhappy both with idealized but impractical ethics and with realistic ethics defined by brute force. Some tried to solve the dilemma by the scientific-seeming method of **utilitarianism**, which seeks a rational assessment and balancing of costs and benefits of behavior. This approach identifies proper behavior because it produces the maximum benefit for the least cost, taking into account the costs and benefits of all concerned. Applied to human research, this means that we must weigh the benefits of the knowledge to be gained against the costs, including those to the subject. However, this approach requires that someone place weights or values on the benefits and costs.

In terms of the Tuskegee Study, what value shall we place on one work-year of forgone treatment for syphilis? How shall we measure the worth of knowledge about racial differences in the development of syphilis, the rationale for the study? Placing values on such intangibles can prove quite difficult, and ultimately this task must move to the political arena for resolution.

The philosophical effort to discover proper behavior by logic and science has not produced a consensus. Researchers want to gain knowledge with minimal resistance. Human subjects want the right to avoid or leave potentially risky research. Not surprisingly researchers and subjects will usually place different values on these differing goals.

Other naturally occurring conflicts in the research process can pose similar ethical dilemmas. For example, the researcher may falsify data or claim the words written by another. These and other types of misconduct result from conflicting interests. Such conflicts, although serious, seldom produce shocking moral tragedies of the magnitude of the Tuskegee Study. Perhaps for that reason efforts to protect human subjects have produced a more detailed body of principles and procedures than the other ethical conflicts in research. As a result we will focus first on these subject protection principles and the procedures designed to uphold them.

Nuremberg Code: The First Legal Effort. In a utilitarian framework, the valuation of costs and benefits will likely depend on the customary beliefs and values of the culture. How does the culture judge the relative importance of the individual subject and the society's right to scientific knowledge? Even in the brief history of large-scale social research, different societies have disagreed on such values and the research practices that flow from them. For example, in World War II, human research in Germany took place under official policy in various concentration camps. After the war, the cruelty of some of this research shocked the Allies. Some of these concentration camp researchers stood trial before the Nuremberg Military Tribunal. This court needed a set of ethical guidelines, from the perspective of the Allied governments' values. The first legal need for such ethical guidelines in social research produced the **Nuremberg Code** (see Table 2–1).

The Nuremberg Code has spawned many sets of ethical principles for the protection of human subjects. Almost every national and world medical and social science organization has devised its own code. These codes have tended to converge on principles that protect the subject's rights to safety and informed consent. By announcing these rules, these groups hope to reduce the uncertainty and disorder that had marked the researcher–subject relationship. However, most of these codes, except for the Nuremberg Code, expressed not laws but guiding principles to which researchers would voluntarily conform.

PROTECTING HUMAN SUBJECTS

To make guidelines serve as more than wishful thinking, someone must back them up by sanctions and external reviewers. For example, point 6 of the Nuremberg Code permits a degree of risk to the subject up to the "humanitarian importance of the problem." This guideline, if left to the researcher, could lead to the subjective overvaluing of the "importance" of the study and/or undervaluing of the subject's risk. Two general enforcement approaches to these ethical principles exist. The first tries to discourage violations of ethical guidelines through penalties. The second uses prior review of research proposals to deny resources for unethical research.

Punishing Human Subject Violations

Legal Remedies. All citizens enjoy the protection of their lives and liberty to the extent guaranteed by state and federal laws. Suppose a demented social researcher physically pulls you off the street and forces you to serve as a subject. In this case you can look to the criminal justice system for the punishment of this violation of the kidnapping laws. However, you are much more likely to encounter unethical research that comes under the civil code. As one example, the Tuskegee Study ultimately concluded with an out-of-court financial settlement of a class action civil suit. The federal gov-

Table 2–1   The Nuremberg Code

1. The voluntary consent of the human subject is absolutely essential. This means that the person involved should have legal capacity to give consent; should be so situated as to be able to exercise free power of choice, without the intervention of any element of force, fraud, deceit, duress, over reaching, or other ulterior form of constraint or coercion; and should have sufficient knowledge and comprehension of the elements of the subject matter involved as to enable him to make an understanding and enlightened decision. This latter element requires that before the acceptance of an affirmative decision by the experimental subject there should be made known to him the nature, duration, and purpose of the experiment; the method and means by which it is to be conducted; all inconveniences and hazards reasonably to be expected; and the effects upon his health or person which may possibly come from his participation in the experiments.

The duty and responsibility for ascertaining the quality of the consent rests upon each individual who initiates, directs or engages in the experiment. It is a personal duty and responsibility which may not be delegated to another with impunity.

2. The experiment should be such as to yield fruitful results for the good of society, unprocurable by other methods or means of study, and not random and unnecessary in nature.

3. The experiment should be so designed and based on the results of animal experimentation and a knowledge of the natural history of the disease or other problem under study that the anticipated results will justify the performance of the experiment.

4. The experiment should be conducted as to avoid all unnecessary physical and mental suffering and injury.

5. No experiment should be conducted where there is a prior reason to believe that death or disabling injury will occur; except, perhaps, in those experiments where the experimental physicians also serve as subjects.

6. The degree of risk to be taken should never exceed that determined by the humanitarian importance of the problem to be solved by the experiment.

7. Proper preparations should be made and adequate facilities provided to protect the experimental subject against even remote possibilities of injury, disability, or death.

8. The experiment should be conducted only by scientifically qualified persons. The highest degree of skill and care should be required through all stages of the experiment of those who conduct or engage in the experiment.

9. During the course of the experiment the human subject should be at liberty to bring the experiment to an end if he has reached the physical or mental state where continuation of the experiment seems to him to be impossible.

10. During the course of the experiment the scientist in charge must be prepared to terminate the experiment at any stage, if he has probable cause to believe, in the exercise of the good faith, superior skill and careful judgment required of him that continuation of the experiment is likely to result in injury, disability, or death to the experimental subject.

H. K. Beecher, *Research and the Individual: Human Studies* (Boston: Little, Brown, 1970), pp. 227–228.

ernment agreed to pay the subjects for their physical and mental stress. Similarly, every social researcher stands liable to lawsuit by human subjects who feel mistreated. Although rare, such suits provide one check on researchers.

Both criminal and civil law provide two essential ingredients for punishment. First, a formal and neutral judge or jury decides whether someone has violated a law or caused a personal injury. Second, the law can levy a financial or other penalty. However, before this judicial process can operate, someone must file a complaint. As shown by the Tuskegee Study, making effective use of the legal system will often prove difficult for the least powerful subjects. In that case, civil action derived not from the subjects but rather from civil rights activists outraged by the study. In less extreme cases of abuse, even well-informed and resourceful subjects may decide that the cost of seeking legal redress exceeds the discomfort caused by their research experience.

Professional Associations.   To provide protection of human subjects while maximizing the freedom of their members, professional associations and universities offer an alternative outside the legal system. Most social research organizations provide their members with ethical guidelines. Anyone, including research subjects or other professionals, can call attention to violations of these guidelines. Indeed the members of these associations have an obligation not only to adhere to their group's standards but also to see that their fellow members adhere to them as well. These organizations and their members can enforce their principles in various ways. Most of these associations own journals and can deny publication of research reports based on unethical treatment of human subjects. Some associations issue public reprimands to unethical members, which can threaten their continued employment and funding. The ultimate sanction that such voluntary groups can impose is removal from the membership.

The human subject portions of the ethical guidelines of three professional associations appear in Tables 2–2, 2–3, and 2–4. They illustrate the similarities and differences across different disciplines. Anthropologists' wide use of field observation methods creates special concern for their key informants and the protection of the general population being studied (often minority or Third World cultures). Psychologists' extensive use of experimental designs explains their special concern with such matters as deception. Psychologists also sometimes use animals in their research, and these subjects are also protected in the American Psychological Association's ethical guidelines (Principle 6.20, not reproduced here). Sociologists' frequent use of archival records and surveys accounts for their emphasis on matters related to confidentiality.

Ideally, scholars will learn and internalize the guidelines detailed in these tables and in turn identify and eliminate threats to human subjects. Sadly, not all members of a discipline obey these codes. Moreover, some of these principles seem unclear. As a result, professional associations sometimes need procedures to clarify and enforce their rules.

For example, the American Psychological Association (APA) has an Ethics Committee that reviews complaints about APA members and reports to the membership on trends in these complaints and their adjudication. Such complaints have increased with the membership from an average of about 57 per year in the 3-1/2 years up to 1980 (Sanders & Keith-Spiegel, 1980) to 88 per year in 1986 and 1987 (Ethics Committee of the American Psychological Association, 1988). However, most of these ethical cases involve issues outside the research domain. The Ethics Committee opened only 3 cases regarding improper research techniques in the years 1990 through 1992 out of 264 total cases in those years (Ethics Committee of the American Psychological Association, 1993).

Given the large membership of APA (over 72,644 in 1992) and the relatively intrusive nature of many psychological experiments, this record suggests little need for concern. However, another report based on a large sample ($n = 19,000$) of the mem-

Table 2–2   Responsibility to People Whose Lives and Cultures Anthropologists Study: Section I of Principles of Professional Responsibility of the American Anthropological Association

Anthropologists' first responsibility is to those whose lives and cultures they study. Should conflicts of interest arise, the interests of these people take precedence over other considerations. Anthropologists must do everything in their power to protect the dignity and privacy of the people with whom they work, conduct research, or perform other professional activities. Their physical, social, and emotional safety and welfare are the professional concerns of the anthropologists who have worked among them.

A. The rights, interests, safety, and sensitivities of those who entrust information to anthropologists must be safeguarded.

1. The right of those providing information to anthropologists either to remain anonymous or to receive recognition is to be respected and defended. It is the responsibility of anthropologists to make every effort to determine the preferences of those providing information and to comply with their wishes.

a. It should be made clear to anyone providing information that despite the anthropologist's best intentions and efforts anonymity may be compromised or recognition fail to materialize.

2. Anthropologists should not reveal the identity of groups or persons whose anonymity is protected through the use of pseudonyms.

3. The aims of all their professional activities should be clearly communicated by anthropologists to those among whom they work.

4. Anthropologists must not exploit individuals or groups for personal gain. They should give fair return for the help and services they receive. They must recognize their debt to the societies in which they work and their obligation to reciprocate in appropriate ways.

5. Anthropologists have an ongoing obligation to assess both the positive and negative consequences of their activities and the publications resulting from those activities. They should inform individuals and groups likely to be affected of any consequences relevant to them that they anticipate. In any case, however, their work must not violate these principles of professional responsibility. If they anticipate the possibility that such violations might occur they should take steps, including, if necessary, discontinuance of work, to avoid such outcomes.

6. Whether they are engaged in academic or nonacademic research, anthropologists must be candid about their professional identities. If the results of their activities are not to be made public, this should be made clear to all concerned from the outset.

7. Anthropologists must take into account and, where relevant, make explicit the extent to which their own personal and cultural values affect their professional activities. They must also recognize and deal candidly and judiciously with the effects that the often conflicting demands and values of employers, sponsors, host governments, and research publications may have upon their work.

Quoted from Council of the American Anthropological Association, 1990, p 1.

bership yielded 5,000 descriptions of ethically troubled human research studies (Ad Hoc Committee on Ethical Standards in Psychological Research, 1973). The number and severity of these descriptions suggest that the association's Ethics Committee may fail to hear many violations. Some psychologists may refuse to report fellow psychologists for ethics violations. The percentage of complaints to the APA filed by psychologists fell from 32 percent in 1983 to 18 percent in 1987 (Ethics Committee of the American Psychological Association, 1988). Perhaps this drop reflects that government policy to protect human subjects may have succeeded in preventing research infractions common in the past.

Table 2–3 Protecting Human Subjects: Standards 6.06–6.19 of the Ethical Principles of Psychologists and Code of Conduct of the American Psychological Association

---

6.06 Planning Research

(a) Psychologists design, conduct, and report research in accordance with recognized standards of scientific competence and ethical research.

(b) Psychologists plan their research so as to minimize the possibility that results will be misleading.

(c) In planning research, psychologists consider its ethical acceptability under the Ethics Code. If an ethical issue is unclear, psychologists seek to resolve the issue through consultation with institutional review boards, animal care and use committees, peer consultations, or other proper mechanisms.

(d) Psychologists take reasonable steps to implement appropriate protections for the rights and welfare of human participants, other persons affected by the research, and the welfare of animal subjects.

6.07 Responsibility

(a) Psychologists conduct research competently and with due concern for the dignity and welfare of the participants.

(b) Psychologists are responsible for the ethical conduct of research conducted by them or by others under their supervision or control.

(c) Researchers and assistants are permitted to perform only those tasks for which they are appropriately trained and prepared.

(d) As part of the process of development and implementation of research projects, psychologists consult those with expertise concerning any special populations under investigation or most likely to be affected.

6.08 Compliance with Law and Standards

Psychologists plan and conduct research in a manner consistent with federal and state law and regulations, as well as professional standards governing the conduct of research, and particularly those standards governing research with human participants and animal subjects.

6.09 Institutional Approval

Psychologists obtain from host institutions or organizations appropriate approval prior to conducting research, and they provide accurate information about their research proposals. They conduct the research in accordance with the approved research protocol.

6.10 Research Responsibilities

Prior to conducting research (except research involving only anonymous surveys, naturalistic observations, or similar research), psychologists enter into an agreement with participants that clarifies the nature of the research and the responsibilities of each party.

6.11 Informed Consent to Research

(a) Psychologists use language that is reasonably understandable to research participants in obtaining their appropriate informed consent (except as provided in Standard 6.12, Dispensing With Informed Consent). Such informed consent is appropriately documented.

(b) Using language that is reasonably understandable to participants, psychologists inform participants of the nature of the research; they inform participants that they are free to participate or to decline to participate or to withdraw from the resarch; they explain the foreseeable consequences of declining or withdrawing; they inform the participants of significant factors that may be expected to influence their willingness to participate (such as risks, discomfort, adverse effects, or limitations on confidentiality, except as provided in Standard 6.15, Deception in Research); and they explain other aspects about which the prospective participants inquire.

(c) When psychologists conduct research with individuals such as students or subordinates, psychologists take special care to protect the prospective participants from adverse consequences of declining or withdrawing from participation.

(d) When research participation is a course requirement or opportunity for extra credit, the prospective participant is given the choice of equitable alternative activities.

Table 2–3   (Cont'd)

(e) For persons who are legally incapable of giving informed consent, psychologists nevertheless (1) provide an appropriate explanation, (2) obtain the participant's assent, and (3) obtain appropriate permission from a legally authorized person, if such substitute consent is permitted by law.

6.12 Dispensing with Informed Consent

Before determining that planned research (such as research involving only anonymous questionnaires, naturalistic observations, or certain kinds of archival research) does not require the informed consent of research participants, psychologists consider applicable regulations and institutional review board requirements, and they consult with colleagues as appropriate.

6.13 Informed Consent in Research Filming or Recording

Psychologists obtain informed consent from research participants prior to filming or recording them in any form, unless the research involves simply naturalistic observations in public places and it is not anticipated that the recording will be used in a manner that could cause personal identification or harm.

6.14 Offering Inducements for Research Participants

(a) In offering professional services as an inducement to obtain research participants, psychologists make clear the nature of the services, as well as the risks, obligations, and limitations.

(b) Psychologists do not offer excessive or inappropriate financial or other inducements to obtain research participants, particularly when it might tend to coerce participation.

6.15 Deception in Research

(a) Psychologists do not conduct a study involving deception unless they have determined that the use of deceptive techniques is justified by the study's prospective scientific, educational, or applied value and that equally effective alternative procedures that do not use deception are not feasible.

(b) Psychologists never deceive research participants about significant aspects that would affect their willingness to participate, such as physical risks, discomfort, or unpleasant emotional experiences.

(c) Any other deception that is an integral feature of the design and conduct of an experiment must be explained to participants as early as is feasible, preferably at the conclusion of their participation, but not later than at the conclusion of the research. (See also Standard 6.18, Providing Participants with Information about the Study.)

6.16 Sharing and Utilizing Data

Psychologists inform research participants of their anticipated sharing or further use of personally identifiable research data and of the possibility of unanticipated future uses.

6.17 Minimizing Invasiveness

In conducting research, psychologists interfere with the participants or milieu from which data are collected only in a manner that is warranted by an appropriate research design and that is consistent with psychologists' roles as scientific investigators.

6.18 Providing Participants with Information about the Study

(a) Psychologists provide a prompt opportunity for participants to obtain appropriate information about the nature, results, and conclusions of the research, and psychologists attempt to correct any misconceptions that participants may have.

(b) If scientific or humane values justify delaying or withholding this information, psychologists take reasonable measures to reduce the risk of harm.

6.19 Honoring Commitments

Psychologists take reasonable measures to honor all commitments they have made to research participants.

Quoted from American Psychological Association, 1992, pp. 1608–1609.

Table 2–4 Disclosure and Respect for the Rights of Research Populations: Section B of the Code of Ethics of the American Sociological Association

Disparities in wealth, power, and social status between the sociologist and respondents and clients may reflect and create problems of equity in research collaboration. Conflicts of interest for the sociologist may occur in research and practice. Also to follow the precepts of the scientific method—such as those requiring full disclosure—may entail adverse consequences or personal risks for individuals and groups. Finally, irresponsible actions by a single researcher or research team can eliminate or reduce future access to a category of respondents by the entire profession and its allied fields.

1. Sociologists should not misuse their positions as professional social scientists for fraudulent purposes or as a pretext for gathering intelligence for any organization or government. Sociologists should not mislead respondents involved in a research project as to the purpose for which that research is being conducted.

2. Subjects of research are entitled to rights of biographical anonymity.

3. Information about subjects obtained from records that are opened to public scrutiny cannot be protected by guarantees of privacy or confidentiality.

4. The process of conducting sociological research must not expose subjects to substantial risk or personal harm. Informed consent must be obtained when the risks of research are greater than the risks of everyday life. Where modest risk or harm is anticipated, informed consent must be obtained.

5. Sociologists should take culturally appropriate steps to secure informed consent and to avoid invasions of privacy. Special actions may be necessary where the individuals studied are illiterate, have very low social status, or are unfamiliar with social research.

6. To the extent possible in a given study sociologists should anticipate potential threats to confidentiality. Such means as the removal of identifiers, the use of randomized responses, and other statistical solutions to problems of privacy should be used where appropriate.

7. Confidential information provided by research participants must be treated as such by sociologists, even when this information enjoys no legal protection or privilege and legal force is applied. The obligation to respect confidentiality also applies to members of research organizations (interviewers, coders, clerical staff, etc.) who have access to the information. It is the responsibility of administrators and chief investigators to instruct staff members on this point and to make every effort to insure that access to confidential information is restricted.

8. While generally adhering to the norm of acknowledging the contributions of all collaborators, sociologists should be sensitive to harm that may arise from disclosure and respect a collaborator's wish or need for anonymity. Full disclosure may be made later if circumstances permit.

9. Study design and information gathering techniques should conform to regulations protecting the rights of human subjects, irrespective of source of funding, as outlined by the American Association of University Professors (AAUP) in "Regulations Governing Research on Human Subjects: Academic Freedom and the Institutional Review Board," *Academe*, December 1981: 358–370.

10. Sociologists should comply with appropriate federal and institutional requirements pertaining to the conduct of research. These requirements might include but are not necessarily limited to failure to obtain proper review and approval for research that involves human subjects and failure to follow recommendations made by responsible committees concerning research subjects, materials, and procedures.

Quoted from American Sociological Association, 1989, p. 3.

Preventing Human Subject Violations

Federal Requirement of Prior Review. Moved by the Tuskegee Syphilis Study scandal, Congress passed the National Research Act in 1974, which led to the establishment of the National Commission on the Protection of Human Subjects of Biomedical and Behavioral Research. Its recommendations in 1978 led the Department of Health and Human Services to issue regulations finalized in 1981.

Because of the seeming inability of the legal system and professional organizations to protect human subjects, the federal government took charge of stopping harmful research practices. Because it provides a large share of the funds for social research, the government can set guidelines that directly or indirectly influence most research. Federal regulations now require that each institution that sponsors any research funded by the Department of Health and Human Services establish local review committees to screen proposals. Even if a researcher could function without federal funds, he or she usually still needs the permission of an institution to use its facilities, subject pool, and graduate assistants.

Institutional Review Boards.   In 1981, the current federal regulations appeared in the *Federal Register*. These guidelines define the types of prior review provided by **institutional review boards (IRBs)**. Although required only for projects with or seeking federal funds, these guidelines usually apply to all research at each institution. Each institution must state how it will review nonfederally funded research. Voluntary agreement to apply the federal guidelines to nonfederally funded research shows the institution's commitment to the protection of human subjects.

Human research proposals fall into three categories of review: exempt, expedited, and full. The first category, **exempt**, includes no- or very low-risk proposals as judged by the investigators and applies to research not requiring formal review by the IRB. A researcher with a proposal that he or she judges to fall in the exempt category need file only an Exempt Registration Form with the the IRB showing evidence that the researcher's department chair or dean has reviewed the proposed research. Exempt studies include the following categories:

1. Research on "normal educational practices"
2. Use of educational tests, surveys, or observations of public behavior unless the subjects can be identified and disclosure of their responses could harm their legal or financial standing or their reputations
3. Use of educational tests, surveys, or observations of public behavior not exempt under the second category if the subjects are elected or appointed public officials or candidates for public office or if federal statutes require that the confidentiality of the personally identifiable information be maintained
4. Study of existing data if the data are publicly available or if subjects cannot be identified
5. Research and demonstration projects conducted by approval of federal agency heads that are designed to promote or improve public service programs
6. Taste and food quality studies not involving additives or with ingredients at levels found safe by federal agencies

The option of researchers to exempt their own research from review has raised concern in those who want maximum federal protection of human subjects (Veatch, 1981). In contrast, others have noted some types of nonexempt research that they believe should have been exempted (Thompson et al., 1981). Finally, remember that the federal procedures define a minimum level of protection to which each institution or IRB can add higher standards.

If the researcher claims no exemption, he or she must submit the research proposal for review by the IRB. **Full review** involves a formal evaluation by the entire IRB. A speedier form of review, called **expedited review**, can be conducted by a single experienced member of the IRB (for example, its chairperson). Expedited review applies to relatively low-risk research involving mainly biomedical techniques such as collecting hair, nail clippings, sweat, small amounts of blood, or dental plaque. Social research techniques considered low risk for expedited review include noninvasive physiological recordings of adults (for example, testing sensory acuity); voice recordings; the use of existing documents; and nonstressful studies of group behavior, perception, and cognition.

Full review applies to proposals that do not fall in the exempt or expedited categories. In full review, the committee tries both to assure no excessive risk of harm and to weigh the relation of benefit to harm in the utilitarian sense. The full review judges the adequacy of the informed consent procedure and the protection of the subjects' identity where appropriate. The IRB must decide whether the subjects have the ability to give informed consent (for example, in studies using children and mentally disabled subjects) and whether the study poses any risk of coercion (for example, studies of students or prisoners in a dependent relationship to the investigator).

Informed Consent.   The matter of **informed consent** often plays a key role in deciding approval for research. Where the researcher can obtain such prior consent, the standards for the procedure seem clear. Ordinarily, the researchers should provide the prospective subject with verbal and written information about the study and a waiver form for his or her signature. An example of such a consent form for exempt research appears in Table 2–5. The information that provides the basis for this consent usually includes the study's purpose and duration, subject confidentiality procedures, risks and benefits, whom to contact for further details, and a statement that participation is voluntary with no penalty for stopping at any time. After receiving and considering this information, the subjects can indicate their consent to participate in writing. This written consent does not waive any of the subjects' legal rights or release the researcher from liability for negligence in the research project.

Federal rules permit IRBs to waive the requirement for written informed consent, but they do so reluctantly and only for very good reason. An IRB may waive informed consent when the research cannot proceed without the waiver. For example, experiments that depend on deception would not succeed if the subjects knew of the deception in advance. In some field studies, the participant-observer can gain entry only by concealing his or her research role. Such studies would become impossible if prior informed consent were needed. The IRB will grant such waivers only if the risk to the subjects appears minimal and warranted by the benefits expected from the study. Usually, the researcher, in exchange for the waiver of prior consent, must provide full information to the subjects at the end of the study.

The IRB's deliberations take place in the context of continuing debate between those who oppose deceptive research procedures on principle (Baumrind, 1985) and

Table 2–5   University of California Irvine Consent to Act as a Human Research Subject

TITLE OF STUDY

NAME, DEPARTMENT AND TELEPHONE NUMBER OF INVESTIGATOR

You have been asked to participate in a research study which is <u>exempt</u> from review by a Human Subjects Review Committee. The purpose of the study, the terms of your participation, as well as any expected risks and benefits <u>must</u> be <u>fully</u> explained to you before you sign this form and give your consent to participate.

You should also know that:

Participation in research is <u>entirely</u> voluntary. You may refuse to participate or withdraw from participation at any time without jeopardy to future medical care, education or employment status or other entitlement.

The investigator may withdraw you from participation at his/her professional discretion.

If, during the course of this study, significant new information which has been developed during the study becomes available, which may relate to your willingness to continue to participate, this information will be provided to you by the investigator.

Any information derived from this research project which personally identifies you will not be voluntarily released or disclosed without your separate consent, except as specifically required by law.

If at any time you have questions regarding the research or your participation in it, you should contact the investigator or his/her assistants who must answer your questions.

If, at any time, you have comments or complaints relating to the conduct of this research or if you wish to discuss your rights as a research subject, you may contact Human Research Administration at 714-856-6068.

You should be given a copy of this consent form to keep.

* *

I consent to participate in this study.

_____

SIGNATURE OF SUBJECT (Age 7 & older)   DATE

_____

SIGNATURE OF PARENT/GUARDIAN   DATE

_____

SIGNATURE OF INVESTIGATOR   DATE

_____

SIGNATURE OF WITNESS   DATE

Rev. 7/93   ***THIS FORM IS FOR USE WITH EXEMPT RESEARCH ONLY*** those who have found significant effects of such ethical requirements on research out-comes (Trice, 1987). Not surprisingly, IRB decisions have varied in response to the so-cial sensitivity of the research topic. In one survey, IRBs were more likely to reject pro-posals that dealt with issues such as racial or sexual discrimination (Ceci, Peters, & Plotkin, 1985). Some researchers who desire more consistent IRB decisions have pro-posed supplying a casebook of actual research protocols to help standardize decisions over time and across different IRBs (Rosnow, Rotheram-Borus, Ceci, Blanck, & Koocher, 1993). For further discussion of ethically troublesome research that an IRB might evaluate, see Reynolds (1979, 1982).

RESEARCH INTEGRITY AND ETHICAL CONFLICTS

Besides the concern for protecting human subjects, several other important ethical dilemmas exist, including ones that arise in socially sensitive research (Sieber & Stan-ley, 1988). Conflicts involving other figures in the research enterprise have led to ad-ditional guidelines. In some cases, these ethics standards elicit little controversy. For other conflicts, guidelines will continue to trigger public and professional debate.

Ethical conflicts in research derive from the variety of players and their divergent self-interests and values. The major players include the researcher, the subject, the fun-der, and society as the consumer of research. Other parties also figure in the process of science, including professional associations, scholarly journals, research institutions such as universities, and government in its regulatory role. The distinctions among these parties are not always clear-cut, since one may play two or more parts—for example, the government as funder, as consumer of research results, as regulator, and as investi-gator (for instance, the collection of census data). In addition, each of these players may have different priorities. Since these priorities sometimes collide, ethical problems can arise between any two parties in the research process. Competing interests may well try to achieve their aims at the expense of the other parties involved.

Researcher Versus Researcher

Plagiarism.   One ethical conflict raises little controversy. Virtually all profes-sional groups prohibit **plagiarism**, and copyright laws provide remedies for stealing an-other author's published writing. However, the explosive increase in scientific journals makes it difficult to catch plagiarized work, especially when it is published in obscure journals. Most cases of research misconduct involve plagiarism (LaFollette, 1992). Just one plagiarist can publish dozens of articles before being caught (for example, the Al-gabti case described in Broad & Wade, 1982).

When he or she is caught, the plagiarist can suffer severe penalties. Jerri Husch, a sociologist, discovered in 1988 that large sections of her 1984 Ph.D. dissertation on Musak in the workplace had appeared uncredited in a book by Stephen Barnes. Dr. Husch initiated a complaint, and in 1989 a committee of the American Sociological As-sociation concluded that Barnes had plagiarized the material. When no satisfaction was obtained from Dr. Barnes or his publisher, the organization raised the matter with Dr.

Barnes's employer, Eastern New Mexico University, where he worked as Dean of Fine Arts. By the end of 1989, Dr. Barnes had left his job (Buff, 1989), apparently, in part, due to this pressure.

Some plagiarism disputes are less clear-cut than using another's published work without permission. The professor who puts his or her name on a student's work shows how research can be "stolen" before the publication stage. In an era of large-scale team research, disputes can easily arise about authorship and the sharing of credit for creative contributions. Such disputes, unless prevented by agreements in the early stages of collaboration, can and do produce long-lasting hostility.

Peer Review of Research.   In contrast to the rules against plagiarism, the ethical codes have achieved less clarity on another potential conflict between researchers. In employment and promotion decisions, in reviews of papers submitted for publication, and in grant requests for research funds, researchers usually receive judgments by their peers on the merits of their research. These decisions can govern which research reports will receive wide publication or none at all and which proposals will receive funding or never be carried out. Such peer review procedures require fairness and objectivity. Suspicion that the peer review mechanism is working with bias could produce interpersonal conflict between competing scholars. Possible abuses in peer review also raise concern about distortions in the substantive direction of future research as decisions favor certain types of research proposals and research careers over others.

The peer review process tries to protect itself by using multiple reviewers. But whereas lawbreakers usually have the protection of 12-member juries, professional researchers are often judged by as few as two to five peers. Research on the peer review process in awarding grants has cast serious doubt on its reliability. One research team had 150 National Science Foundation proposals reevaluated. They concluded that "the fate of a particular grant application is roughly half determined by the characteristics of the proposal and the principal investigator, and about half by apparently random elements which might be characterized as the 'luck of the reviewer draw' " (Cole, Cole, & Simon 1981, p. 885). Research on peer review of manuscripts submitted for publication also suggests low levels of inter-reviewer agreement (Cicchetti, 1980) and only modest relationships between peer judgments of quality and later citation (Gottfredson, 1978). However, "blind" review techniques used by many of the best journals offer some protection against sex, ethnic, or personal bias in manuscript review.

Society Versus Researcher

Fraud.   With great embarrassment, scientists have had to admit that their colleagues sometimes engage in fraud. The problem rarely involves financial fraud, looting the research grant to buy expensive cars and vacations, although perhaps that exists as well. The main problem is falsifying data. The motive to make up or trim data may derive from the desire to gain career success through publications. But the impact of such fraud goes beyond the careers of individual researchers and can reach all the way to socially significant public policy.

Cases of documented fraud, although rare historically, appear to be on the rise

(Broad & Wade, 1982; LaFollette, 1992; Miller & Hersen, 1992). One such case involved Stephen Breuning, a young psychologist whose research was funded by the National Institute of Mental Health (NIMH). Breuning published studies between 1980 and 1984 on the effects of psychoactive drugs on the mentally retarded. His findings influenced treatment practices in some states, including Connecticut. However, "only a few of the experimental subjects described in [some of the investigator's] publications and progress reports were ever studied" (Hostetler, 1987, p. 12, quoting an NIMH draft report). Some of the questionable reports were coauthored by respected researchers who, despite little or no involvement in the research, lent their names to the reports or whose names were added without their permission.

The NIMH investigating panel recommended that Breuning be barred from additional NIMH funding for 10 years and that the case be handed over to the Department of Justice, which subsequently indicted him, the first such indictment in federal court. His institution had to reimburse NIMH more than $163,000 for misspent grants (Bales, 1988). In a subsequent plea bargain, Breuning pleaded guilty, becoming subject to a maximum penalty of 10 years in prison and $20,000 in fines. His actual sentence consisted of 60 days in a halfway house, 250 hours of community service, and 5 years of probation. We may never know the extent of harm done to retarded patients whose treatment was guided by these fraudulent findings. A citation study did track the number of research studies that cited 20 of Breuning's questionable reports (Garfield & Welljams-Dorof, 1990). Out of 200 citations, 80 (40 percent) were self-citations by Breuning or his coauthors. Non–self-citations fell after 1986 when the scandal broke and reflected little apparent impact of his claims.

The Burt Case—Fraud or Politics?   The most famous case of alleged fraud in the social sciences involves Sir Cyril Burt. He died a greatly esteemed scholar in 1971, once called the "dean of the world's psychologists" (Dreger, quoted by Hearnshaw, 1979, p. 227). Burt co-founded the *British Journal of Statistical Psychology* in 1947 and controlled or helped control it until 1963. He studied the source of intelligence—genetic inheritance or rearing and the environment—using identical twins. Identical twins usually score the same on intelligence tests. Because most twins grow up in the same environment as well as sharing the same genes, we cannot tell which source causes their similarity. However, identical twins reared apart have the same genes but grow up in different environments. Scholars who think environment causes intelligence would expect low correlations between the intelligence scores of twins reared apart. Those who believe that genes cause intelligence expect high correlations regardless of environmental differences in rearing. Burt claimed to have found more identical twins reared apart than anyone else in the intelligence area—15 such sets in 1943, 21 by 1955, twice that number in 1958, and 53 in his last report of 1966.

Burt reported high correlations (typically .77) supporting the genetic heritability of intelligence. These findings served as the basis for Burt's defense of British educational policy, which then selected children into higher and lower tracks based on early tests. They also figured in the volatile debate about the relation of race and intelligence. Burt's work roused great animosity from both other psychologists and people in political circles. However, his great stature protected him from charges of fraud until after his death. The first doubts about his work arose from the incredible consistency of his reports, which repeatedly gave the same correlation for intelligence of twins reared apart. Another question concerned publications in Burt's journal on his data by two authors named Howard and Conway. A reporter named Oliver Gillie of the *London Times* tried to contact them in 1976 to get their views of Burt's data. Not able to locate them, he charged that Burt had written the papers himself and assigned authorship to nonexistent people. Other scholars who disliked Burt's genetic views on intelligence added their weight to the charges that Burt had falsified his data. When Hearnshaw, a respected biographer, concluded that Burt had committed fraud, the case seemed closed on the greatest scandal in the history of social science (1979).

In the late 1980s, two independent scholars, with no stake in the genetics versus environment debate, reviewed the Burt case (Fletcher, 1991; Joynson, 1989). They converged on a view that partially exonerates Burt and charges his accusers with character defamation. Burt clearly engaged in misconduct by writing and publishing the papers attributed to Howard and Conway. However, these individuals existed and served as unsalaried social workers who helped Burt with his data collection in the 1920s and 1930s. The lapse in time explains the difficulty Gillie had in finding them. Burt's action in assigning them the authorships may have been his misguided way of giving them credit for their help. As for the identical correlations, it now appears that Burt was simply carrying over findings reported in one article to later articles and not claiming new computations with the same results. The best check on Burt's claims comes from other independent research. At least two separate studies of identical twins reared apart have reported intelligence correlations of .77, exactly the same as Burt (Jensen, 1992). Apparently, both the media and psychologists in leadership positions wrongly accused Burt in order to impugn his views on the heritability of intelligence. In so doing, they not only smeared a leading scholar after he could no longer defend himself, but they cast doubt on the methods he had helped pioneer, such as measurement of mental abilities.

Waste.   We can think of fraud as a special case of waste in which research funds have disappeared without return of valid results. Another kind of waste can occur even when no fraud takes place. An instance of this conflict between funder and researcher appears in the Hutchinson versus Proxmire case (Kiesler & Lowman, 1980). Senator Proxmire waged a campaign to save taxpayers' money from being wasted on trivial research. He publicized extreme cases of such alleged waste with his Golden Fleece Award. Ronald Hutchinson received this embarrassing award in 1975 for his work on aggression in monkeys. Proxmire took credit for stopping Hutchinson's federal funding, and Hutchinson sued Proxmire. The Supreme Court ruled in favor of Hutchinson's claim that he was not a public figure subject to Proxmire's public ridicule and remanded the suit back to a lower court. Proxmire then settled out of court in 1980 for a public apology and $10,000.

Although Dr. Hutchinson won the battle, Senator Proxmire may have won the war. The chilling effect of public ridicule and the power of lawmakers to restrict public research funds surely have an impact on what researchers can explore with public support. No professional association's ethical guidelines define what is "significant" social research. Presumably, individual professionals have freedom to pursue their curiosity. Indeed, an honored intellectual tradition supports pure or basic research for its own sake regardless of its potential uses. On the other hand, the taxpayers' representatives have an obligation to spend scarce public funds wisely.

The allocation of public funds to research must, therefore, take into account the welfare of the entire society and not just the curiosity of researchers. But how should the conflict between the researcher's interests and the social interest be resolved? Researchers often claim that it is shortsighted to limit support to applied research. Since applied research depends on theory and pure research, it will wither in the future if the funders stifle the curiosity of the pure researchers now. On the other hand, we must seek the best possible uses of our scarce research funds and thus pay special attention to our funding priorities (Boulding, 1966, pp. 109–114).

But if politicians guard us from trivial research, who guards against their awarding research grants in their own or other special interests? Awarding government research funds by peer review (juries of fellow scientists) gives no guarantee that funds will spread evenly across congressional districts. Increasingly, lawmakers are pork-barreling research grants to provide jobs in home states and districts (Clifford, 1987). In one instance, a Massachusetts politician took credit for getting a $7.7 million research center for his home district. This occurred over the advice of a technical review panel, which favored another bidder, whose proposal would have cost the taxpayers $3.2 million less (Cordes, 1984). Professional research associations lobby the government to increase the funds put into their fields of interest. Universities and private companies also lobby Congress to give funds outside of the usual peer review process for special interest projects. The value of such "earmarked" projects by Congress increased 70-fold between 1980 and 1992 (Agnew, 1993).

Public Interest Versus Private Interest

Science operates within and reflects society. Science, wittingly or not, often carries out the values of the society, or at least that part of society from which scientists come (for perspectives in the sociology of science, see Barber & Hirsch, 1962). That scientists see reality through the blinders of society's values causes concern for those who want science to understand society in order to make it better. Collecting data within the political and economic status quo will prove irrelevant, it is argued, for the goal of seeing beyond the status quo to a different future (Sarason, 1981).

Private Interests.   In a complex society, no single homogeneous value set exists from which everyone approaches political and social problems. Rather, we find many competing private interests. The government may reflect those private interests that were on the winning side of the last election or coup. Thus, research funded in one administration may be eliminated by the next administration. Just as the government can support research with its funds outside of peer review, it can cut off funding that has earned peer review approval. This can happen when the research topic touches a political nerve. For example, in September 1992 the National Institutes of Health withdrew previously approved funds for a University of Maryland conference on ethical issues related to genetic studies of crime. Opponents of the conference feared that this research would try to link violence to race. Proponents viewed the withdrawal of funds as bureaucratic cowardice in the face of pressure for political correctness (Touchette, 1992). The fear raised by this conference shows the distrust that many hold that science might be used to harm an ethnic or racial group.

A more clear-cut type of private interest is the corporation that can sponsor research to serve its own ends. For example, a tobacco firm may fund research on public attitudes toward smoking prohibition (for example, to prevent laws that outlaw smoking in restaurants). Naturally, the funder has a vested interest in finding techniques that would increase profits by blocking the adoption of such laws. What effect does this natural self-interest have on the researcher's effort? To what extent should such privately employed researchers concern themselves with the "public interest"?

In recognition of this potential conflict, professional associations have provided guidelines regarding research sponsorship. For example, the Code of Ethics of the American Sociological Association calls for identification of all sources of research support or special relationships with sponsors (American Sociological Association, 1989). Similarly, the anthropologists' Statement of Ethics warns that in "working for governmental agencies or private businesses, anthropologists should be especially careful not to promise or imply acceptance of conditions contrary to professional ethics or competing commitments" (Council of the American Anthropological Association, 1990, p. 2).

In recent years, universities have begun to add force to such requirements. Professors often must report their links with private industry and their funding from nonpublic sources. Such reporting permits an assessment of possible conflict of interest, and local boards can provide peer review and guidance in questionable cases.

Public Interest.   Although conflicts involving special interests may seem clear enough, identifying the public interest appears much more difficult. What if the public interest of a nation supported social research that was, arguably, unethical? A notorious example of this kind of research appeared in Project Camelot (Horowitz, 1973), a study that gauged the causes of revolutions in the Third World. Supported by the U.S. military, it sought techniques for avoiding or coping with revolutions. Survey and other methods were to be used in various developing countries after Camelot's conception in 1963.

The uproar over Camelot ignited when a Chilean sociology professor challenged the military implications of the project. The Chilean press and the Chilean senate viewed Camelot as espionage. This criticism resulted in U.S. congressional hearings and the termination of Camelot by the Defense Department in August 1965.

With respect to such research projects as Camelot, Beals (1969) asks "whether social science should be the handmaiden of government or strive for freedom and autonomy" (p. 16). Since the "true" public interest may be in the eye of the beholder, a resolution of this matter will not be simple. Given the increasing importance of science in public policy and social welfare, scientists bear an increasing responsibility to consider the consequences of their work. Just how to anticipate the long-run consequences and how to weigh the potentially different effects on different segments of society (for example, poor versus rich within a society or First World versus Third World nations) has not been worked out in any laws or professional codes. Perhaps for that reason, the movement of "public interest science" will continue as an educational and conscious-ness-raising force before it can be formulated by consensus (see Nelkin, 1979, for a re-view of the emergence of the public interest science movement).

Protecting Research Integrity

In response to the problem of protecting human subjects, the government created preventive procedures such as IRBs for screening research proposals. However, no sim-ilar system exists for preventing other kinds of research misconduct such as plagiarism or fraud. At best, individual whistle-blowers can raise charges when they spot such abuses.

Legal Remedies. Of course, an author can seek legal redress in cases of plagia-rism upon finding that someone has published his or her words without proper credit. Such actions can proceed under the copyright protection laws if the author or publisher has copyrighted the work. A more recent law permits legal action in cases of fraud that wastes public funds.

Under the False Claims Amendment Act of 1986, any individual can bring suit, on behalf of the United States, in a federal district court to recover funds fraudulently paid to contractors or grantees. The Department of Justice may or may not choose to join such suits. But the whistle-blower who brings such a suit may receive a reward up to 30 percent of triple the damages suffered by the government as a result of the re-searcher's fraud (Charrow & Saks, 1992). Thus, if you believe that a researcher is mak-ing up data and misspending a government grant, you can take him or her to court and earn a reward for your trouble if you prevail.

Institutional Hearings. Ideally, researchers will avoid misconduct if they know the rules of proper research. Government research agencies, under congressional pres-sure, have tried to spell out and enforce rules for research integrity. For example, the Public Health Service now has an **Office of Research Integrity (ORI)**, which proposes guidelines for misconduct (for example, prohibiting plagiarism or making up data).

However, when charges of misconduct arise, we must have a means for judging them. The government now expects each research institution to establish its own office of scientific integrity to disseminate the rules of proper research and to judge infractions reported locally. As an example, the research integrity office of the University of Pitts-burgh handled the Needleman case discussed in Chapter 1. Thus, if you suspect that a reseacher on your campus has committed misconduct, you can report it to your local of-fice of research integrity. There you should find established procedures for investigat-ing and judging your complaint. These procedures should help not only the whistle-blower; they should also provide some protection for the accused against loss of repu-tation to false complaints. Because these research integrity offices have appeared on many college campuses only in recent years, some are still working out their proce-dures. We can expect that some cases (for example, Needleman's) will continue on from these local jurisdictions into the courts or to the federal Office of Research Integrity before final resolution. Ultimately, if the federal Office of Research Integrity decides that a researcher has engaged in misconduct, it could withhold future funding as punishment.

SUMMARY

With the advent of large-scale social research came the increased risk of conflicts between different parties in the scientific enterprise. The most notorious examples of such conflict involve the abuse of human subjects, as in the Nazi medical experiments and the Tuskegee Syphilis Study. The publicity attending these scandals helped focus public and professional attention on the problems of protecting human subjects.

Since philosophers of ethics have not been able to derive universal principles, political and professional institutions have tried to regulate research conduct. Professional associations want to preserve the autonomy of their members by helping them conform their conduct to ethical codes without outside intrusion. Criminal and civil legal procedures are also, in principle, available to provide redress to human subjects and other parties in the research process.

However, these legal and professional procedures provide for punishment only after the fact and for only the small proportion of ethical violations brought up for review. To guarantee more systematic and preventive protection of human subjects, the government now requires prior institutional review of research proposals. Under the jurisdiction of institutional review boards (IRBs), researchers must provide in their proposals for informed consent by their subjects and must limit the risks to their subjects. Although IRBs can waive informed consent, they require good reason for such waivers.

Besides the conflict between researcher and subject, other conflicts can arise such as those between researchers, between funder and researcher, and between private interests and the public interest. In some cases, ethical codes already address these conflicts, as in the prohibition against fraud and plagiarism. In other cases, ethical guidance seems less clear, and we can expect continuing political and professional debate about some of these matters (for example, allocation of research resources in the public interest).

Legal means exist for bringing complaints and seeking financial redress in cases of plagiarism and fraud. Because of the recent increase in research fraud, the government now requires institutions receiving its funds to establish offices of research integrity. These offices disseminate the guidelines for ethical research and provide mechanisms for handling charges of misconduct.

EXERCISES

1. Select a social research study with which you are familiar, such as one described in this text. Review this study from the standpoint of its protection of its subjects. Identify any potential problem such as deception, risk of physical or mental stress, and protection of confidentiality. Judge the adequacy of the protection of the subjects and suggest any changes that would have improved this protection without damaging the research procedure.

2. Locate the IRB on your campus and obtain a copy of its application form. Sketch out an imaginary research proposal, preferably one with the potential for human subject violations (many examples can be found in the report of the Ad Hoc Committee on Ethical Standards in Psychological Research, 1973). Based on this proposal, fill out the IRB's application as though you were actively planning to conduct the research. Determine if your proposal would fall in the exempt, expedited, or full review category. If applicable, develop an informed consent form complete with a description of your study for briefing your prospective subjects and for soliciting their written consent. By the standards of your IRB and of relevant professional association codes, would your proposal be found acceptable in its treatment of human subjects?

3. Try to locate a research conflict, other than the protection of human subjects, that appeared recently in your local media (for example, a politician criticizing a researcher's work as trivial, a case of fraud or plagiarism, or concern about researchers concealing their support from private interests). Identify the parties and how their interests conflict (that is, what they hope to gain and what they risk losing). What laws, professional codes, or everyday moral principles, if any, apply to the conflict? What was the outcome of the conflict and was it a desirable outcome in your view? Be sure to spell out your judgment in terms of relative costs and benefits. If it was an undesirable outcome, what could be done to make sure the outcome is more satisfactory in future cases?

4. Contact the office for research integrity on your campus. Ask for a summary of the behaviors that constitute research misconduct. Find out how you would go about reporting a case of misconduct to this office. What protections exist for you as the whistleblower and for the accused researcher?

KEY TERMS

Ethics	Nuremberg Code
Exempt	Office of Research Integrity
Expedited review	(ORI)
Full review	Plagiarism
Informed consent	Utilitarianism
Institutional review boards (IRBs)	

☙ 3 ☙

Finding, Using, and Writing Research Reports
Library Usage and Report Style

Most research projects begin with an idea about a new question or a new method for testing an old question. Often the trigger for such ideas comes from reading another researcher's report. Before starting a new project, the researcher will need to review the past studies on the same question. This review helps establish the originality of the new question or method. It also helps the researcher avoid past mistakes and benefit from past successes with methods or measures. Finally, it forms the basis for the background section that opens almost all research articles. This chapter begins with methods for finding research reports. Then it presents the standard parts of research reports and shows how to make sense of them using an actual journal article.

SEARCHING FOR RESEARCH REPORTS

When you attend class, where do you sit? If you arrive late to a crowded classroom, perhaps you have little choice. Or perhaps you give it no thought and sit wherever your friends sit. Does your choice of seat affect how much you learn or your final grade? By seeking the answer to this question, we can review the library resources available for finding relevant books and journals.

Catalogs for Finding Books

Although some libraries retain their traditional card catalogs, many college and university libraries have computerized their holdings. Such **online** electronic filing systems have become essential for very large libraries, especially those that disperse their holdings throughout different branches. For example, you may do most of your studying in the general library, but you may need to know if your campus has a particular book in the medical library. Universities with several campuses can choose not to duplicate collections at each site. By using an online catalog for the entire system, you can find the location of a needed book across your own campus or hundreds of miles away at a sister campus. In some cases, you may even request the needed book from your computer terminal for delivery by interlibrary loan in a matter of days.

Online library catalogs consist of computers with the catalog stored in electronic memory. As a result, your library may allow access to this catalog at any hour (even after the library has closed) from remote computers. Such personal computers may reside in laboratories, homes, or dormitories. They require only a **modem**, a device for linking your personal computer by telephone line to the host computer.

Such electronic file systems vary from library to library in the details of their use, but most follow a similar logic. Although any system could illustrate the general approach, we will use the one serving the nine campuses of the University of California called MELVYL.[1] Usually, the listings of an online catalog contain books added to the library since a certain date. If you cannot find the book you want with the online catalog, you may need to consult a card catalog for earlier acquisitions not yet entered into the computer.

Traditional card catalogs list the holdings alphabetically by each of several different indexes often stored in different files—author, title, and subject. An online system allows you to look under different indexes but without having to search for the right file or drawer.

If You Know Author or Title.   You might get the name of a likely author from a professor in a course or a likely book title from the reference list in a textbook. Now you need to see if your library has the book you want and if so where to find it. You first need to connect with the library's computer ("log on" in computer jargon), a procedure that varies from system to system. The computer signals its readiness by blinking a particular kind of symbol, called a **prompt**, which also varies from system to system. You can then ask the computer about its holdings by typing your request.

The library's computer can understand your request only if you express it in a standard format. Typically, this format includes three parts: a command, an index, and the key word(s) for which you are searching. If you are trying to find a book, your **command** will be "to find." In MELVYL, for example, you would type FIND or F to indicate that you wanted a search.

Depending on whether you have the author's name or the title, you would then tell the computer to search under the appropriate **index**, that is, by author or title. This step resembles choosing which file cabinet to explore in a traditional card catalog—the one organized by author or the one organized by title. In MELVYL you could type PA, short for personal author, or TW for title words in the space for the index. Other index terms would tell the computer to look in a different way, for example CA for corporate or multiple authorship.

The **key words** consist of the author's name or the book's title, depending on which index you chose. The computer can also combine indexes by using **Boolean operators**, or logical connections that restrict or expand the search possibilities. For example, the operator "and" joining an author's name and some title words would narrow the search to those books that have both the named author and the stated title. Such a search would ignore other works by the same author and other authors of works with the same title.

Suppose you wanted to find whether or not a copy of this text exists in your library. If you are using an electronic catalog that works like MELVYL, you could type any of the following statements after the prompt arrow:

F PA DOOLEY, DAVID <RETURN>
F PA DAVID DOOLEY <RETURN>
F TW SOCIAL RESEARCH METHODS <RETURN>
F PA DOOLEY, DAVID AND TW SOCIAL RESEARCH METHODS
<RETURN>

To signal that you have completed your search instruction, you typically press the RETURN or ENTER key usually represented in text by <RETURN> or <ENTER>. The computer will then report whether it found any books with the indicated author or title. If it does, you can then ask for more details by typing the DISPLAY command D.

Searching by Subject.   If you do not know the authors or titles related to your interest, you would use a similar procedure. Instead of the author or title index, you would use the index for subject, or SU in the search instruction. In this case, the key words depend on the topic you are exploring. To take the example from the beginning of the chapter, suppose you wanted to find out about the effects of classroom seating location on grades. You could try inputting terms related to this topic following the command and index terms, FIND SUBJECT (F SU) followed by the key words for the search.

If you try this, you may find that the computer does not recognize your key words. Most online catalogs use a **controlled vocabulary**, a set of official synonyms, to limit and make manageable the number of terms under which a subject could be filed. How do you know which terms your catalog will recognize? Most online systems use one of the standard terminologies for subject headings. Many online systems, including MELVYL, use the *Library of Congress Subject Headings* (Library of Congress, 1986). Whichever standard applies, you should be able to find copies close to the library's computer terminal. In the subject heading book, simply look up the words that have occurred to you to see whether your online system will accept them as search terms. If not, you should find alternative synonyms that will serve. Such controlled terms as "classroom environment," "spatial behavior," "marking," and "personal space" all appear in the *Library of Congress Subject Headings* and appear relevant to the effect of seating location on grades.

Thus, we could use the following MELVYL command:

F SU CLASSROOM ENVIRONMENT <RETURN>

to locate any books on the subject of classroom environment. In response to this command in August 1993, the MELVYL catalog found 111 different items among the over 11 million holdings in all of the University of California libraries (see the following reproduction of the terminal display):

-> F SU CLASSROOM ENVIRONMENT

Search request: F SU CLASSROOM ENVIRONMENT
Search result: 111 records at all libraries

Type D to display results, or type HELP.

In the display (alphabetical by author) the eighteenth one, located in the library of the Santa Barbara campus (UCSB), appeared most pertinent:

18. DISSERTATION
   Dicks, Robert Henry, 1946–
   An investigation of the relationship between classroom distance
and student outcomes / by Robert Henry Dicks. 1980.
   UCSB Library LB1084 .D534 1980

A request for a long display of this item gives a more detailed description:

Author: Dicks, Robert Henry, 1946–
Title: An investigation of the relationship between classroom
**   distance and student outcomes / by Robert Henry Dicks. 1980.**
Description: xii, 158 leaves, bound : ill. ; 28 cm.

Notes: **Vita.**
      Thesis (Ph.D.)—University of California, Santa Barbara,
       1980.
      Bibliography: leaves 131–138.
      Typescript (photocopy)

Subjects: **University of California, Santa Barbara—Dissertations—**
       Education.
      Interaction analysis in education.
      Classroom environment.
      Educational psychology.
      School children—California—Santa Barbara County—
       Psychology—Case studies.
      Call numbers: UCSB Min Lib LB1084 .D534 1980

The last listing, **call numbers**, tells how to locate this particular volume on the shelves of the library at Santa Barbara. Although interesting, this Ph.D. dissertation deals with schoolchildren rather than college students. In fact, this search turned up no book on the question of seating location and grades in the college classroom. Perhaps research on this question appears in the periodical literature.

Indexing and Abstracting Services for Journal Articles

Standard library catalogs can help you find volumes such as books, dissertations, or bound journals, but they usually do not index particular journals articles. Sometimes the answer to your question requires an article in a recent journal issue. Many tools exist for searching the periodical literature. Some simply index the literature, that is, provide minimal information such as author, title, journal reference, and perhaps some key words about the subject of the article. Other services go further and provide an abstract or summary of the article to help you decide whether it fits your needs. Different disciplines have developed such indexing and abstracting services, for example, *Psychological Abstracts, Current Index to Journals in Education, Sociological Abstracts, Index Medicus* (for more on these and related services, see Reed & Baxter, 1992).

Using Psychological Abstracts. The following sections illustrate the use of one such periodical service—*Psychological Abstracts*. The details of using indexes and abstracts vary from service to service, but most resemble the procedure of *Psychological Abstracts*. Moreover, this service covers hundreds of periodicals in the social sciences in different languages from different countries with, of course, special emphasis on psychological topics.

You can access *Psychological Abstracts* in three different media: as printed publications; as part of the online database called PsycINFO; and in the form of compact digital discs with read only memory (CD-ROM) for the database called PsycLIT. If your library subscribes to PsycINFO you might access it via the same terminal from which you search the library's catalog of holdings. Your library might instead or in addition subscribe to PsycLIT in which case it receives updated CDs readable on personal computers. The printed version of *Psychological Abstracts* has, perhaps, the widest availability, and we will discuss it first.

You follow three steps in finding an article's abstract in the printed version of *Psychological Abstracts:* (1) Find the key word or words in the controlled vocabulary or thesaurus; (2) find an article's reference number in a monthly or semiannual subject index, and (3) find the actual **abstract** in *Psychological Abstracts.* If you know the author's name and the year of publication, you can skip the first step and go directly to the author's index, which corresponds to the subject index and volume of abstracts.

The controlled vocabulary for the *Psychological Abstracts* appears in the *Thesaurus of Psychological Index Terms* (American Psychological Association, 1988). We already have reason to suspect (from the library search based on the *Library of Congress Subject Headings*) that the term "classroom environment" will serve as a key word for studies of seating and grades. Indeed, that term appears as an acceptable search word in the Thesaurus (see Figure 3–1a).

The superscript *73* indicates the year in which this index system first included this term. *PN* refers to posting note or the number of occurrences of this term to date, and *SC* is the five-digit subject code. *SN* refers to the scope note, or definition of the term, which clearly includes the kinds of topics for which we are searching. *B* and *R* refer to broader and related terms respectively and might prove useful in considering alternative descriptors.

Having confirmed that *classroom environment* will serve as an appropriate search term, we can now take the second step by turning to a subject index for *Psychological Abstracts. Psychological Abstracts* is published monthly, and each issue includes a brief subject index for the material abstracted in that issue. Every six months, a cumulative volume index is compiled and published. For purposes of this illustration, suppose we look up *classroom environment* in the index for the July–December 1981 volume. As shown in Figure 3–1b, we find a reference that includes classroom seating position, grades, and college students (#6707).

The third and final step consists of looking up the indicated abstract numbers in the appropriate volume, in this case, volume 66 of *Psychological Abstracts.* See the abstract numbered 6707 (Levine, McDonald, O'Neal, & Garwood, 1980) in Figure 3–1c.

Each abstract provides the following citation information: authors and institutional affiliation of the first author (at the time the article was submitted); article title; the journal in which it was published; and the date, volume, and pages of this publication. The abstract briefly summarizes the entire study. The parenthetical information at the end of abstract 6707, (*8 ref*) indicates that the paper cites 8 other sources. The final note *Journal abstract* indicates that the abstract was the one printed with the article and not written expressly for *Psychological Abstracts.* To find more detail about this study, you could look up the full article in its journal using the citation information provided. You will find this article reproduced in its entirety later in this chapter.

Computerized Database Access. The online electronic database PsycINFO includes the most recent information in *Psychological Abstracts* plus other material such as citations to dissertations in psychology and related disciplines. The electronic format offers great advantages over the manual search using printed versions of *Psychological Abstracts.* For example, you need not consult the numerous volume indexes in order to cover longer time spans. However, for this same reason the electronic index could turn

Classroom Environment [73]
PN 1396   SC 09430
SN Physical, social, emotional, psychological, or
intellectual characteristics of a classroom, espe-
cially as they contribute to the learning process.
Includes classroom climate and class size.
   B   Academic Environment [73]
        Environment [67]
        Social Environments [73]
   R   Classroom Behavior [73]
        Classrooms [67]
        School Environment [73]

(a)

classroom seating position, grades & participation, college students,
6707   pre
                                                                        tec

(b)

6707. **Levine, Douglas W.; O'Neal, Edgar C.; Garwood, S. Gray & McDonald, Peter J.** (U California, Program in Social Ecology, Irvine) **Classroom ecology: The effects of seating position on grades and participation.** *Personality & Social Psychology Bulletin,* 1980(Sep), Vol 6(3), 409–412. —Conducted a 2 phase study to examine the effects of classroom seating position on test scores and participation. When 209 undergrad-uates selected their seats (Phase 1), those in the front performed better on the exam than did those in the rear. There was no effect of proximity on participation. When Ss were randomly assigned to seats (Phase 2), there were no differences in test scores as a function of proximity; however, Ss in the front of the class participated more than did those in the rear. Results imply that the relationship between seating position and grades is mediated by self-selection processes, while participation is influenced by seat location per se. (8 ref) —*Journal abstract.*

(c)

Figure 3–1   (a) From *Thesaurus of Psychological Index Terms* (1988), entry for "Classroom Environment," p. 37; (b) From *Psychological Abstracts Index* (July December 1981), section of p. 238 showing entry 6707; (c) From *Psychological Abstracts,* entry 6707, p. 700, vol 66. (This material is reprinted with the permission of the American Psychological Association, publisher of Psychological Abstracts and the PsycINFO Database. Copyright © 1967–1988 by the American Psychological Association. May not be reproduced without prior permission of the publisher.)

up many references on broad topics, thus requiring you to focus the computer search. You can do this conveniently in PsycINFO and related databases by combining search terms following the Boolean operator procedure. For example, you could restrict your search to classroom environment *and* college *and* grades, thus excluding studies of younger schoolchildren or of outcomes other than grades. The diagram in Figure 3–2 illustrates the logic of such Boolean operators in which the search focuses on the small shaded overlap of all three descriptors. In fact, just two search terms joined by the

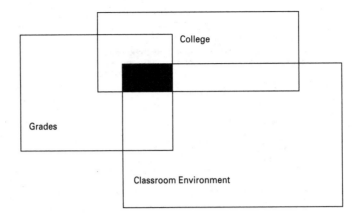

Figure 3–2 Studies of college, grades, and classroom environment.

Boolean operator *and* will often prove sufficient to narrow the search. You can also restrict searches in PsycINFO by excluding foreign language reports or limiting the search to a selected period.

Computer searches can go beyond the controlled vocabulary of the thesaurus and can search any word in the title and abstract to help locate relevant studies. For example, a recent PsycINFO search of the title words "classroom seating position" *and* "grades" turned up the citation of interest here (Levine, O'Neal, Garwood, & McDonald, 1980). Finally, one can obtain interesting abstracts at once, without having to find the relevant printed volume. You can display the abstracts on the computer monitor or make a hard copy of them if a printer is available.

Because the PsycINFO service requires connect time to a computer database, some libraries may not have it available or may charge a fee for its use. However, the same data in the form of CD-ROM may be available at lower cost. This approach permits the cumulative issue of PsycINFO database information in the form of a compact, laser-readable disc, which you can read on a personal computer. Called PsycLIT, this service permits the same kind of focused searches (using Boolean operators) available through the online database.

In addition to PsycINFO, various other electronic databases exist to serve other disciplines (for example, Sociological Abstracts, MEDLINE, and GPO Monthly Catalog for U.S. government documents). For more information on such computer search services see Reed and Baxter (1992).

Citation Index.   Another computer search service deserves special mention—the Social SCISEARCH from the Institute for Scientific Information (ISI). This database provides the electronic equivalent of the *Social Science Citation Index*. A **citation index** has the unique ability to search for reports that cite a particular reference. Using this approach, you can interpret any paper in the context of all the related papers, pro and con, that have cited that study. Suppose you have found an article of special interest and would like to find later articles on the same question, especially those that comment on the original report. You could search for such reports using a service such as *Psychological Abstracts*, but you would need to check the references listed in each discovered article to find whether or not it mentioned your primary report.

To aid this type of search, citation services, or citators as they are called, index articles by their references. Starting with just one article, one could easily multiply the number of pertinent references. Suppose you found that 10 subsequent papers had cited your primary article. Using each of these 10 new references as search keys, you could rapidly find all the other papers that cited any of them. If each of them was cited 10 times, you would have quickly found over 100 potentially relevant references. Citators can also help with author and subject retrieval. As a related service, ISI publishes *Current Contents*. This weekly journal gives tables of contents from thousands of current journals as a convenient way to locate pertinent articles even before they can be indexed and abstracted (for example, in *Psychological Abstracts*).

To follow our continuing example, a citation search was done on the Levine et al. (1980) article on seating and grades using Social SCISEARCH. By 1988, this report had been cited seven times. Of these citations, two seemed especially interesting because they carried a debate about the merits of the original article:

CLASSROOM SEATING EFFECTS—ENVIRONMENT OR SELF-SELECTION— NEITHER, EITHER, OR BOTH
LEVINE DW; MCDONALD PJ; ONEAL EC; GARWOOD SG
PERSONALITY AND SOCIAL PSYCHOLOGY BULLETIN, V8, N2, P365-369, 1982

CLASSROOM SEATING LOCATION, ORDER EFFECTS, AND REACTIVITY
STIRES LK
PERSONALITY AND SOCIAL PSYCHOLOGY BULLETIN, V8, N2, P362-364, 1982[2]

Using the author index to *Psychological Abstracts*, you can easily locate the abstracts of these two papers in order to get a summary of the debate. To get the full details, go directly to the two referenced articles and read the exchange. In the second part of this chapter, you will find a copy of the original article, which triggered this debate. You will have the opportunity to evaluate it yourself while becoming acquainted with the standard format of social science journal articles.

UNDERSTANDING SOCIAL RESEARCH REPORTS

Goals

Purposes of Publishing Research Reports. Obviously, journals exist to make research findings available to interested parties. However, journals meet other goals as well. Professional associations may create journals in order to provide a link among their members and to help define and integrate their community of scholars. Such association journals may carry reports other than research studies, perhaps concerning the organization's financial or professional business—for example, updates of ethical codes.

Journals can also help enforce ethical research practices by requiring that authors who submit papers for publication vouch for the ethical conduct of their research.

Journals may react passively to developments in a research area by publishing papers as scholars submit them. However, journals can also lead research as when editors solicit papers from selected scholars in order to provide guidance to a field. Journals also identify crucial points of contention and can further debate by providing a forum for dialogue between authors holding opposing views (for example, the Levine et al. and Stires exchange in the *Personality and Social Psychology Bulletin*, 1982, noted earlier). By allowing follow-up debate and publishing replications, a journal can become the clearinghouse for settling certain questions.

Perhaps most important, journals provide quality control for the findings that reach the larger public. Scholars have other means to share their results. They can reach the general public by calling a press conference and releasing their findings directly to the news media. They can speak to their colleagues at professional meetings or mail (electronic or hard copy) manuscripts to interested readers. But journals often provide more independent review of the submitted papers than can these outlets. Journals publish only those papers judged sound and sometimes then only after revisions to improve and clarify them. For this reason, scholars usually place more confidence in findings that have undergone such review than those that appear unchecked. An author may choose not to subject his or her findings to review in journals and to disseminate them only through unrefereed outlets. However, we should be cautious of results that seem to skirt such review especially when doubts appear as to their validity. Just such a case arose around the Milwaukee Project for early intervention with children at high risk for mental retardation. Despite questions about its author (who was convicted in federal court of diverting institutional funds), the results of this study managed to enter numerous textbooks without ever facing journal review (Sommer & Sommer, 1983).

Learning to Read Research.   This text should enable you to read social scientific reports and become a discriminating consumer of research. By the end of the course, you should have the ability to understand and critically evaluate most articles in most social research journals. By learning to read research you will have taken the step on the way to conducting your own research. You need to understand previous findings before you can ask a new question or develop a new way of answering an old question.

The weaknesses that you will learn to identify in the reports of others' research are the same ones you will want to guard against in your own research. Scholars try to spot and correct potential problems in their own research as they plan and conduct it. You will want to conduct your project so that the final report will be as immune from criticism as possible. This requires that you serve as your own worst critic by anticipating problems while they can still be corrected.

Learning a New Language.   Reading research consists of two steps: translating and criticizing. Social research, as with any other specialized activity, has its own language. To grasp the ideas of a report, you must first translate the jargon. Social scientific jargon has no more magic or mystery than any other foreign language. Much of this text consists of defining social science terms. Each chapter will introduce new terms and illustrate their use in typical contexts. In this way, you will expand your vocabulary to include the terms and symbols commonly encountered in social research reports.

Some readers feel blocked from reading social science research despite access to translations of technical terms. They believe they cannot understand certain kinds of material. People who fear math or statistical terms have something called **math phobia**. These people may have had bad experiences with math and have developed the habit of avoiding anything mathematical. The sight of a math symbol can make the math phobic anxious and discouraged. Confronted by social science statistics, such people may give up instead of patiently making their way through the material. The math phobic reader can and must learn to get past this kind of block. However, this text deals minimally with statistical concepts and treats them in an introductory way.

Learning to Criticize.   Consuming research reports means more than just translating the jargon into everyday language. It also includes a crucial aspect of science—criticism. Criticism helps ensure that research proceeds both honestly and well, and it consists of pitting alternative ideas against each other. Thus, criticism serves best when it raises constructive alternatives rather than merely pointing out the negatives. Science begins with an assertion and collects evidence to test it. The critical posture challenges whether the evidence best fits the original assertion or can be explained as well by some rival assertion. Criticism by the author or by the readers provides the rival explanations. Authors typically invite criticism of their work before submitting it for publication. The publication process consists of formal criticism of the research report by a jury of experts unknown to the author. Finally, in its published form, the research report becomes fair game for criticism by the readers, who may share their criticisms directly with the author or publicly through letters to the editor of the journal.

Reading critically means trying to come up with the rival explanations for the observed evidence. The theme of identifying and avoiding rival explanations runs throughout this text, usually in regard to one or another type of validity. The threat of rival explanations can influence research designs and reports even when it is not mentioned. The researcher designs and conducts research to avoid the criticism of the work that will follow if someone else spots an uncontrolled rival explanation. The critical reader judges how well the researcher has succeeded in avoiding plausible rivals and so discriminates between better and worse studies.

The Form of Research Reports

Writing Clearly.   The author has the duty to his or her reader of presenting ideas clearly. A common misconception about scientific writing is that it must contain many long or technical words beyond the grasp of ordinary people. On the contrary, the scientific author has an interest in reaching as wide a readership as possible. Indeed, one purpose of research reports is to spell out even advanced procedures in a way that others can understand clearly enough to replicate.

Many writing guides exist (for example, Memering, 1989). Assistance in writing correctly and clearly now comes programmed in many computer word processors. With the advent of spelling and grammar checkers, researchers have little excuse for producing sloppy manuscripts. Beyond the simple aspects of spelling and punctuation, computer software can provide feedback on the overall reading ease of a manuscript. For example, most people find it easier to read material using words of fewer rather than more syllables and sentences with fewer rather than more words that are cast in the active rather than the passive voice. Some software can not only count the words of your manuscript but also provide diagnostics as to the number of syllables per word, the number of words per sentence, and the percentage of passive sentences.

Standard Format.   Beyond writing clearly, the research author must shape his or her report to a standard format. If you compare different articles from the same journal issue or from different journals in the same discipline, you will notice that they follow a similar structure. The references include the same details in the same order. The abstracts all come to about the same length. The tables and abbreviations have a consistent appearance. Such standard format both pleases the eye and, in substantive matters such as stating citations or statistics, assures clarity. To achieve this standard format, the various social research disciplines publish rules for authors submitting papers for publication.

Some professional organizations have developed such extensive rules and examples that they require a separate publication. The *Publication Manual of the American Psychological Association* (American Psychological Association, 1983) spells out the more detailed and widely used of these style systems. This text follows the APA manual when, in the body of the text, it refers to citations in parentheses as follows: (author, year). If you want to look up the full reference, you would go to the References and find the author (listed alphabetically). If the same author has more than one citation you would use the year to identify the particular citation of interest. If the author has more than one reference in the same year, letters help avoid confusion—for example, Smith, 1987a, and Smith, 1987b. Note that the references in this text appear slightly different from those in the Levine et al. article reprinted later. This difference reflects changes in the 1983 style manual, published after the reprinted paper, which followed earlier guidelines.

Most social science journals follow a similar approach although with small differences in details. For example, the American Psychological Association requires the ampersand symbol (&) as an abbreviation for *and* in citations for multiple authors in parentheses (Smith & Jones, 1994), but the American Sociological Association uses the word *and* in the same situation. This small example illustrates the detailed nature of the many rules governing everything from punctuation to paper selection. You will need to follow the appropriate guidelines in preparing a paper to submit to a journal.

Sample Research Report.   With minor variations, all social science reports have the same parts (perhaps with varying titles) in the same order. Research reports typically have four major sections: introduction, method, results, and discussion. Articles in most social science journals also have a brief summary, called the abstract, which precedes the introduction. Following is a very brief report that illustrates this format. Quickly scan this report before reading the commentary about it. Then return to the report and read it more carefully.

Classroom Ecology:
The Effects of Seating Position
on Grades and Participation[3]

Douglas W. Levine

University of California, Irvine

Peter J. McDonald

North Georgia College

Edgar C. O'Neal
S. Gray Garwood

Tulane University

A two-phase study was conducted to examine the effects of classroom position on test scores and participation. When students selected their seats (Phase 1), those in the front performed better on the exam than did those in the rear. There was, however, no effect of proximity on participation. When students were randomly assigned to seats (Phase 2), there were no differences in test scores as a function of proximity; however, students in the front of the class participated more than did those in the rear. These results imply that the relationship between seating position and grades is mediated by self-selection processes, while participation is influenced by seat location per se.

Recent investigations of classroom ecology have indicated a relationship between seating position and a number of classroom behaviors. For example, Becker, Sommer, Bee, and Oxley (1973) found that students' test scores decreased as a function of distance away from the front and center of the classroom. Similarly, other studies have shown that participation (Sommer, 1967) and attention (Breed & Colaiuta, 1974) increase as seating location becomes more proximate to the instructor.

The observed relationship in all of these nonexperimental studies, however, can be explained in at least two ways: (1) seat location per se, and (2) self-selection. It is possible that the location of the seat may lead to better grades, more participation, and so on, perhaps because of the high levels of eye contact with the instructor to which those in front seats are exposed (Argyle & Dean, 1965; Caproni et al., 1977; Goffman, 1963). It is also plausible that the more able and/or interested students may purposely select front seats and, thus, comprise a qualitatively different sample than those who choose seats in the rear (Sommer, 1967). The experimental studies (Caproni et al., 1977; Schwebel & Charlin, 1972) that could

Personality and Social Psychology Bulletin, Vol 6 No. 3, September 1980 409–412 © 1980 by the Society for Personality and Social Psychology, Inc.

clarify this issue have not employed test performance measures. However, their results are congruent with a location explanation, at least for participation and attention behaviors.

In the present study, a two-phase approach was employed in an attempt to distinguish between the location and self-selection hypotheses. For Phase 1, students selected their seats in a large class setting, whereas for Phase 2 the same students were randomly assigned seats. Exam scores and participation were recorded. If students in front seats perform better than do those in the rear in both phases of the study, support for the seat location hypothesis would be indicated, whereas the self-selection explanation would predict that seating position should affect performance only when students choose their seats. Furthermore, these effects should be accentuated in the center of the room.

METHOD

Subjects

The study was carried out in an introductory psychology class composed of 209 undergraduates, 132 males and 77 females. Students who indicated that they had visual or auditory handicaps (n = 2), who objected to being assigned a seat (n = 8), who were using a pass-fail grading option (n = 22), or who were auditing the class (n = 2) were not included in this study. Additionally, 16 students withdrew from the course, leaving a sample of 159 students, 95 males and 64 females. The instructor was a male senior faculty member who was unaware of the experimental hypothesis.

Classroom

The class met in an amphitheater-type room with 10 rows, each containing 25 seats. Each successive row was elevated approximately one foot (.30 m) above and one and one-half feet (.46 m) behind the row in front of it. The instructor stood on an eight-inch (10.32 cm) raised platform approximately eight feet (2.44 m) in front of the first row.

Procedure

During the first week of classes, the instructor informed the students that they would be participating in an experiment within the classroom which would require them to select a seat which they would retain until instructed otherwise. Four weeks later, after their first examination, students were randomly assigned to seats. Again, they were instructed to remain in the assigned seats. Following the second exam, which was given four weeks after the first, students were told the purpose of the experiment and permitted to sit wherever they chose.

Seat selection was employed before seat assignment to maximize the impact of the manipulation. It is possible that if the students had been assigned seats on the first day of class and then told a month later that they could sit wherever they chose, few would have moved. (DeLong, 1973).

Each examination was composed of 50 multiple-choice items. Test scores were determined simply by the number of items answered correctly. Participation data were collected by two observers. Participation was defined as a single occurrence of voluntary initiation of discourse with the instructor. If the discussion continued beyond the initial question or comment, it was recorded as only one participation.

For purposes of analysis, seating positions in the classroom were divided into six areas based on two levels of proximity (front and rear) and three levels of centrality (left side, center, and right side). The two levels of proximity were obtained by dividing the class into two equal parts between the fifth and sixth rows; the three levels of centrality were obtained by dividing the class along the two aisles.

RESULTS

Phase 1

When students selected their seats, those in the front (M = 33.99; n = 72) performed better on the exam than did those in the rear (M = 31.66; n = 87). A 2 x 2 x 3 (sex x proximity x centrality) unweighted means ANOVA indicated the proximity effect was significant $F(1, 147) = 5.33$, $p<.03$. Neither sex nor centrality was reliably related to test score, nor did any of the variables interact.

For participation, the only significant effect was a sex difference, $F(1,147)=4.29$, $p<.05$, with males (M = .25; n = 95) participating more than did females (M = .03; n = 64).

Phase 2

After students were randomly assigned to seats, the proximity effect on test scores evident in Phase 1 was no longer obtained. Students assigned to the front (M = 32.23; n = 83) did not score better than those assigned to the rear (M = 32.89; n = 76), $F(1, 147) = .05$, n.s. Proximity did, however, affect participation, with students in the front (M = .15) participating more than did those in the rear (M = .01), $F(1, 147) = 3.95 = 3.95$, $p<.05$.

Correlations

Scores on the two exams were found to be significantly related, $r(157) = .66$, $p<.01$, while participation across the two phases was not, $r(157) = .03$, n.s. Somewhat surprisingly, no relationship between test scores and participation was evident, either when students selected their seats, $r(157) = .13$, n.s., or when they were assigned to them, $r(157) = .08$, n.s.

DISCUSSION

In interpreting the results of the present study, it would seem essential to distinguish between test scores and participation as indicators of "performance" in the classroom, even though it has often been assumed that they function as parallel measures (Becker et al., 1973). The test score data corroborate the findings of Becker et al. (1973) and provide support for the self-selection hypothesis, rather than the seat location explanation. On the other hand, the participation data appear to be more congruent with the location hypothesis. The significant correlation between the two exams and the lack of relationships for participations across phases lends additional support to this conclusion. Specifically, it seems that "better" students select front-row seats and perform better on examinations. They do not, however, appear to participate any more than do the other students. In fact, the lack of an effect of proximity on participation in Phase 1 implies that the "better" students are relatively immune to pressures to participate because of location. Conversely, when the students in the front and the rear sections of the classroom are comparable because of random assignment, location per se affects participation. This finding is congruent with the experimental evidence indicating that eye contact from the instructor increased participation rates (Caproni et al., 1977).

The lack of centrality effects in either phase of the study was somewhat unexpected and at variance with the results of Becker et al. (1973) and Sommer (1967). This could be due to any of a number of reasons, including class size, classroom configuration, or the relative weakness of the centrality "manipulation." The fact that the present study did involve an extremely large class at the introductory level necessitates caution in generalization. It remains to be determined if these results apply in smaller classes or with more advanced students.

REFERENCES

ARGYLE, M., & DEAN, J. Eye-contact, distance and affiliation. *Sociometry*, 1965, *28* 289–304.

BECKER, F. D., SOMMER, R, BEE, J., & OXLEY, B. College classroom ecology. *Sociometry*, 1973, *36*, 514–525.

BREED, G., & COLAIUTA, V. Looking, blinking, and sitting: Non-verbal dynamics in the classroom. *Journal of Communication*, 1974, *24*, 75–81.

CAPRONI, V., LEVINE, D., O'NEAL, F., McDONALD, P., & GARWOOD, G. Seating position, instructor's eye contact availability, and student participation in a small seminar. *Journal of Social Psychology*, 1977, *103*, 315–316.

DeLONG, A. J. Territorial stability and hierarchical formation. *Small Group Behavior*, 1973, *4*, 55–63.

GOFFMAN, E., *Behavior in public places*. Glencoe, Ill.: Free Press, 1963.

SCHWEBEL, A., & Charlin, D. L. Physical and social distancing in teacher–pupil relationships. *Journal of Educational Psychology*, 1972, *63*, 543–550.

SOMMER, R. Classroom ecology. *Journal of Applied Behavioral Science*, 1967, *3*, 489–503.

Douglas W. Levine is a graduate student in the Program in Social Ecology at the University of California, Irvine. His research interests include nonverbal behavior, helping behavior, and self-awareness.

Peter J. McDonald is an Assistant Professor of Psychology at North Georgia College. His major research interests are in the area of social motivation.

Edgar C. O'Neal is Professor of Psychology and department chairman at Tulane University. His research interests include aggression and person perception.

S. Gray Garwood is an Associate Professor of Psychology at Tulane University. His research centers on the cognitive underpinnings of social development.

Commentary.   The abstract typically condenses the whole article into less than 200 words. Busy readers use the abstract to get the gist of the whole study and to decide how much of the article they need to read or whether they need to read the article at all. The abstract presents the main question(s) or prediction(s), the basic design and measures used to answer the question, and the nature of the results. You may not need to read all parts of each report. For example, once the reader finds the study's outcome from the abstract, he or she may turn directly to the method section to check the nature of the design or measures. Perhaps a scholar is reviewing all studies on a topic. He or she might use the abstract to make sure that the study applies to that topic and then turn to the results section to find the study's outcome in detail. For the experienced reader, the abstract serves as a table of contents. By knowing what kind of material will appear in each section of the report, the reader can skip quickly to the part that he or she most needs to read.

The introduction raises the question or problem under study and presents the background to the problem, including previous studies on the issue. Often this section will state the theory or theories that guide the researcher. The reader learns here what makes this study significant—that is, how it makes an original or socially important contribution.

The authors may have created a new theory or explanation that their study will test. Or they may have identified two or more existing explanations of the same evidence. The conflict between competing explanations may provide the motivation for the study, as in the article reprinted here. The authors cite several studies showing that students seated closer to the front of a classroom perform better academically. But they also note that this result could arise from either of two reasons: (1) Better students choose to sit up front or (2) sitting up front makes students better. The authors make an original contribution by designing a study that will pit the two explanations against each other. They spell out their design in the method section.

The method section tells how the study was done so that others can check it, perhaps by inspecting this section for possible rival explanations that remained uncontrolled by the design. Another way to check a study is to do it over. The method section must give enough detail so that anyone can independently repeat the study. When different researchers, including skeptics with no vested interest in the outcome, repeat the same type of study, the findings will prove more convincing than those from just one study.

The method section describes the collection of measures and details of the study **design**. As in the reprinted study, method sections usually begin by telling about the subjects—their number, their gender, and how many dropped out. Note that the symbol *n* stands for number of subjects. The method section also defines how different concepts are measured. For example, how do the authors define "participation" in the reprinted article (see third paragraph under Procedure.)?

In experiments such as this, the researchers do more than just observe and measure; they also do things in order to provoke a reaction from the subjects. In this case, the researchers did two things. First, they let students pick their own seats, in order to see what kinds of students chose to sit up front. Then the experimenters assigned seats, to see the effect of being made to sit up front. There exist many different patterns or designs for grouping subjects, conducting interventions (that is, doing things to subjects such as assigning seats) and then observing their reactions. Design, like measurement, provides an important source of possible rival explanations.

The results section tells the outcome of the study in numerical terms. This section often makes for difficult reading by those with little statistical background. Even without such background, however, you can learn to make sense of the results section.

Statistics fall into two main categories. Descriptive statistics, as their name implies, describe the subjects on one or more measures. Take as an example the first sentence of the reprinted results section. The 72 students ($n = 72$) who chose to sit up front are described in terms of their exam scores. They received an average score of 33.99 (M = average = 33.99). The 87 students sitting in the rear received an average test score of 31.66. These averages describe each of these two groups as a whole. For example, we expect that a typical member of the "front" group would have a score of 33.99.

Inferential statistics deal with another matter. Do the values 31.66 and 33.99 seem very different to you? Would you infer that students in other courses or other universities would show the same result, that is, that those sitting up front would get better grades than those sitting in back? Since 33.99 exceeds 31.66 by only 2.33 points, perhaps the difference occurred by chance. This small difference suggests a rival explanation of the findings. Maybe the students who were studied do not represent all other students. To infer that their findings generalize to others (and thus to rule out the alternative explanation of chance), the researchers calculated an inferential statistic called an F statistic. The F statistic for the proximity effect (that is, sitting closer is related to higher grades) was 5.33. What are the chances that this value of F could have happened by chance? The probability (p) of getting this F value was less than 3 percent ($<.03$). Thus the expression "$F = 5.33, p <.03$" is the basis for the researchers to infer that the proximity effect reached **statistical significance** (that is, was not a fluke). When p does not fall below .05, we customarily say that the finding is "not significant," symbolized by "n.s." Although not a statistics text, this book will offer some material in later chapters to help you make sense of descriptive and inferential statistics.

The discussion section states the conclusions that the authors draw from their study. This section not only summarizes these conclusions but judges how much confidence they warrant. This estimate of confidence usually comes from the authors' own search for rival explanations. To the extent that one or more rival explanations remains plausible, we have low confidence in the authors' assertion. If the authors have succeeded in eliminating all explanations but one, they will have justifiable confidence in their conclusion. The authors usually close by noting remaining problems or doubts about their finding and speculating about directions for further research.

SUMMARY

The first step in social research is often that of finding out what is already known. Because of the increase in social research publications, you need to learn how to use the most efficient search procedures. Several of them are described in the first part of this chapter. Increasingly, you will find computers used to locate books and journal articles on particular topics. These electronic techniques provide the speed necessary to search huge databases. However, they require that you understand how to find key items in controlled vocabularies and to combine these terms using Boolean operators.

Once you have found a relevant study, you need to read it critically. Fortunately, social research journals follow a fairly standard format, which makes it easy to find the part you need within the whole report. This chapter reprints a brief journal article in order to illustrate the typical format. The standard sections include the abstract, introduction of the theoretical question, methods of measurement and design, results of the statistical analysis, and discussion of causal conclusions.

EXERCISES

1. If you do not already know how to use your library's system for locating books by title, author, or subject, take this opportunity to learn it now. Often libraries offer brief introductions to their procedures with hands-on instruction with computer terminals. Sign up for such instruction or review the library's printed guidelines for finding a book. Then, as an exercise, pick a topic of interest to you and try to find one or more books in your library on that topic.

2. Once you are familiar with your library's catalog system, get acquainted with one of the standard journal indexing or abstracting services. If you are interested in a psychological topic, try finding a journal article on the subject through *Psychological Abstracts*, PsycINFO, or PsycLIT following the procedure described in this chapter. Or, with your librarian's help, pursue a subject using another indexing service. Then try using a citator such as Social SCISEARCH to find articles that have cited the study that you have already located.

3. Once you have found a social research journal article of interest to you, review it critically. Locate each of the major sections identified in the article reprinted in this chapter. Challenge the main assertion of each section, trying to think of rival arguments. You should become so familiar with this standard format that you can go directly to the particular section of any social research article to the information you want—the assertion being tested, the measures being utilized, the numerical results, or the conclusions reached.

4. Obtain a copy of a publication manual for the social science discipline to whose journals you most frequently refer. If appropriate, try casting your next paper in the format prescribed by that manual. If possible, prepare your manuscript using a computer word processor that contains aids such as spelling and grammar checkers and diagnostics for reading ease. Using this software, check your composition and try revising both for better usage and for easier reading.

KEY TERMS

Abstract

Boolean operators

Call number

Citation index

Command   **Modem**
Controlled vocabulary   **Online**
Design   **Prompt**
Index   **Statistical significance**
Key words   **Statistics**
Math phobia

NOTES

1. Registered Trademark of the Regents of the University of California. Copyright 1984 The Regents of the University of California. All rights reserved.

2. Copied with the permission of the Institute for Scientific Information, 1988.

3. Levine, D. W., McDonald, P. J., O'Neal, E. C., & Garwood, S. C. (1980). Classroom ecology: The effects of seating position on grades and participation. *Personality and Social Psychology Bulletin*, Vol. I, No. 6, pp. 409–12. Copyright 1980 by Sage Publications, Inc. Reprinted by permission of Sage Publications, Inc.

4

Theory

Tentative Explanations

CAUSAL LINKS BETWEEN CONSTRUCTS

Diagramming Theories

A Model of Academic Achievement.   Theories state suspected relations among concepts. Figure 4–1 presents a picture of one theory about academic performance (Maruyama & McGarvey, 1980). The words inside the circles name concepts, and the arrows stand for causal links. Thus the arrow from academic ability to academic achievement implies that ability causes achievement.

More precisely, we should say that this arrow indicates that the theorist thinks that ability causes achievement. In reality, achievement may cause ability or both may cause each other or the two may have no connection. Each of these possible patterns would make a different theory from the one we see in Figure 4–1.

The chance that these concepts relate in unforeseen ways reminds us of a most important thing about theories—they are tentative and preliminary. Because we are uncertain about them, we call them theories instead of laws or facts. Theories come before laws in that they provide trial models subject to change and rejection. The theorist might come back to the model in Figure 4–1 and erase an arrow, reverse the direction of an arrow, add an arrow, add another concept, or remove a concept. Theories serve much like an artist's sketches. An artist would not paint in oil or sculpt in marble on the first try. Rather, he or she makes a sketch in pencil or clay and then adjusts it to the reality that the artist wants to portray. Again and again, the artist compares the sketch against the model before fixing the image in a permanent form.

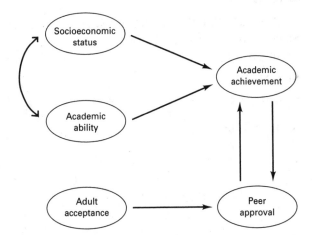

Figure 4–1   Diagram of a sample theory for causation of academic achievement. (Based on G. Maruyama and B. McGarvey. "Evaluating causal models: An application of maximum-likelihood analysis of structural equations," From *Psychological Bulletin*, 1980, *87* 502–522. Copyright 1980 by the American Psychological Association. Adapted by permission of the authors.)

Constructs.   What elements make up theory? Consider the theory in Figure 4–1 which consists of five concepts and their connections. **Concepts** are abstract aspects of reality. They name possible or imagined properties of things, people, or events. Sometimes concepts seem obvious and almost concrete or tangible. For example, we have become used to seeing or feeling such familiar aspects of things as color or weight. Among children's first words are the names for different colors. Although babies cannot define the concept of color, they can grasp that objects have color as one of their aspects or features. In the same way, we all grasp the idea that some objects feel light enough to lift and others feel too heavy to move. When we talk about how tall, fast, pretty, or fearless a person appears, we are gauging that person on abstract dimensions of length, speed, beauty, and courage.

Sometimes we use concepts that are more complex or less obvious than length or weight. Some of our mental images will not appear obvious to everyone. For example, empathy (understanding another person by taking his or her point of view) is one facet of people that we do not directly see or feel. Because we must infer it after observing social behavior, empathy can prove difficult to measure. Think for a moment of the two people you know who illustrate extremes of empathy—the one with the most empathy and the other with the least. What did you see or hear that told you how these two people differed on this concept? Perhaps you responded to facial expressions or voice quality that showed different degrees of sensitivity to others. Would other people consider these same behaviors in judging empathy? Concepts, especially complex, inferred ones such as empathy, often go by the name **constructs**. The term *construct* should remind us that the building blocks of theory are not real, but rather mental constructions.

The five concepts or constructs in Figure 4–1 all involve subtle aspects of persons or social relationships. Socioeconomic status reflects the social class or rank of the individual's parents. Academic ability refers to natural cognitive ability or intelligence. For the moment, we will not concern ourselves with how to measure such constructs. Assume that we translate these constructs into real-world terms and that different people get different scores on the resulting indexes. Thus, a person could be high or low on the continuum of ability, and some measure of ability would reflect this level by yielding a corresponding high or low score. When we measure a construct in a way that gives varying values, we call the measure a **variable**. We reserve the term *variable* here to mean an indicator or measure such as grades in school and **theoretical variable** to refer to an abstract or unmeasured concept or construct such as academic achievement. You need to understand this important distinction. *Concepts, constructs*, and *theoretical variables* all refer to abstract, unmeasured aspects of people, events, or things, which we envision in our mind's eye. *Variables* and *measured variables* refer to the concrete, measured expressions of these aspects, which we can count, categorize, or assign numerical values.

According to the theory in Figure 4–1, the students' social status and academic ability levels came before their achievement. We presume that still earlier constructs caused both status and ability, but a theory has to start somewhere. Theories vary in their range, some including more causal links and some fewer. However extensive, any theory has to choose some concepts as starting points—causes whose own causes are unknown or at least not stated. To such a "starter" concept we sometimes give the name

exogenous construct because its causes originate from outside the theory. Exogenous constructs have straight causal arrows leading away from but not to them. In their measured form, such variables go by the name **independent variables** because they are independent of (not caused by) the other variables in the model.

Figure 4–1 suggests a link between status and ability. That is, high parental status and high ability occur together as do low status and low ability. This linkage has many exceptions, and the degree of the concurrence remains to be estimated. This particular theory does not try to explain the causal link of status and ability. As a result, the figure uses a double-headed curved arrow to symbolize association with no claim of causal direction.

In contrast, the straight single-headed arrows in Figure 4–1 do assert causal linkage, for example, from status and ability to achievement. The theory suggests that these connections are causal in nature. Achievement—the effect in both of these causal relations—is an **endogenous construct** because its causes appear in the model. The manifest or measured forms of endogenous constructs go by the name of **dependent variables** because their values or levels depend on the causal variable(s). The arrow from status to achievement and the one from ability to achievement illustrate simple **direct causal paths**. These particular direct causal paths hold little interest, having neither novelty nor controversy. We expect students with high ability and/or high family status to have high achievement levels. Of course, we know that not all such students will succeed. The theory does not state the strength of these causal connections, only that they exist at a level that we can detect.

This theory should interest us most for the pair of causal links between achievement and peer approval (Figure 4–1). The arrow from peer approval to achievement claims that being liked by same-age people affects learning. If a student feels accepted by his or her classmates, who themselves value high academic achievement, then he or she should adopt the peer group's desire for achievement. Such approval should raise achievement as the individual conforms with peer pressure to try harder. Of course, not all peer groups place a high value on achievement. If the dominant peer value goes against high achievement, the influence model would predict a decrease in achievement as the student adopted the prevailing values. As you can see, just one causal arrow in the diagram can serve as shorthand for a number of assumptions and logical connections.

The right-hand arrow from achievement to approval suggests quite a different causal process. Sometimes referred to as the "star model," this arrow suggests that achievement causes approval, again assuming an environment that places a high value on achievement. High achievers, in such a social setting, should earn the reward of peer popularity.

The presence of both arrows in the diagram says that both the social influence and the star models are working at the same time. Two reverse causal processes, working at the same time, constitute **reciprocal causation**. Suppose a low-achieving student transfers from a low-achievement to a high-achievement school. The reciprocal causation might operate as follows: The student gets acquainted and begins to adopt the harder work habits and achievement goals of the new peer group following the influence model. This harder work should produce higher achievement, which in turn gains the student wider acceptance, following the star model. The new popularity may lead to acceptance by an elite inner group, whose more intense work habits are then adopted. The new work habits lead to still greater success, which in turn causes still greater popularity by our rising star.

Adult acceptance, the fifth concept in Figure 4–1, refers to the degree of approval of the student by important adults such as parents and teachers. Adult acceptance has an arrow going from it but none to it and thus qualifies as an exogenous construct. This model suggests that more adult approval should cause greater peer approval. Since peer approval may cause achievement, adult acceptance also affects achievement by **indirect causation**. When one variable indirectly causes another it does so via a third variable that, like a relay runner, takes the baton from one runner and passes it to the next. This middle variable serves as an **intervening variable**. In our example, peer approval acts like an intervening construct between adult acceptance and academic achievement.

The theory pictured in Figure 4–1 involves only a few constructs and causal connections. Theories can expand to become elaborate systems with not only more constructs but also more and different types of linkages (see Chapter 12 for a review of causal paths). We turn our focus now to the use of theory.

Why Have Theories?

Action. It has been said that nothing is so practical as a good theory. Of course, not everyone thinks of theories as practical. The word *theory* connotes ivory towers where theorists take flights of fancy that have little to do with real life or average people. In fact, most theorists have real-world concerns in mind when they develop their ideas and can justify their efforts by pointing to social choices that their work could affect. If a theory in some basic science area seems impractical, wait a while until applications catch up with it. The pure research of today may well affect daily living tomorrow.

How do we put theory to use? Theories serve us in two major ways. First, they meet our need to act even when we are uncertain. The necessity to act often forces us to guess about how the world works. Until we can replace our guesses with laws, we want to make our guesses the very best that they can be. We can think of theories as carefully reviewed and comprehensive guesses. Good theories have coherence, logic, and internal consistency. More than that, good theories integrate existing thoughts and data, taking into account both agreements and disagreements among observers. Well-researched and well-argued theories can persuade policy makers better than wild guesses. Plausible theories can contribute to important social policy decisions. For example, one link in the theory of Figure 4–1 addresses the policy of school integration. The social influence path from peer approval to academic achievement suggests that moving students from low-achievement to high-achievement schools will raise academic performance by disadvantaged students.

Research. Theories prove useful in a second way by guiding research. Researchers know that theories are only tentative, temporary ways of seeing the world that await further tests. Empirical research collects precise observations in order to answer questions. But the world poses a great many questions. How does one single out any one question? Theory serves to specify the most crucial questions. Better theories point to better questions, that is, those that merit our interest and will yield to our methods. Worthy questions do not already have answers. To pursue an already answered question wastes our time and makes no new contribution. However, we should distinguish redundant studies on an already answered question from those that check research on a question that remains unresolved.

Good questions should also be answerable. Some important questions, such as "What causes poverty?" or "What causes war?," will prove too large to answer in any single study with our present methods. Just as teams of climbers attempt Mt. Everest in stages, so researchers, working in teams, divide great social problems into smaller questions. Good theories provide a series of manageable tasks, which together will solve the great puzzles.

Answerable questions suggest claims that can be disconfirmed. Good theories produce clear predictions that data can support or contradict. For example, the theory in Figure 4–1 proposes that peer approval raises academic achievement, at least in some kinds of schools. We can translate this assertion into a question. In such schools, will students who have more peer acceptance make greater academic progress than students with less acceptance? Since researchers can measure the concepts in this question, such as *academic progress*, they produce a clear yes-or-no answer. If the research uses fair and accurate methods and gives a "no" answer, we will tend to doubt the theory stated in Figure 4–1. In sum, we can falsify or cast doubt on theories with observations that contradict them (Popper, 1987). Good theories run this risk of being shown wrong. If we cannot disconfirm theories, we also cannot confirm them. On the other hand, evidence consistent with a theory does not assure us that all future tests will support it. Even several studies in support of the theory do not give conclusive proof.

How can one tell if a theory can be disconfirmed? Platt (1964) has offered key questions:

> It consists of asking in your own mind, on hearing any scientific explanation or theory put forward, "But sir, what experiment could disprove your hypothesis?"; or, on hearing a scientific experiment described, "But sir, what hypothesis does your experiment disprove?" (p. 352)

Bad theories can prove difficult to disconfirm for various reasons. Sometimes theories consist of vague constructs that we cannot measure in a clear, agreed-upon way. In such cases, different researchers may test the same theory with noncomparable methods. Contrary findings from such different tests bog researchers down in disputes about how to measure the theory's key constructs. Other times, theories fail to give clear predictions. Such "flexible" theories can bend to fit any data. Supporters of such theories can explain away contrary findings by discovering or making up new twists after the fact.

We could try to conduct research without theory but would find it inefficient. Theory serves to organize research. Separate researchers working on the same problem can coordinate their studies within the framework of a shared theory. Guided by theory, a researcher can build a program of research that is greater than the sum of its separate studies. Theory can provide a context that makes each study more meaningful by linking it to others sharing the same constructs and assumptions.

Nomothetic Versus Idiographic Approaches. The role of theory just described fits the **nomothetic** approach. The term *nomothetic* refers to the science of general laws or properties. This approach strives to discover regular patterns that hold in different times and places. Social scientists hesitate to raise one of their theories to the status of law even after repeated supportive findings. Nevertheless, researchers in the nomothetic tradition hope to find general, lawful relationships.

In contrast, other social researchers adopt the **idiographic** approach. This approach focuses on the particulars of the individual person, place, or time under study without trying to generalize or discover universal laws. A pure form of the idiographic approach assumes that each person requires a unique set of descriptors. Scholars taking the idiographic approach to human personality would describe each person as a separate case without reference to any other. On the other hand, those taking a nomothetic approach would try to find traits (such as shyness) shared by all members of a class. If successful, this nomothetic effort would allow the researcher to predict certain behaviors (for example, talking little when meeting strangers) of members of that class (Bem, 1983). This text and the social sciences generally favor the nomothetic approach. That is, we will assume that research can use a common set of concepts or dimensions to describe all persons (for example high, medium, or low on shyness). Nevertheless, we should recall that some social researchers prefer the idiographic approach, as discussed in the chapter on qualitative research (Chapter 13).

THE PROCESS OF THEORY-BASED RESEARCH

Steps in Making and Using Theory

Theory-based research consists of a few repeating steps: induction, deduction, and tests. After testing, the results contribute to another induction, and the sequence begins again. Figure 4–2 illustrate these four steps.

Induction. In the induction phase, we concoct general principles or relationships that might explain specific observations, anecdotes, or research results. In moving from the particular to the general, we are creating theory. What are the sources of the ideas that theorists use to explain or organize their data? Sometimes, we can trace such ideas to earlier theories or analogies borrowed from other disciplines. Other times, inductions appear as new insights invented by the theorist.

Figure 4–2 pictures the inductive process as arrows from data to the conceptual system and abbreviates the theory shown in Figure 4–1. From actual observations of achievement, peer and adult acceptance, status, and ability, the theorist states connections that should apply generally to all students in all schools. Thus, this theory serves the useful purpose of summarizing many separate observations about several different concepts.

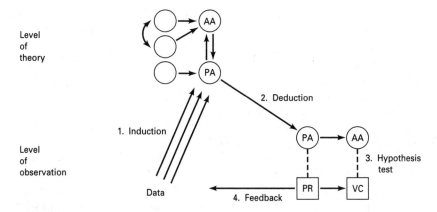

Figure 4–2   Steps in social research.

Theory need not simply summarize observed relationships. Theory can also express the theorist's imagination or intuition about unobserved relations. The theorist may invent new concepts and predict new links between concepts. Thus, theory comes partially from data and partially from speculation. Different theories blend different proportions of facts and imagination.

How do researchers choose topics about which to theorize? The theorist's special interests and training will help orient him or her toward one or another broad area. But within an area, a theorist will likely be attracted to a **paradox**—a situation in which existing theories and data seem to clash. The theorist attempts to reconcile apparently divergent ideas and facts within a more complete framework. The resulting set of constructs and their causal relationships may fit reality better than prior theories do.

Deduction.   **Deduction**, the next step in theory-based research, derives specific assertions or claims from general theoretical principles. A theory that has many constructs and causal paths can provide more than one such claim. Figure 4–2 illustrates deduction with just one link from the theory portrayed in Figure 4–1: the causal path from peer approval (PA) to academic achievement (AA). These two constructs and their connection appear as two circles and a joining arrow. The theory implies that this proposition holds in a general way. If it holds generally for all students in all schools, we expect it to hold for any sample of students from any school. Just as induction goes from the particular to the general, so deduction goes back from general theory to particular claims.

Hypothesis Testing and Operationalization.   To test a theory or any of its components, we must find a way to express the constructs of each proposition and observe them in some particular subjects. In order to translate a construct into a tangible, observable form, we must make an **operational definition**. We can use standard measuring methods to get scores on the peer approval and academic achievement of students

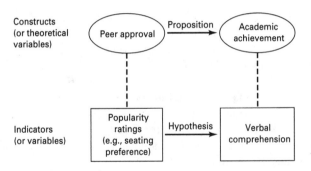

Figure 4–3 Testable hypothesis from theoretical proposition.

from a particular school. The operations or procedures for getting these scores may consist of self-report questionnaires, structured interviews, or standardized ratings by trained observers. In fact, researchers can usually define a construct with any of several different operations. The resulting measures appear as squares in Figure 4–3, which enlarges a section of Figure 4–2.

This distinction between constructs and their operational forms sometimes puzzles students. The present theory includes a link between two constructs—peer approval and academic achievement. These constructs exist as mental notions about which we can think and talk, but they do not have a tangible form. As long as we only think about these aspects of students, we are working with theory and do not need data about the approval or achievement of any particular student.

However, if we want to test the theory's claim that peer approval affects academic achievement we need to observe these two aspects of student experience. How can we measure them in a way that convinces others that we have perceived them accurately? Not any measure will do. Suppose someone measured peer approval with a yardstick in the belief that tall people had more approval. We should reject such a silly measure because height does not reflect what we intend by our concept of peer approval. Indeed, we could imagine hundreds of different measures, many of which would not seem plausible reflections of our construct. Even from among the most plausible measures, we might pick and choose one as better than others. Because a construct can have so many different operational expressions, good, bad, and absurd, we must distinguish the theory level and the hypothesis level. A causal claim about two constructs in a theory may or may not receive a fair translation into measures of actual people. Translating constructs into faithful observations is an important research craft that we explore in Chapters 5 and 6.

When we operationalize a proposition (that is, translate its constructs into observable form), it becomes a hypothesis. A **hypothesis** usually consists of a prediction about the relations among operational terms. Since most constructs can be manifested in more than one way and in more than one sample, any deduction from theory can have many hypothesis tests—one for each set of operational definitions and samples. Figure 4–3 shows how a proposition from the general theory translates into one hypothesis. First we must define each construct in operational form. We could index a student's peer approval by the number of other students who say they want to sit beside him or her in class. We could gauge a student's academic achievement by his or her score on a standard test of verbal comprehension. Then, we can state our hypothesis in these operational terms. For students enrolled in achievement-oriented schools, those whom more students want to sit next to will score higher on verbal comprehension.

Hypothesis testing, the third basic step in social research, brings theory and reality face to face. If the observed data do not fit our hypothesis, we are inclined to reject the hypothesis and to doubt the theory from which we deduced it. Theories should apply generally. Any mismatch of specific data with theory tends to lower our confidence in or falsify the theory, assuming we have conducted the hypothesis test well. Of course, those with faith in the theory may distrust our test methods or measures and claim that they and not the theory are defective in some way.

On the other hand, one instance of a good fit between data and theory does not "prove" the theory. Since theory should hold for all cases within its domain, only tests of the theory in all relevant cases would give conclusive proof. Disproof of the theory always lurks at the next hypothesis test where different subjects or measures might give contrary data. This points up the bias of hypothesis testing. One negative finding saps more support from the theory than a positive finding brings to it. Nevertheless, if the hypothesis test followed good procedures, data that are consistent with the hypothesis do lend some support to the theory.

Since a single hypothesis test cannot prove the truth of a proposition and its parent theory, we often see repeated hypothesis tests for the same deduction. Different researchers, using different samples of subjects and similar or different measures of the constructs, may test hypotheses based on the same proposition. These repeated tests check the generality of the findings, that is, that the proposition holds in different samples. These replications also assure the quality of the hypothesis tests, that is, that the operational definitions and research designs of various tests give consistent results.

Different tests of the same proposition all too often give different results. Different tests may share the same constructs and the same predictions. But these hypothesis tests can vary greatly in the way they operationalize constructs and in the way they demonstrate causal direction. Therefore, researchers try to understand how differences in the designs and operational definitions of hypothesis tests lead to different results. This information helps determine which hypothesis tests to believe and aids in designing still better tests. Much of this book deals with evaluating the quality of measurement and research design.

Feedback.   In the fourth and final step, the results from hypothesis testing feed back to the inductive phase to support or revise theory. Theory serves as a running scorecard for hypothesis testing. As results emerge from hypothesis tests, they become part of the database on which theory stands. New findings that conflict with old theory will trigger new inductive work. Theories may not need adjustment after each study. Over time, however, the weight of evidence from many sound studies will shape and reshape theory.

Consider the hypothesis that greater peer approval leads to increased academic achievement. Numerous convincing findings against this notion could result in removing the arrow from peer approval to academic achievement in Figure 4–1. The other arrows and constructs could remain in place until such time as new research requires their adjustment.

Guidelines for Theory.   Aside from internal logic and agreement with the data, we commonly want our theories to have two properties. One of these is **parsimony**, which we may understand in this context as efficiency. A theory with parsimony employs the fewest constructs and linkages necessary to explain the events of interest. If two theories have equal success in fitting the data, we usually prefer the one with more parsimony. Parsimony does more than save theorists and researchers the trouble of working with extra concepts. Scientists share a faith that underlying causal mechanisms are relatively simple and therefore prefer less complex theories. Nevertheless, some realities, especially social ones, do not seem very simple, and our data may force us to complicate our theories with more constructs and their linkages.

The other property that guides us in revising theory is **generality**. Theorists try to stretch their theories to explain more and more data. Indeed, theory should make sense out of otherwise separate and isolated observations. Theories that explain more findings will prove more useful than less general rival theories. In the absence of theory, our science would consist simply of lists of unrelated facts and thoughts. General theory can take us beyond the already seen and familiar to predict what will happen in circumstances that we have never encountered. Before we had a theory of gravity, humankind made do with a great many unrelated observations of how different objects fell from different heights. But a general theory of gravity made it possible to predict and, therefore, control the falling or orbiting behavior of objects even in places no person had ever visited (for example, the lunar landings). For this reason, theorists strain to extend the generality of their explanations.

We may not always be able to achieve both generality and parsimony. To gain greater generality we may have to accept greater complexity. In order to extend the theory of Figure 4–1 regarding achievement and approval to cover students in other cultures, we may have to add more constructs and causal propositions. Nevertheless, most researchers aspire to a theory that has both parsimony and generality. Such a combination of simplicity and power would have an esthetic appeal that we call *elegance*. An elegant theory will not only prove functional but also has a kind of beauty. For further discussion of social research theory, see Dubin (1978) or Marx (1965).

Testing Theory

Where Are Theories Found?   Statements of theory appear throughout most journal reports. We find them most developed in introductions, because theory provides the rationale for conducting most studies and points to the constructs and questions for research. We also see theory in methods and results sections because the operationalizations and study designs must serve the deductions drawn from theory. Finally, theory often reappears in the discussion section of research articles. Here the work of feeding back the results of the study to the inductive process begins. Thus, most data-based or empirical studies refer to theory throughout their reports and illustrate in miniature each of the research steps.

Theory can appear in a pure form without any hypothesis tests or reports of new data. Such theory statements articulate and defend theory, drawing on and relating existing studies. Such theory papers may require long journal articles or even whole books. Some journals devote themselves to theory (for example, *Psychological Review*) or theory and review (for example, *Psychological Bulletin*). Other journals present a mix of theory and empirical articles (for example, *American Sociological Review*). Chapter 14 discusses approaches to literature review, which often provides the basis for new inductive theorizing. Theory and review papers differ from empirical ones in obvious ways. For example, the former do not include traditional methods and results sections that describe the collection and analysis of new data from research subjects. Rather such papers resemble extended versions of traditional introductions, providing comprehensive overviews of studies along with new ways of relating the pertinent constructs. In the final section of this chapter, we will summarize a portion of such a published theory and then see how it translates into a test.

Unemployment and Mental Disorder.   Scholars have been exploring the links between economic stress and mental disorder for over a century. Some researchers have focused on personal job loss and its connection with symptoms of mental disorder. These researchers have debated whether job loss causes mental disorder (social causation) or existing disorder causes job loss (drift). Other researchers have dealt more with the economic climate and its connection to rates of suicide and mental hospital admissions. Figure 4–4 presents one part of a theory that joins these individual and aggregate perspectives (Dooley & Catalano, 1980). Each of the terms and links in this theory has a basis in prior research or theory, but this review brings these various ideas and findings together in a new way.

The circles in the upper section of Figure 4–4 represent four constructs from the larger model (Dooley & Catalano, 1980, p. 461, Figure 1). Environmental economic change refers to the economy as a whole, not just the job experience of individuals. The arrow from this construct implies that it should influence individually experienced life change, that is, life events felt by particular persons. For example, if a state has a recession, we expect increasing numbers of its residents to have such life events as being laid off. However, another construct might also influence personal life events as indicated by the arrow from the noneconomic sources circle. For example, people with less training or drug abuse problems should have a higher risk of job loss. Finally, the individually experienced life change construct should cause individually experienced symptoms or signs of mental distress. People undergoing great change should feel stress and show signs of it in the form of mental symptoms. Other factors might influence these constructs and they might in turn affect others, but we will attend only to this small part of the full theory.

In order to test this theory, we need to operationalize these theoretical variables or constructs. The vertical lines in the lower section of Figure 4–4 match the constructs with their measured counterparts (in boxes). These particular measures appeared in a test of the theory (Dooley, Catalano, & Hough, 1992). Other tests could have used quite different ways of making these constructs manifest. For example, we might have measured environmental economic change as change in inflation or in surveyed consumer

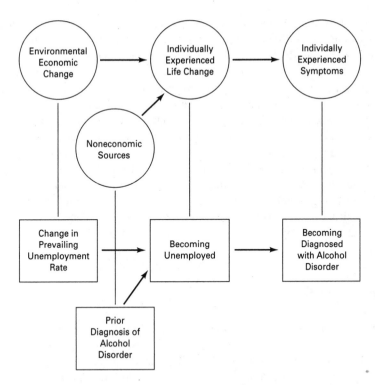

Figure 4–4 A theory of unemployment and alcohol disorder and its operationalization.

confidence. But this hypothesis test used Department of Labor records to measure change from first interview to second interview in the unemployment rate for the communities in which the subjects lived. This study used prior diagnosis of alcohol disorder to express the construct of noneconomic sources of life change in order to test drift, the idea that disorder causes job loss. Individually experienced life change could have appeared as any life event such as divorce or death of a loved one. However, because of its focus on economic stress, this study expressed this construct as moving from working at first interview to receiving unemployment compensation at second interview. The construct of individually experienced symptoms could have appeared as the number or severity of any symptoms including those of anxiety, depression, or schizophrenia. Because it targeted alcohol abuse, this study used moving from no diagnosis of alcohol disorder at first interview to being so diagnosed at second interview. In sum, this study acquired data from different sources that gave numeric values for each of several thousand subjects for each of these four constructs. Other researchers, choosing different ways of measuring these same constructs or using a different sample of people, would have tested the propositions of the theory differently.

You should now have the ability to detect the independent or exogenous variables (unemployment rate change and prior alcohol diagnosis) and the dependent or endogenous variable (becoming alcoholic). Remember that exogenous variables have no arrows leading to them, but they have arrows leading from them to other variables. What kind of variable is becoming unemployed? Since it "intervenes" between unemployment rate and becoming alcoholic, it functions as an intervening variable.

Try stating one proposition from this theory in terms of its constructs and then re-state it as a testable prediction or hypothesis. For example, you might select the proposition that noneconomic characteristics of people affect their life events. In its operational form, it becomes a testable hypothesis for the notion of drift. You could state it as follows: *A person with a prior diagnosis of alcohol disorder will have a higher risk of becoming unemployed.* We have thus taken a small piece of a larger theory and translated it from vague, unspecified concepts into measured variables. Also note that this hypothesis consists of a prediction that could turn out either true or false. A negative or false finding would tend to disconfirm (weaken our belief in) this piece of the theory. A positive or supportive finding would increase our confidence in the theory, but with the reservation that other tests with other measures or subjects might give a different outcome.

SUMMARY

A theory assembles claims about causally related constructs. Theory can help guide research and, in turn, should change as new findings point to improvements. Independent theoretical variables (also called exogenous constructs) have no causes stated in the model. Dependent or endogenous constructs do have causes stated in the theory. An intervening construct links independent and dependent constructs. Two constructs may cause each other in a process called reciprocal causation.

Research proceeds in steps: The researcher first creates general theory from specific data and speculation (induction). Second, he or she selects a causal proposition from a general theory and expresses it as a specific assertion that could be checked in a particular group or setting (deduction). Third, the researcher translates the proposition into operational variables and gathers observations to check the fit between the predicted and the observed relationship (hypothesis test). Fourth, these results feed back into a new inductive step to confirm or revise the theory.

EXERCISES

1. Locate a newspaper or popular magazine article that implies or states a theory and then find its cause and effect constructs. Do any other kinds of constructs intervene between the cause and effect terms? Now, for each construct, state the operation that expresses it in a numeric way. Finally, diagram the theory using circles for the constructs and diagram the hypothesis test with boxes for each operational variable. As in Figure 4–4 join the names of the variables by arrows indicating the supposed causal direction and link each construct to its operational counterpart with a vertical line.

2. When you can diagram simple theories, seek more elaborate ones in the published research literature. Search professional journals in your area of interest. Find ei-

ther a report that tests a theory (for example, Wheaton, 1980, or the article by Levine et al., 1980, reprinted in Chapter 3) or an article stating a theory without any test (for example, Patterson, 1976). In the former case, identify the constructs (with circles) and their associated variables (with boxes) for the key propositions. In the latter case, where there is no test of the theory, select a proposition from the theory and make up your own operational definitions for a hypothesis test. In both cases, note which constructs and variables are independent, intervening, or dependent.

3. Practice making the distinction between constructs and variables. Start by looking at a theory that you found for the previous exercise or the theory in Figure 4–4. For each construct of the theory, see how many different operational variables you can make up. Go a step further and make a list of constructs or theoretical variables that come to mind, for example, length, intelligence, and academic achievement. Then beside each construct write several possible operationalizations or measured variables, for example, for length: feet and inches measured by a ruler; light years measured by astronomical methods; a micron measured by using an electron microscope. Then reverse the process, and make up a list of measured variables and for each one state the construct that it operationalizes. To build confidence with this construct/operationalization distinction, do this exercise with a partner, where one of you states the construct and the other names a variable.

KEY TERMS

Concept	Independent variable
Construct	Indirect causation
Deduction	Intervening variable
Dependent variable	Nomothetic
Direct causal path	Operational definition
Endogenous construct	Paradox
Exogenous construct	Parsimony
Generality	Reciprocal causation
Hypothesis	Theoretical variable
Hypothesis test	Variable
Idiographic	

❧ 5 ❧

Measurement Theory
Toward Validity and Reliability

MEASURING MEASURES

A Case of Mismeasurement

The N-Ray Affair.   Both the social and physical sciences depend on measuring things that are hard to see. An episode in the history of physics shows how much trouble can surround such measurement. As you will see, however, this story tells more about social processes than physical reality.

In 1903, a French physicist named René Blondlot announced that he had found a new kind of radiation, which became known as N rays (Klotz, 1980). A highly respected member of the French Academy of Science, Blondlot was working in an era of rapid breakthroughs, triggered by Roentgen's work on X rays in 1895. Physicists were finding new forms of radiation such as alpha rays, beta rays, and gamma rays, each with new properties that might advance both science and practice.

To detect and then explore a new form of radiation, the physicist needed to develop a good measure. In order to exploit the concept of N rays, researchers needed a standard signal of their presence. Only then could independent work on the new ray proceed rapidly in various laboratories. Blondlot offered such a technique for detecting the N ray.

Figure 5–1 diagrams Blondlot's spark gap method. He claimed that a great variety of objects could emit N rays: electric discharge tubes, the sun, certain types of gas burners, and even cold steel. Blondlot suspected that N rays would reinforce the energy of an electric spark, thus making it brighter.

The researcher would discharge a spark between the points of two wires carrying electricity from an attached battery. The observer would then photograph it or note its brightness directly. Typically, the spark gap detector was enclosed in a light-tight box to keep out the confounding effects of the surrounding light. The spark should appear brighter in the presence of an N ray source than when the source was absent or blocked off. Thus Blondlot had contrived to make the invisible visible.

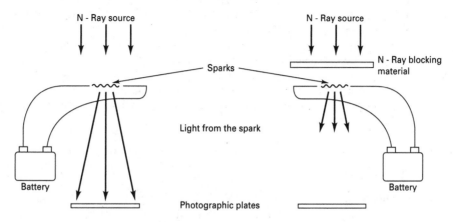

Figure 5–1   Spark gap detector for N rays.

Blondlot's work on N rays led to a host of related discoveries. For example, a respected medical physicist named Charpentier claimed that N rays were produced by the human body and could help study living human organs such as the human heart while it was beating. In less than a year, researchers were competing for the honor of having discovered this promising new radiation. Publications in the *Annals of the French Academy of Science* about N rays jumped from four in the first half of 1903 to fifty-four in the first half of 1904 (versus only three about X rays, for example).

After the sharp increase in scientific papers about N rays in 1903 and 1904, not a single report on them appeared in the Academy's *Annals* in 1905. What had happened to N rays? They had come to the attention of an American scholar and practical joker named R. W. Wood, a professor of physics at Johns Hopkins University. As a hobby, Wood pursued frauds such as spirit mediums. When he tried and failed to observe N rays in his lab using Blondlot's procedure, he became skeptical. He arranged to visit Blondlot's lab at the University of Nancy.

Blondlot and his colleagues very hospitably demonstrated for Wood their various measurement approaches to N rays. For example, they showed him photographs taken by the method shown in Figure 5–1. The researchers exposed the photographic plates for five seconds per trial for repeated trials in order to amplify any sign of N rays. The images of the spark exposed to the N-ray source seemed brighter than those taken with the N-ray source removed or blocked off. But Wood noticed that the technique of making these photos had a serious flaw. The researchers may have exposed the photographic plates for a longer total time when the N-ray source was exposed than when it was covered.

In another display of N-ray effects, this time in a darkened room, Blondlot's staff claimed they could see the rays with the naked eye. When Wood could not see these effects, he devised a practical joke. In this case, a piece of steel served as the source of the N rays. Unknown to the other observers, Wood replaced the steel with a piece of wood, a substance not thought to produce N rays. When Blondlot's staff continued to "see" the N rays, Wood concluded that their belief in N rays was deluding them.

In 1904, Wood published his exposé of N rays and thus ended that line of research outside France. In 1903 and 1904, 20 French scientists had confirmed the existence of N rays, and some of them resisted Wood's conclusions. As Klotz (1980) reports,

> When only French scientists remained in the N-ray camp, the argument began to acquire a somewhat chauvinistic aspect. Some proponents of N rays maintained that only the Latin races possessed the sensitivities (intellectual as well as sensory) necessary to detect manifestations of the rays. It was alleged that Anglo Saxon powers of perception were dulled by continuing exposure to fog and Teutonic ones blunted by constant ingestion of beer. (p. 175)

Most of the French scientists who verified N rays did so in the vicinity of Nancy, suggesting some sort of social contagion or persuasion. To protect the honor of French science the journal *Revue Scientifique* challenged Blondlot to prove once and for all that he could detect and measure N rays. The challenge consisted of two identical boxes, one with a "known" N-ray source such as steel and the other with an equal weight of a non–N-ray source such as lead. The boxes would have different code numbers known only to the staff of the *Revue Scientifique*. Blondlot could use any of his techniques to identify the N-ray source box. After great delay, Blondlot wrote back in 1906 to decline the challenge.

The N-ray affair shows that measuring even the most neutral and objective of physical realities is subject to human distortion. Blondlot saw what he wanted to see and persuaded others to see what he wanted them to see. We do not so much believe what we see; rather, we see what we believe. This problem persists to this day as illustrated by a more recent dispute between Jacque Benveniste, the head of a French allergy laboratory, and the British journal *Nature*. Benveniste claimed to observe an antibody reaction occurring in a solution theoretically too diluted to produce such an effect—suggesting that the solution retained a kind of "memory" of the antibodies it once contained. Doubting the claims of Benveniste, *Nature* sent a review team that included the professional magician James "The Amazing" Randy to study the French laboratory's procedures. The team reported that the experiment failed when the identity of samples was masked from the researchers (Maugh, 1988).

The Threat of Mismeasurement. If researchers have trouble with the neutral, objective concepts of the physical sciences, complex social constructs should prove even more difficult to measure. Almost any social study faces the threat that it has mismeasured its key terms. If the measure we are using does not truly reflect the construct of interest, the study's results cannot address the proposition and theory in question.

Social research constructs often resemble Blondlot's N ray in that they do not seem tangible and prove hard to "see" directly. But we can hope to have some indirect sign or measure of such constructs just as Blondlot hoped that an electric spark would flare up in the presence of N rays. The spark's flare was not an N ray itself but served as a visible indicator of its presence. In the same way, social scientists hope that their measures will reflect the presence and magnitude of such abstractions as social status, empathy, or criminal tendencies.

Sadly, an indicator may measure nothing at all, or it may measure something other than the construct of interest. We now know that N rays do not exist. Blondlot's indicator measured, if anything, the researchers' belief or hope that N rays existed. Blondlot's spark measure seemed to show the presence of N rays only to believers. This phenomenon continues to occur and remains interesting, but it belongs in the realm of social research rather than physics.

Reliability and Validity

As we have seen with the N-ray affair, measures do not always do a good job of reflecting the construct for which they are intended. As a result, in planning or judging research, we must assess all measures. Usually, we will judge the quality of measures on two dimensions: reliability and validity.

Reliability. **Reliability** refers to the degree to which observed scores are "free from errors of measurement" (American Psychological Association, 1985, p. 19). We can gauge reliability by the consistency of scores. Do we find agreement between parallel forms of a test or between different items of the same questionnaire or between different raters using a measure?

Validity.   **Validity** "refers to the appropriateness, meaningfulness, and usefulness of the specific inferences" made from the measures (American Psychological Association, 1985, p. 9). Thus validity belongs not just to a measure but depends on the fit between the measure and its label.

A special research area has emerged to judge and improve the reliability and validity of social science measures. In psychology, this field has the name **psychometrics**. Researchers in this field have invented ways of measuring measures and assigning them scores called reliability and validity coefficients. These numbers tell us how much confidence we can place in the measures (J. P. Campbell, 1976; Nunnally, 1978.)

Measures are rarely perfect and sometimes seem worthless. The value of a measure depends not only on its reliability and validity but also on its specific purpose. Thus a measure with modest reliability and validity may prove adequate for an initial study but too crude for making an important decision about a particular person. Because of the necessity of good research measures, some disciplines have developed standards for reporting new tests and measurement methods (for example, the American Psychological Association, 1985). These standards and the psychometric procedures on which they are based derive from measurement theory.

Errors of Measurement

Decomposing Observations.   Measurement theory begins with the insight that any observation, test score, or outcome of a measurement procedure is imperfect. We can think of the **observed score** (also called the *fallible score*) as the sum of two general components: **true score**, the part that perfectly reflects the concept of interest, and **error**, the difference between the true and observed scores. We can decompose any person's observed score (X):

$$X = T + E$$
where T = true score and E = error.

In this approach, E stands for all of the possible factors that can make our observed score imperfect. Many types of error exist, and their full treatment goes beyond the scope of this introduction (Shavelson & Webb, 1991). For simplicity, we will first approach the error term in a narrow way and later consider other sources of imperfect measurement.

In measuring, we try to assign numbers to objects, persons, or events that reflect the true extent of the construct of interest. That is, we want the observed value X to come as close to T and the error E to come as close to zero as possible. We cannot know exactly how much of any observed score (X) comes from T and how much comes from all other sources (E). In order to resolve this dilemma, we can assume that the error is random. To signify such random error we will use the amended symbol Er. Defining measurement error as random implies that it is unpredictable. This means that Er is as likely to be positive as negative and should add up to zero over a large number of observations. Thus error may favor an individual on one item or test, but over many tests the bad luck should balance the good. This assumption makes it possible to estimate how much of observed scores come from true scores and how much from random error for a whole group of scores.

Random Errors Cancel. Consider an example of measurement error that you have probably encountered. Suppose you take a course that has weekly 10-item, true/false quizzes. To correct for guessing, the instructor subtracts one point for each wrong answer. Now imagine the results of a typical quiz on which you got a score of 8 but knew only 7 of the 10 answers. That is, you guessed on the 3 items that you did not know. You got 2 of the 3 right by chance and 1 wrong. As a result your observed score of 8 consisted of the following components: 7 (true score) +1 (error: 2 right −1 wrong subtracted for guessing).

Now suppose that on the next quiz you get an observed score of 5. Again assume that you knew the correct answer on 7 items. But this time, of your 3 guesses, only 1 was right. This would represent an error of −1 (1 right −2 wrong subtracted for guessing). But you also discover that you skipped one of the questions to which you knew the answer because you failed to read it or to put down an answer. This chance error will also add to the error component: (−1) + (−1) = −2. This time your observed score of 5 consists of the following components: 7 (true score) −2 (error). You could make up other scenarios with different amounts and types of error. Besides guessing and skipping items, other sources of chance error include misreading items, variations in performance due to the timing of the test (for example, having a headache on test day), variations in grading (for example, the grader has a headache while scoring your exam), and variation in the difficulty of the items.

We want to measure true scores but constantly find ourselves with fallible scores. Each time we take a test, the amount and direction of error change unpredictably. We probably have occasions when the errors on a particular test become very small or cancel out entirely, but we cannot know when these occasions occur. At this point, the assumption of random errors comes to our rescue.

Suppose that you could break down all of your quiz scores into true and random error components. Table 5–1 shows what 10 such quizzes might look like, assuming that the true score is always 7 and that the random errors sum to zero over 10 quizzes.

Assuming that measurement errors cancel out (add to zero), the sum and average of observed scores will equal the sum and average of true scores. Of course, 10 quizzes may not provide enough trials for random errors to cancel each other completely. However, the sum of many observed scores should come close to the sum of true scores. For this reason, teachers usually base grades on more than one test and use exams with many items.

Random error causes unreliability. Measures with greater proportions of random error in their observed scores have less reliability. Later we will discuss ways of measuring and increasing reliability.

Bias. The error (E) component of observed scores can include other sources besides random error. **Bias** is one of these nonrandom sources of error. An example of

Table 5–1   Observed, True, and Random Error Scores for Ten Imaginary Quizzes

Quiz Number	Observed Score	= True Score	+ Random Error
1	8	=7	+1
2	5	=7	−2
3	10	=7	+3
4	8	=7	+1
5	3	=7	−4
6	5	=7	−2
7	8	=7	+1
8	10	=7	+3
9	7	=7	0
10	6	=7	−1
Sum	70	70	0
Average	7	7	0

bias occurs in the measurement of height. Suppose that you used a meter stick (measuring 39¾ inches), mistaking it for a yardstick. Everyone you measured would seem to be 3¾ inches shorter than they really were (39¾ inches −36 inches). Thus your observed height measurements would consist of the true heights plus any random error plus this bias. In symbolic form, where B = bias, X would equal $T + B + Er$.

This kind of unchanging, nonrandom error presents less of a problem when all subjects of a study have the same biased measure. If you underestimate everyone's height by 3¾ inches, they will all still stand in the same relation to each other. The tallest person will still have the greatest observed height, and the shortest person will have the smallest observed height. For many statistical purposes, such bias will have no effect. However, if we use the absolute level of a measurement to make a decision (such as diagnosing a patient based on a test score) or if we combine observations with different biases, bias can become a serious problem. In such cases, we need to minimize the bias or to compensate for its effect.

Biases can arise in different ways. Bias can come from a rater or judge (called *rater bias*). In this case, differences among raters can cause consistent biases in their ratings. For example, two teaching assistants may differ in their grading standards. The "hard" grader will give consistently fewer points than the "easy" grader for each subjective essay test answer. Biases can also stem from differences between testing occasions. We would expect a difference in performance between groups if one section of students had to take their quizzes under conditions of noise or exhaustion and the other section always took the same quiz under more tranquil and restful conditions.

How can we make sure to apply measures uniformly so that differences in observations do not come from measurement bias? We can try to standardize measurement so that all methods and raters operate in the same way each time in each place. **Standardization** assures us that any differences in observed scores reflect real individual differences or random error.

The word *standardization* sometimes implies more than measuring in the same way each time. It also suggests a standard against which to compare each local version of a measure. Consider how we measure time. If we think that a clock is running fast, we can compare it with a standard time measure such as that kept by an astronomical observatory.

Error from Measuring the Wrong Construct.

Another nonrandom error component of observed scores comes from individual differences other than those reflecting the construct that we want to measure. In addition to the true score component of an observation (*T*, that relates to the concept of interest), we may have an unwanted measure of another construct. We can label this *Ew* (error due to the reliable score for the wrong construct). Obviously, calling a score's component *T* or *Ew* depends crucially on what we are trying to measure. This situation resembles that of defining a weed. If we are cultivating roses, a stalk of corn rising in the middle of our garden will be judged a weed. But if we are trying to raise corn, a misplaced rose bush will seem the weed.

Imagine an IQ test with very simple questions that just about everybody over the age of six could answer correctly. Now suppose that this easy test were translated into Latin and administered to a sample of adults with normal intelligence. Some people would get very low scores because they could not make sense out of the Latin questions. Some who had studied Latin might get all the answers right. Others who had studied some Latin-based language such as Spanish might get some correct answers to the extent that they could make partial sense of the Latin questions. Thus we would find individual differences in scores, and these differences would be fairly dependable or nonrandom. If the same subjects took another similar elementary test in Latin translation, they would get scores similar to the ones they received the first time.

What characteristic would this Latin IQ test measure? It might seem that the test measures intelligence since it was labeled an intelligence test. If this were the case, the observed score would largely consist of the true score (*T*) for the target construct of intelligence. But we know that the scores in this example varied from high to low not because of differences in intelligence but because of differences in knowledge of the Latin language.

It seems that this "IQ" test measures not so much intelligence as knowledge of Latin. This "IQ" measure does not live up to its name because its observed scores (*X*) include very little of the true score for the target construct intelligence (*T*) and too much for the wrong construct (*Ew*) of Latin. The name of the test misleads us as to which part is dominant. Whether a test measures the concept for which it is named is the question of validity.

Distinguishing Invalidity and Unreliability.

Disregarding the error component of bias (*B*), our symbolic representation of an observed score (*X*) would consist of: $X = T + Ew + Er$. Most observations include all three of these components, and their relative shares determine reliability and validity of the measure.

We typically ask two questions about a measure: Is it reliable and is it valid? The question about reliability really asks how large the random error component (*Er*) is relative to those components that accurately reflect some aspect(s) of the individuals (ei-

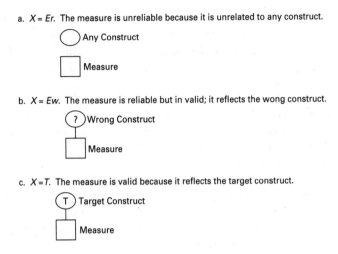

a. *X = Er*. The measure is unreliable because it is unrelated to any construct.

b. *X = Ew*. The measure is reliable but in valid; it reflects the wong construct.

c. *X = T*. The measure is valid because it reflects the target construct.

Figure 5–2 Reliability and validity: Measurement components and construct operationalization.

ther the intended one, *T* or another one, *Ew*). If *X* consists only of *Er*, the test is measuring nothing. Figure 5–2a illustrates this situation (*X = Er*). If we assume that our observations neither contain true scores (*T*) nor reflect any other construct (*Ew*), then we are simply measuring random, meaningless noise. The figure has no connection between the measure and any construct. Such a completely unreliable measure would have no value and would not likely appear in any research report. However, imagine a true/false test written in code or in a very cryptic language with which no subject has any familiarity. Since no one taking the test has any idea what the questions mean, everyone simply guesses on all the items. Since it is a true/false test, everyone might as well flip coins: heads true and tails false or vice versa. Some members of the group will be a little more lucky or a little less lucky. But such random high and low scores will not likely persist over time since they derive from the chance flips of the coins and not any stable aspects of the individuals. To use a radio analogy, this measure would not be dialed to the signal from any station; it receives only static.

On the other hand, if a measure has no random error at all, *X* will equal only *T* or *Ew* or both. In this case, we are measuring one or more dependable traits that can produce systematic or reliable high and low observed scores. Figures 5–2b and 5–2c both show a circled construct (labeled either "?" to indicate a construct other than the one we intend or "T" to indicate the target concept) connected to the measure in the square. In both cases, we have a reliable measure, one that taps something other than random error. To extend our radio analogy, our measure has dialed a station and is picking up a signal.

The second major question involves validity, that is, whether the measure reflects the desired attribute. To be valid, a measure must have good reliability. A completely unreliable measure measures no construct, just random noise. On the other hand, an invalid measure may have high reliability, as illustrated in Figure 5–2b. If *X = Ew*, the measure has no random error. In this case, the measure is doing a good job of measuring something. Unfortunately, it is measuring the wrong construct. The figure shows the measure connected to an unknown construct (?). If the measure were a radio, it would be tuned to the wrong station. This measure has the wrong name. If we could discover what it is measuring, we could make it very useful by renaming it. Validity of measurement always pertains to some particular concept. A yardstick provides an invalid way of measuring weight but a valid way of measuring height. Measures that have poor validity, regardless of their reliability, cannot help us test the theories of interest. If we wanted to study cognitive ability, we would want an "IQ" test that reflects intelligence, not one that measures how much Latin the subjects have studied.

Finally, Figure 5–2c pictures a valid measure because the observed score corresponds to the target construct. Validity is the most important aspect of measurement. High validity implies high reliability and close correspondence of the measure with the target construct. An invalid measure, no matter how reliable, allows a rival explanation of any findings. The observed relationship of an invalid measure does not address the theory and constructs at which the hypothesis test was aimed.

As a practical matter, most measures will have imperfect reliability (at least some random error or *Er*). Also, most measures will have imperfect validity (one or more components from other constructs, *Ew*). Add to this some degree of bias, and you can appreciate that most social science measures are vulnerable to criticism. To conclude our radio example, we want to hear one station clearly but find ourselves hearing it imperfectly over both random static (*Er*) and the competing signals from other stations (*Ew*). The first task for most researchers after they have chosen a theory to test will be to find the best possible measures of the constructs of that theory.

RELIABILITY

Estimating Reliability

Reliability Coefficient.   How does one go about measuring reliability? A measure of reliability should reach its largest value when random error is zero and its smallest value when there is nothing but error. A statistic that meets these conditions is called the **reliability coefficient**. To compute this coefficient, we need the ratio of two numbers, both of which assess variation. The numerator tells the amount of variation (or variability) of the reliable component of the observed score, the true score (*T*) plus that from any other construct (*Ew*). The denominator tells the total variability of the observed score (which includes both reliable and random components). Note that bias does not figure in this ratio of variabilities on the assumption that it is constant, that is, it does not vary. In the absence of random error, the numerator will equal the denominator, and the reliability will equal a perfect 1(a number divided by itself = 1). But if the observed score contains only random error, the numerator equals zero, and the reliability must also equal zero (0 / observed score variability = 0). The reliability coefficient takes on values between 0 and 1, falling as the proportion of random error variability rises.

How do we measure the variability of the reliable component (*T* or *Ew*) when all we actually know are the observed scores in which all components are mixed up? Researchers have learned how to compute the reliability coefficient from the association of two measures of the same variable (Nunnally, 1978). To measure the degree of association we can use a correlation coefficient (see the Appendix for a review). This statistic approaches +1 if the measures agree (that is, tend to be high together or low together) and 0 if the two measures have no correspondence. Different types of variables permit different ways of collecting and correlating pairs of measures, as will be described later.

Uses of Reliability Estimates.   Most often, we will use reliability information to assess a measure in order to decide whether to employ it in a study. In most cases, we will avoid measures with low reliability (say, less than .5).

Sometimes studies go forward with measures of modest reliability (say, .5 to .7). Knowing the reliability of these measures can help in interpreting the findings of such studies. Measures with low reliability will lead to the underestimation of any relationship between the studied constructs, an effect called **attenuation**. Researchers have developed ways of correcting for the attenuation due to unreliability (Nunnally, 1978). These methods use the reliability coefficients of the measures to estimate the association that would have appeared had we measured the constructs with perfect reliability.

Reliability coefficients can also help in estimating true scores, assuming the measure has no component from another construct (*Ew*). An individual's estimated true score (expressed as the difference from the group's average) equals the observed score (also expressed as the difference from the group's average) multiplied by the reliability coefficient. Since reliability almost always falls below 1, the estimated true score will almost always fall between the average of all scores and the observed score. A test score above the mean (for example, +10 where the mean is 0) when multiplied by the reliability coefficient (say .7) will yield a smaller estimated true score ($10 \times .7 = 7$). This implies that the error in this case was positive (estimated error = observed − estimated true score = $10 - 7 = +3$). If you work through this same formula for a low observed score (for example, −10 you will find that the low-scoring person always seems to have had negative error or bad luck.

This pattern of estimated errors suggests a kind of bias. Above-average observed scores will, typically, have gained from error while below-average observed scores will have lost. Evidence for this principle comes from comparisons between scores from earlier tests and later tests for the same persons. On average, people who score high on the first test will get lower scores on the second test. The extent of this change depends on the test's reliability. Tests with perfect reliability do not show this kind of pattern, but less reliable tests will produce greater shifts of this sort. This principle applies to low scorers on the first test as well. Their second test scores will tend to move upward toward the mean. This pattern of test score change has come to be known as **regression toward the mean**, and it causes special problems for studies on human development based on repeated measures of the same subjects (Nesselroade, Stigler, & Baltes, 1980).

Types of Reliability Measures

Within-Test Consistency.   Many measures in social research consist of questionnaires with many items. These include intelligence tests, achievement tests, attitude scales, and health symptom scales. The items of a reliable test should have consistency; that is, they should agree with each other.

How might we measure such inter-item agreement? One simple approach, called the *split-half* method, divides the test into two parts and correlates one half with the other. One form of this approach is called the *odd-even* method from the most common way of dividing a test into two halves—odd-numbered items versus even-numbered items. Thus, on a 10-item quiz, we could compute two scores: the sum for items 1, 3, 5, 7, and 9; and the sum for items 2, 4, 6, 8, and 10. We could then correlate these two scores over all the persons who took the test. The resulting correlation estimates the reliability of either 5-item subtest. The split-half approach to reliability may not work well for short tests because any half of the items drawn at random might not represent the whole test very well.

A more systematic and widely used way of measuring inter-item consistency uses the average correlations of each item with every other item. For example, we could correlate the score from item number 1 of a 10-item test with the score for item number 2 over all the persons taking the test, then with item number 3, and so on. The mean of all these correlations estimates the consistency of the typical item on the test. This average inter-item correlation thus describes the reliability of a single item, but it does not measure the reliability of the whole test by taking all the items into account.

One of the most important lessons from measurement theory teaches that the sum of many items is more reliable than any one item. Assuming equally reliable items, a test with more items will have more reliability than a test with fewer items. Recall the example in Table 5–1 where quiz errors tended to cancel out over many tests. The same principle applies to multiple-item tests. Random errors on each item should cancel out over many items. To gauge the overall reliability of a test, we must take into account both the average reliability of items and the number of items on the test. Different methods exist for measuring test reliability. **Coefficient alpha** appears most commonly for tests in which the items have three or more answer options. When the items use a two-answer or true/false format, we will usually see a related coefficient called KR-20 as the reliability measure (see the discussion of the Spearman-Brown Prophecy Formula, Nunnally, 1978).

Inter-item reliability coefficients such as coefficient alpha and KR-20 estimate how well the test would correlate with an equal-length test composed of similar items taken under the same conditions. Since this reliability coefficient depends both on the consistency among the items and on the length of the test, we can improve it in two ways. First, we could make the test more reliable by substituting items with greater inter-item agreement for the existing items. Second, we could make the test more reliable by adding more items even if they had no more consistency than the existing items. In the case of a test with largely unreliable items, greatly raising its reliability by the second approach might require adding many new items. Thus, we may have to choose between making a test more reliable and not making it too long. The researcher usually accepts an adequately but not perfectly reliable measure of reasonable length.

Other Reliability Coefficients.   If questionnaires were our only type of measure and the only source of random error came from within the test, we would not need other ways to assess reliability. Many researchers do not use multi-item tests. Some rely on raters to count selected behaviors. For example, you might employ three students to count the number of times a professor smiles in class while trying to establish rapport during the first meeting of the course. In the case of ratings, errors may arise in the way different judges observe the same reality. This type of measurement requires us to assess the equivalence of raters or interrater reliability.

Even if the measure consists of many test items, other sources of error exist besides those occurring within a test. Errors can arise from differences between test situations, called between-occasion errors. For example, a subject may have felt ill on the first test and well on the second. Or a group may have taken the first test in a noisy room and the second test in a quiet one. Differences between these two tests stem from the occasions, including all of the stimuli that differed between the two situations. We cannot assign these differences to the true score component because they have nothing to do with an enduring trait of the individual.

We regard such between-occasion error as random but we cannot take it into account in reliability coefficients based only on inter-item consistency for one occasion. If a person performs badly on one test because of temporary illness, the performance reflects both the true score and the illness on that occasion. We have no way to separate true ability from other factors operating during one session. Thus the effect of illness (or noise or an uncomfortable chair or a faulty pen) that operates only in one measurement session shows up as true score rather than random error in one-time within-test reliability coefficients. We must compare test results from more than one occasion in order to account for between-occasion error.

Remember that reliability tells the proportion of variability in observed scores that is not due to random error. If a measure of reliability shifts some variability away from the true score component and assigns it to error, this proportion (and thus reliability) will decline. For this reason, we do not expect all methods of assessing reliability to give the same results. For example, we expect an inter-item reliability coefficient to exceed one that includes both inter-item and between-occasion or interrater error. We will discuss three methods of assessing reliability that take into account different types of error: test-retest, parallel form, and interrater.

Test–Retest Reliability.   Researchers often take the opportunity to give the same test two or more times to the same respondents. The correlation of scores from the same test taken twice measures test–retest reliability. This type of reliability sometimes serves as evidence of the stability of the trait being measured as well as of the quality of the measure itself. For example, if we think of intelligence as an unchanging trait, we would expect people who score high at time one to score high at time two. Unfortunately, evidence based on repeating the same test may not support the claim of trait stability. Subjects may remember their answers from the first test and, wanting to appear consistent, may get the same retest score for reasons other than trait stability.

Parallel Test Reliability.   We can overcome such memory effects by using tests of similar form but with different items, called *parallel forms*. The correlation between parallel form tests over the same individuals measures parallel test reliability. Such tests consist of similar or interchangeable items. If we gave two parallel tests on the same occasion, we would expect them to correlate as well as two halves of the same test. In such a one-occasion case, the correlation of two parallel forms would reflect mainly inter-item reliability. If we gave the two parallel tests on two different occasions, say two weeks apart, we would expect a lower correlation reflecting the added error due to differences between occasions.

Using the same (test–retest) or parallel tests on two or more occasions raises the risk of maturation. Suppose two tests have little correlation after an interval of one year. Does this result prove the unreliability of the measure? No, both the first and second administrations of the test may accurately gauge the construct at the time of testing. The low correlation over occasions could reflect genuine change due to development. When measuring reliability by the test–retest or parallel test methods, you must consider whether the trait might vary with maturation and whether enough time elapsed between the test occasions to permit such maturation.

Interrater Reliability.   The correlation of scores from two observers of the same behavioral sample estimates interrater reliability. For example, the two observers might count the number of smiles produced each minute by the same professor during the same 10-minute period of a class. We could correlate these smile counts between the raters over the 10 one-minute samples. If we had more than two raters, we could report the interrater reliability as the average among all possible pairwise interrater correlations.

A simpler estimate of interrater equivalence reports percent agreement among raters. Suppose the observers were judging a gymnastics performance. For each competitor, any two judges could be said to agree (if they assigned the same score, say 9.5) or to disagree (if one gave a 9.5 and the other gave a 9.6). A measure of their agreement would be the percent of gymnastic performances on which they agreed (say they agreed on 7 of 10 performers, or 70 percent). Although easy to compute, percent agreement poses some problems as an estimate of reliability. For example, if you define agreement as exact agreement, this measure fails to give credit to near misses (often called *adjacencies*). You can solve this problem simply by giving credit for adjacent as well as exact agreements.

However, the percent agreement procedure fails to allow for chance agreements, and chance agreement rises as the number of possible rating categories goes down. Suppose two raters judged 20 performances and each performance could get one of only two ratings, good or bad. Suppose the raters had no idea how to judge gymnastics and simply flipped coins for each performance. If the coins were fair, we would expect to find a pattern such as that in Table 5–2a, that is, an even distribution of good and bad ratings by each rater. Note that the two raters agree on 10 of the 20 performances by chance. Thus with zero reliability (100 percent random error), these two raters achieve 50 percent agreement.

The degree of chance agreement depends in part on the base rate, that is, the frequency of occurrence of the behaviors under study. A behavior with a very high base rate occurs almost all of the time, and any rater would be wise to predict it always or almost always. For example, suppose two trained raters had to predict whether mental

Table 5–2   Interrater Reliability and Chance Agreement

a. Random Ratings by Two Raters for Two Categories

		Rater 1	
		Good Rating	*Bad Rating*
Rater 1	Good Rating	5: agree, both give good ratings	5: disagreement
	Bad Rating	5: disagreement	5: agree, both give bad ratings

b. Ratings by Two Raters for Two Categories with Uneven Base Rates

		Rater 1	
		No Suicide	*Suicide*
Rater 2	No Suicide	985: agree, both predict no suicide	5: disagreement
	Suicide	5: disagreement	5: agree, both predict suicide

patients would commit suicide in the next year based on personality test profiles. We know that suicide occurs rarely, only about 20 per year per 100,000 in the general population in most American cities. Suppose the two raters know that of the 1000 cases they will judge, 10 actually committed suicide in the test year, although they do not know who these 10 were. In this case, the base rate for not committing suicide appears quite high, 990 of 1000 or 99 percent. Suppose the raters did their best to pick out the 10 who would commit suicide and got the results in Table 5–2b. Note that they agreed on 990 of these cases, 985 who did not commit suicide and 5 who did, achieving 99 percent interrater agreement. In order to assess the reliability of these two raters, we need to find out how much of their success came from chance agreement due to the base rate of suicide.

In fact a special coefficient exists that measures agreement adjusted for chance (Cohen, 1960; Hanley, 1987). Called **kappa** (or κ) this measure equals the difference between the observed proportion of agreement (Po) and the proportion of chance agreement (Pc) divided by 1 minus Pc or $(Po - Pc)/(1 - Pc)$. You can compute the proportion of chance agreement from data such as those for suicide prediction as follows: Rater 1's proportion of "not suicide" predictions (990/1000 or .99) times Rater 2's proportion of "not suicide" predictions (990/1000 or .99) plus Rater 1's proportion of "suicide" predictions (10/1000 or .01) times Rater 2's proportion of "suicide" predictions (10/1000 or .01). These data result in the following estimate of proportion of chance agreement: $.99 \times .99 + .01 \times .01 = .9802$. Thus κ equals $(.99 - .9802)/(1 - .9802) = .0098/.0198 = .49$. We see that the raters cannot take credit for most of their 99 percent agreement, but they did improve on chance, and their contribution was almost half of the possible improvement that could have been obtained.

Kappa has become widely used in assessing diagnostic systems that rely on rater judgment. This coefficient has played a central role in recent revisions of the American Psychiatric Association's *Diagnostic and Statistical Manual (DSM)* for classifying types of mental disorder. As a result κ has figured importantly in the debate about the scientific and political meaning of that diagnostic system (Kirk & Kutchins, 1992). For additional discussion of interrater reliability, see Mitchell (1979) and Tinsley and Weiss (1975).

Different Errors, Different Reliability Estimates. Different approaches to reliability estimation reflect different sources of error as summarized in Table 5–3. Each reliability measure has its pros and cons. The research situation will determine which kind of reliability best serves in drawing a conclusion. If the measure depends on subjective ratings, interrater reliability would seem the best method. If your study employs parallel forms of the same test, you would choose the parallel forms correlation to estimate reliability. In sum, the choice of reliability coefficient depends on the situation and its particular combination of occasion(s), test form(s), and judge(s). Since each facet (occasion, rater, item, and form) can contribute error that affects a measure's reliability, the researcher must consider different combinations of these facets. This approach to measurement reliability is called *generalizability theory* because it seeks the accurate generalization from any particular score to the hypothetical average score under all possible conditions (Cronbach, Gleser, Nanda, & Rajaratnam, 1972; Shavelson & Webb, 1991).

We have neither a single best type of reliability coefficient for all situations nor a generally agreed-upon minimum level of reliability. Researchers prefer high reliabilities (in the .90s), but we find lower reliabilities in the .80s, .70s, and even .60s in some published articles. Using measures of low reliability does not cause us to find support for nonexistent relationships but rather causes us not to find support for those that do exist because of the attenuation effect.

Standardization. How can we make measures more reliable? Most often we will employ standardization. For each source of random error in a test score, standardization

Table 5–3 Types of Reliability Coefficients and Sources of Error

Type	Measured by Correlation	Source of Error	Potential Problems
Inter-item (also called *consistency*)	Among items within test	Within test	May not generalize across raters
Test–retest (also called *stability*)	Between two administrations of the same test	Different occasions as well as within test	Confounded by memory of first test and real development
Parallel forms	Between two forms of the test	Different occasions and forms as well as within test	Confounded by real development
Interrater (also called *equivalence*)	Between raters	Differences in raters as well as within test	Beware of interobserver agreement percentages

will tend to reduce that error and increase reliability. For example, inter-item error can be reduced by asking questions in a similar manner (standardizing format and instructions) and about similar content (intentional redundancy).

Standardization also applies to raters, forms, and occasions. Training can reduce rater errors (both within and between raters) by eliminating individual differences in the way raters make judgments. Identical test instructions and inclusion of similar items serve to standardize different forms of a test. Finally, we can make test occasions more standard by using identical test instructions and similar test environments (for example, same room, same time of day, same noise and heat levels).

VALIDITY

Estimating Validity

The Use of Validity Assessment.   Although different types of measurement validity exist, we will focus on the one that tells how well a measure reflects what it is supposed to measure. This kind of validity determines the plausibility of one ever-present rival explanation of research findings. This rival explanation argues that observed links among a set of variables have no bearing on the theory in question because at least one of the variables is invalid (that is, fails to represent its conceptual counterpart in the theory).

Most measures consist of some true score for the target construct, some reliable score for other constructs, and some random error. Validity estimation consists in judging the degree to which the measure reflects the intended rather than the unintended construct (i.e., that the measure is correctly named).

Response Styles and Sets.   What kinds of variables might intrude into social science measures with unwanted Ew score components? Two major sources pose special threats to the validity of self-report measures—response styles and response sets.

Response style refers to a person's manner of responding to test items, independent of item content. One common response style is acquiescence or yea-saying, defined as "a generalized tendency to be agreeable" (Rorer, 1965, p. 151). Operationally, the acquiescence style appears as a tendency to agree with test items, that is, to answer "yes" or "true." Some researchers view response style as a personality trait that will appear on different tests regardless of their content. Other response styles include nay-saying, the tendency to say "no," and extreme response style, the tendency to select the more extreme of the possible answers. A response style does not follow a random pattern but instead appears as an individual trait that persists over situations. As a result, response style contributes an unwanted but reliable component to test scores, thus tending to lower the validity of a measure. A score consisting largely of response style, in effect, measures the response style instead of the target construct.

Recent research has lessened our concern about the effects of a general response style. Content-independent measures of response styles often do not agree with each other, casting doubt on the meaningfulness and generality of this concept. Nevertheless, test builders usually guard against a yea-saying or nay-saying style by balancing item wording so that items are not always scored in the yes or in the no direction.

Response set refers to the tendency of the respondent to answer items in a conscious or unconscious way to give a preferred image. A person with the response set of *social desirability* or *defensiveness* tends to answer items in a socially desirable way. For example, to the item "I have never told a white lie," such an individual might give the socially desirable answer of "true" even if the honest answer would be "false." The social desirability set should have the most influence on measures of personally sensitive topics such as mental adjustment or illegal behavior. Since some people tend to be more defensive than others, this variable could add a reliable component to the observed scores. Many researchers do not doubt that social desirability affects self-report tests but question only "whether a sufficient amount of independent [that is true score] variance remains in the self-inventories to produce other strong factors" (Nunnally, 1978, p. 557).

One defense against the social desirability problem is to use items that do not arouse defensiveness. Another approach uses answer options that do not differ on social desirability. Unfortunately, not all constructs lend themselves to these approaches. A third technique measures social desirability and then removes it statistically. However, social desirability appears to be a complex variable, influenced by the respondent's actual adjustment, self-awareness, and honesty. As a result, statistical control may remove not only the defensiveness component but also some of the true score component as well. Recent research finds that "in most applications, attempts to correct scores for defensiveness or SD do not enhance validity" (McCrae & Costa, 1983, p. 886).

Types of Validity Measures

Various approaches to measuring the validity of measures exist; most fall into three types: criterion-, content-, and construct-related (American Psychological Association, 1985, p. 9). However, the distinctions among these types are not always clear cut, and some have argued that we should think of validation as the single process of hypothesis testing (Landy, 1986). Nevertheless, you need to understand the differences and limits of these three approaches and when to use each one.

Criterion Validity.   An existing measure that we accept as an adequate and valid indicator of the target construct is called a criterion. **Criterion validity** or *criterion-related validity* involves correlating the criterion with the new measure that we are trying to assess. This correlation provides the criterion **validity coefficient**. This coefficient reaches +1 if the new measure and the criterion correspond perfectly. If the two have no relationship ($r = 0$) or only a weak correlation, we regard the new measure as invalid.

Criterion validity has a number of variants. If we measure the new test before the criterion, we call the method *predictive validity*. For example, suppose we define the criterion for success in law school as law school grade point average (GPA). Now we want to check the validity of a measure that tries to predict law school success—the Law School Aptitude Test taken by law school applicants. We would see if this test correlated with (predicted) the criterion of law school GPA years later at graduation. We commonly use predictive validity to evaluate tests designed for selection purposes such as admission to graduate school.

Concurrent validity involves collecting the criterion at the same time as the measure being validated. Collecting the criterion before the measure constitutes *postdictive validity*. Concurrent and postdictive validity coefficients can help in judging whether the new measure can substitute for the criterion. If the criterion measure requires much time or many resources, we would prefer a brief, inexpensive substitute. Suppose we had a highly accurate but costly blood test for screening for a disease such as AIDS. Such a blood test might cost too much for use on millions of persons. A brief, self-report test (perhaps reflecting symptoms or risk factors) that correlated highly with the blood test criterion would be an economical substitute for large scale public health screening.

The criterion validity method has the advantage of providing single, easily interpreted coefficients. However, the simplicity of this approach depends on the assumption that the criterion is valid, which is sometimes doubtful. Consider length of stay on the job as the criterion for job performance, that is, number of months before retiring or leaving for another job. If the personnel director really wants to maximize this variable, he or she will seek a job placement test that predicts this criterion. But staying on the job may not reflect performance on the job. If people who stay are also lazy or inefficient, testing to the criterion of length of stay could give the employer an incompetent staff. The company might profit more by choosing eager and ambitious workers even knowing that such employees may well leave for better jobs.

Content Validity.   Not all measures have criteria, that is, agreed-upon standards. In the absence of a criterion, you can always assess a test's validity by inspecting its content, that is, by judging **content validity**.

We can think of tests as samples of larger domains. For example, a final exam in an economics course should indicate how much knowledge of economics the student has gained. No one expects the test to cover every detail of the course because that would require a test as long as the course itself. Rather, the test should ask a sample of questions that fairly represents the whole domain of all possible questions. We assess the content validity of such a test by judging how well the test's sample of questions represents the domain.

This approach depends on a person's subjective judgment of the domain. As a result, content validity usually does not produce a quantitative coefficient. Although content validity seems appropriate for many achievement tests (for example, course exams), it often proves too subjective and imprecise for many scientific purposes.

One problem is that items with content validity tend to be obvious in their intent, and items that "give away" tests may lead to incorrect measurement. For example, on a test used to select applicants for a very desirable training program (say, pilot school in the military), many applicants would answer such obvious items in a way that increases their chances of being selected. A better screening test would ask items that predicted future success as a pilot (that is, criterion validity) without indicating which answer would help the candidate get admitted. In sum, we may encounter a conflict between face validity and predictive validity.

Construct Validity.   Throughout this text we will emphasize the third form of measurement validation, called **construct validity**. Construct validation asks how well the test or measure reflects the target construct (Cronbach & Meehl, 1955). The abstract nature of constructs complicates this approach (Bailey, 1988). Just as we cannot finally prove theories, so we have difficulty settling the construct validity of measures. At best we can gather evidence that tends to strengthen or weaken our confidence in the construct validity of the measure. Several kinds of evidence can bear on the question of construct validity: the relations among items of a test, the relation of the test to other supposed measures of the same construct, and tests of the links among different constructs within a theory.

One way of assessing the construct validity of a measure uses the statistical procedure called *factor analysis* (Kim & Mueller, 1978). We want to know whether a test measures the intended construct or instead measures some other construct(s). Factor analysis identifies how many different constructs (called factors) are being measured by a test's items and the extent to which each item of a test is related to ("loaded on" in the jargon of factor analysis) each factor. Factor analysis uses the correlations among all the items of a test to identify groups of items that correlate more highly among themselves than with items outside the group. Each such group of items defines a common factor. Ideally, a measure should consist of items reflecting just one construct (that is, unidimensional).

Factor analysis helps answer just part of the validity question. It can tell whether the test measures one construct or more than one construct. But even if a test measures a single construct, we still do not know that this construct is the one we want to measure. We could assess the content covered by the items that load on a common factor, but this checks content not construct validity.

A second approach correlates the test to be validated with other measures thought to reflect the same construct. Suppose we have a new test that we think measures *empathy* (defined as the extent to which a person displays accurate understanding of another person). An empathy measure should correlate with other tests believed to measure empathy, but it should not correlate with tests thought to measure different constructs such as athletic skill. If the several different empathy measures agree with each other and with our new test, we have a kind of construct validity called *convergent validity* (so named because of the convergence of several different tests). If our new empathy test disagrees with tests believed not to measure empathy (such as measures of athletic skill), we have another type of construct validation called *discriminant validity* (since our empathy measure is discriminated from nonempathy measures).

Discriminant validity helps protect against the risk of **method effects**. *Method* here refers to "everything that the investigator does to obtain an array of measurements" (Fiske, 1987, p. 286). Sometimes a measuring procedure brings a component that is not germane to the construct of interest. As a result, measures using the same method may converge even though they should diverge to reflect different constructs. Their agreement with each other stems from their sharing the same method and reflecting some method effect. For example, if we assess both empathy and athletic skill using paper-and-pencil self-report measures, we may find that people rate themselves high on both or low on both despite our view that the two constructs should be unrelated. Perhaps both self-report measures reflect a tendency of people to rate themselves consistently favorably or unfavorably depending on their self-esteem. To check for the presence of method effects, we can measure different constructs with several different methods to produce a *multitrait-multimethod matrix* (Campbell & Fiske, 1959). The term *matrix* refers to the set of correlations resulting when each measure is correlated with every other measure. A measure with little method effect will correlate well with other measures of the same construct using different methods (convergence) and will not correlate well with measures of different constructs based on the same method (discrimination).

This approach of correlating two or more measures resembles the type of criterion validity called concurrent validity. The difference is that in criterion validity, we assume the criterion's validity. In construct validity, we make no assumptions about the existing measures. If the correlations among measures of the same construct prove small, doubt falls equally on the validity of all of the tests. In this case, we require further evidence to identify which, if any, of the tests have validity. Such disagreements among similarly named tests happen from time to time. For example, researchers have reported finding little convergence among several empathy measures (Kurtz & Grummon, 1972).

Even if a test appears to reflect just one construct and has convergent and discriminant validity, we still cannot conclude that the measure has construct validity. Possibly each of the tests showing convergence measures the same wrong construct. Just such misleading convergence occurred in the case of N rays.

The third approach to construct validation assesses the relation of the measured construct to other constructs in the context of theory. Recall that constructs serve as elements in and take their meaning from theory. A measure with construct validity should reflect the concept as understood in its parent theory.

Suppose we have two nonconvergent measures each of which purports to tap the same construct. How can we use the theoretical links between this construct and others to determine which measure has more validity? To make this problem more graphic, suppose the nonconvergent measures are of the construct empathy as understood in Carl Rogers's theory of psychotherapy (1957). Figure 5–3 summarizes this theory.

According to this theory, high therapist empathy should lead to client improvement (arrow 3). The construct validity question asks whether measure *A* or measure *B* better operationalizes the concept of empathy (that is, 1*A* versus 1*B*). The only evidence we have are the observations about links 2*A* and 2*B*. In order to make this choice, we must make two assumptions: that the theory is correct and that the measure of client change is valid (link 4 in the figure). The observed associations 2*A* and 2*B* can help us choose the more valid measure of empathy, link 1*A* or 1*B*. If 2*A* exceeds 2*B*, we conclude that measure *A* reflects the empathy construct as employed in this particular theory better than measure *B*. Measure *A*, in this case, would provide the kind of relationship with client improvement predicted by the theory. In summary, this method of construct validity determines how well the measure being validated conforms to the theory. Just as criterion validity depends on the assumption that the criterion is valid, so

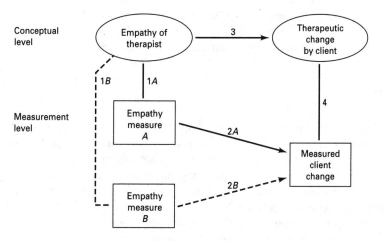

Figure 5–3   Construct validation.

this type of construct validation depends on two assumptions: that the theory is correct and that the measure of the other construct in the theory is valid.

Table 5–4 summarizes the three main types of measurement validation. As with reliability assessment, there is no single right way to validate a measure. The intended use of the measure determines the most appropriate type of validity. The three types of

Table 5–4   Summary of Measurement Validity Types

Type	Method
Construct	Extent to which the measure reflects the theoretical concept it is supposed to measure.
Convergent-discriminant	The measure should agree with other measures of the same construct and disagree with measures of different constructs.
Theoretical-experimental	The measure should be related to other variables in a study in a way consistent with the theory.
Factor analysis	The measure should have the theoretically expectable factor structure (usually unidimensional).
Criterion	Extent to which measure agrees with some other measure believed to be a direct and accurate reflection of the behavior or characteristic in question.
Predictive	Relationship of measure to later criterion (often for selection or forecasting purposes).
Concurrent	Relationship of measure to simultaneously available criterion (often for test equivalence of less expensive measures to existing diagnostic or categorizing criterion measure).
Postdictive	Relationship of measure to previously measured criterion (often for same purpose as concurrent criterion validation).
Content (or face)	Extent to which measure tests or covers the requisite topics, usually based on expert judgment and applied to assessment of achievement tests.

validity have in common a reliance on assumptions. That is, we can claim validity for a measure only in the context of some belief about the validity of other measures or of theory or about the content domain of the construct.

SUMMARY

This chapter has introduced two important ways of assessing social science measures: reliability and validity. Reliability assesses the extent to which a measure reflects some consistent aspect of people or events and not random error. Validity assesses the extent to which the something that is being measured is the intended construct, criterion, or content domain. Measurement theory interprets reliability and validity in terms of the decomposition of observed scores. Reliability decreases as the amount of random error in the score increases. Validity increases in proportion to the amount of the score that reflects the intended true score component.

Reliability measures include different types of correlations: inter-item, test–retest, parallel forms, and interrater. Similarly, validity assessment includes several methods: construct, criterion, and content.

If a measure has high validity, it must also have high reliability, but if it has low validity, it is misnamed and misleading regardless of its reliability. Of the three types of validity discussed here, construct validity often plays the most important role in social research because it addresses the threat that the measures employed do not pertain to the theory in question.

EXERCISES

1. Find a newspaper or popular magazine article that reports a social research study. Identify one test or measure employed in the study and assess its reliability and validity. Consider the extent to which random error could creep into this measure's scores and what could have been done to keep it out. Consider the extent to which this measure might really measure something other than its intended construct. Can you think of some other construct that it might be tapping and why this might be the case? How difficult was this task of estimating the reliability and validity from nonprofessional publications?

2. You probably found the first exercise difficult because articles in the popular press often say little about measurement details, although the measures provide the foundations of the reported research. Now find a professional study that describes the development and analysis of a measure. This report should explicitly discuss reliability and validity assessment methods and results. Such articles occur in journals specializing in measurement and also appear scattered throughout much of the social research literature. If you have difficulty finding such a report try one of these examples: a measure of loneliness by Russell, Peplau, and Cutrona (1980); a measure of test anxiety by Suinn (1969).

KEY TERMS

Attenuation	**Psychometrics**
Bias	**Regression toward the mean**
Coefficient alpha	**Reliability**
Construct validity	**Reliability coefficient**
Content validity	**Response set**
Criterion validity	**Response style**
Error	**Standardization**
Kappa	**True score**
Method effects	**Validity**
Observed score	**Validity coefficient**

⚬ 6 ⚬

Types of Measures
Finding and Using them

CATEGORIZING MEASURES
An Example of Measuring Intimacy
Two Dimensions of Measures

OBTRUSIVE VERBAL MEASURES
Interviews and Projective Tests
Questionnaires

OBSERVATION MEASURES
Unobtrusive Verbal Measures
Obtrusive Nonverbal Measures
Unobtrusive, Nonverbal Observations

ISSUES IN USING MEASURES
Ethical Issues
Computers in Measurement

SUMMARY

EXERCISES

KEY TERMS

CATEGORIZING MEASURES

An Example of Measuring Intimacy

Validity Through Disguise. How would you measure the intimacy of a stranger's disclosure? Your measure should follow some clear rules so that another researcher could use it in a standard way. Moreover, the measure has to have reasonable reliability and validity.

To achieve validity, you may well have to hide or disguise the measure. If you ask people to assess their own intimacy, you will likely hear what they think is appropriate or desirable rather than a frank assessment. Even if all persons gave frank answers, you should expect that different people would have different notions of intimacy or different levels of awareness of their intimacy.

Handwriting Samples. Zick Rubin (1975) used a clever method for measuring intimacy without giving away the study's topic. Rubin's assistants approached adult strangers who were seated alone in airport departure lounges. The researchers provided a sheet and a pen and asked each subject to write something for a class project in handwriting analysis. Each sheet had a sample of the assistant's writing and a space for the subject's sample. The assistants said they wrote their samples to allow a comparison with the subject's writing style. In fact the researchers designed each assistant's "sample" as an experimental stimulus that was intentionally varied in intimacy of self-disclosure. After reading the assistant's writing sample, the subject wrote one or two sentences that served as the data for the researchers' intimacy measures.

In order to score the intimacy of these "handwriting samples," Rubin defined five levels ranging from little or no disclosure (shifted away from self) to intimate disclosure (intimate information on such topics as sex). Two judges independently rated the most intimate part of each sample on this five-point scale. The interjudge correlation reached a satisfactory .77. The Intimacy Rating consisted of the sum of their two ratings (ranging from 2 to 10). Despite their reasonably good agreement, these two raters sometimes disagreed. Rubin tried a simpler, more objective indicator of disclosure intimacy. He counted the number of words in each handwriting sample and found that this measure correlated moderately with Intimacy Rating ($r = .56$).

Rubin's study supported the construct validity of these measures. Studies on verbal openness commonly find reciprocity, the view that more intimate disclosure from one person will evoke a more intimate response from the other person. Rubin found that both Intimacy Rating and number of words increased with the intimacy of the writing sample given as a stimulus by the research assistants.

Two Dimensions of Measures

This chapter introduces the main types of **quantitative measurement**, that is, standardized procedures for representing constructs in numerical form. Another approach to research relies on *qualitative methods*, as discussed later in this text (Chapter 13). So many quantitative measures exist that we can mention only a few examples here and point you elsewhere to find and assess measures as you may need them. Two important dimensions will organize this treatment of measures: (1) **verbal versus nonverbal**; and (2) **obtrusive versus unobtrusive**.

Verbal Versus Nonverbal.   Verbal measures apply to written or spoken messages. Nonverbal measures apply to physical signs, including visual judgments of nonverbal behaviors. Questionnaires produce verbal responses; nonverbal measures can include blood pressure and categories of facial expression. Rubin's Intimacy Rating relied on written disclosures and thus fits in the verbal category.

Obtrusiveness.   Obtrusive measures intrude to a greater or lesser degree into the awareness of the person being measured. Unobtrusive measures do not enter the awareness of the subject. They may be made by an unknown observer or come from verbal records or physical traces produced by the subject but analyzed later or elsewhere. The interviewee or laboratory subject cannot help noticing an interviewer or experimenter. Such research thus falls in the category of obtrusive measurement. A rater who secretly counts behaviors in a city park or who analyzes mortality records is using unobtrusive measures. Rubin obtained his handwriting samples with the awareness of the subjects but kept his purpose secret. Because his subjects did not know he was rating their disclosures on intimacy, his approach remained relatively unobtrusive.

These two 2-level dimensions provide a handy four-way breakdown of measurement types as shown in Table 6–1. This table implies clearer distinctions among these four categories than exist in fact. For example, by custom we label as unobtrusive such records as unemployment rates and census data. While some archival records are unobtrusively collected (for example, birth and death statistics), the data in our census and unemployment records come from questionnaires and interviews that are, by definition, obtrusive. For simplicity in presentation, we will treat such records together here as unobtrusive.

Reactivity.   **Reactivity** refers to the behavior change caused by the measuring procedures, which can threaten research validity. The degree of reaction to a measure depends on the topic being assessed. For example, questions about sexual behavior tend to be more sensitive than questions about the weather. In addition, two other factors influence reactivity.

First, reactivity varies with the extent to which the subject controls the studied behavior. In general, we can control our verbal behaviors better than our nonverbal re-

Table 6–1   Types of Measures

	Obtrusive	*Unobtrusive*
Verbal	Questionnaires	Content analysis
	Projective tests	Process analysis
Nonverbal	Physiological measures	Traces
	Visual ratings	Archives

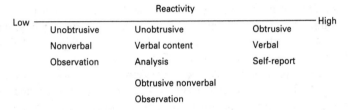

Figure 6–1   Reactivity of measurement types.

sponses. For this reason, law enforcement agencies tend to put more faith in lie detector results (based on physiological responses) than in self-reports. Second, reactivity varies with the subject's awareness of being studied. In general, less obtrusive measures raise less concern about reactivity.

For these reasons, we will find it useful to categorize measures according to their verbal–nonverbal and obtrusive–unobtrusive aspects. As Figure 6–1 illustrates, measures fall on a continuum of reactivity ranging from high (obtrusive, verbal self-report) to low (unobtrusive, nonverbal observation).

The following sections discuss each of the four types of measurement with emphasis on assessing their reliability, validity, and reactivity. Because of the threat of method effects raised in the previous chapter, researchers will often want to use more than one method to measure each construct (Campbell & Fiske, 1959). Thus some studies will draw measures from two or more of these four categories.

OBTRUSIVE VERBAL MEASURES

Interviews and Projective Tests

The Interview.   Even though it is one of the earliest and still most common procedures in human research, the interview does not appear in the typology of Table 6–1. The interview involves different techniques that could place it in any of three of the four categories. The interviewer could observe the subject's number of eye contacts or physical condition, in which case the interview would fall in the obtrusive, nonverbal rating category. Or an observer of the interview might focus on the speed, loudness, or interruptive aspects of the subject's speech pattern, in which case the measure would fall in the unobtrusive, verbal category.

The most common use of the interview, obtaining answers to questions, would locate the procedure in the verbal and obtrusive cell. A highly structured interview, with every question asked in the same words and in the same order, amounts to a questionnaire. Researchers can give such questionnaires in various formats with differing involvement by the interviewer. However, the medium of the questionnaire (in person, by phone, or by mail) can affect the results. The presence or absence of an interviewer and the rapport between interviewer and interviewee can influence the respondent's answers.

Measuring Type A Behavior by Interview.   Type A behavior pattern (TABP), the label given to a personality **trait** linked to coronary heart disease, illustrates the use of interviews to measure a construct. Type A people appear more aggressive, ambitious, and competitive; have a greater chronic sense of time urgency; and have a higher risk of coronary heart disease than their behavioral opposites, called Type Bs (see Powell, 1987, for a detailed review of TABP measurement issues).

The earliest research on coronary-prone behavior used the structured interview (SI). Trained judges evaluated subjects on more than their answer content. They also assessed the emotional tone of responses as shown in such behaviors as interrupting the interviewer during deliberately slow questions. Since a trait consists of an enduring aspect of a person's behavioral style, we would expect people to get similar ratings on this construct over time. In a 10-year follow-up using the structured interview, 67 percent of the subjects received similar A or B ratings (Carmelli, Rosenman, & Chesney, 1987). Other methods of measuring this construct exist, and we will consider some of these rival approaches in later sections.

Projective Tests.   Projective tests use special stimuli to elicit information in interview-like exchanges. Projective testing appears infrequently in social research but is commonly used in psychodiagnosis and sometimes appears in published mental health research, especially case reports.

Projective tests consist of standardized procedures for eliciting responses to ambiguous stimuli. Projective tests provide vaguely defined or unstructured tasks. Such tasks allow the subjects to see, say, or do what they wish with minimal guidance or restriction from the interviewer. Projective techniques got their name from the assumption that the subject "projects" his or her unconscious thoughts and feelings onto the "screen" provided by the unstructured task. Because of their emphasis on the unconscious and their origin in the Freudian movement, most projective techniques are identified with psychoanalytic theory. Nevertheless, the projective method could, in principle, measure other constructs besides analytic ones.

Probably the best known projective technique is the Rorschach inkblot. Rorschach, a Swiss psychiatrist, administered many different inkblots to subjects representing different diagnostic categories. The present Rorschach method consists in showing 10 standard inkblots to the subject who then describes what he or she sees. The test administrator copies down every word of this description for subsequent analysis. Different scoring systems for analyzing Rorschach protocols exist, each designed to differentiate the responses of different diagnostic groups. To improve reliability and validity, modern researchers have tried to interpret Rorschach protocols by computer and to create an inkblot system with parallel forms for group testing (Holtzman Inkblot Test). Despite these advances, the inkblot projective approach has not gained wide acceptance by researchers outside the clinical setting.

Other common projective techniques include the Thematic Apperception Test (TAT), word-association and sentence completion tests, and expressive tests such as the Draw-A-Person Test (DAP). Such projective tests vary greatly both in method and in sophistication. Studies of their reliability have yielded mixed findings. Validity studies have compared diagnoses based on complete case history information (the criterion) with those based on projective test protocols alone. Such comparisons seem to show greater than chance agreement only for experienced clinicians, and even their agreement rates are far from perfect.

Projective techniques have the advantage of being relatively disguised and therefore nonreactive compared with more obtrusive self-report measures. The subject, unless well read in projective testing, cannot infer what answers will produce the desired impression. However, the underlying assumption of projective measures remains in doubt. The projective hypothesis assumes that "the individual's responses to the ambiguous stimuli presented to him reflect significant and relatively enduring personality attributes" (Anastasi, 1976, p. 584). The evidence suggests that the information about such traits is obscured by information about the subject's temporary state and by random noise produced by the ambiguity of the procedure. In sum, projective techniques have not produced satisfactory results on the usual psychometric criteria and seem unlikely to match the widespread use of questionnaires.

Questionnaires

Questionnaires have certain advantages over interviews as illustrated by the measurement of Type A personality. Conducting a Type A interview (SI) requires special training, and only one person at a time can be measured. Public health workers could identify Type A persons more efficiently with a simpler, more automated measure. Several researchers have developed self-report questionnaires by focusing on the answers to the SI. The Jenkins Activity Survey (JAS), the best known and most widely used of these instruments, features computer scoring. The JAS correctly categorized Type A behavior patterns in 73 percent of the cases in one study, using the SI as the criterion (Jenkins, Zyzanski, & Rosenman, 1971). Unfortunately, such questionnaires, despite their reliability and ease of use, miscategorize a substantial number of individuals. Remember that a 70 percent agreement rate with the SI improves only modestly on the 50 percent chance agreement we might expect for a two-category classification (Mathews, 1988). Questionnaires fail to capture some subtle aspects of the TABP construct (Byrne, Rosenman, Schiller, & Chesney, 1985), a topic to which we will return later in this chapter. On the other hand, reliance on the SI instead of questionnaires would greatly increase research costs and hinder longitudinal studies of TABP (Yarnold & Bryant, 1988).

Combining Items into Scales. Questionnaires usually consist of many items that, when combined, produce more reliable measures of constructs than would any single item. Different techniques exist for combining items to produce single scores. Usually, the researcher wants a summary number that reflects a single underlying dimension measured by all of the items, that is, a unidimensionsl scale (Gorden, 1977). More complex methods can create multidimensional scales (for example van der Ven, 1980).

By far the most common method for creating a composite score in social research simply sums the responses to items composed with Likert-style wording. A Likert item consists of a statement followed by a number of possible levels of agreement (for example, from "strongly agree" to "strongly disagree"). If the item had seven possible levels of agreement, the respondent would receive a score between 1 and 7 on each item. The sum of these item scores over all related items produces a summary score or index.

Adding up Likert item scores assumes equal weighting of each question. Researchers sometimes derive composite scores from sets of items that have unequal weights. The Thurstone scale, one example of this latter approach, rarely appears in social research because of the difficulty in constructing it. This method requires that a panel of judges select each Thurstone item from a large pool of items, each preclassified in intensity. The judges must agree on each final Thurstone item's location at some point on an equal-interval scale. Suppose you wanted to measure a respondent's willingness to disclose intimate information. In the Thurstone approach, you would need a set of topics selected to represent different degrees of intimacy (for example, from disclosures about food preferences to those about sexual behavior). The respondent would indicate each topic on which he or she would be willing to disclose. The scale score depends on the weights of the checked items. In theory, the respondent should check all topics at and below the level of his or her most intimate disclosure level and none of the items rated higher in intimacy. The method falters because it has no guarantee that respondents will interpret the items in the same way as the judges. Thus, a respondent who chooses many less intimate topics may get as high an average intimacy score as someone who chooses the most intimate topic but few others.

A related approach combines items that form a **scalar structure**. A scalar structure exists if the subjects choose harder items only if they also choose easier items. Items that satisfy this criterion constitute a Guttman scale. The Guttman scale score depends on the pattern of responses and the intensity structure of the items. Thus a scale score might consist of the value of the "hardest" item chosen, since the scalar structure implies that all easier items are also chosen. However, if some respondents diverge from the scalar structure, such a scoring procedure would be misleading. If more than a few responses differ from the scalar pattern (called errors), we should not score the responses as a Guttman scale. Researchers can measure the extent to which their Guttman scale conforms to the ideal scalar structure by counting such errors and calculating the coefficient of reproducibility. If this coefficient is unsatisfactory (usually less than .90), the same items would produce different scale (value of hardest item chosen) and index (sum of all checked items given equal weight) scores. Even measures designed as Guttman scales and possessing high coefficients of reproducibility may turn out not to be unidimensional (as with Rosenberg's self-esteem scale, Wylie, 1974). In sum, the choice of index or scale scoring can prove complex and will affect item selection, wording, and organization.

Social researchers have designed questionnaires to measure demographic characteristics, aptitude, achievement, attitude, personality, social relationships, and social environments, to name just a few topics. The next four subsections mention a few of the paper-and-pencil tests designed to measure these characteristics and the fifth points to resources for locating existing questionnaires in these and other areas.

Demographic Measures.   Demographic measures reflect fixed aspects of persons such as gender, age, and ethnicity and usually consist of straightforward and highly reliable questions. For example, most researchers have little difficulty in categorizing people as male or female. But even this item can produce some errors, as when a telephone interviewer wrongly records a subject as a male based on a deep-sounding (but actually female) voice.

More complex demographic measures try to reflect constructs for which the respondents themselves may not have ready answers (for example, social class). As an example of standardized social status measures, the Hollingshead Two Factor Index of Social Position locates the respondent in one of seven occupational levels (ranging from higher executives and major professionals to unskilled employees) and one of seven educational levels (from graduate training to less than seven years of school, Hollingshead & Redlich, 1958). The numbers corresponding to the assigned levels (ranging from 7 to 1) are then multiplied by predetermined coefficients: 7 for occupational level and 4 for educational level. The sum of the resulting products gives the index of social position (ranging from 11 to 77). Based on this score, the respondent can be assigned to one of five social class groups. Hollingshead has subsequently revised this index to account for the fact that household status depends increasingly on two working spouses (Hollingshead, 1975). Duncan's Socioeconomic Index, another widely used status measure, ranks occupations on the basis of prestige, education, and income (D. C. Miller, 1991).

Aptitude and Achievement Tests.   Present measures of mental aptitude derive from the Binet-Simon scale developed early in the twentieth century. The French Minister of Public Instruction asked Alfred Binet to study the education of retarded children. Binet and Simon, his colleague, produced a set of 30 problems or tasks arranged from easy to hard, with the difficulty of each problem determined empirically by giving the test to normal children. For example, they identified certain tasks on the test as falling in the 7-year-old level if 80 to 90 percent of normal children at least 7 years old could perform the task. Binet and Simon assigned the mental age of 7 to a child who could pass the 7-year–level parts of the test but not the 8-year–level parts.

Alfred Terman of Stanford revised the Binet for use in the United States producing the Stanford-Binet. Along with this version came the concept of *intelligence quotient* (IQ). The IQ consists of mental age, as determined by the test, divided by chronological age. A 7-year-old child with a mental age of 7 would have an IQ of $7/7 = 1$. Usually we express the IQ as this ratio multiplied by 100, so that an IQ of 100 indicates normal intelligence for one's age.

David Wechsler has produced the most widely used intelligence tests, including those for adults (Wechsler Adult Intelligence Scale, or WAIS), children (Wechsler Intelligence Scale for Children, or WISC), and preschoolers (Wechsler Preschool and Primary Scale of Intelligence, or WPPSI). These scales all sample vocabulary, arithmetic, spatial perception, comprehension, and related verbal and nonverbal performance abilities. Reliabilities for the full scales vary in the .90s, with lower values for individual subtests. The WAIS IQs have correlated in the .40s and .50s with college grades and have predicted subsequent release rate and work adjustment for institutionalized retarded subjects. Of the group-administered mental aptitude tests, college students have most experience with the Scholastic Aptitude Test (SAT) of the College Entrance Examination Board.

One complaint against aptitude tests holds that they are confounded with achievement. We sometimes assume that aptitude tests measure native ability to learn. But most such tests give points for past learning, such as knowledge of vocabulary. Thus, tutoring may increase one's apparent aptitude, thus giving unfair advantage to people who can afford such preparation. Achievement tests, in contrast, assess one's level of acquired knowledge or skill without pretense that all candidates have had equal opportunity to acquire the skills.

You know achievement tests in the form of midterms and finals. Your instructors design such tests to assess your knowledge of material in their courses. In addition, many published tests can measure achievement and advanced aptitude in large populations. For example, college students applying to graduate school must frequently take the verbal and quantitative aptitude tests and one of the advanced achievement tests of the Graduate Record Examination (GRE), or the counterpart tests for law school (Law School Aptitude Test, or LSAT) or medical school (Medical College Aptitude Test, or MCAT).

Personality Tests.   Personality tests measure emotional patterns, motivations, values, and other enduring features of one's psychological makeup. Personality tests can measure attitudes and opinions—that is, the individual's orientation to or assessment of other persons or things. Such attitude measures may help to draw inferences about personality, since such attitudes may reveal something about one's perceptual style.

Personality tests can range from single items to elaborate, multiscale *instruments* (which is another name for a paper-and-pencil measure, not electrical hardware). The widely used Internal-External Scale (I-E Scale) illustrates the multiple-item, personality questionnaire (Rotter, 1966). Rotter thought behavior depended on the belief that it will yield a reward. According to Rotter, individuals differ in their generalized expectancies, that is, their belief about the locus (source) of control of reinforcement. I-type people, or "internals," believe strongly that they control their own fate, and E-type people, or "externals," believe that they are not in control of their own fate. The remaining people fall between these two extremes. Rotter's I-E Scale consists of a 29-item paper-and-pencil test (including 6 filler items designed to conceal the purpose of the test and lower its reactivity). Each item consists of a pair of statements of belief about the locus of control. The subject selects the statement from each pair that most agrees with his or her own general point of view and receives one point for each answer scored in the external direction.

Internal consistency (inter-item reliability) for the I-E Scale has ranged in the .60s and .70s. Test–retest reliability (interim period of one to two months) has ranged from the .50s to the .70s. The I-E has correlated negatively with measures of social desirability. That is, the external locus of control belief statements appear less socially desirable than the internal ones. To test its construct validity, researchers have given the I-E to people known independently to differ on the construct of alienation. Rotter's theory predicts that externals would feel more alienated or powerless. Compared to externals, internals, as measured by the I-E, show more signs of being actively aware of and involved in their environment (Rotter, 1966). For example, they tend to know about and ask doctors about their diseases (in the case of patients with tuberculosis), to take part in civil rights marches and freedom rides (in the case of black college students during the early 1960s), and to be active in a labor union (in the case of Swedish workers).

Personality questionnaires can be constructed in different ways. One approach selects items depending on how well they agree with each other. This approach employs **factor analysis** to make sure that a common factor underlies all of the items of the scale. If an item fails to agree with this common factor, it is excluded in favor of one that does. The introversion–extraversion scale from the Eysenck Personality Inventory or EPI provides an example of such a factor-based scale (Eysenck, 1973). Eysenck thought that compared to outgoing extraverts, shy introverts experience a chronically higher level of mental arousal or responsiveness. Factor analysis has shown that the 24 yes/no extraversion (E) items of the EPI all share something in common with the other items of this scale.

An alternative to factor analysis, the **empirical criterion approach**, selects test items according to their ability to discriminate previously identified groups. For example, the developers of the Minnesota Multiphasic Personality Inventory (MMPI) used the empirical criterion approach. Created in the 1930s, this test has become the most widely used objective personality measure with over 5000 citations in the literature by 1985. The answers to the 550 MMPI questions combine to produce scores on 10 standard diagnostic scales and three validity scales. These latter scales check whether the respondent has answered the questionnaire carefully, honestly, with comprehension, and without any response tendency such as social desirability. Eight of the ten diagnostic scales consist of items that discriminate normal people from one or another of eight clinical groups. Each clinical group consisted of about 50 cases diagnosed at the University of Minnesota hospitals. For example, the test developers contrasted a group of individuals diagnosed as paranoid with a group of normal controls. Only items that were answered one way by the paranoids but the other by normals were included in the paranoia scale.

The empirical criterion approach has opened the MMPI to some criticisms. A subject's scale score takes its meaning from its relation to the criterion group's score. For example, the claim that a person has a paranoid personality type derives from the fact that this person's score on the MMPI's paranoia scale items looked more like that of the paranoid criterion group's than the normal group's. However, the normal and criterion group scores for the original MMPI come from subjects measured in the 1940s and may not apply to the current population. To update the MMPI, a revised version called the MMPI-2 has appeared with some new items and all new norms. While improved in some respects, the emphasis on continuity with the original test precluded any role of modern psychopathology theory in the revised version (Helmes & Reddon, 1993).

Measures of the Social Environment.   Self-report questionnaires can assess a person's social environment as well as his or her personality. An early approach, called **sociometry**, asks subjects to name other persons with whom they have special contact or closeness among all members in a small closed group such as a grade school class (Moreno, 1960). A typical item asks each respondent to name the three persons in the group whom they would like to invite to a party. A person's choice score consists of the number of other people who chose him or her. The sociometric method thus provides data about a person's standing in the social environment independent of his or her own belief about that standing. Unfortunately, the choice scores of the sociometric method may not generalize outside the closed group in which the measures are taken. For example, a child may have a circle of family or friends outside the school setting. A low choice score in this case may not reflect the person's actual social support or level of socializing.

Using another approach, Rudolph Moos developed scales for assessing the social climate of nine different environments, including families (Family Environment Scale, or FES) and college dormitories (University Residence Environment Scale, or URES). He viewed each environment as having a unique "personality." Just as we can judge individuals as having more or less supportive or controlling personal styles, so we may think of environments as being high or low on different dimensions. The URES, for example, allows college students to assess their residence halls, fraternities, or sororities. The respondents answer true/ false questions about their residence, and the resulting answers produce 10 scales such as emotional support, competition, academic achievement, and student influence.

As evidence for the validity of this social ecological approach, Moos and Van Dort (1979) reported results from a study of 1164 freshman college students in 52 living units. A subset of 12 items from the URES was identified as a special Physical Symptom Risk Scale. This scale reflected lack of cohesion or togetherness among residents, lack of emotional support, an excess of competitiveness, and a sense of student powerlessness in the living unit. Living units with high scores on this scale in the fall had greater than expected average health problems by the following spring. A later study also found that URES predicted academic performance but with different patterns for dormitory versus fraternity groups (Schrager, 1986).

Finding Self-Report Measures.   Although researchers can develop new measures for their constructs, they should first search for the best existing tests. Using existing measures can save large amounts of test development time. Moreover, using existing measures improves the comparison of different studies. When studies use the same measure, differences in their outcomes can be traced to design and sample differences rather than to measurement differences.

Two good starting points are Reed and Baxter (1992) and Miller (1991). Chapter 9 of the former lists and discusses a variety of indexes to psychological tests, including some recent ones such as Robinson, Shaver, and Wrightsman's *Measures of Personality and Social Psychological Attitudes* (1991). Miller devotes much of his book to descriptions of measures, including actual questions and answer codings, information on reliability and validity, and references to each measure's original publication. Miller not only cites various compilations but also gives the tables of contents for three earlier volumes by Robinson and colleagues that compare measures of the same constructs in different research areas: political attitudes (Robinson, Rusk, & Head, 1968); occupational attitudes and characteristics (Robinson, Athanasiou, & Head, 1969); and social psychological attitudes (Robinson & Shaver, 1973). The index giving the most thorough analysis of measures comes from the Mental Measurements Yearbook series of the Buros Institute. Although the title implies annual publication, just 11 such "yearbooks" have appeared between 1938 and 1991 (Kramer & Conoley, 1991). This series provides critical updates on numerous measures as well as current references to their applications and has become available electronically in a CD-ROM format.

OBSERVATION MEASURES

Unobtrusive Verbal Measures

Communication consists in transmitting information from a sender to a receiver along any of several different channels: speech, body movements (called *kinesics*), touch, odor, body placement (called *proxemics*), facial expression, and eye movement and contact (called *gaze*). Since communicative behaviors play such a crucial role in social processes, it warrants a large share of social research. This section deals with the study of speech and writing, using content and process analysis. This research tries to draw inferences about the thoughts and feelings of communicators from the form of their messages.

To the extent that people do not know that their communications are being recorded or analyzed, such methods are unobtrusive. Some of the language components studied in process and content analysis are not typically controlled consciously by communicators but are stylistic habits. For this reason, we can regard content and process analysis, even when they are obtrusive, as less reactive than self-report questionnaires.

Content Analysis.   The term **content analysis** refers to methods that count occurrences of selected lexical (related to words) features in samples of text or speech. One use of content analysis appears in journalism research. This approach can quantify the emphasis given to certain kinds of content by counting the number of words or lines of print referring to the topic. The resulting data can then help explore the way the media handle different kinds of issues.

An example of this approach grew out of the "white flight" controversy. In the spring of 1975, James Coleman announced his conclusion that compulsory busing for school desegregation caused white people to move from inner cities to the suburbs. This conclusion provoked a major debate in the social science literature. Two researchers wondered whether the popular print media reflected the criticisms and doubts raised about Coleman's claims as well as they had publicized his initial argument (Weigel & Pappas, 1981). They scanned 200,000 pages of print in 20 periodicals over 6 months from April through September 1975. They copied and content analyzed 69 articles referring to "white flight." For each article, they performed a word count for each of three types of content: uncritical of Coleman, qualified criticism of Coleman, and critical of Coleman. They counted over 26,000 words in uncritical presentations of Coleman's conclusions about white flight against less than 6,000 words of qualified critical or critical reports.

Process Analysis.   Content analyses tend to study words—units that carry the substantive meaning in discourse. But we can also study communication in units such as the sentence or phrase, which can be categorized in terms of form or process rather than topic or content. Verbal communication also includes nonlanguage or *paralanguage* aspects, such as voice quality, pauses, and vocalizations without linguistic meaning. **Process analysis** includes the study of both verbal form and paralanguage behaviors.

Many coding systems exist for process analysis of communication. All such procedures must address the same method issues. One task involves defining the unit of process analysis—the clause, the sentence, the statement, and so on. Process analysts must also provide for the representative sampling of communication. For example, will the analyst draw samples randomly or nonrandomly from early, middle, or late in the conversation or relationship and will he or she take few long or many short samples? How much training will the process analysts receive in order to become reliable coders and what standard of interrater reliability will the researchers set?

Consider a process analytic system designed for studying small group interaction. R.J. Bales (1950, 1969) devised his 12-category Interaction Recorder to count problem-solving verbal behaviors using such response modes as showing solidarity, giving suggestions, asking for opinions, showing antagonism, and so on.

Another technique, called the Interaction Chronograph, illustrates how process analysis applies to paralinguistic behaviors through counting and timing such events as silence, speaking, and interrupting (Chapple, 1949; Matarazzo, Matarazzo, Saslow, & Phillips, 1958). This approach has found that an individual's interaction behaviors appear stable across interviews and so may serve as indicators of personality traits. For example, "initiative," the proportion of possible times that the interviewee communicates again following his or her own last utterance (avoiding silence), correlated positively with self-reported anxiety ($r = .44$).

Application to Type A Behaviors.   Perhaps paralinguistic behaviors in the standardized interview can provide less reactive indicators of the Type A trait than do the answers on the structured interview or the Jenkins Activity Survey. One study compared self-report answers with paralinguistic process measures of Type A (Schervitz, Berton, & Leventhal, 1977). For the criterion of Type A behavior pattern, the researchers obtained standardized interview ratings by a trained interviewer. They then subjected the audiotapes of these interviews to analysis by two auditors. These raters obtained high agreement (90 to 92 percent) in judging three types of paralinguistic process: speaking speed, answering speed, and emphasis. The researchers also gathered JAS questionnaire scores from the same subjects. The best combination of the three speech characteristics correlated better with the structured interview than did JAS.

Finding Content and Process Measures.   Because they require so much time to develop, to train raters in their use, and to apply, process and content analytic procedures have not multiplied as have self-report questionnaires. However, you should scan the existing methods before developing a new and possibly redundant or inferior system. The classic *Unobtrusive Measures* (Webb, Campbell, Schwartz, & Sechrest, 1966) refers to numerous studies of unobtrusive language behavior and conversation sampling (see especially pages 127–134). You might also consult three general guides to content analysis Berelson (1952), Holsti (1969), and Weber (1985). Kiesler (1973) offers a useful compendium of process analytic systems designed for the study of psychotherapy.

Obtrusive Nonverbal Measures

Nonverbal observations can follow either obtrusive or unobtrusive methods, depending on the subject's awareness of being observed. This section covers two major categories: ratings of nonverbal behavior and physiological measures. The inclusion of these measures in this section seems somewhat arbitrary. For example, we might be able to observe nonverbal behavior from behind a one-way mirror, preventing the subject from knowing if he or she is being observed. However, if the one-way mirror resides in a social science laboratory, we must assume that the subject knows of the potential presence of observers. In contrast, physiological monitoring provides an extreme case of obtrusive measurement, in which the subject experiences physical links to mechanical measuring devices.

Nonverbal Behavior Ratings. Previous sections noted that researchers could measure Type A behavior by structured interview, questionnaire content, and paralanguage. We can also use the ratings of nonverbal behavior as indicators of this construct, including greater arm movements, spending less time sitting still, spending more time in exploration, and more frequent gesturing (Hughes et al., 1983). Just as rating systems exist for verbal content and process analysis, so methods have emerged for judging various nonverbal behaviors.

Since Darwin, scientists have tried to assess human emotion from facial expression. Underlying facial anatomy and cross-cultural studies of facial expression of emotion provided the basis for one modern rating approach called the Facial Action Coding System (FACS). The FACS can identify over 7000 different combinations of facial actions (Ekman & Friesen, 1978). As one example of the FACS numerical coding procedure, the code 6 + 12 means cheek raiser and lip corner puller, that is, smiling. Tools such as the FACS might help identify emotion even when its verbal expression is suppressed intentionally (for example by detecting lies) or cannot be verbalized (as in preverbal infants). Such research rests on the assumption that emotion might "leak" out through nonverbal channels such as the face even while blocked or distorted in the verbal channel.

A different approach to facial expressions has studied not whether muscle contractions in the face express emotions but whether they influence emotion. Rather than measuring facial expression, this approach manipulates it unobtrusively by instructing subjects to flex selected muscles. For example, a research group had subjects furrow their brows without trying to produce any emotional facial pattern (Larsen, Kasimatis, & Frey, 1992). The researchers attached two golf tees, one just above the inside corner of each eye, and asked the subjects to touch the tips of the golf tees together. The subjects could do this only by contracting the muscles involved in producing a sad emotional facial expression. In response to viewing aversive photographs (for example, of a starving child), the subjects said they felt more sadness while touching the golf tees together than when they were not contracting these "sadness" muscles. This result for unpleasant affect agrees with prior research that showed that facial feedback operated for pleasant affect (for example, unobtrusive exercise of the smile muscles). In sum, making certain expressions appears to help cause or amplify the feelings associated with those expressions. This type of research illustrates that we can represent constructs not only with nonreactive measures but also with nonreactive experimental manipulations, a topic revisited in Chapter 10.

Within the area of the face, visual contact behavior has received the most research attention. Measures of such behaviors as mutual gaze or breaking eye contact have shown adequate reliability across judges (see Vine, 1971). Individuals seem consistent across partners in their looking behavior, and large differences exist between individuals in their gazing styles (Ellsworth & Ludwig, 1972).

Expressive behaviors include more than visual behavior and facial expressions. Just as we can code facial expression and count gazes, so can we measure the other body movements. **Kinesics** is the study of communicative body motion. Along with speech, several nonverbal communication channels operate more or less continuously, including the kinesthetic one (Birdwhistell, 1970). Head, arm, and other body motions send signals with shared meaning within a society. These signals transmit information by themselves as gestures and in conjunction with other channels as kinesic markers and stress indicators. In one system for recording body motion, "/" symbolizes forward body lean, and "H" indicates a head nod (Birdwhistell, 1970). In some cases, we might record body motions with mechanical devices. For example some researchers have used pressure-sensitive switches mounted in chairs to count the number of times children leave their seats in a study of classroom disruption (Foster & Cone, 1980).

Another approach studies the spacing between people or **proxemics**. We can observe the distance between interacting persons in a laboratory, for example, by asking a person to approach another up to the point at which discomfort is felt. We can also make unobtrusive observations by estimating distances between people in a natural setting. To capture the context in which proxemic behavior occurs, an anthropologist has developed a notational system for recording the gender, posture, orientation, body odors, touching behavior, and voice loudness, among other characteristics, of the observed persons (Hall, 1965).

The research value of such nonverbal behaviors depends on whether they reflect anything important about people or their interactions, such as revealing deception or diagnosing depression. One review of this literature found that measures of facial expression and body movement did correlate with such outcomes (Ambady & Rosenthal, 1992). This review found that measures of the face and body together provided better accuracy than measures of speech or tone of voice and that "thin slices" of behavior (samples of 30 seconds or less) provided as much accuracy as longer samples (up to five minutes).

An Application to the Job Interview.   An example of the use of nonverbal ratings appears in a study of the interaction of race and interview behavior. Observers watched white college students (the subjects) interviewing black and white high school student job applicants (Word, Zanna, & Cooper, 1974). These applicants served as trained confederates of the experimenter, who had coached them to answer questions in a way that made them appear equally qualified. Two judges, behind one-way mirrors, rated four nonverbal behaviors of the interviewers as a measure of *immediacy*, defined as the extent to which behaviors reflect and enhance positive attitudes between two people in interaction. The four immediacy behaviors included (1) physical distance in inches (proximity), (2) forward lean in 10-degree units of angle from the vertical, (3) eye contact measured as a proportion of time spent looking at the job applicant's eyes, and (4) shoulder orientation in 10-degree units from parallel to the shoulders of the applicant. The interrater reliabilities of the judges' ratings ranged from .6 for shoulder orientation to .9 for distance. These measures were combined into a single measure of total immediacy. The results showed that black applicants received less behavioral immediacy, largely because the interviewers placed themselves farther from black than from white applicants. Compared to whites, the blacks also got shorter interviews and received higher rates of speech errors from the interviewers (as judged by two additional raters from audiotapes).

In a second study, the researchers divided 30 white college students (the subjects) into two groups to be interviewed for jobs. Those in the immediate group received the same treatment as the white applicants in the first study—close proximity, longer interviews, and fewer speech errors. The nonimmediate group received the treatment given blacks in the earlier study—greater distance, shorter interviews, and more speech errors. The researchers had trained the interviewers in each case to produce these different styles of interaction. Trained observers rated videotapes of the interviews and judged the college student subjects in the nonimmediate condition as significantly less adequate for the job and less calm and composed. These nonimmediate subjects also rated their interviewers as less friendly.

Psychophysiological Measures.   Many physical measures of the human body can reflect underlying attitudes and emotions. Such measures typically require specialized hardware and training to operate reliably. Several of them depend on the activity of the autonomic nervous system, which controls a host of peripheral (as opposed to central or brain) functions in the body. The **autonomic system** has two subsystems—the sympathetic and the parasympathetic. The sympathetic system tends to dominate during intense emotions such as rage or fear. Autonomic signs of emotion include changes in salivation (for example, dryness of the mouth during stage fright), heart rate, blood vessel constriction, sweat gland activity, electrical skin conductance (for example, sweaty palms), and even dilation of the pupils of the eyes.

Measuring pupil changes with precision requires special equipment and room arrangements. Typically, a subject sits facing a screen and views a first slide to allow the pupil to adapt to the screen's brightness and to provide a base-level pupil size with a neutral stimulus. Then other slides appear with more arousing content, but shown at the same brightness level. While the subject is looking at each slide, a movie camera films his or her eyes. The experimenters can then measure in millimeters the size of the pupils on the screen while the film is projected. The difference in pupil size between neutral and arousing slide conditions indicates emotional response. As validation of this measure, research has shown that in the presence of slides of food hungry subjects show greater pupil dilation than recently fed subjects (Hess, 1973).

Changes in electrical skin conductance (related to sweat gland activity) constitute the galvanic skin response (GSR). An electric gauge measures the GSR from electrodes attached to the skin. The GSR method provides one of the principal parts of the "lie detector", in which false answers typically produce greater autonomic arousal.

Other autonomic indicators include heart rate and blood pressure. One use of such measures appeared in a multimethod study of the effects of traffic congestion (Stokols, Novaco, Stokols, & Campbell, 1978). Employees of a suburban company were measured for heart rate and blood pressure and reported their daily commuting time and distance. The physiological measures correlated with both distance and time of commuting. These physical results paralleled ratings of commuting stress as reported by the subjects on questionnaires.

Autonomic nervous system activity stimulates the adrenal gland, which secretes hormones such as epinephrine and norepinephrine into the blood. These hormones affect various organs of the body in addition to the direct effect of the autonomic nervous system. These hormonal secretions will appear on blood assays and thus can serve as another, still more obtrusive, indicator of emotion or stress. One study attempted to reduce Type A behavior by different treatments and evaluated the outcome both with the usual paper-and-pencil questionnaires (for example, JAS) and also with blood assays (Levenkron, Cohen, Mueller, & Fisher, 1983). The researchers took two blood samples, before and after each stress-inducing task. In partial support of their theory, the researchers found that plasma-free fatty acids (ΔFFA, believed to reflect sympathetic nervous system arousal) declined in the treated groups.

Besides the autonomic system, another large category of human physiological response comes from the central nervous system. Some measures of this system rely on the electrical activity of the brain. The brain generates changing voltages, measurable as wave patterns by the *electroencephalogram* (EEG). Researchers place plate or needle electrodes on the surface of the scalp at points near selected brain structures. Sensitive receptors then amplify the brain's electrical activity and display it on a video screen or as lines on moving paper. This approach has identified some common patterns of brain activity. For example, the 8 to 12 cycles per second (CPS) alpha waves appear when the brain rests with eyes shut. Because alertness and sleep exhibit different EEG patterns, this technique can serve as a tool for the objective study of unconscious internal experiences, such as dreaming during sleep. The EEG has also become widely used in the study of abnormal conditions such as epilepsy.

Electrical activity also occurs in muscles as measured by the *electromyogram* (EMG). As with EEG measurements, EMG measures derive from electrodes placed on the skin near the muscles of interest. The resulting EMG may reflect "mental work." For example, the EMG from the right arm increases if a right-handed subject imagines lifting a weight. Thinking involves linguistic processing, and EMGs from the facial area near the lips increase during silent thought. Researchers have used EMGs to study attitude change—for example, by monitoring the effort of cognitive processing during the presentation of a message that attacks an important set of beliefs (Cacioppo & Petty, 1981).

Positron emission tomography (PET) offers another way to study the central nervous system. This method requires a cyclotron to make glucose mildly radioactive.

When injected into the subject's blood, this glucose is taken up by body cells, including brain cells, that are actively consuming energy. More active brain areas will take up more of the radioactive glucose and in turn emit more gamma rays. The PET device consists of a ring of gamma ray detectors that passively measure radiation coming from different parts of the brain. Computers translate these gamma readings into a picture of the activity of those areas. By giving the subject different mental tasks, the PET researchers can identify which parts of the brain handle different functions. Some researchers have used this technique to test whether psychotherapy produces any change in brain function. One project compared two groups of obsessive-compulsive patients, one receiving drug treatment and the other behavior therapy (Baxter et al., 1992). They found one brain location, called the caudate nucleus, that showed a significant decrease in activity as a result of both types of treatment.

Finding Nonverbal Measures.   You can find nonverbal measurement systems in two handbooks (Scherer & Ekman, 1982; Siegman & Feldstein, 1987), and another book reviews notation systems for nonverbal behavior (Rozensky & Honor, 1982). The specific techniques of physiological measurement depend on the particular model of apparatus used. Thus, you would find step-by-step guidance for such measures in the instructional manuals accompanying the equipment.

Unobtrusive, Nonverbal Observations

The least reactive measures are collected without the knowledge of or verbal reports from the subject. There are three general types of such unobtrusive, nonverbal observations. We have already discussed one type under the heading of observations of nonverbal behavior. This section will consider two other types of unobtrusive measures: physical traces and archival records.

Traces.   Physical **traces** include both *accretions* of and *erosions* in some physical substance. Erosion measurement depends on the principle that people leave evidence of themselves by wearing down surfaces. For example, museum managers have identified the most popular exhibits by the wear on the floor's surface near the exhibits (see Webb et al., 1966).

Measures of accretions follow the same logic. Numbers, locations, and behaviors of people can be measured by their leavings. Erosion can prove difficult to measure with precision, since weeks or months of wear may produce only barely noticeable changes. In contrast, we can more easily count or weigh accretions. Litter provides an example of a frequently measured accretion. Since litter removal costs hundreds of millions of dollars per year and since litter poses fire and health hazards, measuring littering has practical benefits (Geller, 1980). As with any other index, the accretion-of-litter measure must specify the unit of measurement. For example, how small a piece of litter shall we count—as small as a matchbook or only as small as a beer can? Moreover, we must define the physical area of analysis to assure that we observe the same location at different times.

One approach illustrates this method of trace measurement. The photometric index (PI) uses photographic enlargements (for example, of picnic grounds). Researchers use a magnifying glass to study segments of the photos defined by a grid overlay. We can assess such PI litter counts with interrater agreement between different counters or test–retest reliability for the same counter over different occasions. Reliability often reaches high levels with such methods as PI. Since litter is the criterion in such research, validity poses few problems.

However, trace measures do risk both random error and constant bias. For example, is the museum exhibit with greater floor wear located near the entrance where many visitors would pass by on their way elsewhere? Was the measure of picnic area littering adjusted for the time of observation (for example, higher use on holidays, weekends, and warm-weather days)? With proper controls for such unwanted components, trace measures can prove very useful.

Archival Records.   Society keeps many ongoing records for purposes other than scholarship. Called **archives**, these records include vital statistics (for example, births and deaths) and the files of many of our social institutions: health (hospital admissions), law and criminal justice (number of arrests and convictions), journalism (microfilm of all past editions), and politics (number of people registered and voting in each district). Many such archives consist of records obtained unobtrusively. That is, public agencies recorded the events routinely without their clients' awareness that the data would or could serve as research data. On the other hand, some archival records derive from obtrusive, verbal measures (for example, the census), although we will treat them in this section because of their resemblance to other archives.

Besides their relative nonreactivity, archival data offer several other advantages, including convenience and low cost. The collecting agency, often a government office, usually pays for collecting, storing, and indexing the archives. However, some archives, such as ancient records (for example, cuneiform tablets), can require great expense to find, unearth, sort, restore, translate, and classify before starting substantive analysis.

Archives have another advantage—their extensiveness. They tend to cover entire populations rather than small samples and long rather than short time periods. For example, the suicide statistics for a state derive from all death certificates of state residents, not just a sample of a few neighborhoods or cities. Moreover, to the extent that laws and coroners define suicide in a consistent way, the suicide records will permit analysis over many decades rather than just one month or year. These qualities often make archival records the only means for answering certain kinds of questions (for example, has the suicide rate changed over the past 40 years?).

Archival records usually have high reliability and validity based on the routine nature of their data collection. That is, we presume that our public agenices use measuring methods in the same way over time and location. For example, laws and court rules should operate in a standard way across jurisdictions within a state. If so, annual figures on the number of convictions for burglary should allow comparisons between districts and over time. Even when the definitions of archival measures change, the data collectors will sometimes use both the old and the new definition (for example, unemployment rate) for a period of time to permit comparison of the two versions. Archival measures often serve as the criteria for the constructs of interest. For an epidemiologist studying death due to lung cancer, state vital statistics on lung cancer mortality may well provide the most valid as well as the most practical data source.

Scholars have used archives not only to study the obvious theoretical constructs (for example, using records of traffic fatalities to study the safety of different freeway interchange designs) but also as indicators for less obvious constructs. For example, Phillips (1979) used single-car fatalities as a stand-in for suicide on the grounds that some one-car "accidents" are actually misclassified suicides. Thus government records on economics, politics, education, crime, and weather can serve as measures of abstract concepts such as "quality of life" of different cities.

Despite all their advantages, archival records can pose some knotty problems. The first problem arises in finding the proper data set. By definition, agencies collect archival data for purposes other than basic research. After meeting these other purposes, agencies may store, forget, and even lose the collected data. If your first inquiries fail to locate the data you want, do not conclude that the data did not or do not still exist. Perhaps you have not found the right place or the right archivist.

Even after the desired data have come to light, the feasibility of using them may depend on their storage format. For example, you may need to transfer data on paper forms to computer format before analysis, with all the costs of retrieving the forms, key-punching the data into computer spreadsheets, and refiling the forms. If the data already appear in computer form, are they sufficiently summarized or detailed for your purposes? You may have to find data providers who can present the data to you in the format you can afford to analyze.

The archive analyst must discover the errors or changes that have crept into the data from the records system. We must assume that a record system that involves multiple reporting sources and uses changing forms or data-handling procedures will not always perform as planned. Some reporting units adopt and learn new data management procedures early. Other reporting units with less motivation or resources may never fully cooperate in building the archive. You should always wonder "what's in it" for the front-line data gatherers. What incentive do they and their supervisors have to produce comprehensive, accurate records? How well do they screen the data before depositing them in the central file? How vigorously do they apply the formal criteria and definitions of the data? Even records collected in the letter and spirit of the formal archival procedures risk data-handling errors such as miscoding on the original forms, misrecording into computer or other file format, and mishandling in the subsequent analyses.

Sources of Trace and Archival Measures.   Both trace and archival measures receive attention in *Unobtrusive Measures* (Webb et al., 1966, pp. 35–52 and 53–111). Researchers have developed few trace measures for standardized use across studies (such as the PI measure of litter), instead inventing new measures for one-time use in a particular study. So many archival measures exist that no index lists them all. Miller (1991) gives one handy guide that mentions several statistical source books, with special attention to U.S. census data. If you need a public archive, you should visit the nearest government depository, often available in your university library (see Chapter 7 of Reed & Baxter, 1992). You should also consider using social research data from sample surveys collected by other social scientists and by political, consumer, and economic opinion pollsters, who sometimes make their data available for secondary analysis. Many colleges and universities have joined together so that faculty and students of the member schools can obtain access to data collected elsewhere (for example the Inter-University Consortium for Political and Social Research, Miller, 1991, pp. 189–197).

ISSUES IN USING MEASURES

Ethical Issues

Guidelines for Test Makers and Givers.   The sixth ethical standard of the American Psychological Association cautions researchers to protect their subjects' well-being both by seeking their informed consent and by protecting the confidentiality of any information gained from the study's measures (American Psychological Association, 1992). The APA's ethical principles also warn against the misuse of assessment outside of research (standard 2). Specifically, psychologists who use tests must "indicate any significant reservations they have about the accuracy or limitations of their interpretations" and those who construct tests must "use scientific procedures and current professional knowledge for test design, standardization, validation, reduction or elimination of bias, and recommendations for use" (American Psychological Association, 1992, p. 1603). For example, the APA asked some of its members to stop marketing a battery of tests that was found to be below technical standards for test construction (American Psychological Association, 1987, p. 113). To protect the rights of test takers (whether in research, in clinical testing, or in school), there exist a number of standards including the right of test takers to an explanation of test results (American Psychological Association, 1985, p. 85).

Testing as a Social Issue.   Group-administered aptitude tests have taken on increasing social significance. Initially, aptitude tests helped diagnose individuals in order to provide appropriate training and care for the retarded. Now, group tests help screen hundreds of thousands of candidates for admission to higher education and to jobs. For example, 90 percent of all four-year colleges require some kind of entrance exam such as the Scholastic Aptitude Test (SAT), but some critics argue that these tests really measure achievement and not aptitude (Jencks & Crouse, 1982). Ralph Nader's consumer protection group has argued that the testing industry exercises unregulated power and that its products should not be passively accepted as fair and accurate predictors of educational or career success (Nairn, 1980). A group called FairTest has challenged the Preliminary Scholastic Aptitude Test (PSAT) as an unfair basis for choosing semifinalists for the National Merit Scholarship. This group pointed out that although females get better grades in high school and college than males, females win only about 35 percent of the National Merit Scholarships (Shogren, 1993). Because of such apparent sex bias, a federal district court struck down New York's sole use of SAT scores to award state scholarships in 1989.

The most explosive test controversy surrounds IQ differences between racial groups. These findings have led to a bitter debate about the heritability of intelligence and charges of cultural testing bias. From its inception as a tool to aid the mentally disadvantaged, intelligence and aptitude tests have become perceived in some quarters as instruments for preserving social and ethnic class advantage (Cleary, Humphreys, Kendrick, & Wesman, 1975; Cronbach 1975; Scarr & Weinberg, 1976). Ironically, a group of black parents had to sue for the right to have their children receive IQ tests for school placement (Ban on IQ testing of black children lifted, 1992). A U.S. district court had found such tests biased in 1979 because they seemed to place disporportionate numbers of blacks in programs for the retarded. In 1986 the court ordered California not to use IQ tests to assign any students to special educational programs. But a group of black parents persuaded the court to lift the ban so that their children could be assessed for learning disabilities, and the court agreed in 1992. The use of intelligence tests continues to trigger great dispute among educators.

Courts of law have also encountered assessment problems in regard to expert testimony about psychological diagnoses. Clinicians may have to testify about whether or not a murder defendant had a mental disorder at the time of the crime or if an occupational injury had produced permanent disability. Because such testimony often depends on the reliability and validity of assessment procedures, trial lawyers often challenge the quality of these measures and the expertise of their users. This debate has also raged outside the courtroom among psychologists pitting those who doubt that experts can make accurate judgments (Faust & Ziskin, 1988) against those who support the validity of psychological testing (Matarazzo, 1990).

Computers in Measurement

Coding the Data from Measures.   Once data are collected, they must be put in a form suitable for analysis, usually by computer. The data manager first must develop a **codebook**. The codebook names each variable for which data are being recorded, briefly describes it, and tells its location or sequence. Each subject or **case** will have a series of numbers representing that individual's scores for each variable or measure. The resulting database consists of a table of individual names or identification codes (cases) by variables. Your instructor's grade sheet probably resembles such a table, with students' names in the left-hand column and each student's scores on tests and exercises running from left to right in the appropriate row. Entering such a table into a computer file makes it easy to analyze using the relevant statistical software.

Computers in Collecting and Scoring Measures.   We usually think of computers as means for storing and analyzing the results of measuring procedures. However, they can also play other research roles such as gathering data directly from the subjects. For example, some of the physiological measures described earlier in the chapter, such as pulse rate, gamma rays, or brain wave frequency, can involve the continuous flow of information. Such data can go directly into computer storage for integration and analysis. For example, the computer can link the data second to second with other measures and with any special event markers desired by the researcher indicating the timing of different experimental stimuli. Computers can also aid in scoring paper-and-pencil questionnaires. The hundreds of MMPI or MMPI-2 items can be machine scored and the results analyzed by computer. One such analysis compares the MMPI profile of any subject with profiles of previously studied subjects in order to determine which diagnosis fits best.

SUMMARY

The threat of method effects (two measures giving the same results because of shared method rather than shared construct) makes it desirable to use more than one method in measuring each construct. This chapter categorizes measures by two dimensions: verbal versus nonverbal and obtrusive versus unobtrusive. Verbal, obtrusive methods include projective tests and questionnaires. Verbal, unobtrusive measures include communication analyses such as content and process analysis. Nonverbal, obtrusive measures can include ratings of nonverbal behavior and psychophysiological measures. Nonverbal, unobtrusive measures include trace (erosion or accretion) and archival records.

The value of every measure depends on its reliability, validity, and reactivity (the extent to which the measuring procedure produces a change in the behavior under study). Indexes exist that list and assess measures in each of the four categories. Before undertaking the time-consuming task of creating and validating a new measure, you should consult such indexes to find the best existing measure.

EXERCISES

1. Select a measure and evaluate it in terms of its reliability and validity. Try to find it in an appropriate index. For example, you might check a test that you yourself might have to take, such as the Graduate Record Exam (see Mitchell, 1985, Vol. I, pp. 622–626).

2. Define a construct to be measured in an imaginary study. Then try to identify four different measures of that construct, one from each of the four categories of Table 6–1 using the suggested indexes and your own creativity. Compare the measures that you identify in terms of reliability, validity, reactivity, and suitability for different kinds of research.

KEY TERMS

Archives
Autonomic system
Case
Codebook
Content analysis

Empirical criterion approach
Factor analysis
Kinesics
Obtrusive versus unobtrusive
    measurement

Process analysis
Projective tests
Proxemics
Quantitative measurement
Reactivity
Scalar structure
Sociometry
Traces
Trait
Verbal versus nonverbal measurement

7

Survey Data Collection
Issues and Methods in Sample Surveys

This chapter and the next deal with two aspects of an important problem of social research—drawing conclusions about many people based on a subset or **sample** of only a few people. This chapter discusses survey methods for describing a whole population based on a sample from that population. The next chapter covers the statistical inference to a population from sample data, whether those data come from a survey or an experiment.

INTRODUCTION TO SURVEY RESEARCH

A Case of Sampling and Data Collection Bias

Literary Digest Poll of 1936. A survey collects data from a sample of people via a questionnaire. Perhaps the most infamous survey appeared in 1936 when the periodical *Literary Digest* used it to predict the winner of that year's presidential election. The sample came from telephone directories and car registrations, and the magazine collected the returns by mail. The *Literary Digest* predicted that Alfred Landon would defeat Franklin Roosevelt by a wide margin. This error has embarrassed survey researchers and heartened politicians running behind in the polls ever since.

Despite the paradox of judging the whole from a small part, all of us use just this method almost everyday. When served a bowl of hot soup, we taste a fraction of a spoonful to determine how hot the entire bowl is. That is, we measure a sample in order to draw an inference about the whole. Of course, we may take special care in drawing and assessing our sample. Perhaps we stir the bowl well so that a spoonful from one part of the bowl is much like a spoonful from any other part, and we probably take care in touching our lips to the spoon.

The *Literary Digest* poll in 1936 erred for two reasons. First, it failed to draw a representative sample of the voters. In 1936, the United States was suffering in the Great Depression. Many poor citizens, likely to vote for Roosevelt, had less chance to appear in telephone directories (because they could not afford phones) and in automobile registries (because they could not afford cars) than richer voters, likely to support Landon. That is, the pollsters drew their sample in a way that failed to represent the whole population properly. Some observers think another problem with this survey may have caused even more error than did this faulty sampling (Bryson, 1976). *The Literary Digest* sent out some 10 million sample ballots but received back only 2.3 million. That is, only those people with the strongest feelings about the election took the trouble to respond, and the results suggest that those respondents came largely from the anti-Roosevelt minority. Even if the sample had correctly represented the population, this self-selection of respondents would have spoiled the data collection.

Problem of Error. These two problems with the 1936 poll illustrate some of the errors that threaten survey research. Recent advances in controlling such errors have produced growing confidence in political and other surveys. Modern political pollsters correct for such threats by, among other things, drawing respondents that are representative of all segments of society. Survey researchers can exclude inappropriate respondents (for example, those who are below voting age, not registered to vote, or unmotivated to vote) after their identification by careful questioning. They can track late trends in voter opinion by conducting surveys right up to the day of the election—even interviewing voters as they step out of the voting booth. Survey researchers reduce the error from uninterviewed respondents by making special efforts to get high compliance, for example, by phoning or mailing back repeatedly to reach people who did not respond initially.

Such improvements in political survey methods have led to impressive accuracy in recent elections. Some people have expressed concern that polls have too much accuracy. In the presidential election of 1980, the national electronic media polled small samples of voters after they left the voting booths. Based on these postvote, precount surveys, the media predicted the victory of Ronald Reagan over Jimmy Carter hours before the polls closed in the western time zone, and Carter conceded the election before the balloting was complete. Days later, the vote tallies confirmed the accuracy of these surveys and the confidence that people placed in then. However, some people wondered if the survey-based prophesies were self-fulfilling, since they may have demoralized some of Carter's supporters and kept them from going to the polls in the western states. In 1984, Congress asked the national media to refrain from projecting the presidential election winner until the polls closed everywhere. Citing their First Amendment right to free speech, however, the networks have continued to make such projections.

Rationale for Survey Research

Feasibility.   Social science has come to depend on sample surveys because the alternatives to them are either a **census** (that is, a survey of everyone in the population) or no information at all. Social scientists regard the census as impractical since only the national government has the resources to contact everyone and the legal mandate to require that everyone cooperate.

Even the federal government attempts a national census only once every ten years. Although the decennial census tries to reach everyone, it fails to an unknown degree. The census provides valuable descriptive data about the population and often serves as a standard against which to gauge sample surveys. However, when social scientists go beyond demographics to measure more complex constructs, they have to rely on sample surveys. Fortunately, samples need not be very large relative to the population. For example, political pollsters typically sample only a few thousand voters in order to represent many tens of millions of voters. As a result, survey research plays an important role in the social sciences and in consumer market studies as well as in political forecasting.

DESIGNS, MEDIA, AND ERRORS

Design Types

Before exploring survey errors and biases, we must establish as context the basic types of surveys. This section reviews types of survey designs and then turns to the medium of contact—mail, phone, or face-to-face interviews. Each design and medium has different strengths and weaknesses. The most important design distinction in survey research contrasts surveys that measure at one time and those that measure at more than one time.

Cross-Sectional Versus Longitudinal Designs.   A **cross-sectional survey** collects data at one time. We can generalize findings from such one-shot studies to the sampled population only at the time of the survey. A political opinion poll taken two weeks before an election might represent voter sentiment at that time. But we could not assume these results would predict the outcome of the election since events could swing voter sentiment in only a few days.

A **longitudinal survey** takes place over time with two or more data collections and has the benefit of measuring change over time. Longitudinal surveys commonly fall into one of three categories: panel, trend, and cohort.

Panel Surveys.   When a study collects data at different times from the same respondents, the survey employs the panel design, and the respondents are collectively called the panel. The **panel survey** has the major advantage of following changes in particular individuals.

Panel surveys sometimes have difficulty in reaching and reinterviewing respondents. In general, panel studies with longer lags between initial and later interviews run greater risks of **attrition**—that is, losing respondents. Attrition can occur because respondents move, change their minds about cooperating, fall ill, die, or go on vacation. If subjects drop out because of reasons related to the variables under study (for example, health), the attrition may affect the conclusions of the study. For example, the degree of change in the average symptom levels between a first and a later interview may stem in part from the effects of health on the dropout rate.

Pretest sensitization poses a second problem for panel studies in that the experience of the first interview may cause changes in the second interview. For example, a health survey may raise respondents' awareness about health symptoms (say, chronic cough) or health habits (say, smoking). This sensitization by the first interview could lead to behavioral change (decreasing smoking) by the time of the second interview.

Another problem in comparing surveys over time applies to all longitudinal studies, not just to panel surveys—the problem of changes in the measuring procedures themselves. Survey staff may change their interviewing behavior as they gain experience, or new members may join the survey team as old ones leave. Results showing apparent changes in the respondents might really reflect such changes in the interviewers.

Panel designs can employ a short lag between interviews to protect against these problems. However, panel surveys exist with 20-year or longer lags. For example, the original Midtown Manhattan Study surveyed 1660 people from 20 to 59 years of age in 1954 (Srole, Langner, Michael, Opler, & Rennie, 1962). The researchers attempted to reinterview this same group in 1974, thus converting a cross-sectional design to a panel design (Srole, 1975). Of the 1660 candidates for reinterview, the research team located 858 still alive and gathered data from 695 of them.

The comparison of mental symptoms in the 695 respondents who were interviewed 20 years apart shows the unique benefit of the panel design. In 1954, 16 percent of the respondents (age 20 to 59) had mental symptoms that met the "impaired" standard. In the 1974 study, these respondents were 20 years older, aged 40 to 79, and 18 percent met this same impaired criterion. Because of these similar proportions, one might guess that the same individuals who were impaired in 1954 remained impaired in 1974. But the panel design permits a definitive analysis of 1954 and 1974 mental status by individual. Srole (1975) found that over half of those judged impaired in 1954 had actually improved by 1974 and that some persons not judged impaired in the first interview had become impaired by the second.

Panel designs can have more than two interviews as shown in the Panel Study of Income Dynamics, which began in 1968 and continued with annual reinterviews of the heads of households from the original sample of families. The other name of this study suggests the magnitude of this project: Five Thousand American Families (Hill, Hill, & Morgan, 1981). This study shows the special power of its panel design in the test of the hypothesis that those who are poor now have been poor in the past and will remain poor in the future. One-shot surveys can reveal the extent of poverty at a given time but not movement into and out of any social class. The Five Thousand American Families study has shown "that there was not only far more year-to-year change in economic status than anyone had thought, but that there were substantial demographic differences between the very small group of families who were persistently poor and the much larger group who were only temporarily poor" (Duncan & Morgan, 1981, p. 2). Later analyses of these same data gave higher estimates of the persistence of poverty (Bane & Ellwood, 1983; Wilson, 1987), but only such panel survey data can provide the opportunity to answer such questions.

Trend Surveys. In the panel design, the initial sample of respondents represents the population at the beginning of the study. Although the population may change over time, the researchers reinterview the same panel repeatedly. In contrast, the **trend survey** keeps up with changes in the population by drawing a new sample at each measurement point. Trend designs occur commonly in the measurement of political attitudes. Monthly or weekly estimates of the share of the voting population favoring a candidate come typically from new samples, which together constitute a trend design.

Researchers use the trend design in part to avoid having to relocate previously interviewed respondents, thus avoiding the problem of attrition. Follow-up interviews in the panel approach will tend to miss highly mobile types of persons. But in a trend design, each new sample includes some highly mobile persons who happen to live in the area at the time of the survey.

Trend studies also avoid the test reactivity problem of the panel design. Sensitive kinds of survey content (for example, questions about suicidal thoughts) may raise the respondent's self-awareness of problems. Interviewers in such studies sometimes get requests for help from their respondents. Ethically, the interviewer has a duty to provide at least minimal information (for example, the telephone number of a suicide prevention center). Thus the initial interview may provoke change in the respondent. In the trend design, researchers can ask sensitive questions and give appropriate help without distorting later responses. In exchange for these advantages, the trend design gives up some precision in comparing different groups over time.

Differences observed in trend samples do not imply anything about changes in particular individuals.

Another survey of American mental health, which took almost 20 years to complete, illustrates the trend design. This study interviewed 2460 adults in 1957 (Gurin, Veroff, & Feld, 1960), and interviewed a new sample of 2267 respondents in 1976 (Veroff, Douvan, & Kulka, 1981). Although this design could not tell how the mental symptoms of particular persons had changed, as could the Midtown Manhattan panel, it could reflect the changing social climate. For example, the trend survey indicated that the 1976 population tended to deal with unhappiness more by seeking informal social support and less by prayer than the 1957 population (Veroff et al., 1981).

Cohort Designs.   A special case of the trend design is the **cohort survey**, which measures fresh samples, each drawn from the same subpopulation as it moves through time. We call such a subpopulation a *cohort*, and usually define it by birth year.

The cohort survey has special value for scholars in human development. Suppose a researcher wanted to study a personality trait, such as achievement motivation, in adolescents. One could sample and test at one time a cross section of youths ranging in age from 12 to 17. Suppose differences appeared between 17-year-olds and 14-year-olds. We might explain these differences as due to age-specific development. But these adolescents differ on other factors such as belonging to different birth cohorts. These 17-year-olds and 14-year-olds grew up in somewhat different social eras and therefore have had different experiences. In other words, this cross-sectional design confounds age and cohort.

To separate age and cohort effects, we could conduct a series of cohort studies, called a multiple-cohort sequential design. For example, we could study cohorts born in 1955, 1956, 1957, and 1958, surveying each in 1970, 1971, and 1972. This approach makes it possible to assess each cohort's progress over time. The cohort effect equals the difference between cohorts measured at the same age, and the age or developmental effect equals the difference between subjects at different ages within the same cohort. As an example of a cohort effect, one study found that adolescents aged 14 in 1970 had higher achievement scores than those aged 14 in 1972 (Baltes, Cornelius, & Nesselroade, 1979).

The stimulus for such multiple-cohort sequential analyses has come in part from Schaie's (1965) General Developmental Model for separating age, cohort, and time of measurement or period effects. However, this analytic approach can provide descriptive but not definitive causal information (Adams, 1978; Baltes et al., 1979; Kosloski, 1986). In the preceding example, the 1956 birth cohort was 14 in 1970 and the 1958 cohort was 14 in 1972. These two cohorts, controlling for age (both 14 years old), differ in two respects. First, they differ in their birth cohort, which is related to social and cultural differences in the eras in which they grew up. Second, they differ in their period of measurement, which is related to the current events at testing, 1970 versus 1972. Thus measured differences between these two sets of 14-year-olds could stem from birth cohort, period of measurement, or both. Cohort designs, especially multiple-cohort sequential ones, permit useful insights into developmental processes, but cohort and period remain confounded.

Media Types

The term *medium* refers here to the method of gathering data from surveyed respondents—mail, phone, or face-to-face. Each of these media presents special advantages and disadvantages in cost, sampling method, success in gaining cooperation from the respondents, type of content, and format of the questions. We will discuss these different media briefly here and refer to them again throughout the remaining sections. For more detailed treatments of these survey media, see Dillman's (1978) analysis of mail and telephone surveys and Groves and Kahn's (1979) comparison of telephone and face-to-face surveys.

Face-to-Face.   Although still common, the face-to-face medium has become too expensive for many researchers. Reaching people at their residences proves increasingly difficult in an era in which both spouses work. Researchers must make more frequent callbacks to find someone at home while the costs of personnel and transportation are rising.

Nevertheless, face-to-face surveys maximize trust and cooperation between interviewer and interviewee. Face-to-face contact decreases refusals and permits questioning on more intimate topics. In-person contact also allows the use of special aids such as cards showing the questions or answer options. In a personal interview, the interviewer can see and assess the respondent's nonverbal behavior and habitat. Finally, face-to-face interviews can take place with respondents who do not have phones or the ability to read a mailed questionnaire. Were it not for limited resources, most researchers would probably prefer face-to-face interviewing. With personal survey methods priced beyond their reach, social scientists and their funders must often turn to phone or mail surveys.

Telephone.   The telephone interview costs approximately half what a face-to-face interview costs (Groves & Kahn, 1979). Interviewers need not waste their time driving many miles to a residence only to find no one home. The callback to the absent respondent requires only a redial rather than another long trip. Moreover, the telephone method permits unique control because a supervisor can monitor all of the interviewers as they work inside a single complex.

With phones now so widely distributed in society (in excess of 90 percent of all households in urban areas of the United States have phones), relatively few people cannot be reached by phone. Unfortunately, those few probably differ from those with phones. On average, people without phones are poorer, younger, less educated, nonwhite, and female heads of household (Tull & Albaum, 1977).

A potential problem has to do with the fact that many people (20 to 40 percent in some areas) do not list their numbers in telephone directories (Rich, 1977). However, survey researchers can easily reach such unlisted numbers through the procedure of **random digit dialing** (RDD). This method composes telephone numbers by a random process, usually by computer, and can generate unlisted phone numbers as well as a listed one. The RDD method has the potential problem of not identifying the respondent when the call is placed. As a result, the respondent has the option of remaining anonymous even while completing the interview. While less of a problem for cross-sectional research, such anonymity can hinder follow-up interviews required in panel designs. However, one nationwide RDD study reinterviewed 78 percent of the original sample three years later, showing that even panel designs can succeed by phone (Booth & Johnson, 1985).

In addition to keeping their numbers unlisted, phone subscribers also protect themselves from unwanted calls by using answering machines. One telephone survey found that almost 71 percent of the respondents had answering machines, and these people tended to be younger and unmarried and of higher occupational status (Mishra, Dooley, Catalano, & Serxner, 1993). If sampled respondents with answering machines use them to screen out survey calls, the resulting data will not represent such people adequately. For example, even after adjusting for demographic differences, answering machine owners reported less smoking than respondents interviewed without a machine encounter (Mishra, et al., 1993). Without taking into account the effect of answering machines in this case, a phone survey might overestimate the proportion of people who smoke.

After contacting a household by phone, the researcher must choose one household member for the interview. At this point, the interviewer must avoid the temptation to choose the person who answered the phone or who least objects to spending time on the interview. Because some family members spend more time at home than others (for example, retired people and homemakers), the interviewer will want to identify all the household members and then choose one randomly or quasi randomly (Troldahl & Carter, 1964).

Although telephone surveys tend to underrepresent some segments of the population, this problem is rarely great enough to rule out the approach. Remember that even face-to-face surveys tend to underrepresent some population segments. Thus we must choose not between perfect and imperfect media, but between media with different degrees of effectiveness.

Another concern with the telephone medium involves its effect on the frankness of the respondents. Some worry that phone interviews may not yield the same answers as face-to-face contacts, particularly on more intimate and sensitive items. Respondents may terminate the interview, decline to answer certain items, or give a false answer to a stranger on the phone more easily than to an interviewer sitting in their living room. Several studies have compared phone and personal surveys by using the same questions, and some have found small differences in response style. For example, telephone interviewees produce more missing data on income questions, more acquiescence (tending to agree), more evasiveness, and more extreme response bias (tending to select extreme answers such as "very satisfied" rather than moderate answers such as "slightly satisfied"). However, average item scores generally did not significantly differ between the phone and personal interviews (Jordan, Marcus, & Reeder, 1980). When asked their preference, respondents said that they preferred personal to phone interviews and that they would more likely agree to an interview in person than by phone (Groves, 1979).

In some research, data obtained by phone have compared favorably to those collected face-to-face (T. F. Rogers, 1976). For example, one study compared phone and personal surveys of criminal victimization (Tuchfarber & Klecka, 1976). The surveys yielded similar results on demographic characteristics, reports of victimization, and attitudes toward crime-related matters. The authors concluded that in "each instance, the bulk of the evidence supports the contention that RDD yields data of equal, if not superior, quality and reliability to those data collected by a traditional personal interview" (pp. 63–64). The telephone interviews actually yielded higher rates of some crimes (for example, 39 percent greater for household crimes). This finding suggests a greater frankness on the phone than in person on such sensitive topics (Tuchfarber & Klecka, 1976). The telephone medium has become a viable alternative to the face-to-face medium and has achieved success with sensitive, complex, and lengthy interviews.

Mail. Responses for mail surveys have notoriously low return rates, typically in the 20 to 30 percent range for the initial mailing (Nederhof, 1985). How many times have you thrown away the postage-paid, self-addressed return envelope or card begging you to answer a few short questions? Repeated mailings (three or more attempts) can raise the return rate to the 60 to 70 percent range, but the increasing cost of postage tends to eat into the initial cost savings of this method. More important for measurement validity, mail questionnaires provide no control over substitution of respondents. For example, the designated respondent may hand the questionnaire to another person.

Researchers have achieved high return rates for specialized samples for whom the mail survey may work best (Dillman, 1978). For general population surveys, most social scientists tend to limit their choices to personal and phone media. However, mail contacts may play an important supplementary role in such personal or phone surveys. Appointments for or announcements of impending home visits or phone calls could be sent by mail. Researchers can send complex questionnaire materials such as answer cards by mail prior to the phone interview. After recruiting a respondent for a longitudinal survey by an initial personal or phone contact, the researchers can conduct reinterviews by mail. Telephone contacts also can play supplemental roles in surveys in which the primary data collection medium is either mail or personal contact.

Error Types

As with any research method, surveys risk various kinds of error. We will organize our review of survey error along two dimensions. The first dimension includes the two categories of error: random error versus bias or nonrandom error. The second dimension includes the two major parts of the survey process: the sampling phase and the data collection phase. In combination, these two dimensions give four types of error as summarized in Table 7–1.

Table 7–1 Types of Survey Error and the Problems They Present

	TYPE OF ERROR	
Source of Error	Random	Bias
Sampling	Lack of precision of survey estimates	Directionally wrong estimates
Data collection	Lack of reliability of measurement	Lack of validity of measurement

Random Error.   Variable and unpredictable, **random error** has the effect of making estimates based on surveys imprecise and occurs both in the sampling and in the data collection phases. Several different samples of the same size from the same population would almost certainly disagree because small samples rarely represent the entire population exactly. By chance, any given sample will slightly over- or underestimate the true value in the population. Such sample-to-sample variation is called random **sample error**.

Fortunately, we know that many samples collected from the same population tend to converge around a central point. If the estimates of all these samples bunch tightly together, we would say that there is little sampling error. In that case, almost any sample we choose would give a good estimate because all estimates fall so close together. But if the estimates of these many samples differed widely from each other, we would say that there is a great deal of sampling error. In that case, we would have much less confidence in any of the survey estimates. In summary, the problem of random sample error pertains to the extent to which different samples yield estimates that agree (less error) or disagree (more error).

Random error also appears in data collection, as discussed in Chapters 5 and 6. Once some sampling procedure identifies a person, the data collection phase begins, that is, the contact and interview of the respondent. Error that enters this stage contributes to what we have called the *unreliability of measurement*. For example, a sampled respondent might give unpredictably different responses to the same item on different days or to different interviewers. These deviations or errors can arise from interviewer mistakes, from variations in how respondents interpret ambiguous questions, and from mistakes in recording or tabulating the answers. **Data collection error** adds to sampling error to increase the disagreement among separate survey estimates from the same population.

Bias.   When errors push the survey estimate consistently above or below the true value, we call them **bias**. Random sample errors and random data collection errors miss the true population value in either direction with equal likelihood. Such negative and positive errors should cancel each other out given enough chances. If we had only random error to deal with, we could trust the average of many survey estimates as the best overall estimate of the population value. But if bias is present, averaging will not provide a good estimate of the population value. If all sample estimates share the same bias, the average of all these estimates will still differ from the population value by the amount of this bias.

Sample bias occurs when the sampling procedure does not represent the population fairly. Suppose a jar contained marbles, half of them red and the other half blue. If you were blindfolded and picked out ten marbles, you would expect to get an average of five red and five blue marbles. But suppose that someone arranged to put all the blue marbles on the bottom so that you were more likely to select the red marbles from on top. Naturally, your samples would not represent the whole jar accurately.

The same sort of bias occurs in real surveys when one type of person has a greater chance of being sampled than another type. In the case of the *Literary Digest* survey, Republicans had a better chance of being sampled because of their overrepresentation in the telephone books and car registration files.

Even if the researchers draw the original sample in an unbiased way, the final estimate may still become distorted by **data collection bias**. We know that individual differences in response set can lead to biased answers (for example, social desirability). Sometimes the researchers can check such bias. For example, in reinterviews of alcoholics in an experimental treatment, many claimed to be able to drink moderately. However, checks of official records from jails and hospitals cast doubt on these apparent successes (Pendery, Maltzman, & West 1982; see also Heather & Robertson, 1983, for a rejoinder).

We can divide data collection or nonsampling bias into two types. **Observation basis** is data collection bias that arises when the respondent gives answers or when the answers are processed. Observation bias can arise from question wording and can prove to be quite large, as in the job losses claimed by the Bureau of Labor Statistics in the early 1990s. The bureau estimates jobs based on sample surveys of employers. After a questionnaire change in 1991, the number of jobs appeared to drop by 640,000, seemingly due to the 1990–1991 recession. On reanalysis, the bureau found that it had overestimated the number of jobs prior to the recession by counting payroll checks (a worker could receive more than one check for the same job). The revised survey form reflected jobs, not checks, and showed that 540,000 of the jobs thought lost had never existed (Kreisler, 1993).

The second type of data collection bias can occur in the process of contacting sampled individuals. The *Literary Digest* fiasco included an example of this bias. Even if the 10 million people sampled in 1936 had represented the population fairly, the small proportion who returned their mail questionnaires probably did not. The minority who felt strongly enough to mail back their responses seemed to differ from the majority in their distaste for Roosevelt. This type of data collection bias, called **nonobservation bias**, occurs often. For example, researchers expect to find working age people at home less often than retirement age people. Moreover, not all contacted people may agree to be interviewed. And among those willing to be interviewed, some types of respondents will more likely refuse certain questions (especially about private matters such as income). As a result, an unbiased sample may yield a biased set of respondents on one or more items.

Total Survey Error.   **Total survey error** equals the sum of all errors, bias and random, from sampling and data collection. This sum should also equal the difference between the sample survey estimate and the true or population value. Unfortunately, we do not know the population value and thus can estimate total survey error can only by considering each source of error. One source is observation bias or the tendency of respondents to answer falsely. For example, people might tend to claim that they have a library card when they do not. We could measure the existence, direction, and magnitude of this particular error by verifying card ownership with the library. In principle, we could measure all other sources of error and sum them to provide an estimate of total survey error.

In practice, estimates of total survey error can prove difficult to make (Andersen, Kasper, Frankel, & Associates, 1979; *Sociological Methods and Research* 1977). Some ongoing, large-scale surveys, however, do attempt to estimate total error. These include the census (Bailar, 1976) and the Current Population Survey (Bureau of the Census, 1978). Survey researchers want to design the sampling and data collection procedures so as to minimize error and to provide opportunities to check some of the more likely sources of bias or random error.

SAMPLING

Sampling Terms and Designs

Basic Terms.   You will often hear reports of surveys qualified by some statement such as "The survey estimate [for example, of the percentage of voters favoring a politician in an upcoming election] falls within plus or minus 3 percent of the true population value with 90 percent confidence." Another way of saying this is that if the same survey were repeated 100 times, the estimates from 90 of these surveys would fall in the range of 3 percent above or below the correct value. Sampling experts design sampling methods that provide estimates with ever smaller error at greater levels of confidence. To do this, they rely on a sampling theory that uses several basic terms.

Surveys collect data from units, usually individual respondents, each called an **element.** Researchers want to generalize from their sample to all potential elements, termed a **population**. For example, an economist might want to study the population of current residents of the United States who are working or seeking employment—that is, the workforce. To estimate the American unemployment rate, we would select a sample of elements or people in such a way that they represent the population of all American job holders and seekers.

In order to draw a sample in a representative way, we ideally would begin with a list or **enumeration** of all the elements in the population. In practice, we seldom can obtain complete population lists. As a result, we must work with some incomplete list called a **sampling frame**. For example, we might want a list of every resident of a city (enumeration) but might have to settle for a list of residential addresses in the city (sampling frame). Since the sample comes from this sampling frame, any generalizations can be made only to the frame. If the frame does not represent the population fairly (for example, if some homeless job seekers do not have residential addresses), the sample will not represent the population fairly.

Sample Stages.   Researchers draw *single-stage* samples in one step from a sampling frame and *multistage* samples in a sequence of two or more steps. In these steps or **sample stages**, only the last one identifies the elements to be interviewed. For example, we might use a two-stage sampling design to represent the population of college students. First, we could draw a sample of colleges from the population of colleges. The sampling frame for the population of colleges might consist of the list of all colleges accredited by all of the regional accrediting organizations. Then we might draw a sample of students from the students enrolled in the colleges drawn on the first step. The sampling frames for this second stage might consist of the lists of registered students provided by the campus registrars of the sampled colleges.

A **sampling unit** consists of either the element (for example, college student) or the group of elements (for example, college) chosen at a sampling stage. Sampling units consisting of groups of elements are called **clusters**. Clusters usually involve existing groupings, such as areas (city blocks) or organizations (factories, colleges). *Multistage cluster sampling* designs involve several steps: choosing initial sampling units or clusters, listing the elements within the selected clusters, and picking elements from the chosen clusters. Multistage cluster sampling can save resources. Instead of enumerating all the elements in the population, the survey researcher need only enumerate the elements in the selected clusters. Concentrating interviews in certain spatially limited clusters reduces survey travel and personnel time.

Instead of cluster sampling, we could categorize elements by **stratification**. A stratum consists of all the elements that have a common characteristic. For example, the variable gender would define two strata—males and females. Working with strata requires an enumeration of all elements from which a stratum can then be defined. In contrast, one could identify a cluster, such as a block or a college, without knowing the elements it contains.

Depending on our research goals, we could sample in one or more stages from selected clusters or strata or from stratified clusters. For example, we could stratify clusters, consisting of colleges, according to such variables as private versus public, unisex versus coed, large versus small, or urban versus rural. We could then draw particular colleges from each stratum before drawing students (elements) from the chosen colleges. The choice of sampling strategy represents a balance of feasibility (including knowledge about the population, such as an available enumeration) and purpose (including the required measurement precision and hypothesis). For a more detailed treatment of survey sampling methods, consult standard texts such as Babbie (1973), Sudman (1976), or Williams (1978).

Probability Sampling.   Survey sampling has two goals—to provide unbiased samples and to provide sample estimates with the smallest sampling error. First, we will consider the problem of bias and its solution—probability sampling. In a later section, we will see that probability sampling also helps with the problem of sampling error by aiding in its measurement.

Sampling bias, as illustrated by the *Literary Digest* survey, occurs when sampling procedures consistently miss some kinds of elements while overrepresenting others. The *Literary Digest*'s sampling from car registrations and telephone listings illustrates sample-frame bias. Without enumerating the population of voters, the pollsters used convenient, but incomplete listings that favored Republicans over Democrats.

To avoid bias every element has to have an equal chance of being sampled. The *Literary Digest* survey would have needed a different sampling frame, one that did not tend to exclude certain kinds of elements. Beyond defining an unbiased sampling frame, the actual selection of elements from the frame must proceed in a way that gives the elements in the frame an equal probability of selection, a method called **probability sampling**.

Random sampling provides the best way of achieving probability sampling. A lottery in which every contestant has one ticket offers a good example of random sampling. A blindfolded person draws out the winning ticket from a box containing all the tickets. Such random selection seems fair because each ticket has an equal chance of being chosen.

In practice, researchers usually employ **systematic sampling** instead of random sampling. Copying every single element onto slips of paper and putting them all into a mixing drum would prove impractical for a large sampling frame (say, the telephone directory of a large city). To simplify the process, systematic sampling draws every *n*th element from an existing list beginning at a randomly chosen point (for example, every 100th person in a telephone directory starting with a randomly chosen person on a randomly chosen page).

In the case of multistage sampling, the researcher may have to select later-stage samples from different-sized clusters—for example, large colleges versus small colleges. To draw 100 respondents from a university with 25,000 enrolled students and 100 students from a small college with 2,500 students would not give every student an equal chance of being selected. The method of **probability proportionate to size (PPS)** preserves equal probability across all elements in the population. With PPS, the researcher chooses the number of respondents for each cluster in proportion to the size of the cluster. In the previous example, we might draw 100 students from the larger university but just 10 from the smaller.

In some studies, the researcher does not need to represent all elements equally but rather wants to compare and contrast subpopulations, Suppose we want to study the satisfaction of students with their teachers across the range of different-sized colleges. In this case, we might appropriately **oversample** in smaller colleges in order to have enough respondents from each type of campus. Nevertheless, within each subpopulation, stratum, or cluster, we would retain probability sampling by using random sampling or systematic sampling with a random start. If we later wanted to combine the results for such non-PPS samples into an estimate for the whole population, we could statistically correct for any over- or undersampling—a procedure called **weighting**. Thus if students from large colleges had only one-tenth the chance of selection as their small-college counterparts, we would multiply the responses of large-college respondents by ten. Weighting the results from complex survey designs requires more advanced techniques (Lee, Forthofer, & Lorimor, 1989).

Nonprobability Sampling.   The alternative to probability sampling, called **nonprobability sampling**, includes any method in which the elements have unequal chances of being selected. A common nonprobability method, called **convenience sampling**, depends on the convenient availability of respondents. In this procedure, subjects select themselves. Laboratory experiments often sample by convenience from the population of college students eligible or required to participate as human subjects. Students can volunteer for available studies depending on their schedule and interest in the experiment's subject matter. The experimenter typically takes the first students who sign up and makes little or no effort to check whether these volunteers represent the student population.

The experimenter may have little interest in estimating any population characteristic from the sample. Rather, the experimenter wants to split the original group of volunteers into two or more groups for differential treatment. However, the researcher may well make this division of the original group into subgroups by random assignment. Be careful to distinguish random assignment, which divides a sample into subgroups, from random sampling, which selects a group from a population.

Other nonprobability sampling procedures include purposive sampling and quota sampling. In **purposive sampling**, researchers choose respondents because of certain characteristics. For example, we suspect that unemployment is a risk factor for certain stress disorders, but the population includes relatively few unemployed people. Without an enumeration of the unemployed and assuming a 5 percent unemployment rate, a survey using random sampling would have to contact 10,000 persons in the general population to reach 500 unemployed people. If the researchers cannot afford such a large survey, they may resort to purposive sampling. For example, they might interview all people applying for assistance at some unemployment compensation office or all people fired from a closing factory. Unfortunately, we cannot know that these 500 unemployed people from a purposive sample represent all unemployed people. Such a sample may differ from those who did not have unemployment insurance or who lost jobs but whose factories did not close.

In **quota sampling**, the researcher tries to create a sample that matches some predetermined demographic profile such as that of the population, perhaps as measured by the census. For example, suppose we know that 54 percent of the adults in a community are female, and the study requires 100 total respondents. In quota sampling, we might interview the first 54 females and the first 46 males who appear. Quota sampling represents a special case of convenience sampling. For example, in convenience sampling we might select our 100 respondents from those persons entering a particular store. Applying the gender ratio of 54:46 converts it to quota sampling. Elaborating the quota procedure so that respondents fit several different criteria such as sex, age, or ethnicity does not guarantee that the sample will be unbiased on some overlooked but important dimension. For example, if we conduct the survey at a store located in an affluent neighborhood with high Republican voter registration, the sample would not reflect political opinion in the population as a whole.

Random Sample Error

Defining Sample Error.   Survey researchers cannot avoid all sample error, and the term *error* does not imply some sort of mistake. Think of sampling error as sampling variability. More precisely, sampling error equals the square root of the sampling variance (for a review of measures of variability, see the Appendix). The sampling variance consists of the average of the squared differences between each different sample mean and the average of all the samples. We can easily compute this variance whenever we have multiple samples drawn from a population. However, we seldom have multiple samples and so must estimate sampling variance from a single sample.

We could estimate sampling variance by dividing a single sample into a number of subsamples. The variance among the subsamples describes the variability or sampling error for a sample of the size of each of the subsamples. However, larger samples (such as the size of the original sample) have less variability than smaller ones. Think of sampling from your present class in order to represent your class's average grade. A sample of 20 or 30 has a better chance of representing the entire class average than a small sample of two or three. Accordingly, we must adjust downward the sampling variance for the set of small subsamples by dividing by the number of subsamples. This simple approach works for simple random samples, but more complex surveys require more complex calculations of variability that take into account such factors as cluster weights (Lee et al., 1989).

Sampling Variability and Sample Size.   The principle that larger sample sizes give more precise estimates of population values is called the **law of large numbers**. Intuitively, larger sample sizes provide better chances that unrepresentative elements (those much higher or lower than the average for the group) would cancel each other out. This principle helps in estimating sampling error directly from an undivided sample.

In an earlier section, we saw that probability sampling had the advantage of providing more representative, less biased samples. Probability sampling also aids in the measurement of sampling variability. In simple, one-stage random sampling, all elements in the sample frame have an equal chance of selection. Consequently, the variance of elements in the sample can be converted into an estimate of the sampling variance for all samples with the same sample size.

We call this sampling variability estimate based on one undivided sample the **standard error of the mean**. It equals the standard deviation of the sample (square root of the variance) divided by the square root of the sample size. This formula tells how much improvement in sampling precision results from an increase in sample size. For example, quadrupling the sample size will cut sampling error only in half (square root of 4 = 2). Remember that sampling variation or error decreases as sample size increases and that bigger and bigger samples yield diminishing returns for precision.

Confidence Interval of Samples.   The standard deviation of the sample tells how much confidence to place in a sample estimate. Even without selecting and interviewing all possible samples from a population, we know something important about the estimates from many such samples—their distribution. Suppose we took all such samples and plotted their values for the variable unemployment rate. We could think of each sample estimate as a single observation and plot the number of samples that yield each value. The result would look like a frequency distribution such as we usually plot for a single variable measured in a group of subjects. Since each observation comes from a different sample, we call this pattern a sampling distribution. An idealized sampling distribution appears in Figure 7–1.

In the illustration, the sampling distribution takes the shape of a normal (bell-shaped) curve. By a mathematical theorem called the **central limit theorem**, the sampling distribution approaches normality as the number of samples increases. Most sample means congregate near the middle of the distribution with fewer and fewer sample means found at greater distances from the middle. The average of the samples gives the best estimate of the population value, in the present imaginary case, 5 percent unemployment.

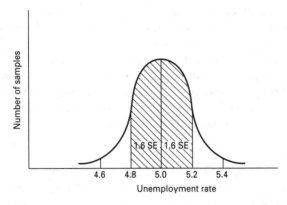

Figure 7–1   Sampling distribution for unemployment rate: Assumed normal distribution with standard error = .11, 90 percent confidence interval (shaded area), and population unemployment rate of 5 percent.

The normal curve has a well-defined shape. We know that about two-thirds of all sample means fall within plus or minus one standard error of the population mean and that 90 percent of the sampling estimates fall in the range between plus and minus 1.6 standard errors. The large-scale survey used to estimate the U.S. unemployment rate has a standard error for the monthly unemployment level of .11 (National Commission on Employment and Unemployment Statistics, 1979). Thus, assuming a true population level of unemployment of 5 percent, nine out of ten samples of the same size would fall in the range 4.82 to 5.18 percent (5 percent plus or minus 1.6 × .11).

Of course, we do not know the population value of unemployment. Instead we must use our sample estimate as the best guess of the population value. We can then specify a **confidence interval** for any desired degree of trust in our estimate. If we want 99 percent confidence instead of 90 percent, we must expand our confidence interval to include 99 percent of the samples. Since 99 percent of all sample estimates fall within plus or minus 3 standard errors of the population value, our 99 percent confidence interval would extend .33 above and below the mean (plus and minus 3 × .11). If our sample had 5 percent unemployment, our best point estimate of the unemployment in the population would equal 5 percent, and we would have 99 percent confidence that the population's unemployment rate would fall in the interval of 4.67 to 5.33 percent.

In summary, sample size and confidence interval width relate closely to each other. As sample size goes up, the standard error comes down. As the standard error goes down, the confidence interval becomes narrower.

Determining Sample Size.   Because sample size affects confidence interval, one could, in principle, select the sample size to yield any given degree of confidence. Formulas exist for computing the required sample size as a function of the desired confidence level, the desired precision or width of the confidence interval, and the population variance as estimated by the sample (for example, Williams, 1978, p. 219).

Unfortunately, this approach has several problems. The formulas require information not usually known until after the survey, such as the estimated sampling variability. Moreover, the formulas rest on such assumptions as the normality of the sampling distribution. Practical problems arise as well. Most surveys measure several different variables, each of which may require different levels of measurement precision and thus different minimal sample sizes. Even when researchers know the ideal sample size, they may have to work with a smaller sample because of budget limits.

Researchers often try for the largest possible survey sample size within the constraints of the survey design (including number of trend samples or panel reinterviews, length of questionnaire, medium, and number of callbacks to complete interviews) and total research resources. Survey planners often make decisions in a zero-sum situation, in which any increase in sample size must come from resource savings in other areas such as decreased numbers of callbacks or reinterviews. How best to buy precision and confidence becomes a problem in the valuation of knowledge, a topic treated elsewhere (Sudman, 1976, chap. 5).

In the absence of precise estimates of required sample size and within the constraints noted earlier, most researchers use rule-of-thumb guesswork to set sample size. One approach sets sample size by reference to earlier surveys of a similar kind. If subgroup comparison seem especially important, the researcher may set overall sample size so as to interview some minimal number of the smallest subgroup of interest.

DATA COLLECTION

Research suggests that nonsampling measurement error typically exceeds sampling error and should, therefore, receive special attention (Assael & Keon, 1982). Bias and random error can occur in each of several parts of the data collection process, and each has a possible remedy. The following sections address respondent contact and cooperation, interviewer training and rapport, and questionnaire construction and processing.

Contact and Cooperation

Completion Rates.   An unbiased sample can yield biased results if interviewers fail to contact or interview some of the sampled elements. The term **completion rate** refers to the extent to which a sample is successfully reached and persuaded to cooperate. A low completion rate raises concern about possible nonobservation bias. If the uncontacted or uncooperative members of the sample differ in some systematic way from those who are contacted and cooperative, the survey will be biased.

Noncompleters reduce the size of the completed sample, which will tend to increase sampling error, but this problem has an easy solution. Researchers can simply draw a sample large enough to yield the required number of completed interviews, allowing for noncontacts and refusals. However, making a sample adequate in size by this approach will not solve the problem of nonobservation bias. In order to measure the attitudes of the kinds of people who dislike surveys, the researcher must gain their cooperation.

Researchers define the completion rate in different ways. In face-to-face surveys, the completion rate typically equals the number of completed interviews divided by the number of respondents eligible for interview. Eligible respondents include those interviewed plus those known to be living at the contacted address but never home or co-operative. In telephone interviewing with random digit dialing, the number eligible proves more difficult to define. An unanswered number may indicate that an eligible respondent is not at home or that the number is in a vacant house or is a pay phone. Researchers have found that most numbers that go unanswered after many calls (say 12 or more) belong to ineligible phones. As a result, some researchers exclude such unanswers phone numbers from the calculation of phone survey completion rates. Some urban telephone surveys have achieved completion rates in the range of 50 to 90 percent (Groves, 1979; Jordan et al., 1980; O'Neil, 1979; Tuchfarber & Klecka, 1976). Face-to-face surveys using the same instruments as used in telephone surveys tend to achieve slightly better completion rates.

Another approach to measuring cooperation involves computing refusal rates, the number of refusals divided by the total eligible. Because of the advent of answering machines, such refusal rates must take into account passive refusals from those who avoid coming to the phone even though they are at home (Mishra et al., 1993). Because completion and refusal rates depend on the definition of eligibles, you must take care in comparing reports of cooperation from different studies.

Checking and Avoiding Bias.   Low completion rates may stem from low *contact* rates (respondents not at home), low *cooperation* rates (refusals), or both. To estimate noncontact bias, researchers have compared respondents interviewed on early attempts with those interviewed on later attempts. This method assumes that those not contacted initially resemble the kinds of people who are never contacted. Respondents requiring more contacts to reach tend to be younger, have more education, live in central cities, and have higher incomes (Dunkelberg & Day, 1973). The tendency to be at home and available for survey contact has been declining steadily of late (Weeks, Jones, Folsom, & Benrud, 1980). To reduce noncontact bias, survey researchers can increase the level of effort by making more callbacks at different hours, especially on weeknights and weekends.

Cooperation depends in part on interview content and interviewer style (topics addressed later). Cooperation also depends on the respondent's characteristics and the data collection medium. Respondents typically prefer face-to-face interviews to telephone interviews and are less likely to refuse a personal than a phone interviewer (Groves, 1979). Information about the personal characteristics of noncooperators comes from comparing initial cooperators with initial refusers who later cooperated or about whom some other data were available. Uncooperative urban interviewees tend to have less education and income and to be older (O'Neil, 1979). In a nonmetropolitan study, noncooperators had less education, more residential stability, and smaller households (Comstock & Helsing, 1973).

To some extent, researchers can persuade initial refusers to cooperate, but ethical guidelines limit such efforts to "convert" respondents. People have a right not to participate in research. Improvements in rater training and in questionnaire design may offer the best methods for improving cooperation. As cooperation rates decline, research to improve cooperation in surveys become more important.

Interviewer Effects and Training

Rapport. Mail surveys have no interviewer, and respondents must decide, based on the written materials, how honestly and thoroughly to answer the questions, or whether to answer them at all. In face-to-face and phone surveys, the interviewer plays an important part in the respondent's decision to cooperate, to answer honestly, and to complete every item. Since the interviewer can affect the completion rate and the validity and reliability of the answers, he or she must try to create a friendly and trusting atmosphere. When the interviewer gains the respondent's confidence and achieves good two-way communication, he or she has established **rapport** with the respondent.

Interviewer style can help establish rapport. A well-groomed and appropriately dressed interviewer has the best chance of getting a foot in the respondent's door. A pleasant manner and a clear and competent-sounding voice will help avoid an early refusal. The interviewer wants the respondent's sincere cooperation and should, therefore, appear friendly, respectful, and honest. Arguments and persuasion have no place in the research interview. The researcher observes the respondent's ideas, opinions, and beliefs without trying to change them.

Random Error. Random error occurs when the interviewer makes haphazard mistakes. Errors can occur as misread questions or misrecorded answers. Researchers have counted such errors in tape-recorded interviews. In one study of very carefully selected interviewers, an average of three reading errors occurred in every ten questions. Some sort of nonprogrammed interviewer speech behavior appeared in over half of all questions (Bradburn, Sudman, & Associates, 1979). Although the interviewer's errors in this study did not greatly distort the responses, such errors have the potential to decrease measurement reliability.

Interviewer training may offer the best solution for avoiding such errors and increasing reliability. Training helps standardize interviewer behavior by instruction and rehearsal. Most professional survey organizations conduct training for their interviewers and provide detailed written instructions in the form of a manual (Guenzel, Berckmans, & Cannell, 1983; Survey Research Center, 1976). The required training varies in length, depending on the complexity of the questionnaire and the interviewer's experience. For example, for the Current Population Survey, new interviewers receive 50 to 60 hours of training in their first three months and then two to three hours before each monthly survey (National Commission on Employment and Unemployment Statistics, 1979).

Bias. Interviewers can bias their survey in various ways. An interviewer may ask certain questions differently or probe more intensively with some respondents than with others based on knowledge of the study's hypotheses. For example, interviewers who expected that their respondents would underreport certain behaviors such as gambling obtained lower reported levels of such behaviors (Bradburn et al., 1979).

Interviewers can also introduce bias by their personal manner. Interviewer effects appear as differences in the average responses gathered by different interviewers. For example, an analysis of surveys of economic outlook found that male interviewers obtained more optimistic reports than did female interviewers (Groves & Fultz, 1985). Although training might help correct bias due to interviewers' expectations, only interviewer selection can reduce bias due to fixed interviewer characteristics.

Questionnaire Construction

Bias and error can also enter the study via the questionnaire. In this section, we will briefly address three aspects of questionnaire construction: individual item clarity, item order, and questionnaire format (also see Sudman & Bradburn, 1982).

Item Construction.   Unclear or badly worded items introduce random error because they force respondents to interpret them. Since different people will place different meanings on the same ambiguous questions, variations in answers will stem from random interpretation as well as from genuine differences between respondents.

Several common problems appear in item wording. For example, the **compound item** squeezes more than one question into a single item. Consider the following question written to evaluate a course: "Do you like the lecturer's content and style?" This item really asks two separate questions, one about content and one about style. Respondents with different views on the two topics must choose which question to answer.

Another problem occurs with **closed-ended questions**, ones that give the respondent fixed answers from which to choose. The respondent can become confused if the provided options omit one or more possible answers or are not mutually exclusive. The following item illustrates both problems: "How often do you feel depressed? (1) Once a year or less; (2) One to four times per month; (3) Once per week; (4) More than once per week." The person who feels depressed four times per month must choose between answers 2 and 3, both of which include the respondent's answer. The person feeling depressed 2 to 11 times a year has no answer. A related problem arises with items to which the respondent has no answer. Some respondents will attempt an answer despite basing it on a fading memory or guesswork. To allow for such cases, answer options should include "do not know."

Items using vague terms force the respondent to guess at the question's meaning. For example, if asked "Have you recently changed your residence?," the respondent might wonder how recent is "recent." A related problem involves wording. Very long questions and ones with difficult vocabulary, negative construction, or convoluted phrasing, may confuse the respondents.

Item composition can also affect the validity of the questionnaire if it increases the chance of bias. Nonneutral wording of questions can produce such bias. For example, in questions about whether respondents favored more assistance for the needy, the words *welfare* and *poor* produced different results. The term *welfare* led to less generous responses, apparently because it suggested waste and bureaucracy (Smith, 1987). For further discussion of how to write survey questions, see Converse and Presser (1986).

Some topics are inherently sensitive, and questions about them lead to more refusals or biased answers—for example, "Have you ever underreported your income on tax returns?" Such items typically yield underestimates of the true level in the population. One approach to this problem would simply omit such threatening items because they may produce not only biased results but also greater terminations or refusals. Another method tries to phrase the questions to minimize the threat even at the cost of precision. For example, respondents may feel more comfortable answering income questions in terms of large categories (less than $20,000, between $20,000 and $50,000, or over $50,000) rather than in exact terms. A third strategy tries to estimate the true population rate from threatening survey items. One such technique, called the random response method, asks the respondent one of two randomly selected questions, but the interviewer does not know which question was asked (Bradburn et al., 1979; Locander, Sudman, & Bradburn, 1976). One question is the personally sensitive one for which the population rate is being sought—for example, "Do you use illicit drugs?" The other question is an irrelevant one for which the population rate is already known—for example, "Is the fourth digit of your phone number less than 3?" Statistical techniques can compute the true population proportion of yes responses to the sensitive item based on the total number of yes responses to both items, the sample size, the ratio of irrelevant to sensitive items in the survey, and the known probability of yes responses to the irrelevant question.

Order Effects.   Virtually all surveys ask more than one question. Sometimes interviews cover several different attitudes or beliefs, each measured by single items. Usually researchers combine several items to measure each variable because the reliability of measurement increases with the number of items used. The limit to the number of items on a questionnaire depends in part on project funding. Interviewers receive hourly pay and must work more hours to go through longer interviews. The limit also depends on the patience of the interviewees, which varies with their interest in the topic. Very boring or threatening questionnaires may prove too long at 10 minutes. On the other hand, questionnaires lasting an hour or more have been used with success.

One issue in writing questionnaires concerns the risk that earlier items may bias the responses to later ones. This threat becomes especially important in comparing answers to the same item across different surveys. Unless the questionnaires follow the same item order, we cannot decide whether differences between the surveys reflect differences in the samples or order effects. To test the order effect, researchers have reversed item order on different versions of the same instrument with samples from the same population. One such analysis studied two abortion attitude items, one specific (in response to a strong chance of a serious birth defect), and the other general (the mother's choice because she does not want more children; Schuman, Presser, & Ludwig, 1981). Respondents expressed up to 17 percent higher agreement with the general proposition favoring legal abortion when that proposition came before rather than after the more specific item. Other research has shown that this effect also depends on the context of the other questions surrounding the items (Bishop, Oldendick, & Tuchfarber, 1985).

One approach to this problem randomizes the order of items within a survey. That is, different respondents would get the same items but in randomly different orders. However, this approach does not guarantee "true" responses to the items in their different orders. It only promises to reduce the bias to an unknown extent in some random orders. Order effects appear strongest for general or summary items because people seem more likely to interpret them with respect to prior specific items. Thus you might avoid general items or ask them before more specific items.

Researchers can also arrange item order to increase respondent cooperation and smooth progression through the questionnaire. You should consider beginning a questionnaire with less threatening and more interesting items to assure cooperation in the crucial early going. Questions on related topics or ones that share the same instructions should cluster together to spare the respondent the confusion of jumping back and forth between different issues or response formats.

Format and Response Recording.   After wording and ordering the items, the next step is formatting the questionnaire and providing for coding and storing the answers. Visually the questionnaire should appear uncluttered. Tiny print, small margins, and multiple items per line can all contribute to reading and recording errors especially for untrained interviewers. The questionnaire design should make clear the flow from item to item. It also can guide the recording of responses so as to aid data management.

Many questionnaires contain sets of items that some respondents need not answer. For example, 20 items might ask about perceptions of one's job. Such items could prove both irrelevant and embarrassing to someone who has recently become unemployed. To skip such items, questionnaires utilize branches. A **branch** occurs when different answers to one question may lead to different paths through the questionnaire. For example, the items about a person's job would ordinarily follow an item asking about current employment status. Employed respondents should go through these job items, but unemployed respondents would take a different branch, skipping ahead to the next section of the questionnaire. Such skips can lead to random errors unless the fork appears well labeled and requires no subjective decision or recall of earlier items on the part of the interviewer.

Recording answers depends on question format. Closed-ended questions come with all possible answers. The respondent (in mail questionnaires) or the interviewer simply marks the code number associated with the chosen answer. As an example of a questionnaire using closed-ended questions and branching, see the Current Population Survey reproduced in Figure 7–2. The government has used this instrument since 1967 to measure employment and unemployment in the American workforce.

Open-ended questions require the respondent to compose the answer and the interviewer to record it. The format for open-ended questions must include ample recording space. Difficult open-ended questions may require the interviewer to probe (that is, ask the same question more than once with variations in the wording). For an example see the question, "What kind of work was [the respondent] doing?", item 23C in Figure 7–2. The list of all possible types of work would be too long to include as fixed answer alternatives. The respondent may not at first think in terms of the kind of categories sought by the question. For this reason, the instrument gives examples in parentheses to help focus the respondent and to discriminate the question from those surrounding it.

While open-ended questions can produce rich and interesting answers, the results require extra time and effort to code. Answer coding means assigning answers to one or more of a number of categories, each of which can in turn be recorded as a brief number code. Only thorough training, precise and detailed coding guidelines, and frequent supervisory checks can assure reliability and validity in this step.

1. INTERVIEWER CHECK ITEM

Only CPS-1 for household .... ○ *(Fill all applicable items on this page)*
First CPS-1 of continuation h'hld. ... ○
Second CPS-1 of continuation h'hold ○ *(Transcribe items 2–13 from first CPS-1)*
Third, fourth, etc. CPS-1 .... ○

FORM CPS-1   **U.S. DEPARTMENT OF COMMERCE** Bureau of the Census
CURRENT POPULATION SURVEY
Form Approved – O.M.B. No. 0607-0049   **MAY 1983**

2. SAMPLE A B C D E ○ ○ ○ ○ ○
3. CONTROL NUMBER

MONTH ○ ○ ○ ○ ● ○ ○ ○ ○ ○ ○ ○ ○   **YEAR** ○ ○ ● ○ ○

10. INTERVIEWER CODE A B C D E F G H J K L M
○ ○ ○ ○ ○ ○ ○ ○ ○ ○ ○ ○
0 1 2 3 4 5 6 7 8 9
0 1 2 3 4 5 6 7 8 9

11. DATE COMPLETED 1 2 0 1 2 3 4 5 6 7 8 9

12. LINE NO. OF H'HOLD RESP. 1 2 3 4 5 6
Non. h'hld. resp.*(Specify)* ○ *(Send Inter Comm)*

4. TYPE OF LIVING QUARTERS

HOUSING UNIT
House, apartment, flat .... ○
HU in nontransient hotel, motel, etc......... ○
HU, permanent, in transient hotel, motel, etc. ○
HU in rooming house .... ○
Mobile home or trailer .... ○
HU not specified above *(Describe below)*.... ○

OTHER UNIT
Quarters not
 HU in rooming or boarding house ○
Unit not permanent
 in transient hotel, motel, etc..... ○
Tent site or trailer site............ ○
Other not HU *(Describe below)*.... ○

5a. LAND USAGE *(TRANSCRIBE from C.C. Item 10 or 11)*
A ○ | B ○ *(Fill 5b)* | C ○
5b. FARM SALES *(TRANSCRIBE from C.C. Item 12)*
A ○ | B ○ | C ○ | D ○

6. PSU NO. | **7. SEGMENT NO.** | **8. SERIAL NO.** | **9. HOUSE-HOLD NO.**

13. TYPE INTERVIEW
Noninterview ○
Personal ... ○
Tel. – regular ○
Tel. – callback ○
ICR filled .... ○

NONINTERVIEW

TYPE A
14. *(Mark reason and race.)*
REASON | **RACE**
No one home ○ |
Temporarily absent... ○ | White... ○
Refused...... ○ | Black... ○
Other – Occ. ○ | All other ○
(Describe below)

15.
Vacant – regular............. ○ *(Fill 16)*
Vacant – storage of h'hld furniture ○
Temp. occ. by persons with URE.. ○
Unfit or to be demolished........ ○
Under construction, not ready .... ○
Converted to temp. business or storage... ○
Occ. by Armed Force members or persons under 14... ○ *(Omit 16–17)*
Unoccupied tent site or trailer site. ○
Permit granted, construction not started........ ○
Other *(Specify below)*.......... ○

TYPE B
Demolished .... ○
House or trailer moved... ○
Outside segment .... ○
Converted to permanent business or storage... ○
Merged................. ○ *(Omit 16–17)*
Condemned............. ○
Built after April 1, 1970 ○
Unused line of listing sheet............. ○
Other *(Describe below)*.. ○

TYPE C *(Send Inter Comm)*

16. This unit is intended for occupancy:
Year round......... ○ *(Fill HVS if HU in Item 4)*
By migratory workers... ○ *(Fill Item 17 below if HU in Item 4)*
Seasonally.......... ○

17. This unit is intended for occupancy:
Summers only........ ○ *(Transcribe as instructed on back of Control Card)*
Winters only........ ○
Other*(Describe below)* ○

SEASONAL STATUS

TRANSCRIPTION ITEMS *Fill 26 to 27E on FIRST CPS-1 of interviewed households*

26. TENURE *(Transcribe from Control Card item 9)*
Owned or being bought.........
Rented.....................
No cash rent...............

27A. TOTAL FAMILY INCOME *(From Control Card item 33)*
A | E | I | M
B | F | J | N
C | G | K
D | H | L

27B. INTERVIEWER CHECK ITEM *(Rotation Number)*
First digit of Segment Number is:
○ 1, 2, 7 or 8 *(Fill 27C)*
○ 3, 4, 5 or 6 *(End telephone transcription)*

USE OF TELEPHONE
27C. Telephone in Household *(Transcribe from item 30a)*
Yes ○ *(Skip to 27E)*
No ○ *(Fill 27D)*

27D. Telephone Available *(Transcribe from C.C. item 30b)*
Yes ○ *(Fill 27E)*
No ○ *(End telephone transcription)*

27E. Telephone Interview Acceptable *(Transcribe from C.C. item 30d)*
Yes ○ *(End telephone transcription)*
No ○

REMINDER Fill items 18A–18I on pages 2, 5, 7, 9, and 11.

NOTES:

CODER NUMBER
A B C D E F G H J K L M
○ ○ ○ ○ ○ ○ ○ ○ ○ ○ ○ ○
0 1 2 3 4 5 6 7 8 9

3–20–83   Fosdic 26.1:1   Page 3

Figure 7–2 Current population survey (form CPS-1). (From the Bureau of the Census, 1978.)

Issues in Conducting Surveys

Ethical Problems.   Sometimes people take offense at surveys because of their content. In one case, complaints from parents and the press led to burning the answer sheets to six personality and youth attitude tests already collected from 5000 ninth graders (Nettler, 1959). The school board found no benefit in such items as "I enjoy soaking in the bathtub" and judged that they might undermine a child's moral character. Researchers should anticipate such fears and be prepared to respond with active public relations efforts (Eron & Walder, 1961).

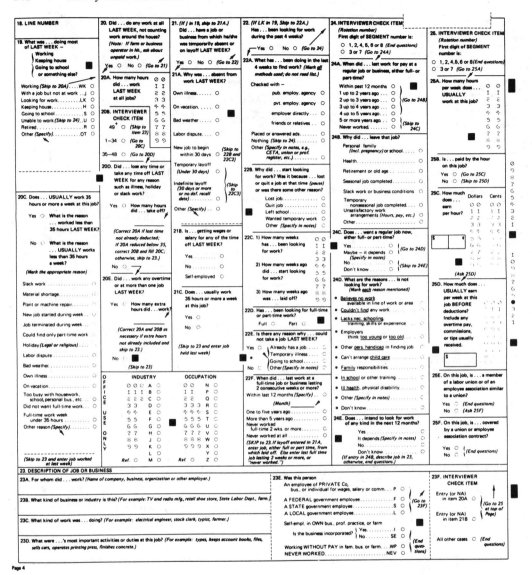

Figure 7-2   (Continued)

Sometimes the debate about social surveys reaches high political levels. In one case, researchers got permission and began a school survey aimed at understanding the causes of dropping out and delinquency (Voss, 1966). Some people in the community believed that the more personal questions were "calculated to plant seeds of doubt about the validity of old-fashioned morality, spiritualism, patriotism, and parental authority" (Voss, 1966, p. 139). Some right-wing critics worried that the federal government had funded the project so that those students "with right-wing tendencies could be committed to institutions as psychotic when they reached their majority" (p. 139). These fears came to the attention of the state senator and state representative for the area, who then expressed their opposition to the superintendent. With a school tax election looming, the superintendent claimed that school approval had not been given properly and halted the study.

Do not suppose that such resistance to social surveys has disappeared with the passing decades. Similar opposition halted a major survey as recently as 1991 (Senate Action, 1991). The National Institute of Child Health and Human Development had, after peer review, awarded $18 million for a national survey of teenage sexual behavior, the American Teenage Study (ATS). However, congressional opponents and others asserted that parents would not want their children to answer questions on sexual practices. Even though the findings of the study might have helped prevent sexually transmitted diseases such as AIDS, the Secretary of Health and Human Services decided to cancel the study.

Computer Use. Once the interviewer has recorded the respondent's answers, often directly on the questionnaire, the next step is data processing. Analyses of large surveys almost always require computer assistance. Answers recorded as pencil marks on paper must be transferred to computer-readable format. In that case someone must read the answer and type it into computer memory. As an alternative, the interviewer could use a machine-readable questionnaire form. In this case, a photoelectric scanner can read the pencil marks into the computer thus saving the manual retyping step.

Still more advanced, the **computer-assisted interview (CAI)** technique allows the interviewer to key answers directly into a computer. This technique avoids not only some data transfer errors but also certain questionnaire administration errors. The interviewer reads the questions not from a printed sheet but from a computer terminal. In the case of telephone surveys, the terminal operates next to a phone station, and the technique is called CATI or computer assisted telephone interviewing. In the case of in-person surveys, the interviewer uses a laptop computer and the technique is called CAPI or computer assisted personal interviewing. In either case, the computer processes each answer as entered, performs the appropriate skips and branches automatically, and shows the interviewer the appropriate next question based on the previous answer. Because of its promise for reducing errors and the economies of telephone surveys, CATI has become very widely used (Groves, 1983; Palit & Sharp, 1983; Sudman, 1983). The CAPI only became possible with the appearance of truly compact computers, but this method is also entering wider use. For example, in 1994, a revised version of the CPS will replace the current version (Figure 7–2) and will employ both CATI and CAPI (Bureau of Labor Statistics, 1992).

SUMMARY

This chapter covered survey designs that fit different research problems and survey methods that minimize bias and random error. Both the researcher who is planning a study and the consumer who is evaluating the results reported from such research must guard against drawing conclusions from faulty surveys. The researcher will want to use probability sampling and to maximize the completion rate in order to minimize bias due to sampling and data collection. Similarly, the consumer of a reported survey will want to check the completion rate and whether probability sampling was used in order to judge how much trust to place in the findings.

Table 7–2 summarizes some of the issues to consider both in planning and in judging a survey. For each problem area, it lists potential difficulties or choices along with possible solutions or diagnostics.

EXERCISES

1. Pick a topic that you can explore in a brief questionnaire (for example, evaluating your instructor). Choose an appropriate survey design (for example, cross-sectional versus longitudinal), construct a suitable questionnaire, draw a sample from the class, and collect the data. Briefly summarize those aspects of the study that a reader should know in order to assess the risk of error or bias in your results, such as the sample method and completion rate.

Table 7–2 Summary of Common Survey Problems and Solutions or Diagnostics

Problem Area	Problem Nature	Solution or Diagnostic
Design selection	Cross-sectional versus longitudinal. Medium: phone, person, or mail.	Does design satisfy inferential requirements of the hypothesis? Is medium appropriate to topic, design, precision requirements?
Sampling error	Random misestimation of population value by sample.	Is the sample size adequate to provide required precision in the required confidence range? (Check sampling error.)
Sampling bias	Constant misestimation of population value by sample.	Is the sample selected randomly from a representative sampling frame?
Data collection error	Interviewers make random reading or recording mistakes.	Are interviewers trained and is questionnaire well formatted?
	Questionnaire has too few items, or items are poorly worded.	Are items clear, well scaled, and sufficient in number? (Check reliability of measurement.)
	Data are miscoded or carelessly managed.	Are data checked for accuracy?
Data collection bias	Respondents with completed interviews are unrepresentative of original sample.	Is completion rate high? Do incompletes or refusals differ from the completes?
	Interviewers, item wording, or item order influence answers.	Are interviewers trained to avoid bias? Are items worded neutrally and ordered to avoid bias?

2. Reports of surveys vary greatly in their detail. Reports in published articles may have only a few paragraphs on the methodology of the survey. Find a published report with as much detail about the survey procedures as possible and, following the sections of Table 7–2, evaluate both the information presented and the information omitted. A behind-the-scenes description of an important survey appears in Hunt (1985, chap. 3).

KEY TERMS

Attrition	**Panel survey**
Bias	**Population**
Branch	**Pretest sensitization**
Census	**Probability proportionate**
Central limit theorem	**to size (PPS)**
Closed-ended questions	**Probability sampling**
Cluster	**Purposive sampling**
Cohort survey	**Quota sampling**
Completion rate	**Random digit dialing (RDD)**
Compound item	**Random error**
Computer-assisted	**Random sampling**
interview (CAI)	**Rapport**
Confidence interval	**Sample**
Convenience sampling	**Sample bias**
Cross-sectional survey	**Sample error**
Data collection bias	**Sample stages**
Data collection error	**Sampling frame**
Element	**Sampling unit**
Enumeration	**Standard error of the mean**
Law of large numbers	**Stratification**
Longitudinal survey	**Systematic sampling**
Nonobservation bias	**Total survey error**
Nonprobability sampling	**Trend survey**
Observation bias	**Weighting**
Oversample	

∞ 8 ∞

Inferential Statistics
Drawing Valid Conclusions from Samples

The previous chapter explored the problem of drawing samples to represent populations. This chapter deals with the problem of leaping from sample data to an inference about the population. We use inferential statistics to judge the trust we can place in that leap. You will make better progress if you know something about descriptive statistics. For a review, see the Appendix before proceeding with this chapter.

INFERENTIAL LOGIC

Example: Academic Performance, Anxiety, and Biofeedback

t = 4.66, p <.01.   Symbols and numbers such as these appear in almost every social research report. The *t* stands for a particular kind of inferential statistic. The number 4.66 gives the value of the *t* statistic in this instance. The *p* stands for *probability*. The expression *< .01* means that such a large value of *t* as 4.66 occurs by chance less than 1 percent of the time. This chapter discusses the purpose of this expression and its uses and problems in social research.

The exact phrase "*t = 4.66, p < .01*" appears in an actual study, which assessed some methods for improving the grades of anxious college students (Stout, Thornton, & Russell, 1980). These scholars believed that a decrease in anxiety would lead to improved grades. To test this notion, they assigned students randomly to three groups: (1) anxiety reduction by biofeedback (BF), (2) anxiety reduction by progressive relaxation (PR); and (3) no treatment (NT). The BF students learned to relax through the use of feedback from a machine (electromyograph) that measured their muscle tension. The PR students learned to relax by taped instruction but without feedback from the machine. The NT subjects received no relaxation training.

Based on this study, would you use biofeedback in order to improve your ability to relax and to raise your grades? To make a judgment about this study, you would need to answer two other questions about its results. First, did the BF group achieve better grades than the NT group in this study? The answer to this question comes from **descriptive statistics** (that is, statistics that summarize information about groups). The scores in a group will differ from student to student. Of the various ways to summarize a group's scores in a single number, the mean appears most often. The mean tells the average, the sum of the scores divided by the number of subjects in the group. To answer the first question, we find that the mean of the BF group (90.33) surpassed the mean of the NT group (79.83). In other words, the biofeedback group performed better than the control group *in this sample.*

The second question looks beyond the present study. Does the difference between the BF and NT groups hold for other college students? To answer this question you must make an inference from the study's small sample to the whole population of college students. This particular study included just 15 BF and 12 NT students. Is it possible that these two groups differed, in some unknown way, from all students? Drawing a conclusion from small samples to large populations requires a leap of faith, or an inference. **Inferential statistics** help us with this judgment.

If the study had included every student, we would have no need for an inference or for an inferential statistic. In practice, scholars rarely get to study whole populations, but they often find that a sample misrepresents its parent population. Suppose that each student in your present class would receive the same grade. Further suppose that this grade would depend not on how well all students did but on how well only a few students did—say just two. Thus, if the two sampled students earned *A* grades, you and each member of the class would get an *A*. If the two sampled students failed, you and everyone else would get an *F*. Would you trust this approach to grading?

In the same way, the sample of 15 BF students in the preceding study could misrepresent all college students who might receive biofeedback. Or the 12 NT students might misrepresent all possible untreated students. This risk threatens the validity of all social research based on samples. Findings may stem from an accident of sampling and fail to reflect the nature of the whole population. We can check this threat with inferential statistics and call this type of validity **statistical inference validity**.

Variability and Inference.   To understand how an inferential statistic is derived (such as $t = 4.66$), you need to recall the meaning of **variability**. We can describe a group's scores in different ways. One way includes the mean or other such measures of **central tendency**. Another way involves variability, that is, the spread of scores within a group. In groups that have a lot of variability, members appear to be spread far apart, both above and below the mean. To display this visually, a **frequency distribution** shows how many members of the group received each possible score. In Figure 8–1, you see two distributions—one with much variability and the other with little.

We want to judge whether the difference between two groups is "real" (that is, holds for the population) or "accidental" (that is, holds only in the sample). This judgment depends on the variability within the groups, not just the difference between the means of the groups. To see this, imagine two different distributions of the study's data (see Figure 8–2) with the difference between the means held constant.

With narrow distributions such as those in Figure 8–2a, note how little the two groups overlap. That is, nearly every student in the BF group did better than any stu-

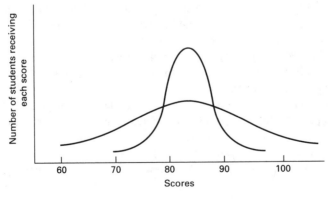

Figure 8–1 Broad and narrow distributions.

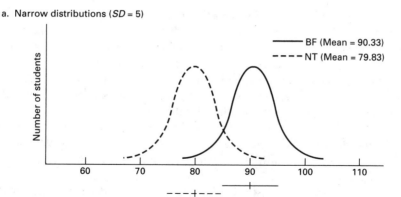

a. Narrow distributions (*SD* = 5)

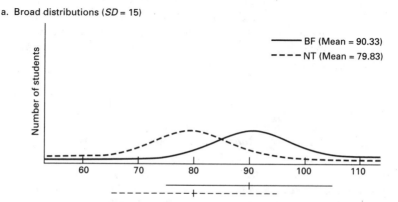

a. Broad distributions (*SD* = 15)

Figure 8–2 Alternative distributions for the biofeedback (BF) and no treatment (NT) groups.

dent in the NT group. Data like those in Figure 8–2a strongly support the view that the treatment improved student performance. In contrast, the wide and overlapping distributions of Figure 8–2b make the difference between the groups seem much less clear. Many students in the control group did as well as the average student in the BF group. In this case, the difference between the two groups might have occurred accidentally. Remember that the population includes students of different ability levels. Perhaps the BF condition received a few more students from the high range, whereas the NT group received a few more from the low range.

The BF sample mean only gives an estimate of the true or population value for all students who might receive biofeedback. Because of sampling error, different estimates (from other samples of treated subjects) would likely form a range or interval of scores in which the true mean would likely fall. Similarly, the NT group mean gives us just one point in an interval in which the true value for all untreated subjects likely falls. If the intervals of possible true scores for the two groups do not touch, the sample findings imply a real difference. But overlapping intervals imply that the samples differ by chance. That is, the true NT value might exceed its estimate in this one small sample and differ little from a true BF value much smaller than its estimate.

To illustrate this, below each group's curve in Figure 8–2 appears a bar with a hash mark at the group's mean. The length of each bar suggests the interval in which the true mean might fall and depends on the variability of the group. The standard deviation (*SD*) measures group variability in terms of the distance of each score from the mean. A small standard deviation reflects that most scores gather close to the mean as in Figure 8–2a with $SD = 5$. Since the scores in this group fall so close together, the true value probably falls near the estimate. A larger standard deviation tells us that the scores have spread out from the group means as in Figure 8–2b with $SD = 15$, and the true score could appear far above or below its estimate. The interval bars reflect these possibilities by extending one standard deviation above and below the sample mean.

The problem of statistical inference consists in deciding whether the data look more like Figure 8–2a or Figure 8–2b. When the data look like Figure 8–2a, we have confidence that chance alone does not account for the groups' difference. Often, however, a study's results present a less clear-cut picture. We need a more precise method to express such results and a clear decision rule for deciding how confident we must be before declaring a choice.

Two Types of Error

Effect-to-Variability Ratio. The problem illustrated in Figure 8–2 requires weighing the difference between the two groups by their variability. The difference between the group means (90.33 - 79.83) expresses the treatment effect in a condensed form. Does this effect exceed the difference we could expect by chance? To answer this question, we must adjust the difference for the variability of the groups. The authors reported the standard deviations for the actual groups as 5.0 for the BF group and 6.3 for the NT group (Stout et al., 1980).

Given measures of effect (difference of two means) and variability (two group standard deviations), we can summarize their relationship in a single number: **effect-to-variability ratio** (that is, effect divided by variability). Since the two groups have different standard deviations, these will have to be combined or pooled before calculating the ratio.[1] One form of this ratio, the *t* statistic, is also called the Student's *t* the pen name used by Gossett, its inventor. Student's *t* has very desirable properties. As the difference between groups grows, relative to the variability, the *t* statistic becomes larger. As the variability increases, *t* becomes smaller. Thus *t* boils down the graphic information such as that in Figure 8–2 to a single number, large for data such as Figure 8–2a and small for those in Figure 8–2b.

If inferential statistics only gave the ratio of effect to variability, they would not meet our needs. The inferential statistic *t*, when calculated for the data in the biofeedback example, equals 4.66. Is 4.66 sufficiently large so that we can conclude that the BF and NT groups look more like Figure 8–2a or 8–2b?

Certainty and Confidence. No magnitude of *t*, no matter how large, can make us absolutely certain. As long as we have only sample evidence, we cannot know the whole population. Unable to speak of certainty or proof, we must deal in terms of probability or risk. If we cannot eliminate uncertainty, we can at least limit it.

Inferential statistics help us choose between two rival hypotheses. In one view, chance or sample error causes the observed difference (likely when the effect is small compared to the variability). We call this the **null hypothesis** (abbreviated H_0) because it implies no real difference between the populations from which the samples came. The other view holds that the difference observed in the samples reflects a real difference in the populations (likely when the effect is large relative to variability).

Suppose for a moment that H_0 were true and that our observed difference is a fluke. The two samples yield a difference that is not really true for the populations. Other groups drawn from the pool of all students and given the same treatments would show no difference on the whole. What are the chances of drawing such unrepresentative samples that t equals 4.66 when H_0 is true? Probability theory can estimate the likelihood of any given value of t when H_0 is true. The expression "$t = 4.66, p < .01$" translates as follows: Samples yielding such an effect-to-variability ratio as $t = 4.66$ appear by chance less than 1 percent of the time from populations that have no real difference. In simpler terms, it seems improbable that the difference comes from sampling error.

Can we be certain that sampling did not cause the observed difference? No, if we reject H_0 as false and assume that there was a real difference, we guess wrong about one time in a hundred. We call this kind of mistake a **Type I error**, that is, rejecting the null hypothesis wrongly. Statistics cannot avoid this error altogether, only limit its risk. A **Type II error** occurs when we wrongly infer that H_0 is true. Table 8–1 summarizes both types of error.

We can set the risk of making a Type I error, called **alpha** (α), before a study begins. Most tests use an alpha level of .05 (see Cowles & Davis, 1982, for the source of this custom). With alpha set at $p < .05$, we consider significant any inferential statistic (for example, a t value) with a chance likelihood of 5 percent or less. A sample finding with **statistical significance** implies a real pattern in the population from which the sample was drawn. Of course, scholars can set the alpha level as they please, such as $p < .10$ or $p < .01$. The risk of making a Type I error climbs when $p < .10$ (10 chances in 100) and drops when $p < .01$ (1 in 100).

Limiting Type I Error. How do we know that a value of t (or other inferential statistic) meets the requirement for some alpha (for example, .05)? In order to serve its function, an inferential statistic, such as t, must have a known **probability distribution**.

Table 8–1 Errors in Inferential Statistics

	Null Hypothesis Is Correct	Null Hypothesis Is False
Null hypothesis is not rejected	Correct	Type II error
Null hypothesis is rejected	Type I error	Correct

That is, the chances of finding each possible value of t (assuming no difference in the population) can be calculated. Because these values vary with the sample size and the alpha, they usually appear in table form. Called **critical values**, these numbers tell the level that the observed t must exceed in order to reach significance at the chosen alpha. To look up the critical values of a statistic, one needs to pick an alpha level and know the **degrees of freedom**. The degrees of freedom depend on the number of subjects or data points, such as cells of contingency tables, used to compute the inferential statistic. The reader of a research report need not find the degrees of freedom and look up the critical value of the inferential statistic. The study's author performs these tasks.

However, you could check the author by looking up the inferential statistic by yourself. Each inferential statistic (for example, t, F or χ^2) has a different set of critical values, but you use the same method with each to judge the significance of the statistic.

To learn this approach, note the critical values of the t statistic in Table 8–2. The eight right-hand columns give the critical values of t for the alphas stated above each column. The left-hand column lists the degrees of freedom from 1 to 100. The critical values of t decrease, for any alpha, as the degrees of freedom increase but change little past 100 as seen by the listing for infinite degrees of freedom (last row). The degrees of freedom for the t statistic in our example equal the sum of the subjects in the two groups minus 2. Since the BF group had 15 members and the NT group had 12, the degrees of freedom equal 15 + 12 - 2 or 25. Think of degrees of freedom as the amount of free information left after computing the statistic. You will sometimes see degrees of freedom reported in parentheses as $t(25) = 4.66$ or as a subscript as $t_{25} = 4.66$.

In Table 8–2, for each number of degrees of freedom, or d.f., you will find a row of critical values of t, one for each alpha level listed along the top row. For example, if we wanted to limit our Type I error to 5 percent, we would choose the alpha column headed by .05 (4th from right). Figure 8–3 shows the distribution of t under the null hypothesis of no difference in the population. By chance, most estimates of t will fall near the middle of the distribution, with fewer reaching very large positive or negative values. Each critical value of t marks an area under the distribution (shaded area in the figure). Higher values of t leave smaller areas under the upper tail of the figure. We choose an area or alpha equal to the largest risk of Type I error that we will accept. This alpha, in turn, defines a critical value of t for the sample's degrees of freedom.[2]

The intersection of the .05 alpha column and the 25 degrees of freedom row gives the critical value of 1.708. We infer that the difference in our samples reflects a real difference in the population since getting such a large t as 4.66 by chance has a probability of less than 5 percent. We could go further and insist on an alpha level of .005 (far right column). Our table shows that the critical value for t_{25} at the .005 level is 2.787. Since the finding of $t = 4.66$ exceeds even this critical value, we decide with some confidence not to accept the null hypothesis. Instead we call this finding statistically significant. Note that we do not claim that our conclusion is certain since there remain about 5 chances in 1000 that our result came through sample error.

Limiting Type II Error.   Just as samples can imply a difference that does not exist (Type I error), so they can conceal a true relationship (Type II error). Social sci-

Table 8–2   The *t* Distribution
(Adapted from Table A6 [p. 681] in Goldman and Weinberg, 1985.)

d.f.	α or Upper Tail Areas for Critical Values of t							
	.25	.2	.15	.1	.05	.025	.01	.005
1	1.000	1.376	1.963	3.078	6.314	12.706	31.821	63.657
2	.817	1.061	1.386	1.886	2.920	4.303	6.965	9.925
3	.765	.978	1.250	1.638	2.353	3.183	4.541	5.841
4	.741	.941	1.190	1.533	2.132	2.776	3.747	4.604
5	.727	.920	1.156	1.476	2.015	2.571	3.365	4.032
6	.718	.906	1.134	1.440	1.943	2.447	3.143	3.707
7	.711	.896	1.119	1.415	1.895	2.365	2.998	3.500
8	.706	.889	1.108	1.397	1.860	2.306	2.896	3.355
9	.703	.883	1.100	1.383	1.833	2.262	2.821	3.250
10	.700	.879	1.093	1.372	1.813	2.228	2.764	3.169
11	.697	.876	1.088	1.363	1.796	2.201	2.718	3.106
12	.696	.873	1.083	1.356	1.782	2.179	2.681	3.055
13	.694	.870	1.079	1.350	1.771	2.160	2.650	3.012
14	.692	.868	1.076	1.345	1.761	2.145	2.624	2.977
15	.691	.866	1.074	1.341	1.753	2.132	2.602	2.947
16	.690	.865	1.071	1.337	1.746	2.120	2.583	2.921
17	.689	.863	1.069	1.333	1.740	2.110	2.567	2.898
18	.688	.862	1.067	1.330	1.734	2.101	2.552	2.878
19	.688	.861	1.066	1.328	1.729	2.093	2.539	2.861
20	.687	.860	1.064	1.325	1.725	2.086	2.528	2.845
21	.686	.859	1.063	1.323	1.721	2.080	2.518	2.831
22	.686	.858	1.061	1.321	1.717	2.074	2.508	2.819
23	.685	.858	1.060	1.319	1.714	2.069	2.500	2.807
24	.685	.857	1.059	1.318	1.711	2.064	2.492	2.797
25	.684	.856	1.058	1.316	1.708	2.060	2.485	2.787
26	.684	.856	1.058	1.315	1.706	2.056	2.479	2.779
27	.684	.855	1.057	1.314	1.703	2.052	2.473	2.771
28	.683	.855	1.056	1.313	1.701	2.048	2.467	2.763
29	.683	.854	1.055	1.311	1.699	2.045	2.462	2.756
30	.683	.854	1.055	1.310	1.697	2.042	2.457	2.750
31	.683	.854	1.054	1.310	1.696	2.040	2.453	2.744
32	.682	.853	1.054	1.309	1.694	2.037	2.449	2.739
33	.682	.853	1.053	1.308	1.692	2.035	2.445	2.733
34	.682	.852	1.053	1.307	1.691	2.032	2.441	2.728
35	.682	.852	1.052	1.306	1.690	2.030	2.438	2.724
36	.681	.852	1.052	1.306	1.688	2.028	2.434	2.720
37	.681	.852	1.051	1.305	1.687	2.026	2.431	2.716
38	.681	.851	1.051	1.304	1.686	2.024	2.428	2.712
39	.681	.851	1.050	1.304	1.685	2.023	2.426	2.708
40	.681	.851	1.050	1.303	1.684	2.021	2.423	2.705
50	.679	.849	1.047	1.299	1.676	2.009	2.403	2.678
60	.679	.848	1.046	1.296	1.671	2.000	2.390	2.660
70	.678	.847	1.044	1.294	1.667	1.995	2.381	2.648
80	.678	.846	1.043	1.292	1.664	1.990	2.374	2.639
90	.677	.846	1.043	1.291	1.662	1.987	2.368	2.632
100	.677	.845	1.042	1.290	1.660	1.984	2.364	2.626
∞	.674	.842	1.036	1.282	1.645	1.960	2.326	2.576

entists tend to emphasize Type I errors and set alpha to avoid them at some precise low level. Type II errors should also concern us, and they increase as we set alpha lower. For this reason, we do not set alpha to extreme levels such as .00001. In order to protect against Type II errors, we must attend to **beta**, the likelihood of accepting H_0 when it is wrong and **power**, defined as 1 minus beta. Power tells the probability of detecting a true effect, that is, rejecting H_0 when it is false.

One kind of research outcome raises special concern about the power of the test used, that in which we find no difference between groups. When a treatment's impact appears not significant at the chosen alpha, can we safely conclude that the treatment had no value? Or should we view the no difference result as due to Type II error caused by a low power test? Did guarding against Type I error increase our risk of Type II error too much? In part this problem concerns the relative costs of Type I and Type II errors. Consider this problem in business terms (Julnes & Mohr, 1989, p. 630): the costs of remaking parts wrongly judged defective versus the costs of shipping defective parts wrongly thought to be sound (errors of wrongly rejecting or accepting the null hypothesis that the parts are sound). We could measure the monetary costs of these two types of errors and set a decision rule for remaking or shipping parts that cost the least. However, in the social sciences, we do not have a clear metric such as money for accounting the costs of both Type I and II errors (Nagel & Neef, 1977). Instead, we too often attend only to Type I error and limit its risk to the standard alpha of .05. As a result, for small treatment impacts and sample sizes, our research produces many more Type II than Type I errors, sometimes in ratios of 10 or more to 1 (Rosnow & Rosenthal, 1989, Table 1). This bias toward Type II error can, in turn, obscure the true pattern of findings over many studies unless we review them properly (Schmidt, 1992).

Although we cannot rule out Type II errors, we can measure their risk through power analysis. Sadly, authors rarely report the power of their studies. One review found that of 64 articles using statistics in the 1984 volume of the *Journal of Abnormal Psychology*, none gave power estimates (Sedlmeier & Gigerenzer, 1989). The reviewers computed the power of these studies finding that it averaged just .37, down from .46 in the same journal 24 years earlier. One can do a power analysis by referring to standard tables for each type of statistic such as t or F (see Cohen, 1988). Different tables for different levels of alpha display the power values according to the number of subjects in the study and the likely magnitude of the effect. For any given type of test and alpha level, the power increases with the size of the effect and the number of subjects.

Because of this link between sample size and test sensitivity, power analysis can estimate the number of subjects needed to yield a significant finding. Research plan-

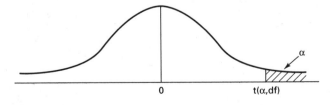

Figure 8–3 Area α under the upper tail of the t distribution for degrees of freedom (*df*) defines critical value of t.

ners want to know the smallest sample that will provide a fair test of their prediction. A no difference finding will warrant interest only if the test had sufficient power to detect the likely effect. Funders of research projects want to avoid granting scarce funds for studies that will miss socially significant effects due to Type II error. Finding more sensitive statistics offers one way of adding power to a study. However, researchers must choose tests that meet the assumptions of the study's data. Thus, a test with low power may appear in a study because it seems the best of those fitting the data. As a result, the researcher's best option to raise the study's power involves increasing sample size. Standard tables exist that give the number of subjects needed for chosen levels of power given different effect sizes and alpha levels (Kraemer & Thiemann, 1987; Lipsey, 1990). For example, suppose you planned to use a *t* test to assess the difference between two groups in an experiment. Assuming you wanted power equal to .80, a commonly used level in such analyses, and set alpha to the usual level of .05, how many subjects would you need? The answer depends on the size of the effect that you find, that is, the difference between the group means divided by the standard deviation. You could pick an effect size based on pilot research. Cohen defines three effect size levels: .2 or small, .5 or medium, and .8 or large. Your study would require only 26 subjects for the large effect size, but 64 for the medium and 393 for the small (see Table 2 of Cohen, 1992).

PROBLEMS OF INFERENTIAL STATISTICS

Math Avoidance

An Obstacle to Learning.   How did you feel as you read the foregoing material on statistics? Many students feel anxious when working with math symbols or statistical concepts. Some believe that they cannot grasp such concepts and admit defeat before even trying to learn. In extreme cases, students seem to switch off their minds and freeze up in the presence of math symbols. If you feel comfortable with statistics, you can skip ahead to the next section. But if the labels "math-anxious" or "math-phobic" fit you, you should read this section.

Math anxiety appears as a continuum, with different people having varying levels of symptoms. Perhaps the most harmful symptom of math anxiety is math avoidance, the flight from settings that involve learning or showing math skills. Escaping classroom situations in which math teachers ask hard questions may serve the short-run goal of blocking fear. Sadly, the long-run costs of math avoidance prove very high. The term **vocational filter** describes the process of people taking themselves out of contention for certain careers or job promotions by avoiding the math skills required for the best jobs.

Do some of the following statements describe you?

I have avoided or postponed taking courses that involve math or statistics.
Because I know I cannot do math, I am trying to find a major or a career that does not require math skills.
When I read assignments that have statistics in them, I get bogged down and have to skip to other sections where the authors tell me what the statistics meant.

If these statements describe you, you probably are not looking forward to the parts of this text that use math symbols. For more details on this problem, consult extended works on the origins of math anxiety (Tobias, 1978) and the treatment of math avoidance (Hollander & Proschan, 1984; Tobias, 1987).

Coping with this text.   I wrote this book's sections on statistics with you in mind and included only the minimum statistics necessary to understand research reports. In reading this text, keep four points in mind. First, you have already discovered that this book focuses on the commonsense meaning of everyday statistics. This chapter should enable you to read (rather than skip) the results sections of standard research reports, not to compute exotic statistics.

Second, guard against telling yourself that you cannot learn this material. Math-avoidant people often give themselves silent messages such as "I'll never understand that concept." This kind of prediction can become self-fulfilling and self-defeating. Be aware of using it as an excuse for not learning the material. You have the right to flounder, fail initially, and try again.

Third, you can learn the scant statistical material given here if you take it in small steps. A value such as the mean or the *t* comes from a sequence of simple calculations, no more difficult than a cookie recipe. Sometimes a statistic seems hard because it uses symbols. If you translate the symbols into verbal synonyms, you can decode even the most complex expression.

Finally, in order to relax with statistical expressions you need to work with them. Later in this chapter, you will learn how to translate statistical results into plain language. You should practice doing such translations with the results sections of actual research reports.

Inferential Problems

Although inferential statistics appear in nearly all quantitative studies, when misused they can mislead us. This section addresses the problems of confusing social and statistical significance, using the wrong statistics, increasing Type I error by using many tests, and confusing statistical significance with causation.

Sample Size and Social Significance.   The number of subjects in a study can help decide whether or not the test statistic reaches significance. Small effects can reach significance if the study has a large enough sample. Consider the anxiety study described earlier in this chapter. The biofeedback group (BF) mean (90.3) surpassed the progressive relaxation group (PR) mean (87.5), but not significantly ($t = 1.31$, n.s. or not significant). Now suppose the study had 10 times the number of students. Replacing the BF sample size of 15 with 150 and the PR sample size of 14 with 140 (assuming the same means and standard deviations) has the effect of raising the *t* value ($t = 4.3$). Also, increased sample sizes mean increased degrees of freedom (288 versus 27), such that the same level of statistical significance requires smaller *t* values (see Table 8–2). As a result, this tenfold increase in subjects allows the finding to reach statistical significance ($p < .01$).

Because an increase in the number of subjects can achieve statistical significance, we ought to assess the size of the effect, not just whether it exists. We need to distinguish trivial but statistically significant findings from socially significant findings. **Social significance** depends on the importance of the variables and the practical size of the effect. The relative strength of an effect can often be judged from the data.[3] The social importance of the variables derives from a subjective reading of personal and social values.

Inappropriate Statistics. Inferential statistics serve diverse purposes with varying types of data. Details about such statistics appear in standard texts (for a brief guide to choosing appropriate statistics, see Andrews, Klem, Davidson, O'Malley, & Rodgers, 1981). The improper use of tests or the choice of a poor test (for example, one with low power) can produce false results. All inferential statistics derive from certain assumptions about the data. For example, statistics designed for interval data (which assign ordered values with equal intervals) may not work well for nominal data (which put observations in unordered categories).

Such data assumptions require checks by the analyst that may or may not be reported to the reader. For example, the *t* test assumes that the two samples being compared come from normally distributed populations. In practice, we often do not know whether the population has a normal distribution and rely instead on a check of the sample's distribution. Whether the data approach "close enough" to their assumed shape depends on the subjective judgment of the investigator. Publications often omit reports of such assumption checks. The authors may have chosen the proper statistic for the problem and applied it well with checks on all the relevant assumptions. The reader must trust the skill of the author or the review of the journal editor.

Authors sometimes violate statistical protocol on purpose, trusting that the statistic is **robust**, that is, relatively immune to distortion by the violation of assumptions or relatively free of assumptions. Other times, an author may overlook the need to check the appropriateness of the statistic. Editors review papers sent to their journals to assure, among other things, correct analyses. However, large quality differences exist among journals and, sometimes, among reviewers for a single journal. Thus journals occasionally report statistical analyses inappropriate to the data.

The Alpha and File Drawer Problems. Earlier we defined alpha as the level of risk of Type I error (falsely rejecting the null hypothesis)—usually set at 5 percent or less. If we run a test just once, 5 percent seems a reasonable standard. However, a problem arises if we conduct the test not one time but, say, 100 times. Five of these 100 tests should be in error, that is, reach statistical significance by accident of sampling. The **alpha problem** appears when a researcher computes dozens or hundreds of tests. Computers can generate exhaustive statistical analyses quickly and cheaply. With numerous groups and variables in a study, all possible pairwise comparisons of groups on each variable will produce a great number of tests. If a few tests reach significance at the alpha level of .05, should we consider them to be good evidence for the hypothesis? Or should we view them as the result of chance? In sum, the alpha problem arises when interpreting a few statistically significant results from many tests.

One approach to this problem estimates the number of "significant" findings expected by chance as a gauge for judging the number observed. If the number of significant findings does not exceed that expected by chance, the null hypotheses would be accepted even for the tests that appeared significant. Another approach sets alpha at a more stringent level (for example, .01 or .001 instead of .05). A third method uses statistics that can combine many tests into a single overall test. Analysis of the many possible subtests proceeds only if that single test proves significant initially. One or another of these techniques can usually prevent an alpha problem in a single study with many tests.

The **file drawer problem** presents a more difficult version of the alpha problem. If a single study reports 100 statistical tests, we can still safely judge a few significant findings. But what if each of 100 different researchers computes one statistical test on the same question? We will see only a few of these tests in the published literature. Journals prefer not to publish nonsignificant or negative findings. In one study, three versions of the same manuscript differed only in the statistical significance of the outcome. The "nonsignificant" and "approach significance" versions were three times as likely to be rejected by the 101 reviewers used as subjects (Atkinson, Furlong, & Wampold, 1982). Thus, many reports of negative findings will wind up in file drawers.

The significant findings that we read in journals represent an unknown share of all studies conducted on the issue. Because we do not know about all the negative findings, we cannot judge whether the significant findings are more or less numerous than would be expected by chance. We fear "that journals are filled with the 5% of the studies that show Type I errors, while the file drawers are filled with the 95% of the studies that show nonsignificant results" (Rosenthal, 1979, p. 636). This file drawer problem consists of the unknown risk that our publications report those studies that by chance reject the null hypothesis. At best we can estimate the tolerance of the published literature to filed null results (Rosenthal, 1979).

Misinterpretation and Replication.   Sometimes, a significant finding in one study seems to imply that a replication would yield the same results. Significant findings can give a degree of confidence about the relationship but do not remove the need for replication. On the contrary, the initial findings in support of a linkage often beget efforts to repeat the study. Ideally, other researchers with different biases working with different samples in different times and places will converge on the same finding. Such replications test predictions under various combinations of researcher, subject type, and situation. Such testing differences reduce the chance that the finding resulted from a coincidence of investigator, sample, and environment. The misuse of inferential statistics (for example, as supplanting replication) has so distressed some researchers that they have called for discarding inferential statistics altogether. For examples of this point of view, see Carver (1978) and Morrison and Henkel (1970).

Finally, inferential statistics cannot by themselves prove a causal connection. Statistics receive more weight in the overall interpretation of research than they deserve. Statistics appear precise, elegant, and decisive. Readers unfamiliar with statistics often skip past the baffling results section to the point where the author concludes that the statistical analysis supported some causal linkage. Dazed readers may agree that the statistics confirmed the causal assertion that *A* leads to *B*. In fact, *A* and *B* can have a statistically significant association without *A* causing *B*. Only careful analysis of the method section can support or reject the numerous rivals to the *A*-causes-*B* explanation. Of the many explanations of the observed results, statistics address just one—that the observation is an accident of sampling. Although relevant, this explanation seldom proves to be the most important rival.

USING INFERENTIAL STATISTICS

Because inferential statistics share the same purpose, you can read them all even if certain of their symbols appear unfamiliar. The following steps teach you to interpret any statistics by focusing on the essential parts of their display. Skip the parts that are not crucial, and you can grasp the essence of the finding.

Descriptive statistics usually prove more helpful than inferential statistics in making sense of research reports. The latter only check one rival hypothesis— whether the descriptive findings happened by chance. The authors could give you the statistical inference in plain language, although they usually do not. When these statistics appear in symbolic or numerical form, you can make your own translation into simpler terms.

Steps for Translating Inferential Statistics

1. *Identify the relationship at issue.* Typically, the inferential statistic pertains to an association of two or more variables or the difference between two or more groups on some variable. Remind yourself which are the independent and dependent variables under study. In the earlier example on biofeedback and grades, the inferential statistic *t* deals with the difference between two groups. The contrast between treatment by biofeedback and no treatment serves as the independent or causal variable. The academic performance of each group, the dependent variable, measures the effect if any.

2. *Identify the statistic(s) that describes the relationship.* For an association, you could look for a correlation coefficient such as the Pearson *r*. This measure would tell you the sign, positive or negative, of the association and whether it appeared large or small in size. For a difference between groups, you would look for a measure of central tendency of the two groups, such as their means. These measures would tell which group did better and by how much. In the biofeedback example, you would check the mean of each group (BF mean = 90.33 versus NT mean = 79.83).

3. *Find the inferential statistic for the relationship and its p value.* Did the inferential statistic reach significance at the level set by the author (usually .05)? In most cases you will find this information in an expression, such as $p < .05$, immediately after the inferential statistic. In other cases you will see a footnote symbol such as * referring to the significance level at the bottom of a table.

4. *Express this probability as the likelihood that the observed difference (or association) occurred by chance.* For example, if $p < .01$, one might say that "the risk of obtaining the observed effect by chance was less than 1 percent." Note that this translation makes no reference to the value of t, its formula, or its degrees of freedom. We do not even need the information "t(25) = 4.66" for our translation.

Examples of Common Statistics

This chapter has explored inferential statistics using an example based on the t statistic. Two other inferential statistics appear often—F and χ^2 (chi square). You can understand each in the same simple terms without learning their origins or how to compute them.

χ^2 for Cross-tabulation.   Table 8–3 shows a cross-tabulation of two variables— depression by undesirable life events. The values in each cell of the table tell the number of persons with each combination of life events and depression. This table does not tell which is the independent and which the dependent variable. However, most researchers treat life events as a cause of depression. Whatever the causal direction, this table describes the association of two variables rather than comparing two groups.

In Table 8–3, no statistic such as the Pearson correlation coefficient describes association. However, the inferential statistic χ^2 tells us whether the two variables are related or independent. The table tells the direction and size of the association. The cell for high undesirable life events and high depression has the largest cell count—123. The low undesirable life events and low depression cell also has a high count of 55, the highest in the low depression column. The concentration of cases in these cells suggests a linkage between greater depression and greater undesirable life events. Could this finding occur by accident or sampling error? The note "$p < .01$" in Table 8–3 implies that the risk of such a large value of χ^2, when life events and depression are really independent, falls below one in a hundred. We did not need the facts that $\chi^2 = 51.91$ and that it had 4 degrees of freedom for this interpretation. Of course the researcher would need them in order to look up the significance level in a table of critical chi square values.

Table 8–3   Cross-Tabulation of Depression and Undesirable Life Events

		DEPRESSION		
		Low	*Medium*	*High*
Undesirable Life Events	Low	55	62	57
	Medium	22	22	36
	High	19	33	123
				$\chi^2 = 51.91$
				$df = 4$
				$p < .01$

F in Regression Analysis. Table 8–4 shows the results of a procedure called multiple regression. The name of the dependent variable (grade point average in this case) typically appears in the heading of the table. Regression analysis attempts to explain this variable as a function of the independent variables (listed here in the Predictors column). Regression can measure the association of two variables while controlling (statistically adjusting) for one or more other variables.

Usually two descriptive statistics measure association in regression analysis—the *b* and the *beta* values. The *b* value tells how many units of change in GPA , in our example, to expect for each unit of change in a predictor. The *b* for hours of study per week (= .106) says that GPA will gain a little over a tenth of a grade point for each extra hour of weekly study. The *beta* value gives the same kind of information for the variables in standardized form. The *beta* permits a better comparison of associations within the study because it adjusts for the fact that different predictors have different scales). The *beta* for hours of study (.31) exceeds that of math aptitude (.09), suggesting that study contributes more than math aptitude to grades. However, such descriptive information does not tell us how much confidence we can place in generalizing from the findings in the studied sample to the larger population.

The *F* test tells the significance of effects in regression analysis, although the *t* test may also serve this purpose. Do any of the coefficients in Table 8–4 reach statistical significance? Hours of study per week reaches significance at the .05 level, as shown by the probability values in the column labeled *p*. The *F* for hours of study per week (4.75) has a probability of occurring by chance of .03. The other two variables have *F* values that we would expect by chance more than 5 percent of the time (8 percent and 38 percent respectively), usually considered not significant. We could summarize this analysis as follows: *As hours of study per week increase, GPA increases, and this association would be expected by chance less than 5 percent of the time.* Note that we did not rely on the other information in Table 8–4, such as the constant and R^2 to assess the statistical inference validity of these findings.

Using Computers to Calculate Statistics

Computers can perform large numbers of simple calculations very quickly. Because complex statistics consist of many simple arithmetic steps, researchers rely on computers for both simple tests and complex statistics involving many variables or subjects. A program for computing statistics consists of a series of commands organized to

Table 8–4 Prediction of Grade Point Average by Multiple Regression

Predictors	b	Beta	F	p
Hours of study per week	.106	.31	4.75	.03
Verbal aptitude	.003	.23	3.75	.08
Math aptitude	.001	.09	1.85	.38
(Constant = -1.02)				
R^2 = .27				

produce the desired result when applied to any set of input data. The user needs to know how to input the data, request the desired program, and read the output.

For ease in applying various analyses to the same data set, packages group together programs designed to compute many different tests. One of the most widely used, easy to operate, and complete packages is the Statistical Package for the Social Sciences or SPSS (Meyer, 1993). You may also encounter packages such as BMDP, SYSTAT, and SAS, all designed along similar lines. Once you define and label data files in the format required by the package, you can easily apply any of its programs to the data. The computation of even very elaborate statistics may require no more commands than naming the desired test. Many of these packager have versions that work well on personal as well as on mainframe computers (Cozby, 1984).

SUMMARY

This chapter has discussed the important but narrow function of inferential statistics. Descriptive statistics can tell whether two variables are related to each other in a sample, for example, the difference between experimental and control group means. But deciding that such a sample relationship holds in a population requires inferential statistics. We will more likely make this inference if the observed effect appears large compared to the variability among the subjects.

Inferential statistics both summarize the ratio of effect to variability and have known probability distributions. The risk of making a Type I error (falsely rejecting the null hypothesis of no relationship) can be limited to some arbitrary, small level called alpha—usually set at 5 percent. If the probability of the observed value of the inferential statistic falls below the alpha, we say the relationship reaches statistical significance. Tables give the critical values of an inferential statistic for varying levels of alpha and degrees of freedom.

The risk of Type II error (falsely accepting the null hypothesis) also exists and requires attention to the power of the statistical test. Power analysis draws increasing attention both to interpret findings of no difference and to plan the best sample size for future studies.

Inferential statistics have numerous problems. Relatively weak, socially insignificant results can reach statistical significance if the sample is large enough. Inferential statistics depend on certain assumptions that, when violated, cast doubt on the results, although some tests appear to be relatively robust or immune to such violations. The risk of Type I errors increases when many statistical tests are run (alpha problem) and when negative findings are ignored (file drawer problem). Ultimately, only replication can confirm that sample results generalize to other samples from the population.

EXERCISES

Many students miss important information in research reports when they skip results sections that contain statistics. Fortunately, you can make sense out of apparently complicated statistics. Following the brief step-by-step guide presented in this chapter, try your hand at interpreting some inferential statistics.

1. Find a popular media report (for example, from a newspaper) of research based on a sample. Determine whether an inferential statistic appeared in the report (typically not). If not state the rival or null hypotheses that an inferential statistic could check.

2. Find a research report in a professional journal that uses an inferential statistic with which you are acquainted (such as the t, χ^2 or F from this chapter). A p value should accompany it. Translate the p value into ordinary language, as illustrated in this chapter.

KEY TERMS

Alpha	**Null hypothesis**
Alpha problem	**p**
Beta	**Power**
Central tendency	**Probability distribution**
Critical values	**Robust**
Degrees of freedom	**Social significance**
Descriptive statistics	**Statistical inference validity**
Effect to variability ratio	**Statistical signficance**
File drawer problem	**Type I error**
Frequency distribution	**Type II error**
Inferential statistics	**Variability**
Math anxiety	**Vocational filter**

NOTES

1.

$$\text{variability of two groups} = \sqrt{\frac{SD^2 \text{ group BF}}{N \text{ group BF}} + \frac{SD^2 \text{ group NT}}{N \text{ group NT}}} \qquad t = \frac{90.3 - 79.8}{\sqrt{5^2/15 + 6.3^2/12}} = \frac{10.5}{\sqrt{5}}$$

= 4.7. The difference between 4.7 and 4.66 is due to rounding.

2. The method pictured in Figure 8–3 describes the one-tailed t test. This test assumes that the researcher has predicted the group that will have the larger mean and knows in which tail of the distribution the critical value of t will fall. When either group could have the larger mean, the resulting t value could have either a positive or a negative sign. In this case, you would use a different approach called the two-tailed test because the critical value could fall in either tail of the t distribution. With alpha at .05, the total risk of making a Type I error divides evenly in the two tails, .025 in the upper end and .025 in the lower end. Therefore, to find the critical value for a .05 two-tail test, you would look in the column headed by .025 in Table 8–2. The two-tail test will always prove more conservative because it requires a greater critical value of t (2.060 versus 1.708 in our example with 25 degrees of freedom).

3. For example, in correlational research, the strength of relationships can be described by squaring the correlation coefficient. If two variables are correlated (for example, $r = .5$), the square of this value $.5^2 = .5 \times .5 = .25$, says that 25 percent of the variability in one variable is accounted for by the other. This also means that 75 percent (100 percent - 25 percent) of the variability is left unexplained. A correlation such as $r = .1$ could reach significance if there were sufficient subjects (at least 400), but such a small correlation carries little information. When .1 is squared ($.1^2 = .1 \times .1 = .01$), we discover that one variable accounts for just 1 percent of the variation in the other. Obviously, to understand the other 99 percent we need further research. If the variable in question had critical importance (for example, the incidence of cancer or suicide), explaining even 1 percent of the variation might justify the effort involved. For other ways of displaying effect magnitude, see Rosenthal & Rubin, 1982).

❧ 9 ❧

Designing Research for Internal Validity

INTRODUCTION TO DESIGN

A Natural Experiment

Three Mile Island. "On Wednesday, March 28, 1979, 36 seconds after the hour of 4 A.M., several water pumps stopped working in the Unit 2 nuclear power plant on Three Mile Island (TMI). [This event] escalated into the worst crisis yet experienced by the nation's nuclear power industry" (Kasl, Chisholm, & Eskenazi, 1981a, p. 472, quoting the Report of the President's Commission on the Accident at Three Mile Island).

These words appear in a study that related the TMI incident to the well-being of nuclear workers. Since no one foresaw this event, Kasl and his colleagues had to design and conduct their study after the fact. Without pretest data, the researchers could not measure health and mood changes in nuclear workers from the TMI plant.

However, the scholars could compare the TMI workers with workers at a distant nuclear plant called Peach Bottom (PB). About 61 percent of the workers from each plant joined the study. They answered a questionnaire that measured perceptions, behavioral reactions, and work-related attitudes (Kasl et al., 1981a) and job tension, health symptoms, and stress (Kasl, Chisholm, & Eskenazi, 1981b).

The Design. The authors called their design a "static-group comparison" (following Campbell & Stanley, 1963) or a "one-shot survey" and considered it rather weak. They found that the TMI workers had more periods of anger, worry, and physical symptoms than their PB counterparts. Did the TMI event cause this difference? The design does not rule out the rival view that the TMI and PB workers differed before March 1979. Without pretest measures from before the TMI incident, we have no evidence showing the two groups to be equal. One must consider the chance that the workers somehow selected themselves differently into the TMI and PB plants. The authors doubt this because "it is difficult to think of processes or variables (other than residential distance) which could select one type of worker into the TMI ranks and another type into PB ranks" (Kasl et al., p. 475).

However, the authors do report some differences between the two groups that must have existed before the accident. The plant at Peach Bottom predated the one at Three Mile Island. Thus, the PB supervisors have more seniority and enjoy higher incomes than the TMI supervisors. Also, the TMI group had a higher percentage of females than the PB group.

The authors handled known differences between the groups (such as gender) by studying separate subgroups (such as males and females). This approch produced few changes from the initial results for the whole sample. For example, females tend to report more such symptoms than males (for example, Dooley, Catalano, & Rook, 1988). As a result of this sex bias, greater TMI symptom scores may come from that group's greater proportion of high–symptom-reporting females. Controlling for sex, however, the TMI females reported more symptoms than the PB females. Thus the sex difference between TMI and PB does not explain the overall results. The risk remains, however, that some other known difference between the groups might explain the findings.

This study shows all of the elements that make up research design:

1. Number of groups (TMI versus PB)
2. Number and timing of the experiences (such as the TMI incident)
3. Number and timing of the measures (such as stress)
4. Information on the equivalence of the groups before the intervention

Together, these aspects of a study decide the risk that rival hypotheses can explain the study's outcome. The major weakness of the TMI study stems from the possible pretest difference of the groups.

Internal Validity and Design Types

The Continuum of Internal Validity.   Validity refers to the truth of claims. For example, one may claim that variable A causes variable B. **Internal validity** refers to the truthfulness of such claims. This kind of validity pertains to the causal linkage of variables that are internal to or included in the design.

Some research designs can provide convincing support for causal claims. Others such as the type employed in the Three Mile Island study, leave us less certain. Thus research designs range along a continuum of internal validity. Designs that permit high confidence in causal inference possess high internal validity. Those that allow many plausible rival explanations have low internal validity.

Consider a metaphor. You may hear a research design called "tight" as opposed to "leaky." A tight bucket has few or no holes in it, and the water cannot leak out. A tight research design has high internal validity, because it has few holes or rival explanations. As Figure 9–1 illustrates, internal validity increases as "unplugged" rival explanations become fewer and less likely.

As named below the arrows of Figure 9–1, different research designs vary in their ability to reduce threats to internal validity. We will review these threats to internal validity later in this chapter. First, we distinguish the major types of designs.

Correlational Versus Experimental Designs.   Two of the requirements for deciding that A causes B include (1) that A and B are associated and (2) that A happens

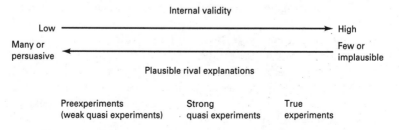

Figure 9–1   Continuum of internal validity as a function of plausible rival explanation.

before *B*. The design of the TMI study satisfied these two conditions. The finding of more symptoms in the TMI than in the PB respondents established association. Measuring symptoms after the TMI incident established temporal precedence of the causal variable.

However, some designs may meet only the association condition. One can find whether two variables co-vary simply by measuring them both at the same time. For example, if you want to find whether or not time spent studying co-varies with grades, you could ask each student in your class to report grade point average and estimated average weekly study hours. Such a study has a **correlational design**, that is, one that measures the independent variable rather than setting it. Chapter 12 explores correlational designs based on quantitative measures in more detail. Purely observational research (that is, without any interventions by the researcher) may also use nonquantitative methods as discussed in Chapter 13.

The second condition for causality requires timing the measures of the dependent variable so that they occur after the presumed cause. We can do this either by making our observation after an unplanned event such as a nuclear plant mishap or by making the presumed cause occur before the observation. The use of a distinct event or intervention as the independent variable constitutes an **experimental design**. Experimental design thus can remove any doubt as to the order of "cause" and "effect."

Within and Between Designs—Preexperimental Types. The term **preexperiments** applies to experimental designs with the least internal validity. Although crude and largely avoided (Campbell & Stanley, 1963), these designs illustrate the kinds of rival explanations that threaten experiments generally. Like stronger types of experimental designs, preexperiments fall into two different kinds: within-subjects and between-subjects.

One sort of preexperiment, the single-group, pretest–posttest design, measures one group at two times, before and after the intervention. Any effect appears within the subjects or group as a change between the pre and post measures, the defining trait of **within-subjects design**. Such single-group designs have a major weakness—the threat of passing time. For example, natural maturation may explain any change. The members of the group may also respond to historical events that happen between pretest and posttest but are unrelated to the study. Observed change may also stem from differences in the conduct of the pretests and posttests rather than from the intervention under study.

To protect against such time-related rival explanations, one could add a comparison group. The TMI post-only, control group preexperiment provides the simplest example of such an approach. Instead of comparing the pretest with the posttest within one group, we compare the posttest of the treated group with that of an untreated group. Measuring the effect as the difference between groups marks this as a **between-subjects design**. Assuming both groups experienced the same time-related influences, the comparison group feature should protect this design from the rival explanations that threaten the within-subject design.

Despite avoiding some threats, the two-group, post-only approach risks threats due to other differences between the two groups, as we saw in the TMI example. Unless the groups differ only on the experimental treatment, we cannot be sure that it alone explains all of the differences observed later. Thus, the untreated group in this post-only preexperiment controls for time-related threats but introduces new threats having to do with group differences.

Although we have discussed designs that manipulate the causal variable either within subjects or between subjects, a design could employ both approaches. In such **mixed designs**, the effect of the independent variable may differ depending on whether we study the within-subjects' or between-subjects' contrast (Erlebacher, 1977).

Quasi Experiments and True Experiments. As Figure 9–1 indicates, two classes of experimental designs can provide better internal validity than preexperimental designs: quasi experiments and true experiments. In a **quasi-experimental design**, the experimenter has more control than in preexperiments. The researcher can collect more data either by scheduling more observations or finding more existing measures. For example, interrupted time-series quasi experiments improve on the one-group, pretest–posttest preexperiment by including more measuring points, both before and after the experimental event. However, in quasi experiments, researchers lack complete control of the situation. In some cases, they cannot arrange for a comparison group. Or, if they can arrange such a group, they cannot assign subjects in a way that makes them comparable before the treatment begins.

Quasi-experimental designs come in various forms depending on the number of groups and the timing of interventions and observations. Chapter 11 describes these designs and their most common threats in more detail. One kind of quasi-experimental design served in another study of the Three Mile Island community (Gatchel, Schaeffer, & Baum, 1985). Researchers took advantage of a planned venting of radioactive gas from the reactor damaged in the TMI accident. Residents of two areas took a battery of measures at four points in time—3 to 5 days before the venting, after venting had continued for 7 days, 3 to 5 days after venting concluded, and finally, 6 weeks after venting concluded. One group came from the community around TMI in Pennsylvania; and the other, demographically matched, came from Frederick, Maryland, about 80 miles away. This design improved on the one used by Kasl et al. (1981a) by measuring the two groups before the experimental event. The later study found that the TMI group reported more psychological symptoms than the Frederick group after the venting but that this difference existed *before* the venting as well. Without the crucial pretests, the posttest results might have led to a wrong conclusion about the impact of the venting.

Despite such improvements, most quasi experiments protect against one threat to internal validity while risking another. A **true experiment** controls for both time-related and group-related threats. Two features mark true experiments—two or more differently treated groups and random assignment to these groups. These features require that the researchers have control over the experimental treatment and the power to place subjects in groups.

True experiments employ both treated and control groups to deal with time-related rival explanations. A **control group** reflects changes other than those due to the treatment that occur during the time of the study. Such changes include effects of outside events, maturation by the subjects, changes in measures, and impacts of any pretests. The term *control* does not mean preventing such effects as outside events or maturation from happening. A control group serves its purpose by detecting such effects. By analogy, in earlier eras, coal miners used caged birds to warn them of odorless, poison gas. A dead or dying bird alerted the miners to their danger. Similarly, a control group can warn of time-related causes of change observed in the treated group.

True experiments control for group-related differences by giving every subject an equal chance of being assigned to any group. You could try to equalize research groups by matching the subjects first, but random assignment serves this purpose better. Chapter 10 explores various true experimental designs and problems with these designs other than threats to internal validity. The next section considers in more detail the main threats to internal validity and the main ways of "plugging" them.

THREATS TO INTERNAL VALIDITY AND THEIR CONTROL

Research designs try to raise our confidence that the independent variable, rather than some other factor, causes the observed change in the dependent variable. If we find no association between the independent and dependent variables, we need not worry about internal validity. Without covariation, the two variables cannot have a causal link. If these variables co-vary, we must consider each of the possible explanations—reverse causation and the threats of time, group, and mortality.

Reverse Causation

Correlational designs that measure all variables at the same time risk the threat of **reverse causation**. Such designs cannot tell us whether the presumed cause came before or after the presumed effect. For example, we might measure self-reported life events and self-reported symptoms of depression at the same time. Does their correlation mean that life events cause depression or that depressed people remember more life events? The problem of reverse causation requires special care in correlational designs as discussed in Chapter 12.

Experimental designs deal with reverse causation by measuring the dependent variable after fixing the independent variable. In experiments, we often create an artificial event as the independent variable. If we could solve the ethical problems, we might give false feedback on a test, randomly telling some students that they passed and others that they failed. Any changes in self-reported depression could not explain the good or bad grades. Only one causal direction seems plausible in this case, from the prior experimental event to the later measure. However, settling causal direction only begins our concerns about internal validity.

Time, Group, and Mortality Threats

After showing association and cause before effect, the third major requirement for causal inference consists of ruling out any other plausible explanation. Protective features in research design can protect against two types of rival explanations, group and time threats. Unfortunately, design elements do not assure protection against a third potential rival, mortality.

Time Threats. **Time threats** consist of changes in the outcome variable, measured over time within subjects, because of factors other than the independent variable. Control groups protect against four time threats—history, reactivity, maturation, and instrumentation—by warning of their presence. In addition, one or more other actions can also control each of these time threats.

We will define the four time threats briefly here and in more detail in Chapter 11 on quasi-experimental design:

1. History refers to the threat that some event unrelated and external to the study, caused the observed change.
2. Test reactivity threatens pretest–posttest studies in which a reaction to the pretest causes the observed change in the outcome variable.
3. Maturation poses a threat when the subjects' normal development causes the observed changes.
4. Instrumentation appears when observed changes in the dependent variable derive from shifts in the way measures are collected.

The first three threats involve real changes that might come from causes other than the experimental manipulation. In contrast, instrumentation involves apparent rather than real changes.

Other procedures, besides using a control group, can prevent each of these time threats. The threats of history and maturation depend on the time between measurement sessions and increase as longer time spans permit more events or maturation to occur. Putting the experimental event and the measures together in one session, reducing the time between them nearly to zero, does away with the threats of history and maturation. Standardizing and carefully monitoring the measurement procedures can reduce the instrumentation threat. Disguising the purpose of the pretest can reduce pretest reactivity, and dropping the pretest eliminates this threat entirely.

Two other time-related threats differ from these four in that a comparison group does not control them. One of these threats, regression to the mean, comes from the tendency of scores from unreliable measures to move toward the mean on retest. This problem can affect one-group studies that select subjects for their extreme scores on the pretest measure of the dependent variable. In this case, change from pretest to posttest might stem from regression, not the intervention. Adding a comparison group will not solve this problem unless the comparison group has the same likelihood to regress toward the mean on the posttest. For this reason, we will consider regression to the mean as a group threat to internal validity. Using highly reliable measures will also reduce this threat (see Chapter 5 for more on reliability and regression toward the mean). To eliminate this problem entirely, avoid selecting subjects on the basis of extreme scores. The other time-related threat not solved by a comparison group is mortality, as discussed later in this chapter.

Group Threats.   **Group threats** include rival explanations based on differences between groups other than the experimental differences created by the researcher. Making groups equivalent before the experimental manipulation protects against group threats. **Random assignment** of subjects to groups offers the best way of assuring equivalence of two or more groups on both measured and unmeasured variables. Random assignment means placing subjects in groups such that the subjects all have equal chances of joining each group. We will define the three group threats briefly here and in more detail in Chapter 11: (1) regression toward the mean, (2) selection, and (3) selection-by-time interactions.

Regression toward the mean threatens multigroup studies when subjects with extreme scores are consistently assigned to different groups, for example, highs in one group and lows in another. Suppose, in testing a new treatment, you select a group of patients for their extremely high scores on a measure of their symptoms. For comparison, you might consider using a group of patients who do not need the treatment because they test low on the symptoms. We would expect the treated group to regress toward the mean, that is, toward a more healthful score to the extent that the measure had poor reliability. For the same reason, the low symptom control group might show a rise in symptoms on retest. Such regression effects would suggest that the new treatment worked even if it did not. But had you divided the high symptom group randomly into treated and untreated groups, any regression to the mean should occur at about the same rate in both groups. As a result, we can credit the treatment for any difference observed between the groups.

Selection explains posttest differences as a function of pretest differences. This threat arises when groups differ before the experimental intervention. The *selection-by-time interaction* threat occurs when observed differences between pretests and posttests stem from the combination of time and prior group differences. Suppose two groups differ in age. One is about to embark on a growth spurt whereas the other has already gone through that growth phase or will not enter that phase for some time yet. If the growth spurt group receives the experimental treatment, shall we credit the treatment or the growth spurt?

Random assignment in true experiments differs from **random sampling**, a procedure used in survey research. Sampling refers to the process of picking a subset of people from a larger group or population. Assignment refers to dividing an already selected sample into two or more groups (for example, experimental versus control). The term *random*, however, has the same meaning in both cases; that is, each individual has an equal chance of being assigned or of being sampled.

Random assignment usually avoids systematic differences between groups but may sometimes fail. **Matching** offers another approach to making groups comparable. In matching for a two-group study, one divides the sample into pairs of people similar on such criteria as sex, age, socioeconomic status, and pretest scores. Assigning one person of each pair to each group assures that the groups will appear about equal on all the criteria used in the matching (for example, the same proportions of males and females). At first glance, matching seems a more certain method of equalizing groups than does random assignment. But matching assures equivalence only on the measures used in matching. Nonrandom assignment of one member of a matched pair to the experimental rather than the control group could cause a selection problem. For example, after matching on sex and age, a nutrition researcher might assign the more sickly looking child of each pair to an experimental vitamin diet in the hope of helping the sick children. No matter how many criteria are taken into account, matching may fail to equalize on some important variable not considered by the researcher. Random assignment has the advantage of avoiding systematic groupings on all criteria, including those neither measured nor thought of. One can get the benefit of both random assignment and matching by combining them. After creating matched pairs, one could make the assignment to groups by some random process (for example, flipping a fair coin).

Mortality: Construct or Internal Validity.   **Mortality** refers to the loss of subjects from a study because of death (literal mortality) or any other reason such as refusal to cooperate or change of residence. Such attrition can affect a single-group study if dropping out of the study is related to the dependent measure. In that case, comparing the pretest mean for the whole group with the posttest mean of the survivors may wrongly give the appearance of change. Consider a drug treatment program with a high dropout rate. Continuing patients at posttest look like successes, much better than the average incoming patient at pretest. But the drug program failed to "cure" a high proportion of admitted patients. It only selected or "creamed" the easiest, most motivated patients while letting go of the problem cases.

Adding a control group will not solve the mortality problem if the treatment somehow provokes the dropping out. The treatment will appear effective when compared to the control group because the treatment may drive out more of the problem cases than does nontreatment. In general, when "leavers" differ on the pretest measure from the "stayers," we must question any between-group differences. Mortality can threaten any design that lasts long enough to have dropouts. As a result, one solution keeps the study short enough to avoid losing subjects. This type of control cannot serve many of the most interesting research questions that require more than brief or one-shot designs. In longer studies, you will have to monitor mortality carefully. Because neither control groups nor random assignment prevents mortality, this validity threat differs from the group and time threats to internal validity.

We might better think of mortality as a threat to measurement construct validity. Consider the earlier example of "creaming" the best patients in the evaluation of a drug program. The posttest mean for the remaining patients fails to reflect the true posttest score of all entering patients. To have more confidence in any resulting findings about the program's effectiveness, we would need to improve the measurement of the improvement construct. To achieve a more valid measure, we might follow up the dropouts as well as the participants still in the program. Thus, although mortality often appears as a problem in internal validity, we can be better handle it as a problem in measurement.

Table 9–1 summarizes the major problems in internal validity—reverse causation, time, and group threats—and notes alternative control procedures for each.

Table 9–1 Threats to Internal Validity and Their Control

Threats	Design Control	Other Control
Reverse Causation	Intervention prior to posttest	
Time Threats to Within Designs		
History	Control group	Limit intersession period
Maturation	Control group	Limit intersession period; avoid rapidly maturing samples
Instrumentation	Control group	Standardize
Reactivity	Control group, omission of pretest	Disguise pretest; use unobtrusive pretest
Group Threats to Between Designs		
Selection (confounding)	Random assignment	Check pretest equivalence
Regression	Random assignment	Use reliable measures; avoid grouping on extreme scores
Selection-by-time	Random assignment	Check pretest equivalence; apply controls for time threats

DIAGRAMMING DESIGNS

Rationale

Why Diagrams? Whether you read others' research reports or plan your own studies, you will need to appraise designs. You may want to categorize designs as being of one type or another: correlational, true experimental, preexperimental, or quasi-experimental. Beyond applying such broad labels, you will need to identify designs as falling in certain subtypes of these larger groupings. For example, it matters whether a preexperimental design has one group or two groups. The first type risks time threats, and the other risks group threats. Different subtypes of designs have more or less internal validity. Recognizing a design's type gives you more than just a handy name to call it. It also tells which threats to consider. Diagramming makes it easier to identify a research design and, in turn, its chief strengths and weaknesses.

Symbols. To diagram a design means boiling down a study to its basic elements. To aid this process, design diagrams employ just three symbols. We could symbolize the three elements in different ways, but these symbols follow the nearly standard approach of Campbell and Stanley (1963).

O stands for observation or measure
X stands for experimental intervention or manipulation
R stands for random assignment to groups

These three symbols, used together, tell us the type and vulnerability of the study.

How many differently treated groups or treatment conditions does the study have? Each differently treated group appears as a separate line of Xs and Os, representing different treatment and measurement points. Subjects may experience the conditions of the study individually or together with other subjects. The diagram tells only how many different types of experiences occur in the study. For example, in a group dynamics study, one could have ten sets of eight subjects. If five sets received one kind of instruction and the other five received no instruction, how many design groups would you have? You might be tempted to say ten, because the subjects worked in ten sets. But from the design perspective, only two different conditions (that is, with or without the instruction) exist. Therefore, this study's diagram would show just two different lines of symbols. You would consider each eight-person set a design group only if you thought of it as an experimentally different condition (for example, different group leaders).

When did the researcher collect the measures (O)? This step does not refer to the number of tests or items collected at any time. Rather, it refers to when, relative to the experimental manipulation (X), the subject responded to the measures. Suppose a researcher used 10 tests at the first session, carried out the intervention in the second session, and collected 20 more tests in the third session. You would not put 10 Os at time 1 and 20 Os at time 3. Rather, you would focus on how many time points have measures. Thus you would put one O at time 1 (representing 10 scales) and another O at time 3 (representing 20 scales): $O X O$.

What groups have interventions and what groups do not? An X indicates that the group has received an experimental manipulation. A single X might represent a complex series of treatments lasting weeks. The absence of an X indicates that the group has received no treatment from the researcher, that is, a no treatment control group. Studies need not employ a no treatment control group nor have only two groups. Complex studies may use more than one kind of intervention and require more than two groups. Differently treated groups may appear as Xs with different subscripts. For example, X_1 might reflect treatment with a vitamin pill of minimum dosage, and X_2 might indicate treatment with a vitamin pill of a larger dosage. A single X with more than one subscript could also stand for a combined treatment. For example, X_{VR} could signify a health program using both vitamin supplements (V) and running (R). You may use multiple Xs to show the timing of different interventions in the same group. For example, X_1X_{10} could reflect two successive treatments, the first with a standard dosage, and the second with 10 times the usual dosage.

Did the researcher use random assignment to create the groups? An R indicates that all subjects had an equal chance of assignment to each of the groups. These subjects came from some larger pool of subjects, available for this study. The presence of the R does not imply that this pool resulted from random sampling. Rather, the R implies that however biased a sample this pool may be, it was divided randomly into each design group or condition. Typically, laboratory studies draw on biased (that is, not randomly chosen) samples such as college student volunteers. Once such a pool of people has been identified, however, random assignment does ensure that each group resembles every other group in the study. In the absence of an R, the groups may have been equalized by some other method such as matching. But no method other than random assignment will qualify the study as a true experiment. For clarity, a diagram might have lines drawn from the *R* to each group to indicate precisely the groups randomly composed. You may also see a dotted line separating those groups that are randomly assigned from other groups drawn from a different sample.

In sum, the three symbols *O*, *X*, and *R* can tell the number of design groups, the number and timing of measurement points, the number and group assignment of different interventions, and the random assignment of subjects to groups. These symbols do not tell how many subjects joined the study, whether they worked individually or in clusters, how many tests they took at each measurement point, the exact intervention, or how biased the subject was. Although important, these pieces of information do not appear in the diagram in order to focus on the basic parts of the research design.

Diagramming Different Types of Designs

Independent and Dependent Variables in Correlational Designs.   By hypothesis from some theory, one variable causes another variable. We call the presumed effect the dependent variable. We expect that its value depends on the level of the causal variable. We always observe the dependent variable, never manipulate it. As a result, we always use some measure, symbolized with an *O*, to represent the dependent variable. We call the presumed cause the independent variable. We expect its value to be independent of the outcome variable. We may either observe (*O*) or manipulate (*X*) the independent variable.

Because correlational studies do not have experimental interventions, *X* never appears in their design diagrams. Having no manipulation, correlational designs need no control group. In such studies, the researcher measures not only the dependent but also the independent variables. The diagram of a one-shot correlational study appears as a single *O*, showing that all subjects gave their responses at one time point.

Sometimes correlational designs seem to have multiple groups. For example, a researcher may divide a group of subjects on some personal variable such as sex. The analyst may even describe the "effect" of sex as the difference between males and females on some outcome variable. Avoid the trap of using two *O*s in this case, each on a different line and representing one gender group. In fact, this study has no difference between the two sex groups in their treatment. You should diagram this study with a single *O*. With no experimental event in the study, no *X* should appear in its diagram. Only the presence of differently treated groups justifies using multiple groups in the diagram. That the researcher analyzes the data by groups based on sex, age, or other prior characteristics does not change the study's design.

If the same untreated group has measures at two or more time points, it becomes a panel design and we call the group a **panel**. Test–retest reliability studies, in which respondents take the same test(s) twice, often rely on the panel design. To diagram a panel design, simply place two *O*s on the same line: *O O*.

Independent and Dependent Variables in Experimental Designs.   The experimenter either manipulates the independent variable or takes advantage of a natural event. Usually, the researcher defines the independent variable as the contrast between two or more experiences. Often, the independent variable has two levels—treatment or no treatment. But treatments can have more than two on or off levels. They may involve several dosage levels. For example, the researcher might select three levels of a drug (perhaps, 0, 1, and 2 milligrams) or four levels of a training procedure (perhaps 0, 2, 5, and 10 hours of instruction). In such cases, the researcher has *fixed* the independent variable at the selected levels.

An experimental independent variable has the special property of being clearly independent of the measured dependent variable. That is, the experimental variable can cause but cannot be caused by the outcome variable or something correlated with it. In the clearest case, the experimenter creates the independent variable, making it occur before the dependent variable is measured. Less clearly, in the case of natural experiments, the experimental variable comes not from the researcher but from the unplanned, sometimes unexpected, flow of events. At minimum such objective, natural "interventions" must appear prior to the measurement of the outcome variable. An event such as a tornado would qualify as being independent of subsequent measures of distress.

Contrast such experimental independent variables with the measured "independent" variables used in correlational designs. For example, a common way of studying the effect of stress asks subjects to recall their recent life events. One survey found that subjects who reported more economic life events such as job loss also admitted more symptoms such as anxiety and depression even after adjusting for other kinds of life events such as divorce (Dooley, Catalano, & Rook, 1988). In this case, the stress variable appears as "independent" only by hypothesis or assumption. It would not qualify as an experimental independent variable since the recall of personal events might depend on, not cause, the level of symptoms. Perhaps feeling depressed or anxious causes people to try harder to recall recent events in order to explain their problems. One could also study the concept of economic stress using a natural experimental design. In such a study, researchers found that a factory was about to close and arranged to study the symptoms of the workers before and after (Kasl & Cobb, 1979). Here, the plant closing, much like a natural disaster, serves as an objective experimental independent variable.

Sometimes, studies include both types of independent variables—experimental and measured. A study of stress and the common cold illustrates this combination (Cohen, Tyrell, & Smith, 1991). First, the researchers asked 394 healthy subjects to report their recent stress on such measures as life event counts. Next, the subjects received nasal drops with either a cold virus or a sterile saline solution. Finally, the subjects were quarantined and monitored for signs of infection. Giving subjects different nasal drops clearly served as an experimental independent variable. In contrast, the subjects' perceived stress scores served as a measured independent variable of the type used in correlational studies. As predicted, in subjects exposed to a cold virus, the rates of infections increased with the degree of self-reported stress at pretest. Why can we not regard such a life event measure as a natural experimental variable such as a nuclear accident or volcano? Despite being measured before the virus exposure, life event stress might not be independent of the disease process. For example, the authors wondered whether some other factor might link life event stress and risk of getting a cold. For this reason, they adjusted their findings for smoking, alcohol consumption, exercise, diet, sleep, white-cell counts, and such personality variables as self-esteem. Although none of these variables affected the results, the chance remains that some other unmeasured factor connects the tendencies to catch a cold and to have or recall stressful life events. In sum personal measures do not have the key ingredient possessed by objective changes in the environment (such as a plant closure or earthquake)—clear independence of the outcome measure.

Because of the special nature of the experimental independent variable, it has its own symbol X. Thus the one-group, pretest–posttest preexperimental design has the following diagram: $O \ X \ O$. With two groups, as in the posttest-only, two-group preexperiment (for example, the TMI study), the design requires two lines, one for each group:

$$XO$$
$$O$$

Any claim about the impact of X requires at least two measures, one showing the state of affairs after the X and one for the state of affairs prior to or in the absence of the X. The two preexperimental designs accomplish this either by the contrast of pretest and posttests in one group or by the contrast of posttests in the two-group case. A single measure design as $X \ O$ does not permit such a contrast and, therefore, has no use.

True Experiments and Group Equalization.   True experiments offer the highest internal validity of all the designs. True experiments have both multiple groups (to control for time threats) and group equivalence (to control for group threats). One simple true experiment, the pretest–posttest, control group design has the following diagram

$$O \ X \ O$$
$$R$$
$$O \quad O$$

The R symbolizes that the two groups were randomly assigned from the same pool of subjects. Any difference between the groups in the posttest measures should come from the treatment X, not from preexisting differences. This design permits the comparison not only of the two groups on posttest (between-subjects) but also within each group between pre- and posttest (within-subjects). True experiments always permit between-subjects tests, because they must have multiple groups. But they do not necessarily provide for within-subjects tests. Because random assignment makes groups comparable, true experiments do not require pretests. The post-only control group design thus provides no way to measure change within subjects:

$$X \ O$$
$$R$$
$$O$$

In summary, experimental designs range on internal validity from the weakest ones, called preexperiments, through quasi experiments to the strongest ones, called true experiments. Another aspect of experiments involves whether the experimental contrast occurs between groups of subjects, within subjects in a single group, or both in the same design. Table 9–2 shows the nine possible combinations of these two 3-level dimensions. As noted earlier, true experiments always have the between-group feature, thus explaining the "NA" (not applicable) in the within-subjects row. Preexperiments do not have any mixed forms, that is, combining between and within features.

Hybrid Correlational and Experimental Designs. Correlational and true experimental approaches can work together in the same study. An example of such a hybrid design appears in a study of a relaxation treatment to reduce student anxiety in a statistics course (Bartz, Amato, Rasor, & Rasor, 1981). First the students were divided into low- and high-anxiety groups by means of a pretest. Then the high-anxiety group was further divided by random assignment into a treated and a control group. The experimental treatment consisted of a "do-it-yourself desensitization" procedure. The resulting three-group design had, for each group, a pretest, a posttest (midterm exam), and a follow-up test (final exam).

$$
\begin{array}{ll}
O\ X\ O\ O & (1) \\
R & \\
\rule{4cm}{0.4pt} & \\
O\quad O\ O & (2) \\
O\quad O\ O & (3)
\end{array}
$$

Groups 1 and 2 alone would form a simple true experiment based on just the high-anxiety subjects. Groups 2 and 3 alone would constitute a correlational design assessing the consequences of low versus high anxiety over time in the absence of an experimental treatment. Combining all three groups in a single study allows the additional contrast of Groups 1 and 3, asking whether high-anxiety students with the treatment fare as well as untreated low-anxiety students.

This example illustrates how subjects grouped, or "blocked," on a measured independent variable can then be further assigned to different levels of an experimental independent variable. Complex designs can involve **blocking** on more than one measured variable and assignment of subjects to levels of more than one experimental variable. A **factorial design** assigns each subject to just one or another combination of two

Table 9–2 Types of Experimental Design

	Preexperiment	*Quasi Experiment*	*True Experiment*
Between subjects	XO O	NA	R XO O
Within subjects	OXO	OOOOXOOOO	NA
Mixed	NA	OXO O O	R OXO O O

or more different experimental independent variables. We can use subscripts to show multiple factors. For example, a two-factor quasi experiment (no random assignment) with treatment A, treatment B, both, or no treatment could have the following diagram:

$$
\begin{array}{ccc}
O & X_A & O \\
O & X_B & O \\
O & X_{AB} & O \\
O & & O
\end{array}
$$

ISSUES IN APPLIED EXPERIMENTAL DESIGN

Ethical Issues

A Case in Point: An Experimental Prison.   The Stanford mock prison study illustrates one ethical problem arising in social experiments (Zimbardo, 1975). The researchers converted a psychology department lab into a "prison." Young, healthy men, selected for their stability, volunteered as subjects and were randomly assigned either a prisoner or a guard role. The experimenters made great efforts to achieve realism through rules, uniform clothing, and nonviolent punishment such as exercise and isolation. The study began on a Sunday night when the Palo Alto police "arrested" the subjects, but it ended just six days later because of stress. All ten "prisoners" reported mental anguish, and half of them had to be released early because of depression, anxiety, or psychosomatic illness. The principal investigator said he allowed this study to become so intense as a result of the research team's " 'group think' consensus which had isolated us from external normative standards and from our own moral and human values" (Zimbardo, 1975, p. 44). Although the study produced results that helped improve the prison systems of various states, it illustrates the danger in experimental research for harming human subjects. As indicated in Chapter 2, the federal government has applied stringent safeguards in the last two decades to prevent such harm.

Effect of Giving Consent.   Of these safeguards, the most important protection for subjects requires that they give their informed consent before joining the study. This procedure has become so widespread that journals often demand that authors give signed assurances of subject protection before publishing their results. In some cases, articles report their human subject protection procedures as part of the methods section. An example comes from the stress study that exposed subjects to a cold virus: "The trial was approved by the Harrow District Ethical Committee, and informed consent was obtained from each subject after the nature and possible consequences of the study were fully explained" (Cohen et al., 1991, p. 607).

There remains some dispute, however, about the informed consent requirement. Some researchers believe that certain hypotheses cannot be tested if the subjects are fully informed, and they therefore support the occasional use of deception. Other researchers argue that deception cannot be justified and that nondeceptive research strategies can and should be employed (Baumrind, 1985).

Ethical safeguards can have measureable effects on research results. One example of this appears in studies of distracting, uncontrollable noise and proofreading performance. A researcher varied the timing of the information that the subjects had the right to withdraw from the study (given either 10 weeks or just before the study). The study also included two levels of noise controllability (whether or not the subjects had the right to turn down the volume but stay in the study). The results showed that "having subjects sign the withdrawal option close to the time of the experiment has a similar effect to providing an experimental manipulation giving subjects potential control over the aversive event" (Trice, 1987, p. 127).

Ethics of Random Assignment.   Ethical concerns also arise in the random assignment of subjects to different conditions. The comparison of two surgical treatments for breast cancer illustrates this problem. In the usual design, researchers would assign a woman with breast cancer to one of the treatment conditions only after informed consent (Marquis, 1986). In one such study, not enough patients agreed to participate, apparently because of a reluctance to leave their surgical treatment to chance. To get enough subjects to complete the study, the researcher used a different procedure called **prerandomization**. In this approach, potential candidates for the study get assigned to treatment conditions *before* consent and thus know which treatment they will receive if they agree to participate. This procedure appears to gather subjects more rapidly than the standard procedure because the subjects receive information only about the assigned condition. However, some critics have attacked this approach on the grounds that the patients are receiving inadequate information about their alternatives and thus are not giving fully informed consent (Marquis, 1986).

Another ethical problem arises when a community objects to the denial of urgently needed treatment for purpose of achieving experimental control. Politically sensitive research may require special efforts to consult with the community. This approach appears appropriate in the case of clinical trials for the treatment of AIDS (Melton, Levine, Koocher, Rosenthal, & Thompson, 1988). When the drug AZT was the only one approved for experimentation, AIDS activists challenged the research protocol of denying patients the only possible treatment. In this context, the double-blind, placebo-control design appeared cruel. In response, researchers can seek a partnership with the relevant community and even "overdisclose" the nature and risks of the research. This approach both empowers the community and protects the validity of the research design.

Computers in Experimentation

Subject Assignment.   Computers play an ever increasing role in all phases of social research. Of course, once the data are gathered, computers will likely calculate the statistics. But in experimental research, they may serve in three different phases before data analysis: assigning subjects to groups, controlling the procedure, and gathering data.

Computers can easily generate random numbers for assigning subjects in a true experiment. In the absence of an appropriate computer, the researcher could use a random number table available in the back of most statistics texts. But if the researcher wishes to match subjects (whether or not randomly assigning them), a computer may prove essential in sorting subjects according to the chosen features (for example, grouping by gender and age).

Sequencing the Interventions.   In some studies, the researcher wishes to give many different stimuli to each subject and must control the sequence of these stimuli precisely. In such projects, a computer could time the stimuli, starting and stopping them in the planned order. The computer may even provide the experimental tasks. For example, a subject may receive a proofreading task with the manuscript presented on a computer screen (see Cozby, 1984, pp. 147–148).

Collecting the Data.   In some cases, computers can collect the research data directly during the experimental procedure, called **online data collection.** The computer is connected electronically to the sensory apparatus monitoring the studied behavior. In the proofreading example, the subject could note any errors in the manuscript by correcting them from the computer keyboard. At the end of the session, the computer could count and store the number of errors found, the number of missed errors, and the amount of time expended by the subject. Such online data collection saves the time of the researcher (who otherwise might have to monitor the subject's performance) and helps prevent errors in both data collection and data entry.

SUMMARY

In this chapter, you have learned a shorthand method for diagramming research designs. Design groups or conditions (sets of subjects given different treatments) are indicated by different lines. A measure is symbolized by O, an independent variable manipulation by X, and random assignment by R. These symbols can portray correlational designs and the whole range of experimental designs, including preexperiments, quasi experiments, and true experiments.

Diagramming serves to identify threats to internal validity that are left uncontrolled by design features. Control groups protect against the time-related threats that endanger within-subject designs. Group equalization by random assignment protects against group-related threats that can arise in between-subjects designs.

EXERCISES

Practice with actual research reports to build your confidence in identifying and diagnosing validity threats. Try the following four kinds of practice:

1. Diagram studies. Made a diagram using Os, Xs, and Rs as appropriate for a study. Start with this made-up study:

A group of 90 students was divided into three groups by class standing: freshmen, sophomores, and juniors. The freshmen received a special tutorial on study methods that lasted a total of six hours. The sophomores received a short version of the same course in one 2-hour session. The juniors received neither treatment. Not planning to assess the course, the trainers collected no pretest measures. Later, however, they decided to evaluate the intervention by comparing the final course grades of the three groups. Diagram this study and then repeat this exercise for research reports in professional journals.

2. Make up a study to fit a design diagram. Imagine and name the variables and procedures that would fit the following diagram:

$$
\begin{array}{c}
O\ X\ \ O\ O \\
O\ \ \ \ \ O\ O \\
R \\
O\ O \\
O
\end{array}
$$

Repeat this exercise by making up arbitrary diagrams and then fitting studies to them.

3. Diagnose a study. Name threats to the internal validity of the design that are controlled and tell how they are controlled by the study. Name threats that are not controlled and tell how they might have been controlled by a change in design. Do this step for the designs in exercises 1 and 2.

4. Make up a story about each uncontrolled threat you find in the previous exercise. That is, tell how it might come about by identifying a particular extraneous cause that could lead to a false inference of causation. Tell what direction this misleading effect would take. That is, would the dependent variable tend to move up or down because of this cause? For example, if maturation were the threat, we would expect cognitive ability increases in young people over time.

KEY TERMS

Between-subjects design
Blocking
Control group
Correlational design
Experimental design
Factorial design
Group threats
Internal validity
Matching
Mixed design
Mortality
O
Online data collection

Panel
Preexperiments
Prerandomization
Quasi-experimental design
R
Random assignment
Random sampling
Reverse causation
Time threats
True experiments
Within-subjects design
X

❧ 10 ❧

True Experimentation
External Validity and Experimental Construct Validity

VALIDITY QUESTIONS IN TRUE EXPERIMENTS

True experiments protect against both time and group threats to internal validity by randomly assigning subjects to treated and control groups. However, all experiments, including true experiments, risk threats to the construct validity of the experimental variable. Moreover, all research studies, both experimental and correlational, may fail to generalize to other groups, places, and times. This chapter will use the true experiment as the context for treating these validity problems.

An Example of a True Experiment

Drug and Placebo Effects.   As more of our population reaches retirement age, we must become more concerned with the problems of the aged. We can all hope for a new medicine that lifts mood or improves physical performance—a chemical shield against the effects of aging. One true experiment tested the impact of the drug amphetamine on the mood and psychomotor performance of 80 hospitalized patients with an average age of 66 (Ross, Krugman, Lyerly, & Clyde, 1962). This study shows how one design dealt with a special kind of construct validity.

The authors wanted to assess the "pure" effects of 10 milligrams of d-amphetamine. Thus, they had to separate the effects of the drug from any **placebo** effects caused by the method of giving the drug (for example, by pill or injection). Placebo effects might result from the patients' beliefs, which could be raised by seeing any medical equipment connected with healing in the past. Such raised hopes might lead to a better mood or more energetic physical movement even without effects from the drug. To measure both the placebo and drug effects, the authors randomly assigned the subjects to four different groups:

1. Pill with amphetamine
2. Pill without amphetamine—the placebo
3. Amphetamine disguised—no pill
4. No pill, no amphetamine

Each group received orange juice. Groups 1 and 2 drank the orange juice after the pills. For group 3, the orange juice contained dissolved amphetamine, unknown to the subjects. The researchers told all four groups that their orange juice preference would guide the hospital's kitchen staff. This was a "cover story" to get the groups, especially group 3, to take the orange juice without creating doubts that might have affected their behavior in the study. To make this cover story work, all groups answered some questions about the flavor of the orange juice. This questionnaire also tested whether the amphetamine made group 3's orange juice taste any different from group 4's. It did not.

The two "pill" groups (groups 1 and 2) received neutral instructions: "This is a study from which we hope to gain information about the effects of this drug upon mood, the way that you feel, and your eye–hand coordination" (Ross et al., 1962, p. 384). These subjects received these pills in a hospital in the same context that they received their own medicine. Therefore, we can assume that they expected the experimental drug to help, perhaps even more so than older, less advanced drugs. These subjects answered a variety of questions, including a six-factor mood scale. Figure 10–1 shows the mean comfort index scores based on the mood measures for each group. A high score reflects feeling friendly and energetic and clear thinking.

The results showed two different and opposite effects—one from the drug and the other from the pills. The drug effect appears as the contrast between the subjects with and without the drug, controlling for the pill effect. In the case of the two pill groups, those with the drug averaged 12.6 points less on the comfort index (327 - 314.4). In the case of the two no-pill groups, the drug group averaged 11.6 points less than the no-drug group (312 - 300.4). In both contrasts, the drug *lowered* reported comfort.

On the other hand, the pill seemed to *improve* mood. The pill effect appears as the contrast between subjects with and without the pill controlling for the drug. Without the drug (placebo versus nothing), the pill raised the comfort index 15 points (327 - 312). Similarly, in the two groups with the drug, the pill raised the comfort index 14 points (314.4 - 300.4). In sum, this study shows a harmful drug effect and beneficial placebo effect.

We rarely get to separate the drug or experimental effect from the pill or placebo effect in such studies. Only the presence of all four groups in this design allowed us to measure these two effects in such a convincing way. More commonly, studies provide just two groups. For example, a naive researcher might have conducted this study with just groups 1 and 4. The experimental group would have received the drug in pill form. The outcome of this pill-plus-drug group would then be compared with that of a "control" group receiving nothing—neither the drug nor the pill. What might we have concluded from such a two-group study? Figure 10–1 gives the comfort index for these two conditions. The pill-plus-drug group (314.4) would have looked slightly better than the no pill–no drug group (312). We might have concluded that amphetamine helped the elderly if only modestly (by just 2.4 points).

From the four-group study, we know this conclusion would be incorrect. The observed improvement in mood in the drug-plus-pill group over the no drug–no pill group is entirely due to the positive effect of the pill (approximately 14.5 on average), which exceeds the negative effect of the drug (about -12).

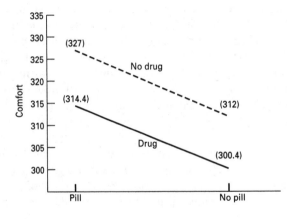

Figure 10–1 Comfort index for four experimental groups. (From Ross, S., Krugman, A.D., Lyerly, S.B., & Clyde, D.J. Drugs and placebos: A model design. (1962). *Psychological Reports, 10,* 383–392. Reprinted with permission of the author and publisher.)

Experimental Construct Validity.   As this example shows, true experiments do not assure us of **experimental construct validity**. We define experimental construct validity as the extent to which the contrast of experimental and control conditions truly reflects the causal construct under study. Do we know that the experimental and control groups differ only on the independent variable reflecting the causal construct of our theory? In the naive two-group, drug-plus-pill versus no drug–no pill design, we saw that the two groups differed in two ways. One way involved the construct of central concern—the dosage of amphetamine. In the other way, the pill effect confounded the effect of interest. The two-group design can tell us only the net result of those two different interventions. A diagram of this study could represent both of these interventions as separate Xs—one for the drug X_d and one for the pill X_p as in Figure 10–2a.

Intrasession history consists of both the planned interventions and any other events incidental to the research procedure. The experimental study would always include the intervention itself, the effect of which we want to observe. However, many other events can occur within the research session that might affect the outcome. Our primitive two-group drug experiment fails to control for one bit of intrasession history—the pill. We want to find the pure effect of the drug after sorting out the effect of the pill. This goal leads to either of two designs. In one we could give the drug in a concealed form so that no pill appears in the study to produce a placebo effect. This design, diagrammed in Figure 10–2b, consists of groups 3 and 4 in the original four-group study by Ross and others. Here, removing one extraneous event, the pill, reduces the threat of intrasession history. In practice, such a design could violate the subjects' right to informed consent.

To avoid this ethical problem, a more common two-group design uses the placebo control group appearing in Figure 10–2c. This approach consists of groups 1 and 2 in the original four-group study. Including the pill-taking event in both groups solves the intrasession history problem by exposing all subjects to it equally. As in the no-pill design of Figure 10–2b, the two groups differ only by the presence of the drug in the treated group.

Experimental construct validity depends not on random assignment but rather on the operational definition of the experimental variable. To assure that the study tests the desired causal construct, you may have to include a special control group such as the placebo control pictured in Figure 10–2c. Experimental construct validity has two main types of threats to be considered in more detail later: control group contamination and

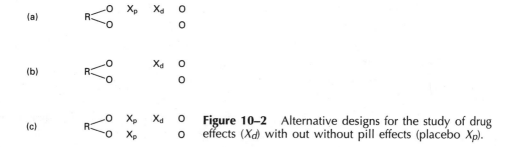

Figure 10–2   Alternative designs for the study of drug effects (X_d) with out without pill effects (placebo X_p).

experimental group contamination. Both types of threats involve confounding events that occur within the research process or intrasession history.

The next section briefly reviews the most common true experimental designs. Later sections will revisit in more detail the threats to experimental construct validity and their solutions. Finally, we will turn to external validity, or the extent to which the findings of a study can generalize.

Variety in True Experiments

Basic Designs and Their Variants.   Many designs could satisfy the criteria for a true experiment, namely, random assignment to multiple, differently treated groups. The following three examples show both this variety and the different ways of handling one internal validity threat—that of pretest reactivity. These controls for pretest reactivity also serve as models for securing experimental construct validity. Figure 10–3 diagrams these basic true experimental designs.

These designs represent only the simplest versions of their types. Adding one or more follow-up measures as in Figure 10–4a or one or more pretests as in Figure 10–4b only makes these designs more elaborate. Finally, these designs could accommodate one or more additional experimental groups as in Figure 10–4c.

All three of the basic designs in Figure 10–3 control the common threats to internal validity. Each tests a comparison group at the same time(s) as the experimental group in order to control for such time threats as history and maturation. Each has random assignment to groups which, if successful, will rule out such threats as selection.

Although usually successful, random assignment sometimes fails its purpose of making the groups equivalent. When that happens, the design becomes a quasi-experimental design. Because random assignment may fail to achieve group equivalence, you may prefer true experiments with pretests over those without. The pretests permit a

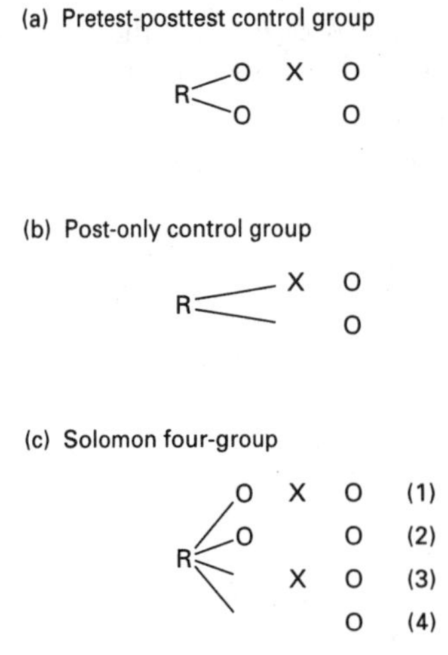

(a) Pretest-posttest control group

```
      O   X   O
R <
      O       O
```

(b) Post-only control group

```
          X   O
R <
              O
```

(c) Solomon four-group

```
      O   X   O   (1)
      O       O   (2)
R <
          X   O   (3)
              O   (4)
```

Figure 10–3   Three basic types of true experimental designs.

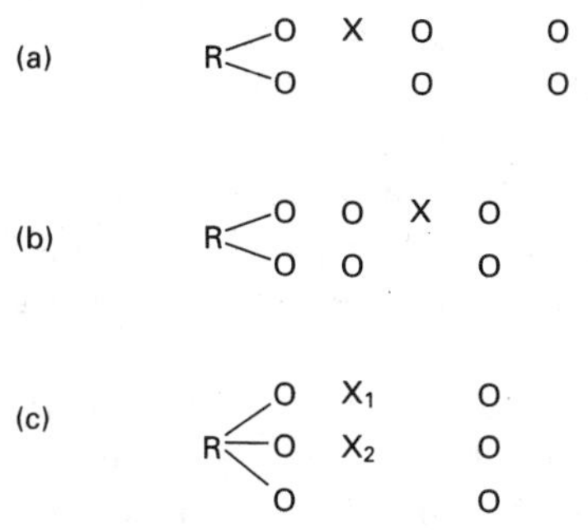

(a) $R\!\!<_{\,O}^{\,O}$ X   O   O
                        O   O   O

(b) $R\!\!<_{\,O}^{\,O}$ O   X   O
                        O   O   O

(c) $R\!\!<$ O X_1 O
                 O X_2 O
                 O   O

Figure 10–4   Some variations on a simple, true experimental design.

check on equivalence before the intervention X is introduced. If the groups prove not to be equivalent on pretest, the pretest scores can be used to adjust statistically for the non-equivalence.

Test Reactivity and the Need for Different Designs.   One reason for having the three different types of true experiments in Figure 10–3 has to do with test reactivity. The pretest may act as an unwanted "active ingredient" much like an unwanted but impactful external event, as in the history threat to internal validity. Both of these kinds of events take place outside the experimental treatment. The pretest occurs before the X, and the history threat occurs outside the treatment session although at the same time. The pretest can add to or subtract from whatever effect comes from the experimental intervention X. Although by custom we treat pretest reactivity as an internal validity threat, its control serves as a model for intrasession history events that confound experimental construct validity.

A study of psychiatric interventions illustrates the effect of testing in relation to the placebo effect (Frank, Nash, Stone, & Imber, 1963). The researchers studied the short-term and long-term effects of a placebo on patients' discomfort. A psychologist, using paper-and-pencil symptom checklists, initially tested adults diagnosed as neurotic for about 90 minutes. A psychiatrist then took measures of autonomic functions and collected for the second time the discomfort measures before offering the patient a placebo pill (the treatment).

While the pill was "working," the patients took some more paper-and-pencil and autonomic tests. They then returned to the psychologist who collected the discomfort measure for the third time that day. The patients returned after a week for a fourth round of testing. The following diagram summarizes this design, where X represents the placebo and the Os represent the repeated measures of discomfort:

$$O\ O\ X\ O \qquad\qquad O$$
Day 1   1 Week Later

The results of this study agree with previous research on the placebo. On different measures and for two different groups, the average discomfort level declined from the first test to the final test one week later. Surprisingly, much of this change happened *before* the placebo (that is, by the second measure on day 1). These patients showed a further decrease in discomfort directly after the placebo (that is, between the second and third measures on the first day). At follow-up, one week later, the average discomfort level increased somewhat but remained significantly lower than on the first test.

Without a control group, we cannot safely interpret the relative effects of placebo pills and test reactivity. However, it appears that patients reacted favorably to testing. Possibly some of the initial discomfort stemmed from stage fright in the presence of unfamiliar psychologists and psychiatrists in a clinical setting. After talking with these clinicians in the initial testing, the patients would naturally become more comfortable. These patients may also have felt that the impressive array of tests would help diagnose their problem and lead to a solution, thus raising their spirits. Finally, the tests involved kind attention from high-status experts who patiently allowed the subjects to express themselves in repeated tests. By more than one theory (for example, systematic desensitization, client-centered counseling, psychoanalysis), this kind of exchange should have therapeutic value. By any or all of these different mechanisms, the experience of testing may have caused a real change in the outcome variable.

In sum, we must regard testing not as a neutral event but rather as a kind of intervention with a power that can rival that of the main treatment. For this reason, true experiments attempt to control for the effects of pretests. In a similar way, the packaging of the main treatment (as in a pill) can also serve as an intervention. The controls for pretest reactivity suggest ways in which to manage intrasession history threats such as placebo effects.

The pretest–posttest control group design includes the pretest in both the treated and the control group. A simple or main effect of the pretest should show up in the posttests of both groups, just as would any other time threats such as maturation. The difference between the posttests of the two groups should derive only from the treatment effect. The posttest-only control group design controls for pretest reactivity by eliminating the pretest entirely. Assuming that random assignment made the two groups equivalent before the treatment, any posttest differences between the groups should come solely from the intervention.

These two ways of controlling pretest reactivity also deal with intrasession history, any stimuli occurring along with or carrying the experimental treatment. One approach excludes the intrasession event from both groups, as the posttest-only design excludes pretests. The other includes the intrasession event in both groups. Will these two approaches yield the same results? The answer is yes if pretest reactivity or intrasession history operates independently of the intervention. However, if the intervention has a different effect when the pretest (or a placebo) is present than when it is absent, these two designs will yield different posttest effects.

How can we tell if the treatment behaves differently depending on whether the pretest or placebo is present? To answer this question, we must use both kinds of designs at the same time. This combined design requires four groups, as diagrammed in Figure 10–3c, and is called the Solomon four-group design. Compare the posttests of groups 2 and 4 to see the impact of the pretest absent the treatment. Compare groups 1 and 3 to show the effect of the pretest when both groups have the intervention. If these two contrasts give the same results, we conclude that the pretest's effect does not vary with the presence of the treatment or X. But different results from the two contrasts would alert us to a combined effect of the pretest and treatment, a problem to which we will return later in the section on external validity.

EXPERIMENTAL CONSTRUCT VALIDITY

Doubts About the Independent Variable

The manipulated independent variable has experimental construct validity when it reflects the intended causal construct and nothing else. Threats to this validity derive from contamination of the experimental variable. **Contamination** means the presence of some intrasession events, which raise doubt that the experimental and control groups differ in only one respect—the causal construct. Unlike the pretest, which occurs prior to the intervention, intrasession history can be difficult to separate from the theoretical causal variable.

One type of contamination affects the experimental condition and raises doubt about whether the treated group received any stimuli beyond the intervention intended by the researcher. We can see this in the study by Ross and others in the difference between the effect of the drug alone (X_d) and the effects of the drug plus the placebo pill ($X_d + X_p$). The pill casing, X_p, contaminates the experimental condition by adding something to the treatment beyond the chemical under study.

The other type of contamination affects the control condition. If the control group experiences any part of the experimental treatment, it will fail to serve as a clear contrast. In the next subsections, we will first consider experimental group contamination and then control group contamination, along with their causes and controls.

Confounding in the Treated Group

Experimental group contamination appears in two related forms—demand characteristics and experimenter expectancy. **Demand characteristics** include any cues, such as placebos, that affect research outcomes by guiding subjects' perceptions of the goals of the study (Orne, 1962). **Experimenter expectancy**, in contrast, consists of the ways, other than the intervention itself, by which an experimenter influences the subjects to get results consistent with his or her hypothesis. However, experimenter expectancy bias does not include intentional data fraud.

Experimenter expectancy sometimes operates through demand characteristics. That is, the experimenter's conviction can lead her or him to provide subtle behaviors or demand characteristics. The subjects, in turn, interpret these clues as guides to the behavior they should provide. However, experimenter expectancy may operate through mechanisms other than demand characteristics. Experimenter expectancy emphasizes the experimenter's beliefs and behaviors that point the subject, human or animal, to the researcher's hypothesis. Demand characteristics emphasize human subjects' perceptions and their desire to do "well" in the research situation. As a result, demand characteristics include all the clues in the experimental setting that can guide the subject whether or not they derive from the experimenter's expectancy. A research situation might give unintended demand characteristics that guide the subjects away from the researcher's pet theory.

Experimenter Expectancy.   Also called the self-fulfilling prophecy and the Pygmalion effect, experimenter expectancy has received the most attention from Rosenthal (Rosenthal, 1976; Rosenthal & Rubin, 1978). It comes as no surprise that researchers have some attachment to their hypotheses and care whether their findings support or reject their beliefs. Our scholarly system rewards researchers who get the results that they predict. Ethical guidelines usually restrain researchers from creating their results by fraud. Until the evidence for experimenter expectancy became convincing, researchers assumed that they would prevent their beliefs from affecting their results. Now we know that ethical scholars can, without intention, influence the behavior of their subjects to get hoped for results. This effect has even appeared in animal studies.

Cordaro and Ison (1963) randomly assigned 17 college students to three conditions. In each condition, these student "researchers" studied a pair of primitive organisms called planaria. They observed their planaria in a small V-shaped trough filled with water, fitted with electrodes, and exposed to an overhead lamp. The five high-expectancy (HE) students understood that their planaria had already been conditioned to show a high response rate to the light preceding the electrical shock. They expected these planaria to show marked contractions or head turns when the light but not the electrical current came on. The five low-expectancy (LE) students believed that their planaria had not yet been conditioned and did not expect much activity from them. The remaining seven students had high expectations for one planarian and low expectations for the other (called the high and low expectation, or HLE group). In fact, all 34 planaria had received the same training—50 trials, each consisting of three seconds of light alone followed by one second of light plus electrical shock. We can see that this study concerned not the planaria, but rather the students as subjects and their different induced beliefs.

The experimenters conducted 100 trials (three seconds of light alone followed by one second of light accompanied by shock) with each planarian. Each experimenter served as his or her own observer by recording the head turns, contractions, or lack of response of the planaria. Compared to the LE students, the HE students found 20 times more contractions and almost 5 times as many head turns.

Perhaps this difference derives from the way the experimenters performed their observer role. Imagine trying to detect a slight head or body motion in a small organism during a three-second period. The observers may have employed different criteria, depending on their expectations. Rosenthal (1976) argues that such measurement bias differs from experimenter expectancy and cannot account for all of the animal studies of this type. Within the Cordaro and Ison (1963) study, the HLE group partially controls for measurement bias. The HLE experimenters observed both "trained" and "untrained" planaria and should not, therefore, observe with such different criteria. Although the difference between the high- and low-expectation planaria is smaller in the HLE group than the difference between the HE and LE groups, it still strongly favors the high-expectation planaria.

In research with rats labeled "bright" or "dull," similar expectancy results occur even though such experiments offer less ambiguity in the outcome measure. Rosenthal (1976) concludes that the experimenters must be changing the behaviors of their subjects to conform them to expectations. Such influence might operate through physical treatment of the animals (for example, more handling of "smart" than of "dumb" rats or closer attention and thus greater physical closeness to "trained" than to "untrained" planaria). Such experimenter behaviors constitute intrasession history, that is, events that might affect the outcome but are not part of the causal construct under study.

If such experimenter effects occurred only in animal studies, social researchers might feel less concern about this problem. However, experimenter expectancy has appeared in human research as well. Probably the most dramatic and discussed test of the self-fulfilling prophecy comes from Rosenthal and Jacobson's *Pygmalion in the Classroom* (1968). The researchers told teachers that certain children, based on mental testing, would become late bloomers. The researchers made this false claim to mislead the teachers. Although the "late bloomers" did not differ from other children in the beginning, they appeared to make greater intellectual progress than their peers. Rosenthal and Jacobson argued that the teachers' beliefs led them to behave differently toward their students. In particular, teachers may have provided more attention to "late bloomers" and set lower goals for the progress of children not labeled as late bloomers. The Pygmalion study aroused criticism (Elashoff & Snow, 1971; Jensen, 1969), which has been rebutted, and later research has provided more support for the self-fulfilling prophecy (Rosenthal, 1976, pp. 437–471; Rosenthal & Rubin 1971).

Other research has asked how teachers' expectations develop under natural conditions and whether they translate into differential educational treatment. For an example, see Rist's (1970) longitudinal study of primary grade teachers and students and the studies of teacher bias by Babad, Inbar, and Rosenthal (1982a, 1982b). Interpersonal expectancy may operate through the voice tone of the camp counselor (Blanck & Rosenthal, 1984) or therapist (Rosenthal, Blanck, & Vannicelli, 1984).

Preventing Experimenter Expectancy Effects.   At least four methods can stop experimenters from fulfilling their own prophecies by influencing subjects' behavior. One approach keeps the hypothesis from the person conducting the study, called the **naive experimenter** method. It requires that the persons who guide the subjects through the experiment and measures remain ignorant of the literature and theory behind the study. Unfortunately, the naive experimenter may, after seeing the first subjects respond to the experiment, cease being naive. He or she will likely begin to expect certain responses. This expectation, whether consistent with theory or not, can contaminate the study.

The second approach requires that the experimenter remain ignorant not of the hypotheses but only of the subject assignments. We call such an experimenter **blind** in that she or he cannot tell whether a given subject is receiving the experimental treatment or the control experience. This technique appears commonly in studies of drug effects, where drug and placebo pills can be prepared to look the same. Unfortunately, many treatment procedures may not fit in such convenient packages. Also, some treatments may cause side effects that identify the experimental subjects. This information spoils the effort to keep the experimenter from knowing the subjects' group assignment.

A third technique consists of experimenter **standardization**. In this approach, all of the experimenter's words and behaviors strictly follow a script used with all subjects. An observer can monitor this approach to assure its success. Unfortunately such standardization may not extend to subtle nuances of voice tone and nonverbal expression that may transmit the experimenter's expectancy as powerfully as words.

Fourth, extending standardization, the experiment could proceed without an experimenter entirely. Audiotapes and printed handouts could give all instructions to the subjects, an approach called the **canned experimenter**. This procedure works only for experiments that can take place in the highly controlled environment of laboratories. To succeed, the same canned instructions appear in all conditions. A study of two kinds of canned therapists makes this point clearly. The tape condition using a warm voice tone produced better results than the cold voice tone tape using the same script (Morris & Suckerman, 1974). We must seriously consider the threat of experimenter expectation in studies that use none of these four remedies.

Demand Characteristics.   Where experimenter expectancy emphasizes the researcher's beliefs and behaviors, demand characteristics, in contrast, emphasize the subject's beliefs and all the signals in the experimental setting that guide these beliefs. Demand characteristics can include both interpersonal influence by the experimenter acting on his or her expectancy and experimental cues of a physical nature, such as pills containing the active ingredient in drug studies. Any such cue present in the experimental condition but absent in the control condition offers a potential rival explanation of the outcome.

Demand characteristics guide subjects by providing hints about the study's purpose and the responses wanted from them. Two assumptions underpin the demand characteristics mechanism. First, the subjects must be curious about their experiment and must attempt to figure out what is wanted of them. Second, having guessed the study's purpose, subjects must be motivated to change their behavior to accord with (or under some circumstances diverge from) the research hypothesis.

Demand characteristics may cause subjects to behave differently than expected by theory. For example, Turner and Simons (1974) predicted that the presence of weapons would increase the number of shocks given by subjects to a provoking partner. Instead, the more the subjects knew about the study (that is, awareness that the study was about their reactions to the weapons), the fewer shocks they gave. This emphasizes how independent subjects can be in using demand characteristics to form conclusions about how to act.

Frequent reports have noted subjects' curiosity about and motivation to respond to cues in research studies. Perhaps the most famous of these reports gave social science the term **Hawthorne effect**, named for the Hawthorne plant of the Western Electric Company in Chicago. This plant served as the site of an extensive study, conducted from 1924 to 1933, of the effects of physical and social conditions on worker productivity (Roethlisberger & Dickson, 1939). The Hawthorne study consisted of several quasi experiments using different sets of workers in different settings on different tasks and different experimental interventions. Researchers outside of industrial psychology remember this study for the incidental observation of the Hawthorne effect.

We can now regard the Hawthorne effect as a myth, because it lacks sound empirical support. One version holds that the Hawthorne workers increased productivity because of the attention they received from the researchers. Some evidence suggested that the workers increased their output in the illumination experiment after each manipulation, whether the lighting was increased or decreased. Because the workers responded so oddly to the presumed causal variable of lighting, some theorists claimed they were showing the energizing effects of being observed by high-status strangers.

Close analyses of the Hawthorne data in recent decades have cast doubt on the Hawthorne effect. Productivity did not increase regardless of the nature of the manipulation of experimental variables and of other external events. Careful analyses of the data have connected variation in outcomes over time to causes such as personnel changes and external events like the Great Depression (Franke & Kaul, 1978). Although these findings have not gone unchallenged (Bloombaum, 1983), other studies have failed to replicate the Hawthorne effect (see Cook & Campbell, 1979, p. 66).

The Hawthorne effect may have endured because it appeals to our intuition. The Hawthorne investigator, Roethlisberger, observed that human subjects are likely to notice that they are being studied and to form feelings and attitudes about being studied. These reactions may in turn influence the outcome of the research. How the subject interprets the experience becomes crucial.

For example, placebo effects may depend on the subject's belief that the pill will make one feel better or different. The study that began this chapter (Ross et al., 1962) got subjects to take amphetamine or a placebo without instructions about what to expect. The same research team added some new instructions to this procedure in a follow-up study (Lyerly, Ross, Krugman, & Clyde, 1964). Some subjects got capsules described as likely "to make you feel a little livelier than you feel now, or maybe more pepped up, or even a little tense" (Lyerly et al., 1964, p. 323). Some of these capsules really had amphetamines, but others, the placebos, contained only lactose. In addition, other subjects received no instructions and got either the amphetamines in disguised form (dissolved in orange juice) or nothing at all, not even a placebo. The instructions produced strong effects. The placebo group with these instructions reported slightly more comfort than the disguised amphetamine group. Interestingly, the instructions seemed to amplify the chemical effect with the instructed amphetamine group reporting much more comfort than the disguised amphetamine group.

Such instruction effects can appear with interventions other than capsules and chemicals. Johnson and Foley (1969) compared three groups of students who received the same structured discussion of the same subject matter. The group that heard that it was in an experiment and that the treatment would help (experiment–expectation) did best on the outcome measures. The group that heard that it was experimental but without basis for predicting whether the procedure would help (experiment–no expectation) did no better than the group kept unaware of being in an experiment (no experiment).

One behavior observed in experiments has special importance for demand characteristics. **Evaluation apprehension** refers to the anxiety generated by being tested (Rosenberg, 1969). Subjects feeling evaluation apprehension try to look good, intelligent, normal, or well. Under some circumstances, research makes subjects suspicious (McGuire, 1969). Knowledge that some studies have used deception or unpleasant stimuli such as mild electric shock motivates subjects to avoid being "fooled" or hurt. Such subjects guard themselves in experimental settings against such procedures. Both evaluation apprehension and suspiciousness come from the subjects (as opposed to experimenter expectancy) and serve to motivate them to react to the cues provided in the experimental setting.

In some cases the subject may believe that he or she can look best by behaving in a way that supports the researcher's theory (as guessed from demand characteristics). In this case, evaluation apprehension should bias the results in favor of the theory. On other occasions, looking good may conflict with the experimenter's hypothesis. As an example, subjects not wanting to look overly aggressive or vengeful confounded a prediction that the presence of weapons would lead subjects to give more shocks (Turner & Simons, 1974). The research shows that subjects would rather look good (evaluation apprehension) than meet the researcher's expectations if the theory requires looking bad (Silverman, 1977).

Despite such motives as apprehension and suspicion, researchers continue to recruit volunteers prepared to serve the cause of science. Volunteer subjects tend to respect science and trust in the wisdom and authority of scientists (Rosenthal & Rosnow, 1969). Such attitudes will likely lead to the subject's compliance not only with experimental procedures but also with demand characteristics (Orne, 1969).

Preventing Demand Characteristic Effects.   The drug study discussed at the beginning of the chapter illustrates the best defense against demand characteristics—the use of a placebo control group. We know that placebos can influence a variety of human responses including reaction time, grip strength, pulse rate, blood pressure, short-term memory, self-perceived relaxation, and activation. Moreover, some research suggests that neurologic changes such as the release of endorphins may mediate such effects (Ross & Buckalew, 1983). As a result, we will often want to know the effect of a treatment in contrast to a placebo control that reflects the demand characteristics of the situation. These demand characteristics might include therapeutic elements not specified in the theory being tested but of interest nevertheless (Bowers & Clum, 1988). Such nonspecific or placebo effects may appear in contrast to the experience of another kind of group—one receiving no treatment.

A placebo control differs from a no treatment control in that the former group receives something that looks like a treatment. For example, if the treatment of interest involves an argument for an attitude change presented in written form, the placebo control could receive some equally interesting and long reading material on another topic. Such an "attention placebo" can help prevent the controls from perceiving that they are controls. This method can keep subjects "blind" to their condition, even though they all know they belong to an experiment. When neither the subject nor the experimenter knows the condition to which subjects are assigned, we call the study *double blind*. This procedure will minimize both experimenter expectancy and demand characteristic threats.

A second approach keeps the subjects from knowing that they are in a study at all. This method requires studying subjects in a natural setting. If the subjects do not know that they are subjects, they will not experience evaluation apprehension, become suspicious, or try to comply with possible demand characteristics. Ethics limit this type of research to mild interventions, for example, noting whether passers-by will return an intentionally dropped letter or wallet.

In a third approach, subjects may know that they are in an experiment, but not when and how they will be observed. This unobtrusive measure approach may serve when the study concerns a voluntary behavior. If the subject produces this behavior only to conform to the demand characteristics of the study, she or he is less likely to produce it "off stage." An example comes from the experimental study of hypnosis, a very difficult concept to pin down. Both hypnotists and subjects can have difficulty telling when the hypnotic state has appeared. In a study by Orne, Sheehan, and Evans (1968), each hypnotized subject received the posthypnotic suggestion to touch his or her forehead upon hearing the word "experiment." Unknown to the hypnotist, the researchers had used a test to sort subjects into groups of those either easy or hard to hypnotize. The researchers asked the hard-to-hypnotize group to act hypnotized in order to trick the hypnotist into thinking that he had succeeded. In effect, the researchers made overt the demand characteristics to "go along" with the hypnotist. Unknown to the subjects, the hypnotist's receptionist acted as an unobtrusive observer. She said the word "experiment" casually three times and counted the number of correct (touching forehead) posthypnotic responses. Only the good hypnotic subjects consistently touched their foreheads at this prompt, but subjects from both groups touched their foreheads when the hypnotist said "experiment." In other words, the subjects faking hypnosis dropped their act when they thought they were no longer being observed.

In a fourth approach, the experimenter can try to deceive the subjects about the nature of the study. Telling the subjects the study's true hypothesis might bias their behavior. Thus some researchers try to distract the subjects from guessing the study's purpose by giving them a false **cover story**. An example comes from the placebo study discussed at the beginning of this chapter. The researchers told the subjects that the study concerned consumer preferences in orange juice. Deception studies have a major drawback: They violate the subject's right to informed consent. In addition, the deception may fail. To check the success of the deception, studies may end by questioning the subjects about their beliefs about the study.

The fifth option enlists subjects' aid in not guessing the hypothesis. In the **faithful subject** method, the researchers tell subjects that knowing the real hypothesis would destroy the value of the study. For the good of the project, subjects are asked to comply with the research procedures and to suspend or avoid any hunches they may have about the study's purposes. However, we cannot know whether such subjects will permit themselves to look abnormal, unhealthy, or incompetent for the sake of science. Thus, this approach may work best when subjects need not fear the outcome of the experimental treatment.

Confounding in the Control Group

Control group contamination consists of unplanned or extraneous stimuli in the control group that spoil the experimental contrast. In this case, the control group experiences something other than the absence of the studied treatment. Something other than the treatment could have caused any observed difference between the groups. If the experimental and control groups do not differ at posttest, we cannot conclude that the experimental intervention had no impact. Control group contamination can misestimate the true impact of the experimental treatment in either direction. **Compensatory contamination** produces underestimation, and **exaggerating contamination** produces overestimation.

Compensatory Contamination.

In the typical two-group experiment, the treated subjects receive the intervention, but the control subjects do not. Withholding a treatment does not guarantee that the control group receives no treatment. "No treatment" control groups may obtain the intervention or something like it in various ways.

Control subjects will feel motivated to acquire a withheld treatment that they perceive as desirable or needed. In mental health research, this problem comes under the heading of **spontaneous remission**. Suppose a pool of subjects consists of 100 clients seeking help for depression at a mental health center. A true experiment might randomly assign half of these clients to the new treatment and half to the control condition. For ethical reasons, this procedure works best when the number of clients exceeds the supply of service. That is, some clients would have to wait for treatment in any event, and the random assignment gives everyone a fair and equal chance for immediate or delayed care. The researchers would place the control subjects on a waiting list to receive treatment when therapists become available at the end of the experiment. Such studies often find that the waiting list clients show improvement at the end of the experiment but before they have received the treatment. Research suggests that this remission or improvement may not occur spontaneously but rather because of treatment received outside of the study (Bergin & Lambert, 1978).

People in anguish will not likely sit idly by for months while they wait their turn for help. Highly motivated help-seekers will find assistance either from professional mental health workers or from friends and family. Typically, the experimenter knows neither the amount nor the quality of this therapeutic intervention. As a result, the experiment fails to provide a clear contrast. Instead, it pits a group receiving known treatment against a group receiving unknown treatment.

If the control subjects know that they are being denied treatment that others enjoy, they may take a competitive or vengeful interest in compensating for the denial of treatment. Even without an intrinsic motive to acquire treatment, intergroup rivalry may incite the control group to match the performance of the experimental subjects. This rivalry seems likely when naturally competitive production units receive different experimental assignments.

Another form of contamination occurs through diffusion, for example, by exchanging information. Experimental and control subjects who know each other outside of the study may contaminate the study by sharing their experiences.

Compensatory contamination can occur not only through the control subjects but also by the managers of the study. When the withheld intervention provides a public good or service, political pressure may come to bear on the study. The controls and their allies can argue on equity grounds that everyone should receive a perceived benefit (for example, an innovative educational program). Program managers or sponsors have sometimes bowed to such pressures, sacrificing the experimental distinction between groups. The anticipation of such pressures often accounts for the resistance of program managers to experiments with no treatment control groups. Such managerial compensation should prove less misleading than individual subject compensation of an unknown nature. We can simply ignore studies in which the planned difference between treatment and control subjects has failed.

Preventing Compensatory Contamination.   First, and especially important in assessing a public program, you should check the feasibility of withholding the intervention from the controls. To avoid the later collapse of the study, the evaluator needs to confirm the project manager's commitment to the design against the likely pressures to give the treatment to the control subjects. If the control subjects will not receive the focal treatment on purpose, you must protect against compensatory contamination.

If you expect the control subjects to replace the denied treatment with one found outside the study, several strategies may help. First, consider offering the control group an alternative treatment such as a placebo. To succeed, the placebo must satisfy the subjects' desire to get some kind of help for their problem. It may also serve the purpose of keeping the subjects blind to their condition. However, this method may risk ethical problems for informed consent and subjects' welfare.

A second way of dealing with contamination accepts that control subjects will seek outside help. You can still try to measure such help both sought and received outside the study. Such data could prove useful for experimental subjects as well and would help in assessing and adjusting for the degree of compensatory contamination.

A third approach deals with interventions that easily transfer. To prevent diffusion, you can either use subjects who do not know each other or separate treated and control subjects during the study. If none of these remedies proves feasible, you may have to consider other designs such as within-subject time-series designs rather than between-group designs.

Exaggerating Contamination.   Exaggerating contamination makes the control group's experience even more different from the treated group's experience than planned. While compensatory contamination can disguise real effects, exaggerating contamination can produce false effects. A treatment may appear effective because of changes in the control group. If, for example, the control condition seems less desirable than the experimental condition, the control subjects may feel a "resentful demoralization" (Cook & Campbell, 1979, p. 55). Instead of competing with the experimental group, the demoralized control subjects feel apathetic, surrender, and perform badly. The treated group, even if they do not improve, will appear better off than the untreated group, which shows a loss. Whether subjects will react to a situation in a spirited or an apathetic way depends on the subjects and the study's context.

The same methods that deal with compensatory contamination can serve for the threat of exaggerating contamination. The placebo control method might help keep subjects from knowing whether they are in the control or experimental condition. Such "blind" subjects should not feel underprivileged. Absent a placebo control, the study should monitor the feelings and actions of the control subjects. Pilot research could indicate whether control subjects will react competitively or apathetically. In either case, the researcher could adopt the faithful subject method and share the rationale of the design. If the subjects understand the random procedure, they may take their group assignment less personally. Where possible, the researcher should assure the control subjects that if the treatment is found effective, they will receive it in due course.

Diagrams can help summarize the two types of control group contamination. The control group subjects might get access to the X_d treatment intended just for the experimental subjects. This case illustrates compensatory contamination.

$$R \quad \begin{matrix} O \; X_d \; O \\ O \; (X_d) \; O \end{matrix}$$

The intervention X_d should appear only in the treated group (top row), but, by contamination, it also appears in the control group (X_d). This reduces any difference between the two groups and hides any effect of the treatment

On the other hand, contamination may lead the control subjects to behave in ways opposite to those produced in the experimental group. By harming the control subjects' performance, this effect will increase the apparent benefit of the intervention. Thus we can diagram exaggerating contamination as a negative treatment, indicated by $(-X_d)$ in the control group.

$$R \quad \begin{matrix} O \; X_d \; O \\ O \; (-X_d) \; O \end{matrix}$$

Weak Treatment

When the Manipulation Fails. Until now, the discussion of experimental construct validity has focused on contamination. Another threat arises when the manipulation is too weak to reflect the intended causal construct. Suppose a researcher predicts that decreased anxiety will produce better test scores in a math class. To reduce anxiety, the treated group receives 10 minutes of relaxation training. On the final exam, the researcher finds that the experimental group did no better than the control group. Should we interpret this result to mean that anxiety does not disrupt test taking? Or, should we suspect that a mere 10 minutes of relaxation treatment might not reduce anxiety enough to have an effect? A weak treatment may not give a fair test of the theory.

Checking the Manipulation. To assure that the manipulation has good experimental construct validity, researchers follow two procedures: pilot tests and manipulation checks. In a **pilot test**, the researcher tries the experimental treatment out on small samples before the actual experiment. If it does not produce sensible results, it can be modified and retested until it performs properly. The test anxiety researcher could try out several different levels of relaxation training, each with a different small group, say one 10-minute session, one 60-minute session, or five 60-minute sessions. The main study could proceed after finding the training dosage that produces adequate relaxation.

Since pilot test and study conditions may differ, the manipulation may not function the same way in both. To make sure that the treatment operated as hoped in the actual study, researchers often employ **manipulation checks** in the measures or **debriefing** after the intervention. Suppose you wanted to study the effects on seventh-grade boys of violent versus nonviolent video games. You might begin by choosing video games for their face validity as violent or not. You might then pilot test the games on some children to see if they produced the kinds of effects you expected, such as different changes in pulse rates. But how could you be sure than the actual sample of seventh graders would perceive the games as violent or nonviolent? You could ask manipulation check questions about the perceived violence of the study's games, both in absolute terms and compared to games the subjects commonly play. Manipulation checks usually involve standard test items or other measures confirming the impact of the intervention. In contrast, debriefing consists of less formal conversation in which the subject and researcher can ask about each other's views of the study. Both of these procedures can help identify the kinds of subjects on which the treatment has more or less impact.

EXTERNAL VALIDITY

Doubts About Extending the Findings

Generalizability.   **External validity** consists of the extent to which research findings generalize to other populations, other times, and other settings. Whereas internal validity pertains to the truth of causal inference within a particular study, external validity pertains to the truth of the causal inference in another situation or population. A true experiment should have high internal validity. But its results may apply only to the subjects, setting, and particular events of the study and thus have low external validity.

Interactions.   To understand external validity you must grasp the idea of an **interaction**. Two independent variables interact if the effect (on a dependent variable) of one depends on or varies with the level of the other. Recall the discussion of pretest reactivity earlier in this chapter. In a group with both a pretest and an experimental intervention, either or both could affect the outcome. The Solomon four-group design (Figure 10–3c) provides a technique for separating the pretest effect from the intervention effect. The pure pretest or reactivity effect appears as the difference between the posttests of the two groups without the experimental intervention. Any difference must stem from the fact that one group has a pretest and the other did not; see groups 2 and 4 in Figure 10–3c. The pure intervention effect, similarly, appears as the contrast between the posttests of the two groups without pretests. Any difference here must come from the fact that one group has the intervention and the other one did not (groups 3 and 4). In each case, we can see the isolated or *main* effect of just one factor, either the pretest or the intervention, controlling for the other.

Sometimes, only main effects appear, and the intervention's effect remains the same whether the design has a pretest or not. In this case, the posttest difference without a pretest (group 3 versus group 4) should equal the difference with pretests (group 1 versus group 2). However, these two differences sometimes prove unequal. The effect of the intervention (*X*) may expand or contract depending on the presence of a pretest. In this case, we say that the intervention and the pretest interact or that we have an intervention-by-pretest interaction.

Such an interaction seems to have occurred in one study of AIDS education (Wenger et al., 1992). The researchers wanted to reduce risk behaviors for AIDS in heterosexual college students. They evaluated an hour-long, small group training session that involved videotape, doctor's lecture, role-play, discussion, and written materials. The researchers randomly assigned 435 students to one of three groups: training session only, training session plus HIV testing, and no training or testing. One aspect of the training dealt with asking sexual partners about their HIV status. At posttest, the training plus HIV testing group did question their partners about HIV status (56 percent) significantly more than the training only (42 percent) or the control (41 percent) group. The lack of effect of the training alone surprised the researches because they carefully designed it to exceed the kinds of AIDS training usually found in public health programs.

What could have caused this finding? The three-group design cannot rule out the chance that the HIV testing alone (as a main effect) produced the success of the training plus testing group. We would need another control group with the HIV test alone in order to check this possibility. However, an interaction of the test with the training seems likely in this case. First, the training, unlike the testing, specifically addressed the behavior of asking about partners' HIV status. HIV testing alone would not have sent any messages about the need and method for talking with partners. Second, the HIV test may have amplified the training by motivating the subjects to remember and apply their learning. The researchers noted that all of the subjects received negative results from their HIV test (that is, not infected). However, each subject may, for a period of time, have feared getting positive results with the profound costs they would bring. Perhaps this fear made the training material more personal and vivid.

Assuming that the HIV testing and AIDS training interacted, what has this to do with generalizing or external validity? Suppose this study had not had three groups but rather the simpler two-group design comparing the tested and trained group with a control group. The results would have indicated that the experimental training worked, and readers of the study might try to apply the training module in other settings. Some of these programs might not include the HIV testing element because of expense or ethics (need to draw blood sample, fear of breaking confidence about the results). In these latter programs, the training module would likely fail just as in the training only group. In short, the findings from this study only generalize when all of the necessary conditions are present. The original research results might have low external validity because of the presence of the interaction. The apparent training effect, thought of as an independent or main effect, would not generalize. Rather, it seemed to hold only for the situations in which subjects received the augmenting pretest.

External validity threats always involve an interaction of the treatment with some other factor. Threats to external validity fall into three main categories, depending on the factor interacting with the treatment: setting, population, or history. In each case, the researcher must judge whether a finding holds only for the specific setting, sample of subjects, or period of time studied or applies more generally.

Setting Interactions

The **setting**, narrowly defined, includes the experimental arrangements in the study. More broadly the setting can include the whole physical and social context. Both senses of the term apply to the threat of interactions with the treatment.

Experimental Setting. The experimental setting includes all experiences of the subjects due to the experiment, whether planned or unplanned, including the pretest or other Xs (experimental manipulations). In order to keep all of the X-by-other factor interactions together under one rubric, we will treat interactions with experimental setting factors as threats to external validity.

The AIDS education study offers one example of a setting interaction threat to external validity. Another setting experience is that of a second experimental manipulation. If the study has only one manipulation, it makes no sense to consider one treatment interacting with itself. Sometimes, however, we can view a single manipulation as more than one treatment. For example, a drug intervention includes both the active ingredient and the delivery method by pill or hypodermic. As shown by the placebo research example at the beginning of this chapter, the chemical ingredients and the pill casing can have opposite effects. In the example, these two effects proved independent, and the placebo main effect fit the category of threat to experimental contrast validity. But such variables could have interacted. Although some authors would also consider such interactions as threats to experimental construct validity (Cook & Campbell, 1979), we find it more convenient to consider them as threats to external validity. That is, any setting experience that moderates or changes the effect of the principal treatment meets our definition of a threat to external validity. Some research designs intentionally include more than one intervention: The experimental group receives a series of different Xs. The presence of different treatments raises the possibility of multiple-X interactions that can also threaten external validity. For example, a treatment that has success only in the presence of another treatment will not generalize elsewhere without that accompanying treatment.

The control group plays a crucial role in interpreting the effect of multiple interventions. Suppose the treatment group has two interventions X_1 and X_2. If the control group receives neither intervention, the difference between the two groups could come from the main effect of X_1, the main effect of X_2, and/or the interaction of X_1 with X_2. Suppose the control group had one of the interventions, X_1. Now any difference at posttest between the experimental and control group cannot come from the main effect of X_1 since both groups would have received this effect. But the difference between the two groups still has two explanations: the main effect of X_2 and the interaction of X_1 with X_2. You can determine the correct explanation only by designing the experiment to include all the different combinations of Xs. To further complicate this picture, you may have to consider the order of the different Xs. Drugs X_1 and X_2 may interact when X_1 is ingested first but not when X_2 is ingested first. Controlling for and measuring the different effects of different orders of multiple Xs is discussed under the heading of within-subject designs in the next chapter on quasi experiments.

Context.   Just as a treatment may interact with another aspect of the experiment, so may it interact with the larger environment. Any study must take place in some context, whether a laboratory or a field location such as a street corner, factory, grade school, or home. Subjects will react to the treatment in terms of its surround. For example, a study that tape-records family discussions in response to different manipulations by the experimenter may get different results if the recording takes place in the family's home rather than in a university laboratory. The researcher runs the risk that the results will apply only to the study setting and not elsewhere.

Highly controlled laboratory research can appear artificial because all the cues remind the subject that he or she is in a research rather than a natural situation. As a result, lab-based research may have special problems with external validity. To the extent that laboratory conditions fail to represent the "real" world, lab-based results may not generalize to everyday life. For this reason, critics of laboratory studies have urged that social research try to achieve more **ecological validity**. A study with high ecological validity takes place in a research situation representative of the natural or "real" social environment.

A closely related concept is **mundane realism**. This term refers to the resemblance of the research setting to a natural setting. Presumably, research conducted under conditions of mundane realism will promote ecological or external validity. On the other hand, ecological validity may come at the cost of measuring subtle causal mechanics that require precise controls. Moreover, some think that the experimenter should not seek superficial mundane realism. Rather researchers should pursue **experimental realism**, that is, the arrangement of procedures such that the subjects become fully engaged in the experience. Each researcher will have to decide whether such involvement requires physical similarity to natural situations (that is, mundane realism) (Berkowitz & Donnerstein, 1982).

Identifying Setting-by-Intervention Interactions.   Weak external validity means that results from one study might not apply to other cases. In general, we prevent such wrong generalizations by discovering those settings, populations, and eras to which the findings do or do not apply. Perfect external validity would require replication of the research in all combinations of populations, places, and times. In practice, of course, no research team can carry out so many replications.

For the problem of treatment-by-experimental setting interactions, researchers can fairly easily manage such replications by adding groups or conditions to the design. The Solomon four-group design illustrates such a test for the interaction of the treatment with the pretest. Similarly, a design could include multiple groups to test for interactions involving multiple treatments.

Merely adding groups in a single study will not, however, solve the problem of intervention-by-context interactions. For such interactions, you need to replicate the study over different locations in which the theory says the cause–effect relationship should hold. Absent such replications, you must limit the generalization from a study to similar contexts.

History or Selection Interactions

A treatment can interact with the type of subjects or with the time period in which the study is conducted. A study conducted on 18-year-old, middle-class, male college students may not generalize to young children or elderly adults, to young people raised in the culture of poverty, to females, or to high school dropouts. The way researchers choose subjects for a study may also affect external validity. For example, not all male college students enroll as social science majors, and not all social science majors volunteer for social science research. If the treatment works, perhaps it does so only for the kinds of people who willingly join social research studies. The result may not hold on replication for differently selected subjects with different personal traits.

Just as a cause–effect relationship may appear in one type of subject but not others, so it may appear in one time period but not another. If the study takes place at a time when a major public event occurs, might the experimental results depend in part on the unusual external event? For example, a study of depressed mood might produce different results on the day after a popular public figure has died than after the local sport team has won a championship.

Identifying History and Selection Interactions. Researchers should not generalize beyond their specific population of subjects and period of study. To support wider generalization, researchers should replicate their studies in different populations and time periods. One way of increasing external validity without full-scale replication would be to include a variety of subjects in a single study. Theory and past research might help identify the blocking variables on which to diversify the sample. Each subgroup (for example, young males, young females, old males, old females) represents a built-in replication.

Similarly, long-term longitudinal studies allow replication over occasions or eras. Many true experiments involve brief treatments that must necessarily occur at particular times. To represent many different times, you must repeat the study in later months or years.

Fortunately, science has become a cooperative and cumulative enterprise. Often a researcher has colleagues working on the same or similar problems in other locations, at other times, or with different kinds of subjects. When different studies vary with respect to setting, sample, and time, systematic differences in the literature may emerge and point to improved theory.

SUMMARY

While true experiments have a high degree of internal validity, they may risk other validity threats. This chapter discusses threats to experimental construct validity and to external validity. Table 10–1 summarizes some of the more common threats to these validities and the methods for dealing with them.

Table 10–1 Threats to Experimental Construct and External Validity

Type	Threat	Possible Remedies
I. Experimental construct validity threats		
A. Experimental group contamination		
1. Experimenter expectancy	Observed effect is due to self-fulfilling prophecy— experimenter affects subject behavior.	Naive, "blind," standardized or "canned" experimenter, debriefing to check subject awareness of hypothesis.
2. Demand characteristics	Observed effect is due to motivated subjects reacting to their interpretation of cues about the study's meaning.	Placebo control, "blind" subject, naturalistic context, unobstrusive measures, false cover story, "faithful" subject, debriefing to check subject awareness of hypothesis.
B. Control group contamination		
1. Compensatory contamination	Observed absence of effect is due to acquisition of experimental treatment or its equivalent by control group.	"Blind" subjects, administrative adherence to no treatment control design, "satisfying" placebo control, monitoring control group's behavior outside of experiment, minimum contact between experimentals and controls.
2. Exaggerating contamination	Observed effect is due to harmful awareness of denial of experimental treatment.	"Blind" subjects, explanation of assignment procedures, promise of experimental treatment later, monitoring of reactions of controls for resentful demoralization.
II. External validity threats		
A. Setting-by-intervention interactions		
1. Experimental settings	Observed effect of X is due to its combination with some aspect of the experimental arrangements.	Identify by inclusion of multiple groups to test for interaction (e.g., with pretest, other X).
2. Context	Observed effect of X is due to its combination with some aspect of the social or physical environment.	Identify by replication in different types of settings. Increase realism of setting.
B. History-by-intervention interaction	Observed effect of X is due to its combination with some recent event or with the particular era.	Identify by replication at different times.
C. Selection-by-intervention interaction	Observed effect of X is due to its combination with some aspect of the particular subject sample.	Identify by replication in samples from different populations or by inclusion of population "blocking" variable, i.e., grouping by age or sex. Use representative subjects.

EXERCISES

Unlike the threats to internal validity discussed in the previous chapter, one cannot automatically identify all experimental construct and external validity threats from a study's design. Using Table 10–1 211   211
as a checklist, you should critically review some true experiment for each listed threat to experimental construct validity and external validity. Repeat this review for several true experiments until you can do it quickly and routinely.

KEY TERMS

Blind	External validity
Canned experimenter	Faithful subject
Compensatory contamination	Hawthorne effect
Contamination	Interaction
Cover story	Intrasession history
Debriefing	Manipulation checks
Demand characteristics	Mundane realism
Ecological validity	Naive experimenter
Evaluation apprehension	Pilot test
Exaggerating contamination	Placebo
Experimental construct validity	Setting
Experimental realism	Spontaneous remission
Experimenter expectancy	Standardization

∽ 11 ∽

Quasi Experimentation
When Multiple Groups and Random Assignment Are Not Possible

INTRODUCTION TO QUASI-EXPERIMENTAL DESIGNS
An Example of Quasi Experimentation
Quasi Experiments and True Experiments

TYPES OF QUASI EXPERIMENTS
Nonequivalent Control Group Designs
Interrupted Time Series Designs
Variations on the Time Series or Within-Subjects Design

SUMMARY

EXERCISES

KEY TERMS

INTRODUCTION TO QUASI-EXPERIMENTAL DESIGNS

An Example of Quasi Experimentation

Head Start.   The federal government launched the Head Start program with an enrollment of a half million children in the summer of 1965. By 1967, Head Start had become "the country's biggest peacetime mobilization of human resources and effort" (Brazziel, quoted in Payne, Mercer, Payne, & Davison, 1973, p. 55). This program aimed to increase the learning readiness of poor children entering the earliest school grades and became the centerpiece of the war on poverty in the 1960s.

In the mid-1960s, the Bureau of the Budget established the Planning, Programming, and Budgeting System (PPBS) to ensure the critical assessment of all federal programs (Williams & Evans, 1972, p. 252). To provide a timely, independent analysis of Head Start, the government gave a contract to Westinghouse Corporation and Ohio University in 1968. Conducted by Cicirelli and colleagues and referred to as the Westinghouse Study, this project produced the most influential early evaluation of Head Start (Westinghouse Learning Corporation & Ohio University, 1969). In his Economic Opportunity Message to Congress in early 1969, President Nixon alluded to the initial results of this study by concluding that "the long-term effect of Head Start appears to be extremely weak" (quoted by Williams & Evans, 1972, p. 255). Ever since, the debate over Head Start has raged in both the political and scientific arenas (Campbell & Erlebacher, 1970, versus Cicirelli, 1970; Kantrowitz & Wingert, 1993; Magidson, 1977, versus Bentler & Woodward, 1978; Smith & Bissell, 1970, versus Cicirelli, Evans, & Schiller, 1970).

How did a social science study provoke such a heated and lasting dispute? In part, the program became politically and economically important to many people. Another factor was the nature of quasi-experimental research design. Because of the urgency to provide an assessment, the researchers used an after-the-fact or **ex post facto design**. They had no time to assign children randomly to Head Start and non–Head Start conditions and then wait several years for results. Almost a decade later a consortium of researchers would begin to collaborate on the analysis of such longitudinal evaluations of preschool programs (Zigler & Muenchow, 1992). But in the initial studies, the researchers could only gather test data on children who had enrolled in Head Start several years before. This design, despite its careful application, permits rival explanations that have raised doubts for over two decades.

Suppose you had the job of evaluating Head Start soon after it began. You have access to thousands of current first, second, and third graders who joined Head Start when they were four years old. You must measure how much, if anything, these early Head Start students have gained. You can test these treated children and their untreated counterparts, but comparing them will prove your hardest problem. You expect all children, whether in Head Start or not, to show some gains over time through maturation. That is, normal development should produce some cognitive gains in all children. You must determine how much *more* the Head Start children gained than they would have gained without Head Start.

A simple solution to this problem would use as controls the children who did not receive Head Start. You might simply compare the posttest scores of the Head Start and non–Head Start groups of children. However, this method would certainly prove wrong for Head Start and for most other compensatory programs (that is, ones aimed at making up the deficit of one group compared to another). The Head Start children have, by definition, a disadvantage when compared to the untreated children. Head Start children started out at a lower level and would have to gain much more to reach parity on posttest.

Instead, you might use gain scores. In effect, you would compare the Head Start gains with the gains due only to natural maturation without Head Start. Although widely used, this approach assumes that the normal maturation rates of the Head Start and control children are the same in the studied period. But this assumption will almost certainly prove false in this case. Given that the Head Start and control children differ at pretest, they must have been gaining at different rates prior to pretest and might well continue at different rates. Thus the natural gains of the non–Head Start children should exceed the natural gains of the Head Start children (see Figure 11–1).

Any effect of Head Start should appear as a gain beyond that expected for children who are similar to Head Start children except that they did not receive the Head Start experience. Unfortunately, we do not know the natural maturation gain for this subgroup of disadvantaged children. The control children's gains will misestimate gains expected for disadvantaged children not receiving Head Start. They will lead us to expect too much. If Head Start has no effect and Head Start children make normal gains

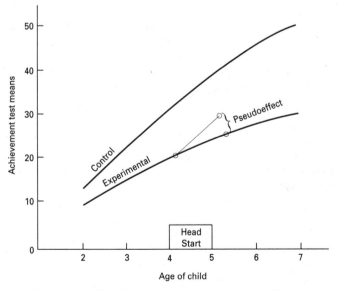

Figure 11–1 Pseudoeffect due to assuming equal growth rates. (Reprinted with permission from J. Hellmuth, ed., *Disadvantaged Child, Vol. 3: Compensatory Education: A National Debate.* New York: Brunner/Mazel, 1970), p. 198.

due to maturation, their achievement will fall short of the control children's. We call this difference the **pseudoeffect** of Head Start. As pictured in Figure 11–1, the *apparent* effect of Head Start makes treated children seem *worse* off than if they had not entered Head Start at all. If Head Start had a positive effect on children, we would not notice it unless it made up for the pseudoeffect that makes Head Start look bad. Judging whether Head Start has a negative or positive effect depends on the assumption made about the natural maturation of poor children.

    A Statistical Adjustment.   The evaluation of Head Start by Cicirelli and colleagues avoided both of these methods (comparing posttest scores or comparing change scores). The Westinghouse Study used a statistical technique to deal with the non-equivalence of the Head Start and non–Head Start groups. After matching on age, sex, race, and kindergarten attendance, they applied **analysis of covariance**. This method uses pretest data on parent's occupation, education, and per capita income to adjust the posttest scores. By these procedures, they tried to equalize the two groups that had not originally been assigned by randomization.

    Unfortunately, they may not have adjusted enough for social class (parent's occupation, education, and income) as shown in a simulation by Campbell and Erlebacher (1970). The reason has to do with one of the threats to internal validity that is most troubling in quasi experimentation—**regression toward the mean**. Extreme scores on unreliable measures tend to move toward the mean on subsequent tests. Campbell and Erlebacher said that Head Start children came from an entirely different population from that of the control group children. The Head Start test scores will thus move toward a different mean than that of the control group children. The analysis of covariance technique used in the Westinghouse Study did not take into account the unreliability of the measures. Later studies using newer techniques for handling unreliable measures have disagreed on whether Head Start had a significant effect (Bentler & Woodward, 1978; Magidson, 1977).

    The debates about adjusting for nonequivalence and the value of Head Start go beyond the scope of this text (see McKey et al., 1985, for a review of hundreds of Head Start studies). You should remember that the failure to assign subjects randomly to treatment and control conditions makes the interpretation of findings more difficult and can cause lengthy disputes about the results. This chapter will explore the major threats to the internal validity of the most common quasi-experimental designs.

Quasi Experiments and True Experiments

    Random Assignment to Groups.   Quasi experiments differ from true experiments by the absence of random assignment of subjects to different conditions. Quasi experiments have in common with true experiments that some subjects receive an intervention and provide data likely to reflect its impact.

    Quasi experiments appear similar to true experiments when diagrammed. For example, in the diagram that follows, a true experiment appears as two groups composed by random assignment of subjects (*R*). Each group had measures or tests at two times (*O*), and the groups differed by the intervention (*X*).

$$
R \quad
\begin{array}{ccc}
O & X & O \\
O & & O
\end{array}
$$

The quasi-experimental version follows. Again two groups, each with measures before and after, apparently differ only in their experience of the intervention. The absence of random assignment makes a crucial difference. Without it, we doubt the equivalence of the groups before the *X*.

$$
\begin{array}{ccc}
O & X & O \\
O & & O
\end{array}
$$

Given the importance of random assignment, why don't all studies use true experimental designs? First, not every researcher finds it feasible to conduct a true experiment. The evaluation of Head Start illustrates this problem. Because of political urgency, the Head Start evaluators could not wait several years to retest the students. The researchers had to use an ex post facto design to compare groups created after the treatment.

Other reasons besides haste sometimes make true experiments difficult or impossible. Researchers may want to study variables that they cannot anticipate (earthquakes) or manipulate (economic cycles). Sometimes, politics prevents the manipulation of the independent variable. For example, we can imagine court-ordered school desegregation staged with half of the school districts randomly desegregated in the first year for comparison with the remaining half, to be desegregated later. However, the conflict between the forces opposed to each other on this emotional issue would likely block such a plan. In sum, many constructs of interest to social scientists prove unsuitable for true experimentation. Their uncontrolled occurrence does not permit random assignment of subjects.

A second hindrance to true experimentation comes from ethical standards. Suppose you want to know the effects of trauma—either psychological (such as terror) or biological (such as starvation). You may not inflict terror or severe starvation on human beings. As a result, the study of these stresses can only proceed with people not randomly assigned (disaster victims). Moreover, it is also unethical knowingly to allow harm to continue. Thus you may not deny a treatment to someone who has a disease in order to study the course of the disease.

Advantages and Disadvantages.   For ethical and practical reasons, true experiments could proceed for certain topics only by using stand-in variables (as in simulation studies). For example, we cannot ethically assign humans randomly to conditions of inmates or guards in real prisons. However, we might role-play some of the conditions of a prison for a short time with volunteers. If simulations of danger really produce duress or threat, they must, for ethical reasons, promptly stop. Zimbardo, Haney, Banks, and Jaffe (1975) reported that they had to end a mock prison study after one week instead of the planned two weeks because the experience became too real. To the extent that such simulations produce no harm, they may not reflect the construct of interest. Thus quasi experiments may have the advantage of experimental construct validity in tapping real situations.

On the other hand, nothing guarantees that quasi experiments will prove superior to true experiments. Both risk some of the same threats. If the dependent measure has poor reliability or badly represents the construct of interest, neither design will give useful results. If the independent variable has a transparent or intrusive operationalization, both types of study raise doubts about experimental construct validity. Both designs risk the possibility that observed differences between the experimental and control subjects arise from chance, a threat checked by inferential statistics.

Although quasi experiments have some advantages over and share some of the same potential problems with true experiments, they face a set of threats to internal validity that do not trouble true experiments. These threats fall into two clusters called time and group.

Time threats include history, maturation, instrumentation, and pretest reactivity. In these threats, something changes over time in the behavior of the subjects or in the measuring process. Because the comparison group feature of true experiments protects against them, time threats mainly concern single-group quasi experiments such as *interrupted time series*. We will treat each time threat in a later section and then review an example of an interrupted time series study.

The group threats to internal validity include selection, regression toward the mean, and interactions of selection with time threats such as maturation. These threats concern designs in which subject assignment fails to ensure group equivalence. To multigroup studies without random assignment we give the label *nonequivalent control group designs*. The following section discusses each of these threats briefly and presents an example of the nonequivalent control group design.

TYPES OF QUASI EXPERIMENTS

Nonequivalent Control Group Designs

Threats.   In true experiments, we expect random assignment to ensure the equivalence of the groups. However, even matching and random assignment do not guarantee equivalence. An example of this failure comes from a study of college students working as group leaders with mental hospital patients (Rappaport, Chinsky, & Cowen, 1971). The study included 40 groups, each with 8 patients. Thirty-two of these groups were randomly assigned to the experimental (*E*) condition and received group counseling by college student volunteers. The remaining 8 groups did not actually meet but served as controls (*C*).

Time did not permit matching on pretest measures of the dependent variables. Instead, the researchers tried to ensure the similarity of the *E* and *C* groups before random assignment by matching patients on five variables that tend to relate to the outcome variables: age, length of hospitalization, education level, marital status, and diagnosis of paranoia. This matching should have yielded 40 groups that were nearly equal before the group treatment on cognitive and behavioral performance. The random assignment of groups to E and C conditions should have eliminated any remaining group differences on pretest performance levels, including any selection bias from the researchers.

After the data came in, the researchers checked their assumption of E and C group equivalence on pretest performance. The results shocked the investigators, who discovered that on 15 of the 16 pretest performance measures, the C groups looked better than the E groups and that 6 of these differences reached statistical significance. In the words of the researchers,

> The failure to have achieved a satisfactory pretest matching of Es and Cs was both perplexing and embarrassing. It was damaging to the basic design of the study and necessitated a series of improvisations, none initially anticipated, and each less than fully satisfactory. Considerable thought and effort was [sic] invested in the matching procedure beforehand and the method selected seemed defensible not only at the time, but even in retrospect. Unfortunately the facts of the situation are otherwise. Despite considerable effort, it is difficult even after the fact, to identify sources of systematic error that could account for the pretest differences between Es and Cs. However unsatisfactory or unenlightening it may be to say so, the authors consider it likely that the pretest matching breakdown was essentially a chance phenomenon. Whatever the explanation, it is clear that this breakdown had serious, negative implications for all subsequent data analyses. (Rappaport et al., pp. 89–90)

This chance failure of random assignment to equalize the conditions converted a true experiment into a **nonequivalent control group design** for purposes of analysis. The simplest, two-group nonequivalent control group pretest–posttest design has the following diagram:

$$O \ X \ O$$
$$O \quad \ O$$

If the two groups differ at pretest, several rival explanations could explain any posttest difference. One such threat to internal validity holds that the posttest difference simply reflects original differences. We call this threat **selection**. That is, the researchers selected different kinds of subjects, intentionally or unintentionally, into the different groups. This difference, rather than the treatment, may account for later differences.

Regression toward the mean, another rival explanation, arises when groups are composed by assigning subjects by their extremely high or low pretest scores. For example, suppose we test a group of students for math anxiety and assign the students with high scores to a course in relaxation, with the low-anxiety students serving as untreated controls. If the relaxation students show a greater decrease in anxiety than the control students, this "improvement" may stem from either the relaxation course or regression toward the mean.

Regression toward the mean involves an automatic tendency of extreme scores to move toward the population mean on retest. The less reliable the measure, the more the retest will shift. A test score consists of the true score plus some error. As the random error portion of a score becomes larger compared to the true score, the test will have less reliability. This random error can cause the same person to get different scores on two attempts on the same unreliable test. A high score on a test may reflect both a high true score and some lucky random errors. On retest, that person should get the same high true score but will not likely get the same lucky random errors. Thus the retest score will tend to decrease, on the average, for people scoring above the mean the first time. For the same reason, people who scored low the first time will enjoy, on the average, better luck and higher scores on the retest.

Regression can make good programs look less effective or make harmless programs look harmful. The Head Start study with which this chapter began makes this point. Instead of pretesting and sorting one sample into highs and lows, the Westinghouse Study compared children from two different populations (higher income, no Head Start versus lower income, given Head Start). These two samples began with different levels of learning readiness. On later tests, each group should regress toward its respective mean. The method used for adjusting their initial differences may not have worked with unreliable data. Thus regression toward the mean may have made Head Start look worse than it was because of failure to control fully for regression toward different means.

Finally, initial group differences can interact with time-related changes such as maturation, a threat called the **selection-by-time interaction**. Suppose a fifth-grade teacher tries a new way of teaching spelling and measures the average number of new words that the class learned (change from beginning of year to end of year). The principal decides to compare these results with the results obtained in the fourth-grade class taught by another teacher, who used a different method of spelling instruction. If the fifth-graders learned more words than the fourth-graders, should we credit the fifth-grade teacher's new spelling approach? The rival hypothesis remains that the fifth graders had more mature learning skills than fourth graders and would have done better even without the new technique. Thus the nonequivalence of these two classes became confused with the treatment and, in this case, makes the intervention look successful. An opposite situation arose in the case of the Head Start evaluation. The higher income, non–Head Start control students may have had a higher cognitive development rate because of their home and school experiences. In contrast, the Head Start children may have had a slower cognitive development rate. Head Start would have had to make a significant impact to overcome this maturational rate difference before it could seem to provide any benefits. In this case, maturational nonequivalence worked against the Head Start intervention.

Casa Blanca Nonequivalent Control Group Study. When none of the group threats of selection, regression, and selection-by-time threat interactions seems plausible, a nonequivalent control group design can yield persuasive results. Singer, Gerard, and Redfearn (1975) used such a design as part of their study of school desegregation. They tested the prediction that disadvantaged minority children would make greater educational progress in an integrated school. Other effects of busing may appear, including beneficial effects on the racial attitudes of whites (Cook, 1985) and on public opinion toward schools (Raffel, 1985), but the present study did not address such issues.

In Riverside, California, the school board ordered the desegregation of minority schools beginning in the 1966–1967 school year. A true experiment would have compared two randomly assigned groups of students—one group to integrate and the other group to remain for a time in their unintegrated schools. However, the researchers could not employ a true experiment in this case. The original plan aimed to bus 712 minority grade school students out of three segregated schools in the fall of 1966. It so happened that half of the students of one of these schools (Casa Blanca School) could not keep to this schedule but had to wait until the following year. Thus circumstances permitted a natural experiment involving the two phases of busing of Casa Blanca children. This Casa Blanca experiment did not qualify as a true experiment because the two groups were not randomly assigned. On the other hand, the two "waves" of Casa Blanca students seemed reasonably similar in the 1965–1966 period before busing began. The two groups did not differ on IQ tests or grades. The children had similar popularity (peer sociometric ratings), socioeconomic background, and education of the heads of their households. However, on standardized achievement tests collected in 1965–1966, the group desegregated in the fall of 1967 did score significantly higher than the group desegregated in the fall of 1966.

The researchers measured the learning of the children with state achievement tests. They standardized students' scores, that is, expressed them relative to other students within each grade level. The reading scores for the two Casa Blanca groups appear in Table 11–1. The diagram of this design for the pretest year of 1965–1966 and the two following years appears in Table 11–2, with X indicating the beginning of busing from Casa Blanca to an integrated school.

The two groups did not differ significantly with respect to changes in reading ability. In 1966–1967, both the experimental (desegregated in 1966–1967) and the control (not desegregated until 1967) groups showed *decreases* in reading achievement. However, a delayed effect of desegregation might not reveal itself until later. This delay hypothesis found no support. The experimental group did not gain significantly more than the control group in 1967–1968, and neither regained the positions they enjoyed before busing. The authors concluded that "as is clearly evident, there was no apparent short-term effect of desegregation" (Singer et al., 1975, p. 78).

Might the results derive from some uncontrolled aspect of this quasi-experimental design? The 1967 desegregation group controlled for time threats. If maturation or

Table 11–1 Reading Achievement for Two Groups of Mexican American Students Desegregated from Casa Blanca School*

Group	Year Desegregated	1965–66	1966–67	1967–68
Experimental	1966	92.8 (113)	90.3 (77)	91.2 (75)
Control	1967	97.4 (107)	94.6 (105)	95.2 (111)

Numbers in parentheses are the sample sizes on which the mean reading achievement scores are based.
*From Table 4.1 (p. 78) of Singer, Gerard, and Redfearn (1975).

Table 11–2 Casa Blanca School Research Design

	1965–66		1966–67		1967–68
Experimental	O	X	O		O
Control	O		O	X	O

outside events affected the experimental group, they should also have appeared in the control group. Absent random assignment, however, the group threats offer a more likely challenge to this study. Luckily, the near equivalence of the groups on the pretests of 1965–1966 makes the selection threat less plausible. The regression threat also seems implausible. The researchers did not use pretests to select the two groups for extremely high versus low scores. Moreover, the experimental group had slightly lower pretest scores and should have been more likely to regress upward. Thus, if regression operated, it should have favored the treated group. Finally, the threat of an interaction of selection with, for example, maturation seems unlikely because the two groups had the same average age and should not mature at different rates. Perhaps the slight difference in pretest scores between the two groups reflected a lower maturation rate for the experimentals. This selection-by-maturation rival, although possible, seems rather doubtful and complex.

A different kind of threat—mortality—could occur in this case. The experimental group had a substantial dropout rate. We would expect attrition in this type of study. About one in four Southern California families changes residence every year. Perhaps the number or type of dropouts from one group differed from the dropouts of the other group. In fact, more high-status minority children tended to move away. The authors judged that this movement had little effect on the outcome of the study. Moreover, the researchers repeated the analyses with just the students who took all the tests and found no differences. Again, one could imagine a very complex interaction combining the attrition and the pretest differences of the experimental subjects that could have disguised a true positive effect of busing. However, such a complex argument remains less persuasive than the simpler explanation of the results—that busing simply had little or no effect in this case.

In conclusion, this particular nonequivalent control group study escaped threats such as selection and regression. On the other hand, we must not generalize the results too far. The findings apply only to Mexican Americans, in one southern California school system, and with one form of busing (one-way busing). Integration of other minorities, in other school systems, in other parts of the country, and using other methods (for example, two-way busing) might yield different results. Moreover, the sample and design of the study might have influenced the outcome. A review of the literature on desegregation and achievement for African Americans has suggested that beneficial effects of busing are more likely to appear under two conditions: (1) for students who begin in desegregated classes as opposed to students with one or two years in segregated classes before being desegregated, and (2) with random assignment of experimental and control groups (Crain & Mahard, 1983). For an extended debate about the effects of school integration by busing, see Armor (1972), Miller (1980), and Pettigrew, Useem, Normand, and Smith (1973).

Interrupted Time Series Designs

Threats. In time series designs that use one group, community, or subject, the group threats of selection and selection-by-time interaction cannot apply because we do not compare different groups. Regression could threaten single-group designs if the group is selected for extreme scores on some test. However, time-series designs usually risk one or more of the four time threats: history, maturation, measurement decay, and test reactivity.

History refers to events that coincide with the intervention and account for the observed change over time. **Maturation** refers to normal development in the subjects. **Measurement decay** involves changes in the measurement process over time. **Test reactivity** occurs when subjects respond to a pretest. How can we check these threats or reduce them in a single-group design? In a control group study, the control group reveals any maturation, history, or other time-related changes that might confound the treatment effect. In single-group designs, the studied group serves as its own control. We can compare changes in earlier pairs of observations with the pair of observations just before and just after the experimental manipulation. Such pretest changes provide a baseline by which to judge the effect of the intervention. Figure 11–2 shows how pretests serve as surrogate (substitute) controls. The first two pretests should reflect such influences as maturation or test reactivity that might also operate between the measures before and after the manipulation. We would expect the change from just before to just after the treatment to exceed the change between pairs of earlier pretests. Otherwise, we doubt that the intervention added anything over and above time effects.

Interrupted Time Series Designs. The single-group, **interrupted time series design** employs multiple measures before and after the experimental intervention (*X*). In this regard, it differs from the single-group preexperiment that has only one pretest and one posttest. Users of the interrupted time series design assume that the time threats such as history or maturation appear as regular changes in the measures prior to the intervention. This assumption seems plausible for some time threats but less so for others. Test reactivity, maturation, and regression toward the mean (the latter from the group threats cluster) should all reveal themselves in the early tests. Suppose we witness a greater jump in scores from just before to just after *X* than between the first two pretests. To argue that this greater jump in scores came from test reactivity requires a rather complicated explanation involving some delay in the test reactivity effect. In the absence of evidence for such a delayed test reaction, the test reactivity threat appears unfounded. Similarly, to argue that the greater jump came from maturation requires us to believe that the maturation rate suddenly spurted or slowed just at the time *X* was administered. Again, this explanation assumes a rather elaborate coincidence and requires additional evidence. The same reasoning applies to the threat of regression to-

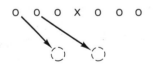

O   O   O   X   O   O   O

Figure 11–2   Interrupted time series—pretests as surrogate controls in single-group designs.

ward the mean. The interrupted time series design controls for each of these threats by measuring a baseline of change before the X is administered. Of course, you could handle each of these threats in other ways. You could apply highly reliable, unobtrusive measures to subjects known not to be undergoing significant developmental changes.

The two remaining time threats, history and measurement decay, pose generally more serious threats to the interrupted time series designs. In contrast to the other time threats, history and measurement decay effects tend to include irregular, unpredictable shifts in addition to any regular, foreseeable changes. Irregular changes can confound experimental interventions with which they coincide. History includes effects of environmental change other than the intervention. For example, suppose you were evaluating a new safe driving media campaign by measuring decreased deaths from auto accidents. You would have a problem judging your findings if, at the same time, driving decreased because of higher gas prices. Instrumental decay includes apparent changes in the target variable due to changes in the measurement procedures rather than in the phenomenon itself. For example, suppose a government job training program (X) aimed at lowering unemployment rates coincides with a change in the definition of unemployment used by the Department of Labor. How will you know whether your program worked or the new definition produced the outcome?

Time series designs (those with observations at many time points) have the special power to separate regular or repeating variation from the irregular variation that might come from the intervention. Regular patterns include **trends** and **cycles**, which are repeating effects of one or more maturational, historical, or other processes. Trends consist of persistent increases or decreases commonly found in long-term processes such as population growth or economic development. For example, a variable such as annual car accidents depends in part on the number of people who can afford to drive cars, a number likely to rise with an ever-growing population. A cyclic pattern, in contrast, appears as alternating rises and falls. Variables associated with seasons or business patterns often move in cycles (for example, monthly counts of people employed in agriculture rising in the summer and falling in the winter). As illustrated in Figure 11–3, linear trends (1), curvilinear trends (2), cycles (3), and combinations of trends and cycles (4) can be detected with sufficient observations. These four lines show equal decreases from one time point before to one time point after the intervention (X). We could interpret each as showing a downward impact of X except that each more likely continues a pattern established before the intervention. We can project these patterns past the intervention to see whether the intervention X adds any effect beyond the trend and cycles.

Figure 11–4 shows two time series in which there appear to be effects of the intervention X along with the linear trend (line 1) or cycle (line 2). The dotted lines show the post-X pattern expected from the pre-X trend or cycle in the absence of X. As can be seen, these expected lines differ noticeably from the observed (solid) lines.

Researchers who work with trends or cycles often remove the regular changes from their data in order to see the irregular changes that might come from their interventions. For example, instead of analyzing annual death counts, you might study annual death rates (that is, deaths per 100,000 population). This adjustment allows a researcher to detect a decrease in the death rate (for example, because of a public health

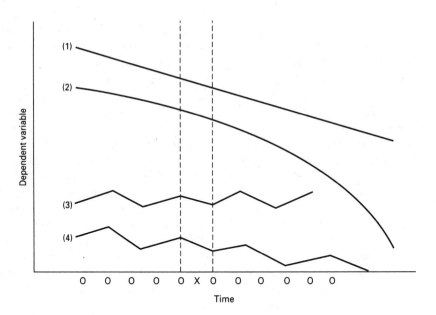

Figure 11–3 Trends and cycles.

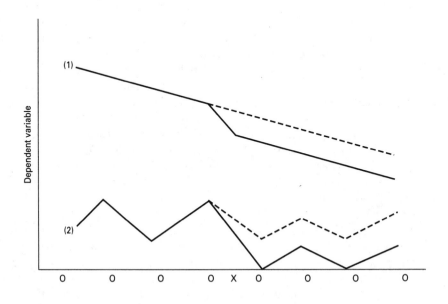

Figure 11–4 Intervention effects in trend and cyclic patterns.

education campaign) otherwise concealed by an increase in the death count stemming from an increase in population. Other techniques that **detrend** and **deseasonalize** (remove seasonal cycles from) time series go beyond the scope of this chapter. However, these techniques have in common the assumption that factors causing the trend or cycle continue over the period of interest.

Once the effects of regular trends and cycles are taken into account or removed, the effect(s) of the intervention come into sharper focus. Figure 11–5 shows several different kinds of effects that interventions can have on the outcome variable. The pretest baselines appear as straight, flat lines to emphasize that upward or downward trend and cyclic waves have been removed. The multiple pretests serve the purpose of assessing and removing the regular changes due to continuing processes.

Outcomes of interrupted time series can take different shapes as shown in Figure 11–5: (1) a simple step change; (2) a permanent change in slope; (3) a delayed step change; (4) a step change followed by a return to the former baseline level; and (5) an increase followed by a larger step decrease. This variety of possible effects emphasizes the importance of multiple post-X measurements. The only plausible counterexplanation of the observed changes that follow X is that some irregular, one-time change other than X also occurred. Although such a coincidental, unique event may seem unlikely, this design cannot entirely rule it out.

Both history and measurement decay can produce such irregular coincidental changes. Consider an evaluation of a community police department's effort to prevent rapes. Perhaps several teams of police officers change assignments from other details to work full time investigating rapes or carrying out a community outreach campaign. The dependent variable for this evaluation might consist of the number of crimes of rape

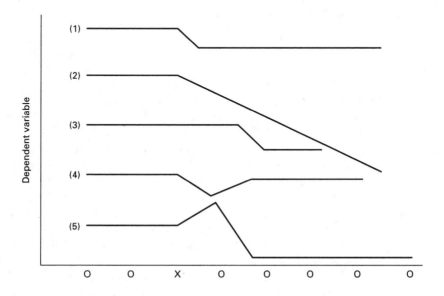

Figure 11–5   Possible intervention effects in time series.

brought to trial each month starting 12 months before the new policy began. After removing regular trend and seasonal changes, suppose pattern 1 of Figure 11–5 appears. That is, the number of rapes going to trial sharply decreases and levels off at a new rate. This pattern could provide evidence that the program to decrease rapes is working.

On the other hand, you must consider possible history or measurement rival explanations. Perhaps as a result of the public concern that led the police department to make its change, the city council also voted to improve lighting in high-crime areas of the city. Perhaps the new lighting accounted for the decrease in rape arrests and trials—an example of a history threat. Alternatively, a closer inspection of the district attorney's policies may reveal a change in the outcome measure. The same outcry against rape may have persuaded the elected DA to increase the conviction rate in rape cases. To get a higher rate of convictions, perhaps the DA now brings to trial only the cases most likely to yield convictions. The remaining cases may settle by plea bargaining to lesser assault charges. Thus the measure of rape may shift in a way that explains the observed change even if the actual rate of rape remained the same.

History and measurement effects can also work against the intervention. Suppose, in our example, the DA had decided to bring more rape cases to trial rather than to settle them through plea bargaining. As a result rape would seem to increase (as measured by rape trials) as a result of the crackdown. Actually, such an increase might communicate that rape is no longer tolerated in the community and serve as a useful step to a long-term lowering of the rape rate (as in line 5 of Figure 11–5).

In summary, irregular history or measurement changes that coincide with interventions will pose the most difficulty for interrupted time series designs. In the absence of a control group, only careful attention to the surrounding events and measurement methods of the study can identify such threats.

Boston White Flight: An Interrupted Time Series Design.   Busing students to integrate schools initiated the "white flight" controversy. James Coleman led the project resulting in the influential report *Equality of Educational Opportunity* (Coleman et al., 1966; Hunt, 1985, chapter 2). This study found learning gains for minority children who studied in integrated schools. Proponents of busing often cite this report as evidence for their view. In 1975, Coleman announced his findings on the extended effects of school desegregation. He concluded that desegregation in large central cities increased the loss of white students from the public schools of those cities. This finding became a prominent feature in antibusing legal actions. Coleman's findings suggest that busing, whether good for minority children or not in the short run, defeats itself because white flight will make integration difficult or impossible in the long run. The remaining whites cannot provide an integrated experience for the minority students, who will find themselves in the majority. This white flight thesis and its policy implications have triggered extensive research and rebuttal (see Pettigrew & Green, 1976, versus Coleman, 1976).

Researchers have used interrupted time series methods to test the white flight thesis. Christine Rossell (1975–1976) concluded from her analysis that little if any white flight results from desegregation. In a later critique, Diane Ravitch (1978) took exception to Rossell's method of measuring white flight. Ravitch concluded that at least in the case of Boston, desegregation increased white flight.

Rossell measured white flight as the change in percentage of white enrollment, using the total number of students as the denominator:

$$\frac{\text{white enrollment last year}}{\text{total enrollment last year}} - \frac{\text{white enrollment this year}}{\text{total enrollment this year}}$$

Using Rossell's method, if whites were 80 percent of the enrollment in 1972 and 75 percent in 1973, this would represent a change of 5 percent. Ravitch argued that this method

will show small declines even in the face of large absolute movements. Consider, for example, a school district with 250,000 pupils, 200,000 whites (80% of the total) and 50,000 blacks (20% of the total). If 40,000 white pupils were to leave the district in a single year, it would then have 160,000 whites (76.2% of the total) and 50,000 blacks (23.8% of the total). Rossell would say that the change in percentage white was –3.8% that is, a drop of 3.8 percentage points. *But what has actually happened is that 20% of the white pupils have left the district* (since 40,000 is 20% of 200,000). (Ravitch 1978, p. 140; italics in original)

Ravitch proposed a different measure, which considers absolute change in white enrollment and uses white enrollment as the denominator:

$$\frac{(\text{white enrollment last year} - \text{white enrollment this year})}{\text{white enrollment last year}}$$

We can see how the interrupted time series method works for white enrollment changes comparing the Rossell and the Ravitch methods for the city of Boston. Figure 11–6 presents the change in white enrollment from year to year before and after the two phases of Boston's busing program. The two lines reflect Rossell's measure (solid line = percentage of total) and Ravitch's measure (dashed line = percentage of the previous year's white enrollment).

Both measures of white flight show a pattern of white flight *before* busing, and both reach their peaks during the first two years of busing in 1974 and 1975. White enrollment declined from 69,400 in 1964 to 57,358 in 1972 (the year before the filing of the suit to bus) to 36,243 in 1975 (the second year of busing). Despite using the same data, the Ravitch method reveals much more white flight than the Rossell measure.

Another approach to this question uses a variant of the interrupted time series design. Armor (1980) estimated the portions of white flight that came from two different sources. He separated nonbusing factors (accounting for white flight before and continuing after busing) from the part that began with busing. Using the prebusing white flight data, he projected the loss of white enrollment assuming no busing. He then compared this projection with the actual white enrollment loss (see Figure 11–7).

Armor divided the total loss of about 28,000 white Boston students from 1971 to 1977 into 16,000 due to busing and 12,000 due to nonbusing factors. He also found that minority enrollment stopped growing in 1975, contrary to projections, and suggests that this may represent a case of "black flight" (Armor, 1980, p. 205).

These studies by Rossell, Ravitch, and Armor illustrate several points about interrupted time series analysis. First, the method can separate regular preintervention patterns of change from postintervention patterns. For example, the premeasures show that prebusing white flight existed at high levels. The postmeasures show that the rate of white flight rose from the baseline level with the advent of busing. Whether this difference in white flight rate appears significant depends on the measure used. Each of these analyses risks the threat of some irregular, unprojected cause of white flight coinciding with the 1974–1975 beginning of busing. It remains to be seen whether anyone can suggest a nonbusing threat, for example, a historical event or change in record keeping, that could plausibly account for the observed increases in white flight.

Absent plausible rivals to the white flight hypothesis, the debate about the impact of desegregation on white enrollment no longer focuses on whether whites leave the school system. Rather, the concern has shifted to the timing and magnitude of

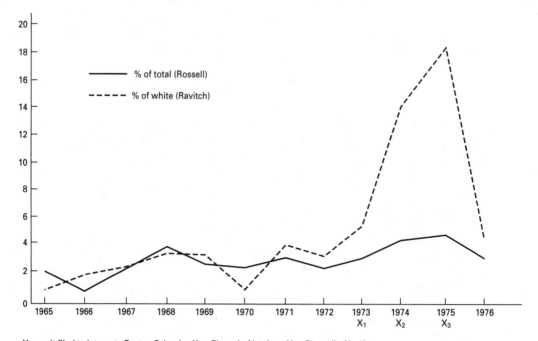

X_1 = suit filed to integrate Boston Schools; X_2 = Phase I of busing; X_3 = Phase II of busing.

Figure 11–6   "White Flight" in Boston: Two measures from 1965 to 1976. (Based on Table V, p. 143 of Ravitch, 1978. Reprinted with permission of the author from *The Public Interest, 51* (Spring, 1978), 143. Copyright © 1978 by National Affairs, Inc.)

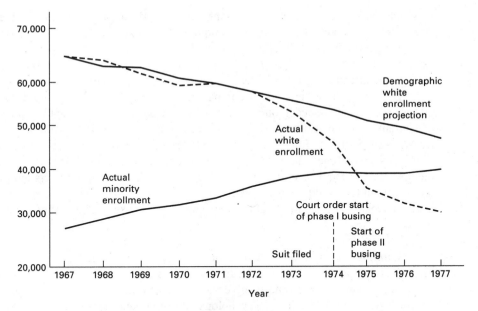

Figure 10–7   Projected and actual enrollment for Boston. (From D.J. Armor, White flight and the future of school desegregation, in W. G. Stephan & J. R. Feagin, eds., *Schools Desegregation: Past, Present, and Future*. New York: Plenum Press, 1980).

the flight and its response to particular aspects of the desegregation procedure (Welch, 1987; F.D. Wilson, 1985, 1987).

Variations on the Time Series or Within-Subjects Design

The interrupted time series design can take a very simple form, consisting of one group, one intervention, and several measures. Several variants of this basic design can help protect against the main threats to its validity—irregular coincidental changes, especially those of history or measurement.

Multiple Groups.   One variation simply adds one or more comparison groups:

00000 X 00000
00000   00000

The comparison group serves the same function as in the nonequivalent control group design. It controls for coincidental events such as history threats. If an apparent effect of *X* appeared in the treated series but not in the control series, the threat of history or other time-related explanations recedes. In order to cast doubt on the internal validity of this design, one would have to argue that the coincidence that caused the effect had two properties. First, the event could not have appeared in the measures prior to *X*, that is, it was irregular. Second, the event could not have appeared in the control community or group, that is, it was unique to its locality or subjects. Although such local, irregular events could appear, we might well ask for supporting evidence of their existence. In terms of internal validity, this combination of interrupted time series and nonequivalent control group elements rivals the true experiment.

Extending the logic of such comparison group time series, we could gather several treated and untreated groups in order to "average" out any irregular, local factors that might occur in just one group. Just such multigroup analyses were performed by Rossell (1975–1976), Ravitch (1978), and Armor (1980) in their analyses of white flight. They combined data from several desegregated school districts and compared them with those from several undesegregated school districts. Any effects unique to just one community should "wash" out in the average of many similar communities over different years. The result should reveal any "pure" busing effect after canceling out random factors.

Multiple Interventions.   Up to now, we have considered one or more groups, each receiving just one intervention. In some kinds of studies, we can give the same intervention more than one time or give more than one kind of intervention to the same group. In experimental clinical psychology, the individual rather than the group often serves as the unit of analysis. The *n* = 1 or **single-subject design** represents a special case of time series research using **multiple-intervention design** to control the time threats to internal validity. Two of the more common *n* = 1 designs are the reversal or ***ABAB* design** and the **multiple-baseline design**.

In the *ABAB* design, the manipulation (*B*) occurs twice:

$$O\ O\ O\ X\ O\ O\ O\ X\ O\ O$$
$$A\ B\quad\ \ A\ B$$

Before each intervention (*B*), the baseline condition of no treatment (*A*) is measured. If the treatment has an effect, the evidence of the effect should appear after the first intervention. The effect should decrease or disappear when the treatment is withdrawn and appear again when the treatment occurs again. The first appearance of the effect might come from a coincidental event (for example, the subject receiving some treatment elsewhere, unknown to the researchers). But the disappearance and reappearance of the effect requires a very unlikely and complex set of coincidences.

Although popular in clinical research, the *ABAB* or reversal design (Kazdin, 1978) can also serve in group- and community-level research. For example, Jason, Zolik, and Matese (1979) used a reversal design in a study of community behavior that may interest public health workers, city managers, and policy makers. They studied the effects of two interventions to encourage urban dog owners to pick up after their pets as a way of controlling animal-carried germs and parasites. They used signs (intervention *B*) and prompting (intervention *C*). Their design fit an *ABCAC* pattern: baseline, signs, prompting, baseline, and prompting. They reported that signs had little effect but that prompting led to an increase in owners picking up after their dogs. This picking-up behavior decreased somewhat on reversal (no prompting) and increased when prompting resumed.

The second most common $n = 1$ design is the multiple-baseline design (Kazdin, 1978). This design uses different interventions aimed at different outcomes. This design requires multiple measures—at least one for each type of behavior to be studied. The first intervention (X_1) aims at one behavior. Only that targeted behavior should respond significantly, and the other behavior(s) should remain unchanged. The second intervention (X_2) aims at the second behavior and should have little effect on the first behavior. The following diagram illustrates a simple multiple-baseline design:

$$0\ 0\ 0\ X_1\ 0\ 0\ X_2\ 0\ 0\ 0$$

Each measuring point (0) includes at least two measures. Measure 1 should respond to X_1 immediately after its introduction. Measure 2 should remain unaffected until after X_2 occurs. Rival explanations of such effects must resort to complex coincidences. An example of multiple-baseline research comes from mental health work. The interventions X_1 and X_2 may be operant conditioning procedures aimed at shaping different aspects of behavior. Such targets might include improving the ability of a regressed psychotic patient first to dress him- or herself (X_1) and then to talk appropriately (X_2). Measures of both appropriate dressing and talking would be taken at each observation (for example, the nurse's daily ratings). Dressing should improve after X_1, but talking should improve only after X_2. The multiple-baseline design could serve at the community level as well. For example, you could use this method to assess traffic congestion campaigns targeted first at bus ridership (X_1) and then at car pooling (X_2).

Within-Subjects Designs.   All time-series designs are within-subjects designs because they measure changes within subjects or groups of subjects. Multiple intervention within-subjects designs fall in two major categories: complete and incomplete. In **complete within-subjects designs**, each subject receives all possible orders of the various treatments, sometimes several times. Complete designs have two requirements. First, the researchers must have few interventions or be able to apply them quickly if they are numerous (for example, tests of reaction times to different pitches of sound). Second, the impact of each intervention on the subject must quickly evaporate with little lingering effect. Thus complete designs appear commonly in studies of perceptual, physiological, or cognitive processes with many stimuli applied quickly and in all orders to each subject.

Incomplete within-subjects designs may serve when the researcher can give only one stimulus or stimulus sequence to each subject. Thus one subject may experience three conditions in the order X_1, X_2, X_3. The apparent effect of X_3 may come in part from the preceding exposure to X_1 and X_2. As a result, we cannot separate the true effect of any stimulus from the order of presentation of all the stimuli felt by this one subject. For example, the prior experience of visual (X_1) and tactile (X_2) stimuli may affect reaction time to noise (X_3). To control order effects in such an incomplete design, we must use more than one subject so that the group of subjects taken as a whole experiences all possible orders of the stimuli. By this method, we can pit the effect of X_3 following X_1 and X_2 in some subjects against the effect of X_3 occurring first or second in other subjects. Order effects will concern us most in studies of treatments that produce lingering effects (for example, teaching methods that can change the impact of later manipulations). Such interventions may produce exhaustion, heightened sensitivity, practice effects, or other results that could make the last treatment look more or less effective than it would have if it had come earlier. We call this effort to produce all possible orders of Xs over all subjects taken as a whole **counter-balancing**.

SUMMARY

Quasi-experimental designs either have no comparison group or fail to compose experimental and control groups by random assignment. Although less internally valid than true experiments, quasi experiments sometimes offer the only feasible or ethical way to study certain questions.

Nonequivalent control group quasi experiments have two or more groups that cannot be assumed to be equal on all relevant characteristics. Matching (composing groups by exchanging members until the groups are equal on measured characteristics) does not assure equivalence on unmeasured characteristics. In such cases of nonequivalence, the group threats to internal validity raise special concern: selection, regression toward the mean, and selection-by-time interactions. Methods exist for the statistical adjustment of nonequivalence, but they remain controversial (for example, the Head Start debate).

Interrupted time series quasi experiments usually have just one group. However, they employ many observations before and after the treatment to control for the time threats to internal validity: history, maturation, instrumentation, pretest reactivity, and, sometimes, regression toward the mean. These numerous observations over time help distinguish regular and recurring change (such as trend and cycle) from the effects of the intervention. Unfortunately, single-group time series with a single intervention remain vulnerable to irregular events (for example, history or instrumentation) that coincide with the intervention. Variations of time series designs can control for such irregular threats with comparison groups or multiple interventions (*ABAB* or multiple-base-line designs).

EXERCISES

Threats to internal validity pose special problems for quasi experiments. Find an example of a quasi-experimental study and categorize it as a nonequivalent control group or an interrupted time series design. Then check its vulnerability to the most likely threats to internal validity. Repeat this exercise for a study using another type of quasi-experimental design. Continue until you can quickly and routinely scan any experiment for the common group and time threats to internal validity.

KEY TERMS

ABAB design
Analysis of covariance
Complete within-subjects design
Counter-balancing
Cycles
Deseasonalize
Detrend
Ex post facto design
History
Incomplete within-subjects design
Interrupted time series design

Maturation
Measurement decay
Multiple-baseline design
Multiple-intervention design
Nonequivalent control group design
Pseudoeffect
Regression toward the mean
Selection
Selection-by-time interaction
Single-subject design
Test reactivity
Trends

∽ 12 ∽

Correlational Methods
Controlling Rival Explanations
Statistically

INTRODUCTION TO CORRELATIONAL ANALYSIS

An Example of Correlation

Health, Wealth, and Age.   In correlational research we study variables that we do not manipulate. That is, we observe variables taking their natural values rather than being fixed as in experiments. In some cases, we cannot make individuals take chosen values of the variable (for example, age). In other cases, we choose not to control a variable for ethical reasons (for example, health). In still other cases, we might control a variable, but we seldom do because of the cost (for example, personal income). Finally, we may avoid ethical and affordable treatments because they appear so artificial that they endanger external or construct validity.

If we do not manipulate such variables as age, health, and income, we can at least measure them. However, drawing causal relations from the associations of these measured variables can prove difficult. Correlational designs pose some internal validity problems that experimental studies avoid. To see the nature of these problems, consider the following made-up example. Imagine a survey that asks subjects to reveal their age, their income, and their recent symptoms of ill health. To simplify the analysis, we can divide the subjects into those who rate high or low on each measure. Any relation will appear in a cross-tabulation if subjects with high scores on one measure also tend to score high (or low) on the other measure.

First, what relationship would you expect between income and symptoms? If these variables have a link, what causal hypothesis might explain it? Perhaps income causes health status. For example, we might expect that high income allows better health care and, thus, would occur with low symptoms. We note to our surprise that in Table 12–1 high-income subjects have more symptoms.

With some effort, we can create theories that agree with our findings. Perhaps wealth causes ill health because of the stress of the hard work required to earn high in-

Table 12–1   Cross-Tabulation of Income Level and Frequency of Recent Health Symptoms

| | | SYMPTOMS | |
		High	*Low*
Income	High	11	9
	Low	9	11
			gamma = .20

Note: The relationship of income and symptoms is summarized by the descriptive statistic called gamma. It ranges from -1 (perfect negative relationship) through 0 (no relationship) to +1 (perfect positive relationship).

come. Or maybe wealth permits us to attend to symptoms that poor people ignore. Or we could reverse the causal path and ask whether ill health causes higher income by motivating people to earn the wealth needed to cover their medical costs. Although not very plausible, these explanations illustrate a problem common to correlational studies. Data such as those in Table 12–1 appear consistent with several different theories. The correlational researcher has the problem of choosing a single best hypothesis from the several that fit the data.

Reverse and Spurious Causation.   The rival explanations of the results in Table 12–1 fall into two major types that pose basic threats to the internal validity of many correlational designs: reverse causation and spurious causation.

Some of the farfetched explanations illustrate the problem of **reverse causation**. According to one, income causes health, but another has health causing income. Even if these peculiar ideas had an appeal, we could not choose between them based on the data in the table. That is, cross-sectional data (observations taken at the same time) cannot, by themselves, tell causal direction.

Experimental designs rule out reverse causation by using a manipulated causal variable. But correlations have more difficulty with reverse causation. We could resort to theory to decide that a variable must serve as the cause rather than the effect. Or, we could design correlational studies to take measures at different times to find the causal direction.

Although this dilemma seems bad enough, we face still another threat to the internal validity of correlational designs. Sometimes an observed association stems from some third variable—a threat called **spuriousness**. True experiments handle this threat by randomly assigning subjects to different groups. Without random assignment, such groups may differ before the intervention, and the design would have the problem of group threats to internal validity (for example, selection). This same problem afflicts correlational research. An unknown third variable could cause both the "independent" (supposed cause) and the "dependent" (supposed effect) variable. If we could somehow remove the effect of the third variable, we would see that the association disappears.

Dealing with Spuriousness

Statistical Control and Multiple Causal Paths.   Look again at the data relating income and symptoms, this time controlling for the third variable of age. Here *control* means to hold constant. To hold constant the effect of age, we need to look at income and symptoms within different age groups. In our example we have two such groups, younger and older subjects, giving the two cross-tabulations presented in Table 12–2.

Note that income relates to symptoms in the same way in the two control tables. Next note that these controlled relations appear opposite in direction from the uncontrolled version in Table 12–1. The relationship had a positive sign in Table 12–1 but a negative sign in the control tables. Now it appears that higher income people have lower

Table 12–2   Cross-Tabulation of Income and Symptoms
Controlling for Age

OLD

SYMPTOMS

		High	Low
Income	High	10	4
	Low	5	1

gamma = −.33

YOUNG

SYMPTOMS

		High	Low
Income	High	1	5
	Low	4	10

gamma = −.33

symptoms after controlling for age. For example, 71 percent of older, high-income respondents report high symptoms versus 83 percent of the older, low-income respondents. In the same way, 17 percent of the younger, high-income respondents report high
symptoms versus 29 percent of the younger, low-income respondents. In contrast, Table
12–1 gave the high symptom rate as 55 percent in high-income subjects versus only 45
percent in low-income subjects.

Controlling for a third variable does not always lead to such opposed results. It
may strengthen an observed pattern, reduce it to zero, or as in the present case, reverse
its sign. One of these effects will occur only when the third variable correlates with both
the other variables. If the third variable has no relationship to one of the other variables,
removing it will not change the finding. We can see in Table 12–3 that age correlates
positively with income (a) and symptoms (b).

We can summarize the pattern of connections among age, income, and symptoms
visually. Figure 12–1 shows a set of causal paths that agree with the observed data. To
such a set of possible relationships, we sometimes give the name **model**.

This model includes two different channels by which income may affect symptoms. The first consists of the spurious association based on the fact that both income
and symptoms relate positively to age. This third variable of age tends to make income and symptoms appear positively related. This spurious association conceals the
second way in which income may relate to symptoms, the direct negative effect that
we expected.

Table 12–3   (a) Cross-Tabulation of Age and Income

		INCOME	
		High	*Low*
Age	Old	14	6
	Young	6	14

gamma = .69

(b) Cross-Tabulation of Age and Symptoms

		SYMPTOMS	
		High	*Low*
Age	Old	15	5
	Young	5	15

gamma = .80

Remember that the causal diagram in Figure 12–1 pictures a guess or hypothesis. As noted in the earlier comments on reverse causation, the negative arrow from income to symptoms might also run in the opposite direction. To get more confidence in the causal connections of Figure 12–1, we would need more information than that found in our simple cross-tabulations.

Partial Correlations and Path Coefficients.   Each of the arrows in Figure 12–1 could also carry a number telling the size of the association. For the arrow from age to income, we could use the measure called gamma, which has the value .69 in Table 12–3a. But what measure shall we use to describe the path from income to symptoms in Figure 12–1? We cannot use the initial correlation from Table 12–1 (gamma = .20) because we now know that this value includes the spurious association due to age as well as the direct effect controlling for age.

We might use the two gammas from Table 12–2, each of which holds for one of the two age groups. Each of these adjusts for age and reflects the direct connection of income and symptoms with the effect of age removed. However, using two different numbers to describe a single path will prove less convenient than using a

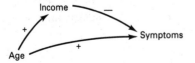

Figure 12-1   Possible causal model for age, income, and symptoms.

single number. With more than two control levels (for example, young, early middle, late middle, early retired, and very old age groups), we would have to deal with even more coefficients. Although the two age groups in our example have the same gammas (-.33), we cannot expect such coefficients always to have equal values across control groups.

Combining two or more such coefficients into a single value could solve our problem. A single number that measures an association controlling for another variable is called a **partial correlation**. In the present case, the partial gamma has the value -.33, the same as the two control gammas (because they had the same value and derived from equal numbers of respondents). A measure of partial association that describes the size of a causal path is a **path coefficient**. Although a path coefficient resembles a partial correlation, it has a different calculation. By convention, a path coefficient consists of the standardized regression coefficient produced in **multiple regression** analysis. See the Appendix and Chapter 8 for examples of regression analyses and how to read them.

TYPES OF RELATIONSHIPS

Direct Causation Versus Other Relations

Direct causation refers to the effect of one variable on another after removing other causes. Although we often seek direct causal relations in correlational studies, the data may not permit such simple findings. As the preceding example shows, a seemingly plain two-variable relationship can appear quite different with the inclusion of a third variable. By random assignment, true experiments control for the effect of any causal variable left out of the design. Usually this method equalizes treated and control groups on measured and unmeasured variables. Thus third variables do not threaten the internal validity of true experiments. A different situation occurs in correlational research where the omission of a third causal variable can lead to serious mistakes. As a result, correlational research must consider the effects of many variables in different patterns.

Multivariate research consists of the combined analysis of three or more variables. In multiple regression (the most common approach to multivariate research), the omission of important causal variables has a name—**specification error**. We regard the observed pattern of relations as wrong to the extent that we have omitted any important causal variable. The danger of missing an important effect makes multivariate research not just desirable but a real necessity in correlational studies. The task of correlational research goes beyond simply noting that two variables have an association. Rather this approach seeks to explain the causal links by which all of the variables produce the association.

Suppose we expect that variable *A* leads to variable *B*, a case of direct causation. As support for our hypothesis, we observe that *A* correlates with *B*. Before concluding that *A* simply and directly causes *B*, we must consider the other sources of the *AB* cor-

I. A causes B directly

A ─────────────────► B

II. A does not cause B

    a. Descriptive association--causation not established

    b. Measurement association--both reflections of the
       same latent variable

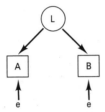

    c. Reverse causation--B causes A

A──────────────B

    d. Spuriousness--a confounding variable causes both

Figure 12-2   Types of causal and non-causal connections producing correlations.

relation. Figure 12–2 provides a graphic summary of the various types of relationships that could account for our observed correlation. Only the first diagram (I) portrays simple direct causation. We must guard against various noncausal types of associations as described in the next section. These include descriptive associations, measurement associations, and the two already mentioned threats to internal validity—spuriousness and reverse causation (diagrammed in section II of Figure 12–2). Even if we can rule out these noncausal sources, the impact of A on B may take more complex, nondirect forms as discussed in the subsequent section. These include reciprocal, indirect, and interactive causation (diagrammed in section III of Figure 12–2).

III. A causes B reciprocally, indirectly or interactively

    a. Reciprocal causation--each causes the other

    b. Indirect causation--effect passes through an intervening variable

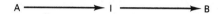

    c. Interactive causation--effect of one variable modified by another

      A x M   B

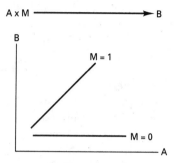

The A to B relationship is strong when M has the
value 1 but weak when M has the value 0.

Figure 12-1   (Continued)

Noncausal Associations

Descriptive Associations.   Observing a correlation between two variables does not imply any causal connection. Inferring causation from a correlation requires some added information. Such information might include knowledge that the presumed cause came before the presumed effect. Absent such information, we need not draw a causal inference. Often theories develop after and, in part, from descriptive correlational research. Thus we may present an observed correlation but avoid premature causal inference. As shown in Figure 12–2 (IIa), we can portray a noncausal, **descriptive association** with the use of a curving two-headed arrow.

An instance of such a descriptive association comes from a public health study of the factors linked to breast self-examination (BSE). The researcher surveyed women at high risk for breast cancer (Howe, 1981). Frequency of BSE behavior correlated positively with BSE knowledge, BSE attitude, and education and negatively with a measure of modesty. The author concluded that since the data came from a cross-sectional, retrospective survey, "BSE knowledge and a positive BSE attitude could precede, follow, or develop concomitantly with the adoption of the monthly practice of BSE" (p. 254).

Absent a causal connection, the correlation between BSE knowledge and attitude would appear linked by the curving double headed arrow of Figure 12–2 (IIa). Theories may have one or more noncausal relationships built into them along with any single-headed arrows representing direct causal connections. Such descriptive correlations invite future research to find the direction of any causal sequence.

Measurement Association.   Suppose that in a paper about depressed mood, you found a correlation between an item asking about suicidal thoughts and one asking about hopelessness. Would you make the claim that based on this finding, one of these caused the other? Some researchers would not explain such a correlation as a sign of direct causation. Rather, they would see the link between such items as a case of **measurement association**. Two items measuring the same construct (for example, depressed mood) should agree with each other. Their correlation only shows the extent to which they succeed in reflecting the same reality.

If we want to think of this measuring process in causal terms, we can do so as pictured in Figure 12–2 (IIb). In this case, the two measures *A* and *B* appear in boxes to show that they consist of observed variables. The arrows pointing to them come from a **latent variable** symbolized by the circle. We conceive of the latent variable as the underlying construct that shows itself in the form of actual measures. This ideal or perfectly reliable factor "causes" the unreliable measures that we observe. To show that our observed measures have measurement error, the figure shows arrows labeled "e" for error pointing to *A* and *B*. Sometimes researchers collect only one measure of each construct or combine multiple items into a single score. In such cases, we may forget that the observed variables represent more general concepts. However, studies that distinguish measured and latent variables will often show them as in Figure 12–2(IIb). For example, one study pictured the latent variable of depression (in a circle) with arrows pointing from it to four different measures (in boxes) including self-reported hopelessness and death ideation (Aneshensel & Frerichs, 1982).

A problem arises when we try to explain the correlation due to measurement association as though it came from a causal process. Two different variables may reflect the same latent variable or they may represent two different constructs that have a causal connection. For example, suppose you found a correlation between the number of friends and perceived support reported by people in a survey. You might try to explain this association as due to a causal process, perhaps number of friends causing perceived support. However, your efforts in this regard would have to withstand the rival view that both measures derive from an underlying latent variable called social support. In fact, these measures have appeared as indicators of the social support construct (Aneshensel & Frerichs, 1982).

Reverse Causation.   As illustrated earlier in the health, wealth, and age example, reverse causation appears when actual causal direction moves opposite to that expected. As pictured in Figure 12–2 (IIc), the causal path proceeds from *B* to *A* rather than the predicted *A* to *B*. Often the data cannot settle the question of causal direction. This problem arises commonly in studies that take measures of both variables at the same time.

In such cases, the researcher can only assume the direction and may or may not make this assumption explicit. However, research that collects measures at more than one time can check for reverse causation.

An example comes from the previously cited study of depression that used latent variables (Aneshensel & Frerichs, 1982). This project collected data four times from a sample of people with follow-up interviews at 4, 8, and 12 months. Although the authors supposed that loss events would cause depression, they allowed for the possibility that depression could somehow cause later loss events. Using their four data points, they were able to show that depression is related over a four-month period to an increase in stress. This finding did not preclude the expected finding that recent stress was related to depression in the same interview. Nevertheless, the reverse path from depression to stress warns researchers in this area to take care with their assumptions of causal direction.

Spuriousness.   The threat that a supposed causal relation is spurious lurks behind all observed association. One can always wonder whether the evidence of a causal link would disappear if we controlled for a **confounding variable**. A confounding variable causes both of the variables and accounts for their association. As pictured in Figure 12–2(IId), the direct causal path, indicated by dashes, would drop to zero and disappear when the confounder's effects are taken into account. The risk of spuriousness invites an analysis that controls for the alleged confounding variable.

One example of possible confounding comes from research on suicide and its predictors. Some research suggests that feeling hopeless may lead to suicide. Note that this approach treats hopelessness and suicide as separate constructs not as measures of a single latent variable, as in the earlier section on measurement association. However, this possible causal link must face another threat. The alleged causal connection from feeling hopeless to thinking suicidal thoughts would be spurious if some third variable caused both of them. Research has proposed such a confounding variable—the tendency to answer in a socially desirable direction. People high in this tendency will report neither hopelessness nor suicidal thoughts, even if they have them. Those low in social desirability will admit some feelings of hopelessness and suicidal thoughts of the common variety that many people sometimes have. To check for confounding, one study had subjects fill out the Bell Hopelessness Scale, the Suicidal Behavior Questionnaire, and the Edwards Social Desirability Scale (Linehan & Nielsen, 1981). Hopelessness correlated positively and significantly with risk of future suicide among those seriously suicidal in the past ($r = .39$). Social desirability correlated negatively with both hopelessness and future suicide. Controlling for social desirability, the partial correlation of hopelessness with future suicide dropped to .14, a level below statistical significance. Other researchers have reported that controlling for social desirability does not entirely explain the hopelessness with suicidal thinking association and that social desirability may serve as more than a confounder of this relationship (Holden, Mendonca, & Serin, 1989).

The threat of confounding produces a good deal of research controversy. An example comes from the study of lead and intelligence with which we began this text. The original study compared the intelligence scores of children rated high or low for lead exposure based on lead in their shed teeth (Needleman et al., 1979). Both intelligence and lead levels can correlate with such potential confounders as age and socioeconomic status. Critics have pointed out that the 1979 study did not include age as a control variable, raising questions about the validity of the findings (Ernhart, Scarr, & Geneson, 1993). Needleman rebuts that he controlled for age by using age-adjusted IQ scores and that, in any event, controlling for age in later analyses did not destroy the association between lead and intelligence (Needleman, 1993).

Complex Causation

Reciprocal Causation.   Sometimes a variable can have a causal impact on another variable but in ways other than simple direct causation. Clarifying these more complex causal relations can aid both in theory development and in applications. As one instance of this complexity, evidence for direct causation going in one direction does not rule out reverse causation going in the other direction. Indeed, for many pairs of social variables, **reciprocal causation** seems plausible. In reciprocal causation both direct causal paths exist as diagrammed in Figure 12–2 (IIIa). The two straight, parallel, single-pointed arrows go in opposite directions to indicate that each variable influences the other.

As an example of reciprocal causation, consider the connection between the violence of protestors and police at political protest rallies. Kritzer (1977) collected data from a sample of 126 protest demonstrations with observations about the violence levels of both sides, the extent to which heavy police equipment was available, and the degree of commitment of the protestors to nonviolence. We might expect that the protestors provoked the police or vice versa. The reciprocal causation model suggests that each provoked the other in a cyclic way—each increment of violence from one side drawing more violence from the other. Testing reciprocity requires advanced techniques and unusually rich data. When Berry (1984) reanalyzed the Kritzer data with these methods, he confirmed the finding of reciprocal causation.

Indirect Causation.   **Indirect causation** refers to the causal path from an independent variable to a dependent variable via an **intervening variable**. Figure 12–2 (IIIb) pictures this case. The initial variable produces its effect by two simple, direct causal links. If the analysis omitted the intervening variable, the first variable could, if of sufficient impact, appear as the direct cause of the outcome variable. Multivariate analysis reveals the more complex causal sequence involving three variables. The causal linkage between two variables may involve only direct, only indirect, or partly direct and partly indirect effects.

How can we compare the sizes of direct and indirect effects in correlational results? We can measure the direct effect of one variable on another by the association between the two after partialing out the effect of the intervening variable(s). We can measure the indirect effect as a function of the two (or more) direct links passing through the intervening variable(s). If we use regression analysis, the indirect effect consists of the product of the path coefficients for the links involving the intervening variable.

Whether two variables relate directly or indirectly concerns both theorists and policy makers. Theorists want to understand causal process as completely as possible. When scientists find an association without an explanation, they sometimes refer to the missing link as a "black box." One variable appears to start an effect, and the other appears to respond. Between the two, inside the black box, one or more intervening variables must exist to transmit the causal influence. Scientists devote a good deal of their research trying to open such black boxes.

Adding intervening variables to a study may help find an otherwise unnoticed connection between two variables. Indirectly related variables can have a small **bivariate association** (or two-variable correlation), which can fail to reach statistical significance. The two variables may, however, have links with an intervening variable, each of which reaches significance. Because an indirect effect's size depends on the multiplication of the intervening paths, each modest direct effect weakens further when it passes along the next path. A survey showing little effect of earthquake experience on amount of earthquake preparedness illustrates this process (Dooley, Catalano, Mishra, & Serxner, 1992). Experience had a small effect on earthquake concern (path coefficient = .21). Concern had an even smaller effect on whether any preparations were made (.08), which in turn had a moderate connection to amount of preparation (.46). Although each of these three paths reached significance, they yielded a small indirect effect of just .008 (.21 × .08 × .46).

Interest in intervening variables also comes from policy makers who want to apply research findings. You might suppose that such planners would not care about the black box between cause and effect. However, they may not be able to change the first variable in the sequence. In that case, they will want to know the intervening variable and whether they might change it. For example, suppose we observe that parental social status has a causal connection to criminal behavior. Since we have little hope of changing parental status, the criminologist will look for an intervening variable that offers more chance of control, such as educational performance.

A correlational study analyzed these variables in the records of 3421 Danish males (McGarvey, Gabrielli, Bentler, & Mednick, 1981). Occupational prestige measured parental status, and the subject's highest grade level and score on a draft board screening test measured his educational performance. To measure criminality, the researchers used the number of arrests and the severity of the crimes by the time the sample reached an average age of 26. The results showed no direct path between parental status and criminal behavior controlling for educational performance. The negative bivariate association between parental status and criminal behavior appears due to the indirect path from parental status (path coefficient = .46) to educational performance (-.39) to criminal behavior. The product (-.18) of these path coefficients (that is, .46 × -.39) estimates the magnitude of this indirect effect.

Interactive Causation.   **Interactive causation** occurs when the effect of one variable depends on the level of another. Two variables may combine to produce an interaction when neither variable alone has a direct effect, when either does, or when both do. Figure 12–2 (IIIc) shows an interaction in two ways. The first part shows a causal arrow from the interaction term $A \times M$ leading to the outcome B. By custom, we symbolize the interaction as the multiple of the interacting variables. The second part of the figure shows one kind of interaction in which the relation of B (values on the vertical axis) to A (values on the horizontal axis) depends on the value of M. In this case, we can think of M as modifying the effect of A on B. When a variable adjusts the causal connection between two others, we call it a **moderating variable**. When M has the value 0, B does not vary with changing values of A. But when $M = 1$, B rises sharply with increases in A. In this example, M can take only one of two values, perhaps gender. In practice, the interacting variables can take more than two values, for example scores on a continuous measure.

In experimental research, we test for interactions by manipulating two or more independent variables in a factorial design. In correlational research, we look for interactions by checking the effect of a term created by multiplying the two interacting terms (for example A and M in Figure 12–2 [IIIc]). We can assess this product term $(A \times M)$ in a regression analysis as long as the separate effects of A and M are included. If $A \times M$ reaches significance, we can then explore the nature of the interaction to see how one variable modifies the other. We can do this by comparing the associations of two variables (such as A with B) at different levels of a third variable (M). An example of such an analysis comes from research on physical fitness as a moderator of the adverse health effects of stressful life events (Roth & Holmes, 1985). Subjects reported their recent life changes, took a bicycle test of fitness, and, nine weeks after the first session, reported their health problems. The researchers found that stressful events, fitness, and their interaction each predicted the sum of the severity ratings of later health problems. The interaction term took the form of the lower part of Figure 12–2(IIIc) with health problem severity on the vertical axis (B) and life stress on the horizontal axis (A). The researchers divided the subjects into two levels of fitness with the low-fitness group corresponding to line $M = 1$ and the high-fitness group to line $M = 0$. That is, health problems rose with increasing life events for the low-fitness group but not for the high-fitness group. In this study, fitness seemed to *buffer* or moderate the effect of stress on health.

Interactions may include more than two independent variables. Higher order interactions can involve three, four, and more variables, although explaining such complex effects can prove difficult. An example of a three-way interaction comes from a study of self-esteem in young people (Jensen, 1986). Table 12–4 summarizes the results of this research. One hypothesis holds that young people will have lower self-esteem if they view themselves as troublemakers. Mild support for this prediction comes from the first subtable for the entire sample (gamma = -.20). The next two subtables analyze boys and girls separately and show that this negative association comes largely from the girls (gamma = -.37). In this two-way interaction, gender moderates the effect of troublemaking on self-esteem. Jensen went further and considered the effect of another variable, that of status resources such as school performance or material possessions. For boys low in such resources (the last subtable), high self-esteem and high troublemaking actually go together (gamma = +.42), an example of a three-way interaction.

Problems with Causal Inferences

Indirect Causation versus Spuriousness. Correlational data can never give final proof of causation. The same set of data can agree with more than one causal model. Recall that in correlational research, we often name variables as independent or dependent in an arbitrary way. No experimental manipulation assures us that the "independent variable" indeed functions as a cause. Similarly, a third variable in multivariate analysis receives the label "intervening" or "confounding" according to some theory. Consider the two causal models in Figure 12–3.

Figure 12–3a describes an indirect causal path from *A* through *Q* to *B*. We earlier saw an example of this in Figure 12–2(IIIb) where the intervening variable had the label *I* instead of *Q*. Figure 12–3b describes a case of spurious association between *A* and *B*, which disappears when the confounding variable *Q* is controlled. This diagram appeared earlier in Figure 12–2(IIb) except that the confounding variable had the label *C* instead of *Q*. The two causal diagrams of Figure 12–3 differ only in the direction of the link between *A* and *Q*.

How can we tell which of these two models best fits the data? If we compare the simple correlations between *A* and *B*, both models would give the same result. That is, *A* and *B* have a nonzero correlation $r(AB)$, and the associations have the same magnitude in both cases. To check for indirect causation, we test the partial correlation between *A* and *B*, controlling for *Q*, symbolized as $r(AB.Q)$. Without the intervening vari-

Table 12–4 Associations Between Troublemaker and Self-Esteem

	TROUBLEMAKER		
	High	*Low*	
Entire Sample	High 44%	55%	Gamma = −.202
Self-esteem	Low 56%	45%	
Boys Subsample			
Self-esteem	High 50%	53%	Gamma = −.043
	Low 50%	47%	
Girls Subsample			
Self-esteem	High 40%	59%	Gamma = −.370
	Low 60%	41%	
Boys Low in Conventional Status Resources			
Self-esteem	High 56%	34%	Gamma = .420
	Low 44%	66%	

Boys high in conventional status resources, gamma = −.309
Girls low in conventional status resources, gamma = −.321
Girls high in conventional status resources, gamma = −.370

From Gary Jensen (1986), *Dis-integrating integrated theory: A critical analysis of attempts to save strain theory.* Paper presented at the Annual Convention of the American Society of Criminology, Atlanta.

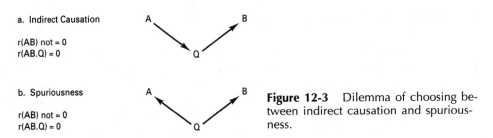

Figure 12-3 Dilemma of choosing between indirect causation and spuriousness.

able Q, the A to B association disappears, and $r(AB.Q)$ falls to zero. To check for spuriousness, we also check the partial correlation. Again if Q accounts entirely for the AB relationship, $r(AB.Q)$ should also become zero. Thus we get the same simple and partial correlations in both cases. In sum, our analysis cannot tell us whether to believe that indirect causation or spuriousness accounts for these results.

Weak Inference.   Deciding whether two correlated variables have a causal relation depends on our view of causation. One meaning of causation (called the **generative theory**) refers to a mechanism by which a cause produces an effect. In contrast, **weak inference** of causation requires only that the presumed cause and effect still covary after removal of confounding variables. Weak inference relies on the **regularity theory** of causation. Generative theorists dislike the use of weak inference. They argue that regularity does *not* "constitute an explanation of that covariation, but merely justifies the rather weak claim that the causal event is statistically (that is, causally) relevant to the consequent event" (Baumrind, 1983, p. 1296).

According to the generative theory, correlational designs can test only the fit of a given causal model to a set of data. Such a fit does not provide sufficient evidence for the model. A poor fit between a model and the data would tend to cast doubt on the model. But a good fit does not rule out other, equally good-fitting models. As an example, the two models in Figure 12–3 fit equally well. Regularity theorists who fit complex models to correlational data often use the method of path analysis, as discussed in the following section.

CONDUCTING CORRELATIONAL ANALYSIS

Summarizing Relationships

Approach.   **Path analysis** uses coefficients and diagrams to express the causal paths that link variables (Asher, 1976; Heise, 1975). Even before collecting data, you may find it useful to clarify your theoretical model in the form of a diagram that uses arrows to connect constructs. An exogenous variable, a variable with causes from outside the theory under investigation, has no arrows leading to it. Causal arrows lead to endogenous variables, the presumed outcomes of prior causes. Endogenous variables may also cause other endogenous variables, in which case they serve as intervening variables.

To estimate the sizes of the causal effects, path analysts usually perform regression (Schroeder, Sjoquist, & Stephan, 1986). Each endogenous variable requires one regression equation. The regression produces standardized regression coefficients. These become the path coefficients placed on the matching arrows of the diagram. Each sign tells the direction of association, and each value tells the strength of the relationship compared to coefficients on other arrows.

In addition to measuring the strength of each path between two variables, we will want to know the overall fit of the model to the data. That is, we can ask the extent to which all of the causally prior variables explain the variation in the endogenous variables. Two equivalent values provide this information for each outcome variable—R^2 and the residual. The R refers to the multiple correlation coefficient, which measures the best association of a dependent variable with all of its causal variables. The square of R (R^2) expresses the percentage of information in the dependent variable accounted for by all of the causal variables taken together. The **residual path** provides a related kind of information but on an arrow pointing to an endogenous variable from no variable. This residual arrow portrays the effect of all the unmeasured forces outside the model. The value placed on this residual path reflects the difference between perfect explanation (that is, when $R^2 = 1$) and the explanation observed in the present model (R^2 observed) or $1 - R^2$. The actual value placed on the residual path consists of the square root of this difference or $\sqrt{(1 - R^2)}$. Thus a good fit between model and data will result in a large R^2 (approaching the value 1) and a small residual path coefficient (approaching zero) for each endogenous variable.

Example of Educational Attainment. Figure 12–4 presents a path analysis of women who were Wisconsin high school seniors in 1957 (Sewell & Shah, 1967). The data came from a large panel study of the students' educational plans and family socioeconomic status. Intelligence scores came from archives of a standard test administered to all Wisconsin high school juniors. Reinterviews in 1964–1965 measured the educational and occupational attainments of one-third of these same women. Educational attainment had the following codes: 0 = did not attend college, 1 = attended but did not graduate from college, and 2 = graduated from college.

A persistent debate concerns the relative influence of parental social class versus the students' ability on later attainment in education, occupation, and adult social class. This debate touches a political nerve because we justify the unequal distribution of wealth on the grounds of merit. Individuals with greater ability and effort deserve larger slices of the societal pie. However, some critics have claimed that entry into high-status careers depends not on individual ability but rather on inherited social status.

Figure 12–4 addresses this debate by summarizing two different regression equations. One used socioeconomic status (SES) and intelligence to predict college plans. The second used SES, intelligence, and college plans to predict educational attainment. The results show that both sides of the debate have some basis in fact. Both SES and intelligence affect college plans. However, the SES effect appears larger in this sample.

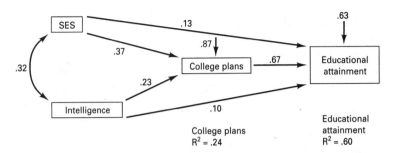

Figure 12-4   Path diagram for effects of socioeconomic status (SES), intelligence, and college plans on educational attainment in women. (From W. H. Sewell & V. P. Shah, Socioeconomic status, intelligence and the attainment of higher education, *Sociology of Education, 40,* 1967, 1–23).

In turn, college plans strongly influence ultimate attainment. Both SES and intelligence affect attainment in two ways—directly, controlling for each other and for college plans, and indirectly via college plans. The total SES effect on attainment is the sum of the direct effect (.13) and the indirect effect (SES to college plans times college plans to educational attainment or $.37 \times .67 = .25$). This total SES effect ($.13 + .25 = .38$) exceeds the total intelligence effect ($.10 + .23 \times .67 = .10 + .15 = .25$).

Did this model as a whole provide a good fit to the data? The R^2 or residual path can tell us the fit of each equation but not the overall fit of the full model. Fortunately, procedures that provide tests of overall fit do exist for complex models. Two previously mentioned studies used such a method—the relation of social class to criminality (McGarvey, Gabrielli, Bentler, & Mednick, 1981) and the relation of stress to depression (Aneshensel & Frerichs, 1982). These studies employed maximum likelihood analysis of structural equations (Bentler, 1980; Maruyama & McGarvey, 1980).

Computer software for structural equation modeling has become widely available, including LISREL (Joreskog & Sorbom, 1981) and EQS (Bentler, 1989). These statistical procedures provide single tests (based on the chi square statistic) to assess overall model fit (see Bentler & Bonett, 1980). This method can also use multiple measures of each construct to study the underlying latent variables. Illustrated in Figure 12–2(IIb), this latter approach controls for measurement error and helps consolidate many measures into a more parsimonious set of constructs. Although widely used, structural equation modeling has not resolved the basic problem of correlational analysis. Finding a model with a good fit to the data does not rule out the possibility of many other models that could fit equally well (Breckler, 1990). In fact the model pictured in Figure 12–4 could be recast in a variety of ways, each with an equally good overall fit (Stelzl, 1986).

The correlational researcher can predict the ways in which each variable relates to every other variable in the model. The researcher then analyzes the data to estimate the strength of each predicted path and to test the overall fit between model and data. Paths with small coefficients should disappear, and whole models with poor overall fits should give way to theories that better explain the data. However, even if a model fits the data well, the wise researcher remembers that correlational designs only yield weak causal inferences.

To strengthen the conclusions from a correlational study, the researcher will have to attend to the study's design. For example, in order to claim support for a causal inference, the researcher will want to measure variables with known temporal sequence. That is, the supposed cause should occur prior to the supposed effect. When the studied variables do not have a natural order, the researcher can seek a longitudinal design that measures the variables at different times. Another measurement aspect that can affect conclusions involves the degree of aggregation of the data. The following section surveys the issues that arise in different types of designs, whether longitudinal or cross-sectional and individual- or aggregate-level.

Types of Designs

Definitions. Experimental designs have a longitudinal aspect in that the researcher manipulates the independent variable before measuring the outcome. In contrast, the most common correlational designs use cross-sectional data. In **cross-sectional correlation** the researcher measures the "independent" and "dependent" variables at the same time. For example, the 1990 census questionnaire asked questions about age, housing, and other personal matters all at one time. In contrast, **longitudinal correlation** applies to data collected at different times. For example, a survey researcher might interview a group of subjects and then reinterview the same subjects one year later to assess changes in their housing, finances, or health.

Individual-level data include measures of particular persons. The researcher studies one or more people with the individual subject as the unit of analysis. In contrast, **aggregate-level data** include measures of groups of persons. We can define the group by space (for example, the average educational level by state) or by time (for example, the average educational level by decade). The analysis may use a spatial unit of analysis (for example, studying education levels across different states in 1990). Or the analysis could use a temporal unit of analysis (for example, the education level of the American population over the decades of this century). In either case, we cannot know about any particular person in the studied samples. The educational attainment of each individual disappeared in the aggregation by state and year.

Typology by Time and Level of Analysis. Table 12–5 describes the division of studies by time and level of analysis. Each of the four cells displays one set of design attributes, either cross-sectional or longitudinal and either individual or aggregate level. To show the differences among these designs, each cell asks a common question: "Does economic stress cause suicide?" Because each cell operationalizes this problem in a different way, each approach may support a different inference. For the actual research that corresponds to each cell, see the reviews by Dooley and Catalano (1980, 1986).

The typology of Table 12–5 should help us avoid making two different kinds of errors. One type involves wrong causal inferences across levels of analysis. The other involves wrong inferences with respect to cross-sectional (static) or longitudinal (dynamic) studies. The following sections examine these two types of problems.

Cross-Level Inference and the Ecological Fallacy. A **cross-level inference** draws a conclusion at one level of analysis from research at another level. The most common cross-level inferences leap from aggregate-level data to individual-level claims. We now know that the correlation between measures at the aggregate level can differ greatly from that of the same variables measured on individuals. The term **ecological fallacy** describes this false individual-level interpretation of aggregate-level findings.

Robinson (1950) used 1930 U.S. census data to study the relation of race to literacy. He found that this correlation was much larger at the aggregate level (spatial grouping by region of the country) than at the person level. Firebaugh (1978) reanalyzed these same data to show that the grouping variable plays an important part in the cross-level bias. Literacy varied greatly across regions for both blacks and whites (lower for both races in the South). Moreover, race interacted with region. Blacks in the South had higher illiteracy rates than blacks in the North. After taking into account the direct effect of region and the interaction between race and region, the net connection between race and illiteracy became quite small.

A basic cause of the ecological fallacy involves group effects. We combine data within groups such as the spatial units of northern and southern regions in Firebaugh's reanalysis of Robinson. Such groups may add their own effects over and above those

Table 12–5 Typology of Correlational Studies by Longitudinal–Cross-Sectional, and Level of Analysis: Illustrated by Question: "Does Economic Stress Cause Suicide?"

	Individual Level	
Unit: Individuals at one time		*Unit:* Individuals measured over time
Sample Question: Does current suicidal intention correlate with current economic		*Sample Question:* Does change in suicidal intention correlate with recent economic life
Cross-Sectional 1	3	Longitudinal
Unit: Spatial aggregate (e.g., state) 2	4	*Unit:* Temporal aggregate (e.g., year)
Sample Question: Does the suicide rate correlate with unemployment rate over states?		*Sample Question:* Does the suicide rate correlate with unemployment rate over years?
	Aggregate Level	

of the individual-level variable. In the case of the literacy study, region correlated with race because different regions had different racial compositions. Thus, the aggregate measure of race served as a proxy or stand-in measure for region of the country. A high score on racial composition was tantamount to a high score for being southern on the dimension of region. Studies finding a connection between race and literacy really described a link between region and literacy. Firebaugh (1978) suggests that this grouping effect operated indirectly on illiteracy. Through history, the direct causes of illiteracy, such as quality of schools, became linked with region.

Individual and aggregate correlations will differ when the grouped measure of the causal construct reflects some important aspect of the group over and above the individual causal variable. Individual- and aggregate-level associations will give the same results (that is, no ecological fallacy) only when the grouped causal variable adds nothing to the individual causal variable. Robinson (1950) got a strong relationship in the aggregate between race and literacy because his analysis included the effects of unmeasured aspects of his regional grouping variable. With this group effect removed, as in individual-only analysis, individual race and literacy appear much less strongly related.

Cross-level interpretive errors can operate both ways. Robinson (1950) focused on the errors of going from the aggregate to the individual. However, we should not assume that individual-level data describe aggregate-level relations. We might call this latter error the atomistic fallacy. In the literacy example, if we were to generalize from individual data to groupings by region, we would miss the interaction effect of race and region on literacy found in the aggregate-level analysis.

This discussion of cross-level inference shows how a research question translates in different ways according to level of analysis. The question of association between individual race and individual literacy falls in cell 1 of Table 12–5 (individual, cross-sectional). In that cell, the question would become, "Does race correlate with literacy across individuals?" But at the aggregate level (cell 2—aggregate, cross-sectional), the question becomes: "Does the racial composition of a region correlate with the literacy rate over regions?" These two questions produce quite different answers. For the same reasons, the question about economic stress and suicide in Table 12–5 can yield different answers depending on how we ask it. For example, social factors linked with aggregate poverty (say, social disintegration) may have a strong impact on suicide rates over spatial units that group by poverty. But at the individual level, personal poverty may have a weaker link to suicidal risk (for a discussion of the greater aggregate effect of social disintegration, see Leighton, Harding, Macklin, Macmillan, & Leighton, 1963).

Inferences from Cross-Sectional and Longitudinal Studies.   Both cells 1 and 2 of Table 12–5 include cross-sectional or static studies. Such studies collect measures at one time for both "independent" and "dependent" variables. Such static research has the problem of ruling out reverse causal connections. Absent independent information about causal sequence, the analyst points causal arrows by theory, not evidence. Collecting data over time offers one way to find temporal order.

In Table 12–5, cells 2 and 4 appear to differ only in that cell 4 improves with dynamic data on the static nature of cell 2. However, crossing the line between static and dynamic research, even within the same level of analysis, can greatly change the question. We can see this in studies of the same relationship with the same data organized in two ways—cross-sectionally and longitudinally. An example comes from data from India on the relation of birthrate to literacy (Firebaugh, 1980). This study compares the approach of cell 2 using spatial units with that of cell 4 using time units. In the former case, the spatial units consist of districts of the Punjab measured at one time. Firebaugh replicated this spatial analysis 11 times, once for each of 11 years of available data. In the latter case, the time units consist of years over which a particular Punjabi district varies. Firebaugh also replicated this analysis 11 times, once for each of the 11 districts.

We would expect these two different methods to give the same answer. Increasing birthrate should correlate, if related at all, with either increasing literacy or decreasing literacy. To our surprise, the two approaches gave opposite answers. The ecological relation (based on spatial units, cell 2) appeared positive, with high-literacy districts having high birthrates. The same pattern appeared in each of the 11 years studied. In contrast, the over-time analysis (cell 4) produced a negative relation. Within a district, year-to-year increases in literacy accompanied decreases in the birthrate. This relationship appeared in each of the 11 districts.

How can we make sense of these contrary findings? Although arbitrary, let us assume that literacy operates as the cause of birthrate. If the time-unit approach gave the correct result, increasing literacy produces decreasing fertility. If this inverse relation between literacy and fertility has operated through time, we should find a similar negative relationship between these variables in the ecological analysis for any one year. At any time, the districts that have enjoyed the greatest gains in literacy should have the lowest birthrates. Less fortunate districts with less advanced educational systems should have the greatest birthrates. Such a pattern ought to produce an inverse effect over spatial units similar to that over time units. That we do not get this harmonious result warns us that we have made a false assumption.

We supposed that the process observed over the 11 years of the dynamic study must have operated prior to the study. This assumption flies in the face of the facts. In the first year of the observations, districts with high literacy also had high fertility, and districts low in literacy also had low fertility. This pattern of differences between units is called the **unit effect**. Some historical process(es) must have led to this positive association of the variables of literacy and fertility across spatial units. Perhaps the wealth produced by favorable agricultural land supported both a high birthrate and investment in education. Districts with fewer resources may have had lower birthrates and less support for education. Whatever the process leading to the spatial differences, the pattern must have changed. At the time of Firebaugh's dynamic analysis, increasing literacy appears connected to decreasing fertility. We can speculate that the new causal process involves changing means of production and distribution. Since this inverse pattern operates in each district, all the districts will tend to move down in birthrate as they move up in literacy. As a result of this parallel process, the districts will preserve their relative standing. Even if a district decreases its fertility as a function of increased literacy, it can still retain the relatively high (or low) position on both fertility and literacy that it had in 1961.

In sum, crossing the border between static to dynamic research designs can transform the original question, just as does changing levels of analysis. We must take care to make inferences appropriate to both the data level and the time design of the analysis.

SUMMARY

Correlational research can provide only weak support for causal linkages. Two variables may correlate for reasons other than the hypothesized one. We may describe an association without knowing that a causal link accounts for it. Two measures might correlate only because they reflect the same underlying construct. The two most serious threats to causal claims involve reverse causation and spuriousness. We can assume causal direction based on theory or decide it by evidence that establishes temporal priority as in longitudinal research.

When a causal process does account for an association, it may operate in a complex way. For example, variables measured at the same time may cause each other (reciprocal causation). Or, the causal process may pass through an intervening variable (indirect causation). Finally, one variable may cause another but only conditionally on the level of one or more other variables (interactive causation).

Statistical procedures can check for spuriousness by controlling for the confounding variable(s). But statistics cannot decide the true causal pattern based on correlational data. Different models may fit the observed data equally well. At best, we can compare a theory with correlational data using such techniques as path analysis.

In interpreting correlational findings, note the study's level of analysis (aggregate versus individual) and time span (static versus dynamic). Beware of generalizing from one level to another as from aggregate to individual (risking the ecological fallacy). Nor can you generalize from one time span (for example, cross-sectional) to another (for example, longitudinal).

EXERCISES

1. Since the interpretation of correlational research depends on the statistics that describe association, you should read the part of the Appendix dealing with correlations and the way associations are summarized graphically. Then identify several studies using the correlational approach, that is, using passively observed, nonmanipulated causal variables.

2. Select a simple correlational study on a topic of interest to you. For example, the results might appear in one or more tables (or matrices) that summarize the simple or partial correlations of interest or in the form of a path diagram. Choose a pair of variables that you or the author suspect to be causally related. Assess the evidence in support of the causal relation and judge such rivals as reverse causation and spuriousness.

3. Using the same study, decide which design type it belongs to: cross-sectional or longitudinal and individual or aggregate level. Then consider whether the inferences fit these design characteristics. For example, does the author risk the ecological fallacy?

KEY TERMS

Aggregate-level data
Bivariate association
Confounding variable
Cross-level inference
Cross-sectional correlation
Descriptive association
Direct causation
Ecological fallacy
Generative theory
Indirect causation
Individual-level data
Interactive causation
Intervening variable
Latent variable
Longitudinal correlation
Measurement association

Model
Moderating variable
Multiple regression
Multivariate research
Partial correlation
Path analysis
Path coefficient
Reciprocal causation
Regularity theory
Residual path
Reverse causation
Specification error
Spuriousness
Unit effect
Weak Inference

❧ 13 ❧

Qualitative Research
Participant Observation

SEEING PEOPLE IN THEIR OWN SETTING
An Example of Qualitative Research
Defining Qualitative Research

RATIONALES FOR QUALITATIVE RESEARCH
Models of Knowing
Feasibility

METHODS OF QUALITATIVE RESEARCH
Ethics
Techniques
Validity Threats

SUMMARY

EXERCISES

KEY TERMS

SEEING PEOPLE IN THEIR OWN SETTING

An Example of Qualitative Research

> Prophecy from planet. Clarion call to city: Flee that flood. It'll swamp us on Dec. 21, outer space tells suburbanite. (Festinger, Riechen, & Schachter, 1956, p. 30)

This headline appeared on September 23, during the mid-1950s, over a short article in the back pages of a midwestern city newspaper. The prophecy came in messages received through automatic writing. Beings from the planet Clarion were using a suburban housewife's hand to write their messages. Besides warning of earthquake, flooding, and general calamity, the Clarion beings also described a complete belief system.

Other predictions about the end of the world have appeared and some have produced serious harm. For example, a doomsday sect in Korea believed that they would enter heaven on Wednesday, October 28, 1992, in the Rapture predicted by the Book of Revelations. At least four members committed suicide and others burned their furniture or gave away their savings. One thousand believers, who were issued special identification cards to keep out doubters, entered their church on the evening of the Rapture for services. Some 1,500 riot police stood guard around the church to protect against mass suicide. The next morning, after nothing happened, some members said that "God lied to us," but others said "we'll keep waiting" (Watanabe, 1992, p. A10).

Dissonance Theory.   In contrast, the Clarion news story did not cause an evacuation or even very much interest in the general community. The story did spark great interest in a small group of social researchers who were hoping to field-test a theory. These scholars wanted to study the aftermath of a failed prediction. Sometimes a religious group increased their recruitment (proselytizing) following the failure (disconfirmation) of an important belief. The researchers wanted to confirm this response by direct observation and to test their theory for it. They based their hypothesis on *cognitive dissonance*, which holds that two inconsistent (that is, dissonant) ideas produce an uncomfortable tension. In order to reduce this tension, the person will strive to change one of the ideas to make it compatible with the other or to reduce the importance of the difference.

These researchers thought the September 23 prediction of a December 21 flood offered a good test of this theory. They thought that after December 21 they would witness great dissonance between the belief in the prediction (the Clarion messages) and the fact that the prediction had failed. On the basis of past doomsday groups, the researchers expected the members to retain their belief and increase their efforts to recruit new members: *"If more and more people can be persuaded that the system of belief is correct, then clearly it must, after all, be correct"* (Festinger et al., 1956, p. 28; italics in original).

What determines whether a believer responds to dissonance by giving up the belief or by seeking new converts? The researchers suspected that social support determined the outcome. In isolation, a believer cannot hold out against the fact that the world has gone on or withstand the doubts of the nonbelievers. For example, the Korean sect that had expected the Rapture in 1992 disbanded within a week of the failed prediction, in part because its leader was in jail for swindling the members (making investments that would not mature until after the predicted end of the world). In contrast, the Clarion believers who stayed together for almost three weeks after disconfirmation could draw on each other for support in an effort to retain faith and recruit new members.

We can use quantitative measures and experimental designs to study cognitive dissonance and reactions to disproved predictions. However, those predicting the end of the world have no interest in subjecting their beliefs to study by skeptical social scientists. The researchers decided to test their theory by using the method of qualitative research. Since they could not bring the doomsday sect into the laboratory, they joined the Clarion group as observers. They could not use questionnaires with these subjects without giving away their identities as researchers. As a result, they gathered data by looking, listening, and secretly recording their observations as the occasion permitted.

Observing the Faithful.   Beginning in early November, the research team began approaching the Clarion believers. They gained entry in various ways. Usually they expressed interest in the messages from Clarion. Sometimes they reported a fictitious dream or mystical experience that would be of interest to the believers. These participant observers did not tell the believers that they were studying them and their reactions to disconfirmation. The research team included the three authors and four assistants who had contact with the believers until the group split up into subgroups and dispersed on January 9. The team observed 33 persons, produced 1,100 pages of transcribed materials, and summarized their findings in the book *When Prophecy Fails* (Festinger et al., 1956).

The observers witnessed three distinct disconfirmations surrounding the cataclysm predicted for December 21. The believers expected flying saucers to pick them up on the afternoon of December 17, then at midnight of the 17th, and finally at midnight of December 20. The observers saw a variety of responses to the failure of these predictions, including an increase in proselytizing, especially among those committed believers who had the most social support.

Defining Qualitative Research

Observing Without Numbers.   The term **qualitative research** refers here to social research based on field observations analyzed without statistics. The subjects may or may not know that they are being observed for social research purposes. The degree to which observers participate actively in the lives of the subjects may vary. However, the term **participant observation** often stands as a synonym for qualitative research, and it implies some involvement in the observed setting. Qualitative research always takes place in the field, that is, wherever the subjects normally conduct their activities. For this reason, qualitative research often goes by the name of **field research**. The term *field research* is somewhat misleading because quantitative research can and frequently does also take place in the field. For example, survey researchers often conduct interviews in their subjects' homes, and standardized observations may occur on street corners or in schools as part of experimental research.

The situational factors that may require qualitative observation and the techniques of this approach affect both research design and subject sampling. As a result, we can explore qualitative research in terms not only of construct and inferential statistical validities, but also of internal and external validities. We will consider these validities at the end of the chapter as they apply to qualitative research.

Advantages of the Qualitative Approach. Qualitative research entails direct observation and relatively unstructured interviewing in natural field settings. The researcher attends to the social transactions that occur in the setting and may also collect pertinent documents and artifacts. Qualitative data collection appears spontaneous and open ended and usually has less structure and planning than quantitative research.

Quantitative researchers sometimes see this flexibility and the tendency of observers to become personally involved in their field setting as threats to reliability and validity. However, qualitative researchers regard these same features as strengths of the method. The involvement and naturalness of the observers reduces their disruption of the setting and group under study. After getting used to the observer's presence, the subjects can return to their normal routines. The observer who looks, listens, and flows with the social currents of the setting can acquire perceptions from different points of view. Interviews with different subjects and observations at different times and places in the same social network should defeat any effort to "fake" behavior. This approach has the advantage of **triangulation**, which compares different interviews and perceptions of the same subject or behavior. Faulty understandings, which might elude any single measure, will become apparent in the contrast of divergent vantage points.

Qualitative researchers point to these strengths of nonreactivity (little impact on the natural setting) and triangulation as setting the standard by which to judge other research methods. That is, the data of the qualitative observer may provide more detail and less distortion than those of other approaches. Perhaps the quantitative criteria of reliability and validity should not apply to qualitative data. For a more extensive debate about the relative merits of quantitative and qualitative methods, see the exchanges of Becker and Geer versus Trew in McCall and Simmons (1969). As will be seen, however, a research approach must provide more than valid observations. It must satisfy the other validity criteria that pertain to drawing causal inferences, including those related to its design.

Design. Qualitative research usually consists of passive observations with no intent to manipulate the causal variable. On occasion, however, qualitative designs can take the form of natural experiments. For example, *When Prophecy Fails* (Festinger et al., 1956) resembles an interrupted time series quasi experiment. Consider the experience of disconfirmation of belief as the independent variable. The believers encountered three such disconfirmations in a period of four days. The disconfirmations (Xs) occurred at 4 P.M. (X_1) and midnight (X_2) of December 17 and at midnight of December 20 (X_3). Prior to, between, and following these disconfirmations, the observers monitored the proselytizing behaviors of the believers. These behaviors included calling the press with news releases, welcoming outsiders for persuasion sessions, and making greater efforts to increase the faith of marginal members. We can diagram this sequence of observations (symbolized by O) and disconfirmations as follows:

$$\ldots O\ O\ O\ X_1\ O\ X_2\ O\ O\ O\ O\ X_3\ O\ O\ O\ \ldots$$

If we can understand qualitative research as a variant of experimental or correlational designs, why treat it as a separate class? For one reason, the nature of qualitative research complicates and blurs the design, as you will see later. The second reason, explored in the next section, pertains to the philosophy of knowledge. As will be seen, some qualitative researchers do not share the positivist views of most quantitative researchers.

To see how the qualitative method blurs research design, consider the timing and nature of the observations or Os in the example. Ordinarily in quantitative research, the measures consist of items or scales administered at fixed time point(s) to all subjects. In *When Prophecy Fails*, the observers wanted to gather data continuously but could not for practical reasons. At the beginning of the study, several different researchers gained entry at varying times to the inner circle of believers in two different locations. After entry, an observer could monitor the believers only at those times when he or she could join them. At times, the observers had to leave to record their notes or to sleep. Thus the apparent completeness and regularity of the observations implied by the sequence of Os understates the gaps in the data stream.

Aside from such gaps, the observers varied over time in what their understanding, roles, and fatigue allowed them to see. As participants, their roles changed from curious strangers to full members to potential leaders. Believers sometimes asked the observers to conduct group meetings and even wondered if the observers were aliens from Clarion come to judge them. In sometimes lengthy meetings, the observers no doubt became weary and wavered between boredom and emotional arousal.

More variation in their perceptions came with the growth of the observers' acquaintance with and comprehension of the people and situations under study. For example, the investigators wanted to measure increases in proselytizing behavior. But what should or could they consider increased proselytizing behavior? The range and classification of potential proselytizing behaviors grew and crystallized with researchers' experience in observing the group. The regularity of the Os in the diagram fails to reflect the actual disordered, dynamic, and uncontrolled measurement process. Thus, although qualitative research may resemble quantitative research designs, it has much less order and is much more prone to validity threats.

Differences from Other Approaches.   On a continuum of researcher's control, true experiments would fall at the high end and qualitative research at the low end. In true experiments, researchers assign subjects to groups that receive different experiences chosen by the researcher. In contrast, the qualitative researcher can only visit the subjects in their natural habitat (with their permission) and observe them. Such researchers must constantly adapt their strategy to the rhythm, style, and preferences of the subjects.

The most obvious difference between quantitative and qualitative research appears in the system used to report the findings. Tables, figures, and statistics appear in the results sections of quantitative studies. In contrast, qualitative research reads like a story written in everyday language. A stranger enters a group or community, gets acquainted, has experiences and relationships, and then shares the insights gained on reflection.

RATIONALES FOR QUALITATIVE RESEARCH

How does one choose between quantitative or qualitative methods? To some extent, researchers simply follow their training and use the method that feels most comfortable. But two other factors also influence the choice of method. One of these involves the scholar's philosophy of science as it favors one or another method of gathering and presenting information. The other reason has to do with the practical limits on the way researchers can operate. As mentioned in the previous section, strategies vary in the amount of control required of the researcher. Sometimes qualitative research emerges as the most or only feasible method, given the nature of the subjects and their environment.

Models of Knowing

Positivism.   To this point, this text has presented an approach to knowing that shapes most of quantitative social research. Growing out of the tradition of positivism, it seeks to understand the general principles (or laws) that govern any set of specific events or experiences. This approach assumes that an objective reality exists independent of the perceiver and that we can come to know it, however dimly. Social research in this tradition proceeds by offering tentative laws (called theories) and then attempting to disconfirm them through their testable implications (called hypotheses). For more detail on this approach, see Cook and Campbell (1979) and the appreciation of Campbell's views in Brewer and Collins (1981).

Research methods that use numbers will prove most convenient for summarizing results, assessing measurement reliability and validity, testing inferences from samples (statistical inference validity), and planning precise research designs with high internal validity. As a result, qualitative methods will come to be used only under two circumstances. One of these conditions, given positivist assumptions and goals, occurs when quantitative procedures prove impossible. In such a case, we must test our hypotheses with qualitative data. As will be seen in the next section, participant observation can offer the sometimes essential advantage of little or no reactivity.

Phenomenology.   The second condition occurs when the researcher does not subscribe to positivist assumptions (for example, Patton, 1980; Smart, 1976. Some researchers do not accept that there exists, or that they have the responsibility of seeking, an objective, underlying reality. Rather, they have more interest in understanding daily life and activities from the actor's subjective point of view. The concern with the subject's point of view derives from different sources. One source, which has given its name to a style of research within sociology, is called **symbolic interactionism**. This perspective emphasizes that

> (1) human beings act toward things on the basis of the meanings that the things have for them; (2) these meanings are a product of social interaction in human society; and (3) these meanings are modified and handled through an interpretive process that is used by each person in dealing with the things he/she encounters. (Meltzer, Petras, & Reynolds, 1975, p. 54)

If no objective reality exists or if we cannot know it, then reality becomes what the actor thinks, feels, and says that it is. This view implies that we have no reason to impose an external theory on the subjective views of the actors. Preconceived hypotheses, constructs, and measures will only hinder the researcher in understanding the actor from the actor's point of view. This focus on the subject's point of view agrees with the philosophy called **phenomenology**. When applied to the social sciences, it emphasizes that social "facts," unlike physical facts, are "characterized by and only recognizable because of their meaningfulness for members in the social world" (Smart, 1976, p. 74). It follows that the researcher should try to discover the meaning of things and events to the members of the social group of interest.

Phenomenology has had particular appeal in anthropology, expressed in an approach called **ethnography** or ethnomethodology. Although the term suggests a general method for describing (*graphy*) a cultural group (*ethno*), it has come to mean the particular technique of describing a social group from the group's point of view: "The ethnographer tries to obtain the cultural knowledge of the natives" (Werner & Schoepfle, 1987a, p. 23). Such an approach has special relevance to anthropology because that social science must deal with the problem of **ethnocentrism**, perceiving other cultures from the perspective of one's own cultural biases. How far some ethnographers have distanced themselves from the positivist perspective is shown by the following definition: "Ethnomethodology is not a method of pursuing the truth about the world. Rather, it examines the many versions, including its own, of the way the world is assembled" (Mehan & Wood, 1975, p. 114). Carried to its extreme, this approach requires an immersion in the studied group: "the researcher must begin by first becoming the phenomenon. . . . a full-time member of the reality to be studied" (Mehan & Wood, 1975, p. 227).

The ethnographic approach of necessity consists of qualitative techniques. Consider the classic study *Tally's Corner* (Liebow, 1967). Elliot Liebow, then a graduate student in anthropology, wanted to understand the nature of life among a small group of poor black men centered on a corner in an inner city. Tally was a 31-year-old man who became one of Liebow's **key informants**, that is, a source of interview information and a main link between Liebow and the rest of Tally's social circle.

Liebow wanted to describe "lower-class life of ordinary people, on their own grounds and on their terms. . . . [The data] were to be collected with the aim of gaining a clear, firsthand picture . . . rather than of testing specific hypotheses . . . [with] no firm presumptions of what was or was not relevant" (Liebow, 1967, p. 10). He made explicit his avoidance of objective general laws: "The present attempt, then, is not aimed directly at developing generalizations about lower-class life from one particular segment of the lower class at a particular time and place but rather to examine this one segment in miniature" (Liebow, 1967, p. 16).

Liebow's analysis of time perspective exemplifies his aim to see the world through the eyes of the actors. He notes that one theory explains lower-class behavior in terms of a defect—the absence of a well-developed future time orientation. Liebow attempts to understand the same behavior not from the standpoint of a theory but from that of the men. He takes the side of his subjects and tries to persuade the reader also to see through their eyes: "Thus, when Richard squanders a week's pay in two days it is not because, like an animal or a child, he is present-time oriented, unaware of or unconcerned with his future. He does so precisely because he is aware of the future and the hopelessness of it" (Liebow, 1967, p. 66). Liebow quotes Richard's rationale: "I've been scuffing for five years from morning till night. And my kids still don't have anything, and I don't have anything" (p. 67). Liebow concludes that the "apparent present-time concerns with consumption and indulgences—material and emotional—reflect a future-time orientation. I want mine right now is ultimately a cry of despair, a direct response to the future as he sees it" (p. 68).

Hypotheses: Before, After, or Never.   In sum, qualitative research may serve within either framework—positivism or phenomenology. In the latter case, interviews and observation seek in-depth understanding with neither prior theory nor the goal of general laws that go beyond the setting studied. In this case, qualitative research will not test hypotheses. The researcher may speculate, after collecting and interpreting the data, about the implications for wider segments of the population. However, such a researcher would not proclaim any universal laws.

When research attempts only to portray phenomena without testing for causal patterns, we call it descriptive. Because this text focuses on causal rather than descriptive research, we will have more interest in qualitative research that tests hypotheses in the positivist tradition.

Confirmatory research consists of causal research that tests prior hypotheses. Research that begins without hypotheses but with only a general question is **exploratory research**. In this case, the data lead to the hypotheses. We may then test such post hoc hypotheses in the usual confirmatory way.

A clear example of the confirmatory, hypothesis-first type of qualitative research appears in our opening example from *When Prophecy Fails*. Early on, the authors state five conditions under which they expect to see increased proselytizing following disconfirmation. These conditions express testable hypotheses (Festinger et al., 1956, p. 4).

In contrast, exploratory research seeks to build theory rather than test it. In commenting on this exploratory process, one qualitative researcher noted: "Model building is an ongoing process. Because a participant-observer does not go into the field with a hypothesis, the end point of such a study is not always obvious. The construction of the model signals the end of the study, and first attempts at model building usually are made long before the researcher leaves the field" (Browne, 1976, pp.

81–82). As illustrated by *When Prophecy Fails*, qualitative research sometimes tries to confirm theory. However, at the beginning of truly original projects, existing theory may seem inadequate or even misleading. In such a case, the researcher meets the data with an open mind in order to create fresh theory.

An example of the exploratory approach comes from another study of a cult predicting the end of the world. A graduate sociology student wanted to know how cults recruit and retain members in the face of a disapproving and even hostile society (Lofland, 1966). Almost single-handedly, he observed the group for about fifteen hours per week for the first nine months and for four days per week as a live-in participant for another three months. He not only described the formation of this cult but also produced some general principles that could serve as testable hypotheses. For example, Lofland authored a series of conditions for recruitment into a cult that together represent a theory of conversion (1966).

Exploratory qualitative research can also fill in the gaps in existing theory. For example, research has documented the overarching connection between poverty and low academic achievement. Some researchers have explained this relationship using the self-fulfilling prophecy. That is, low expectations for poor students help cause their low performance. However, the initial research in support of this theory did not spell out the process by which the self-fulfilling prophecy took place within actual teacher–student interactions. One researcher took as his goal "to provide an analysis both of the factors that are critical in the teacher's development of expectations for various groups of her pupils and of the process by which such expectations influence the classroom experience for the teacher and the student" (Rist, 1970, p. 413). Rist observed one class of children from kindergarten through second grade and then offered a number of general propositions and processes. Other researchers can translate such explanatory ideas into testable hypotheses. Quantitative researchers can then test this theory by operationalizing the constructs as standard measures.

In summary, qualitative research may or may not entail hypotheses. Qualitative research from the tradition of phenomenology describes social process from the point of view of particular actors rather than testing general causal claims. But a researcher from the positivist tradition will need some hypotheses. This researcher will pursue causal laws that apply to whole populations and will either test prior hypotheses (confirmation) or generate new ones (exploration).

Feasibility

Qualitative research may offer the only alternative when hypotheses do not translate well into quantitative terms. One instance occurs when a new theory cannot provide well-defined hypotheses or its constructs have no adequate measures. A more common problem occurs when the natural social setting provides the only or best location for research but will not permit the usual standardized measures. For example the actors under study may change their behavior or expel the researcher when they become aware of the measurement process. In such cases, the qualitative approach may serve well. This approach does not require well-developed quantitative measures and generally proves less reactive by not constantly reminding the actors of their being observed. Qualitative methods even allow participants to conceal their observer status, making them unobtrusive.

Nonreactive Data Collection.   The participant observer joins in the natural social processes of the setting. To the extent that observing these processes changes them, the research loses value. The qualitative approach surpasses most quantitative methods in its nonreactivity. Nevertheless, there always remains the risk that the actors will change their behavior or conversation in the presence of the observer. As Becker says, the researcher "must learn how group members define him and in particular whether or not they believe that certain kinds of information and events should be kept hidden from him. He can interpret evidence more accurately when the answers to these questions are known" (Becker, 1958, pp. 655–656). If we cannot rule out reactivity entirely, perhaps we can adjust for it in the final analysis.

However, participant observers have good reason to believe that their presence will not greatly distort their data. Researchers who gain entry to the setting and acceptance by the key informants have achieved a large measure of trust. Had the actors wished to conceal themselves, they would have found it much simpler and more effective to deny the observer entry than to sustain a charade. Qualitative projects may require hundreds or thousands of hours of the observer's presence in the setting. This long duration, the multiple informants, and the many cross-checks of observations and interviews (or triangulation) all tend to discourage any sustained reaction on the part of the actors.

Consider Rist's two-and-one-half years of observing the same students in kindergarten, first grade, and second grade. However reactive his presence may have seemed initially, the class must have accepted and ignored him after the novelty wore off. A quiet observer would not likely have much effect on five- and six-year-olds pursuing their own games, lessons, and friendships. Similarly, Lofland's (1966) involvement with his doomsday cult must also have passed through an early reactive stage. However, after months of involvement, approval by the leadership, and resident status in the group, his presence would produce little reaction.

Despite the reasons for trusting the accuracy of qualitative research in general, some authors have challenged it in special cases on grounds that the actors misled the observer. One of the most controversial of these challenges appeared in Derek Freeman's critique of Margaret Mead's research in Samoa. In 1925, Mead was studying adolescence, a developmental period known in American and European cultures for its emotional stresses and conflicts. Mead reported, in contrast, that Somoan adolescence appeared more relaxed because that culture permitted promiscuity before marriage. This finding agreed with her belief that adolescent turmoil came not from biology but rather from cultural restrictions. Freeman contends that Mead erred in her assessment of Samoan adolescence because Samoans place a high value on female virginity. Mead was misled, Freeman argues, by her young female informants, who were simply teasing her (Freeman, 1983, pp. 288–291). Mead went on to become a world-famous anthropologist, but, now dead, can no longer defend her fieldwork. However, the fact that such doubts can arise about informants points to an inherent risk in this method.

Unobtrusive Participant Role.   To avoid reactivity and to gain entry into otherwise forbidden settings, the researcher may have to work in an **unobtrusive** way, that is, operate without informing the actors of his or her research role. Again, as summarized by Becker (1958), if the observer works undisclosed, "participating as a full-fledged member of the group, he will be privy to knowledge that would normally be shared by such a member and might be hidden from an outsider. He could properly interpret his own experiences as that of a hypothetical typical group member" (p. 655).

Commonly, the participant observer's role will remain unknown or unclear to at least some actors. For example, as Liebow (1967) moved among Tally's circle of friends, they might recognize him as Tally's acquaintance, with whatever that implied. However, not all the actors knew that Liebow was compiling extensive notes on their conversations and actions.

Lofland's (1966) experience shows the potential cost of working as a known or obtrusive observer. Although the group tolerated him at first as a self-identified observer, it finally excluded him when it became clear that he was not going to convert. Apparently, the cult allowed entry only in order to recruit him.

Lofland's exclusion stands in contrast to the outcome in *When Prophecy Fails* (Festinger et al., 1956). That research team chose to enter the cult as participants not identified as observers. The Clarion cult became more concerned about its public image and fearful about its possible persecution in its final days. As a result, the group might well have denied the observers access to the aftermath of the disconfirmation had it known they were conducting research.

METHODS OF QUALITATIVE RESEARCH

Ethics

Ethical Issues.   Unobtrusive studies raise serious ethical problems. Some research cannot proceed if the observed know of the study and have to give informed consent. In planning unobtrusive studies, the researcher and the human subject protection committee that reviews the plan must assess the subjects' risks and the researchers' ability to protect their confidentiality.

Sometimes field researchers have to go to court to protect their field notes. One example involves a sociology student named Mario Brajuha who had been working and observing in a restaurant that later burned down (Thaler, 1985). A New York State grand jury demanded to see his notes for an arson investigation, but he refused. The court dismissed the case against Brajuha after the state accepted an edited version of his research journal. However, the Brajuha case did not settle the right of qualitative researchers to protect their data. In a later case, a U.S. District Court held in contempt a graduate student named James Scarce for refusing to reveal information given him in confidence by animal rights activists. Scarce was studying these activists as part of a long-term project on radical social movements, and a federal grand jury wanted his information for their investigation of break-ins at university laboratories. The American Sociological Association supported Mr. Scarce by providing a friend of the court brief arguing for the right of social researchers to protect the identity of their sources (Levine, 1993). However, the U.S. Court of Appeals for the Ninth Circuit upheld the District Court's contempt ruling thus sending Mr. Scarce to jail on May 14, 1993 (Scarce remains in jail, 1993). He did not receive his release until October 18, 1993, having neither revealed his sources nor established the legal right of researchers to protect their sources (Scarce released from jail, 1993).

Even if no grand jury demands confidential data, disguised field observations can raise ethical concerns. Such methods deceive subjects about their being observed and may expose behaviors of the most private and intimate sort. The most famous example of such research concerned homosexual acts by men living otherwise "straight" lives. Laud Humphreys (1970) observed homosexual encounters between strangers in public restrooms—the "tearoom trade." He was able to do this by playing the role of lookout for anyone approaching, also known as the "watchqueen." He noted the license numbers of the cars driven by his subjects and obtained their names and addresses from motor vehicle records. A year later, disguised and claiming that he was doing a health survey, he conducted home interviews with 50 of these same men, 27 of whom were married. Humphreys took extensive precautions to protect his subjects' identities. He notes that "I even allowed myself to be jailed rather than alert the police to the nature of my research, thus avoiding the incrimination of respondents through their possible association with a man under surveillance" (1970, p. 171). However, others worry that no one should possess such potentially harmful data given the risk that a subpoena could force disclosure (Bernard, 1988). In a later edition of his work (published in 1975), Humphreys himself expressed second thoughts about the wisdom of his methods.

Techniques

We can divide qualitative research into a series of steps: (1) gaining entry; (2) category definition and observation; (3) data recording; and (4) analysis. The following brief discussion will address each of these steps. For detailed guides to participant observation, see the treatments by Bernard (1988), Lofland (1971), Patton (1990), Schwartz and Jacobs (1979, Part II), and Werner and Schoepfle (1987a; 1987b). You can find examples of the problems and procedures of qualitative research in Glazer (1972) and Golden (1976).

Gaining Entry and Finding a Key Informant.   The field researcher must attend the setting during the interactions of interest and occupy a role that does not cause the actors to change their natural behavior. Of course, the researcher can attempt to gather data by interview only. Sometimes, one or more key informants will provide information to the interviewer. However, data drawn only from informants leave the risk that they will mislead the researcher (as alleged in Freeman's critique of Mead noted earlier). Even if the informants speak in good faith, one might doubt their accuracy. For example, what kind of person would offer to serve as a key informant to a stranger come to study his or her group? Some key informants may be deviant members of their own community and, therefore, not well placed to describe it to others (Bernard, 1988).

Although helpful later in suggesting important areas of observation and interpretations of data, informants initially serve as contacts linking the researcher to the informant's network. Thus the researcher typically begins the **entry** process by persuading one or more members of the setting to accept him or her. If an observer can define his or her role in a satisfactory way, other members of the setting will permit entry as well. For example, Lofland (1966) and the Festinger team (1956) both gained acceptance by approval from central leadership of each cult under study.

The method of gaining acceptance by key members of a setting varies with the nature of the setting. Sometimes, the key informants may know the observer's role (for example, Tally in *Tally's Corner*). In others, acceptance may require that the observers conceal their research interest (for example, *When Prophecy Fails*). In both cases, the researcher's role must permit him or her to be curious and in need of instruction by other members. Sometimes such a student role will seem natural, as in the case of prospective recruits to a cult's belief system. In other cases, the observer may "purchase" his or her entry and continued presence in some way. For example, the researcher may offer aid, as Liebow offered to one of Tally's friends in a legal matter or by serving as watchqueen in Humphrey's study. After a while, the observer may enjoy the bond of friendship with one or more of the setting's members. Possibly one or more actors will become interested in the researcher's task and support the activity out of curiosity or a desire to produce the best possible report about his or her own setting.

Although entry into a new setting may seem an enjoyable process of making new friends, some researchers find it harrowing. Some settings carry risks (for example, Humphrey's arrest for loitering near a public restroom). First contact with a truly different subculture may inspire either excitement or "the desire to bolt and run" (Bernard, 1988, p. 163). Even if the initial contact goes well, the qualitative researcher may feel "some form of depression and shock thereafter (within a week or two). One kind of shock comes as the novelty of the field site wears off and there is this nasty feeling that anthropology has to get done. . . . Another kind of shock is to the culture itself. Culture shock is an uncomfortable stress response, and must be taken very seriously" (Bernard, 1988, pp. 164–165).

Category Definition and Observation.   In the typical quantitative study, category or variable definition precedes data collection. In contrast, participant observers have only general questions as their guides and cannot translate them into standardized measures. As a result, the qualitative researcher both observes and chooses what to observe at the same time. For example, the Festinger team (1956) knew at the beginning that they wanted to study proselytizing. But they only discovered how proselytizing would appear in behavioral terms in the process of observing. Thus, such acts as being more or less responsive to callers from the media came to be included in the category of behaviors representing proselytizing.

The alternating process of observing and defining categories will repeat throughout the study and helps to avoid blinding preconceptions and rigid measurement procedures. The flexibility and sensitivity of this approach may allow profound penetration of the subject matter. As counterparts to these advantages, this method faces the threats of unreliable measures, instrumentation shift, and observer bias.

Recording Data.   What is to be observed will vary from study to study, depending on the topics, and over time within a study, evolving with the definitions of the categories and the researcher's interests. Lofland has noted that different levels of analysis may interest the observer, ranging from brief acts up to entire settings, and that recorded observations provide either static cross-sectional or longitudinal descriptions (Lofland, 1971, pp. 14–15). In light of this complexity, how does the observer make sure to cover and record the full range of categories?

Comprehensive observation requires the observer's presence at the times and places of the actions of interest. Unless the observer knows in advance when these activities are going to occur, he or she must take up virtual residence in the setting. If information comes from interviews, the interviewer has more control of when and where the interview will take place. Still, how can the interviewer ask about each point of interest? In the absence of standardized questionnaires, the interview at least can follow some preset guidelines. A written or memorized **interview guide** provides a checklist of topics that the interviewer wants to cover. These checklists include reminders about the categories of interest to the researcher in an order that seems likely to promote rapport (usually holding more threatening questions until later). The guide provides only a general approach. The actual questions are composed on the spot to fit the natural rhythm of the dialogue and to promote maximum, unbiased disclosure by the interviewee. The art of such interviewing requires a sensitive ear and the ability to gently probe without suggesting any desired answers.

The researcher must record the observations and interview material either by audiotape or by handwritten notes. Although taping one's notes and interviews may seem faster initially, transcribing them from tape may take six or more hours for each hour of interview. In either case, the resulting transcripts should have labels with basic information such as the interviewee's identification (name or code number), demographic characteristics, and location in the social network under study along with the time and place of the interview or observation. Bernard reminds us that "the difference between field work and field experience is field notes" (1988, p. 183), and he offers five rules for good notes (1988, pp. 181–183):

1. Make many shorter notes instead of a few long ones.
2. Separate notes into four types: (a) field jottings done on the spot, (b) field notes based on the jottings, (c) field diary about personal reactions that can later help interpret the notes and reveal oberver bias, (d) field log of how time was spent.
3. Take field jottings all the time.
4. Do not fear that you can offend people by jotting notes.
5. Set aside time before the end of each day for writing up all notes.

In the case of unrecorded interviews and of observations of behaviors in the setting, the observer must make the notes as extensive and accurate as possible. Make field notes as soon as possible after observation. One exception to Bernard's fourth rule about not offending people with note taking involves disguised research. Since conspicuous note taking could spoil the observer's accepted role, the unobtrusive researcher may have to make brief notes of key words and phrases in fleeting moments of privacy (for example, going to the bathroom or stepping out for a walk). As soon as possible thereafter, and certainly before going to sleep, the researcher must construct fully detailed notes from the jottings and recollections.

Whether originally taped or handwritten, the notes should then be typed with multiple copies. One copy can serve as a permanent record of the raw data. The analyst can rearrange or annotate other copies as part of the interpretive process. One type of annotation involves coding each observation with a number that allows you or others to quickly look up all instances of any behavior type. For example, if you were studying cult recruitment, you might devise a code number to put in the margin of your notes next to every instance of recruiting behavior. For such a note-coding system, some anthropologists recommend using the Outline for Cultural Materials (Murdock, 1971). Because qualitative research may extend for months and the researcher does not want to omit any potentially useful details, the resulting documents can easily run to hundreds or thousands of pages. Given such massive data sets, qualitative researchers increasingly record their field notes and codes in a computer database to enable fast relational file searches.

Analysis.   The analysis of qualitative data begins with the first observation. As the observation phase winds down, analysis becomes more intense. Analysis organizes the hundreds of pages of raw notes into a meaningful pattern. It interconnects discrete observations and locates these connected events within a small number of conceptual categories. As with a jigsaw puzzle, the researcher fits and refits the pieces according to a variety of tentative models until few unconnected pieces remain and the fit seems subjectively and logically satisfying.

A final report gives the resulting "jigsaw" picture as clearly and convincingly as possible. A common reporting method combines quotations from interviews with anecdotes from the field observations to illustrate and support the analyst's general argument. In support of a causal model, the analyst may report the approximate frequency and distribution of the different categories of observation (for example, high versus low proselytizing) as evidence. Such event counts may even support basic statistical analysis, but the qualitative researcher seldom relies as heavily on statistics as does the quantitative researcher.

Validity Threats

The causal analysis of qualitative data poses serious problems (Becker, 1958). Bernard (1988) points out that the qualitative researcher has become immersed in the setting and may well adopt the perspective of the key informants. At the same time, the researcher must retain an outsider's skepticism in interpreting the data. In practice, the analyst must switch back and forth between these perspectives, checking for consistencies and inconsistencies among the various informants and observations. In this final section, we will review qualitative methodology from the standpoint of each of the four main types of validity: construct, internal, statistical inference, and external (also see Kidder, 1981; LeCompte & Goetz, 1982).

Construct Validity.   This text has defined different kinds of construct validity—measurement and experimental. Both face threats in qualitative research, but measurement construct validity is especially vulnerable. By definition, participant observation does not use standardized tests. As a result, observations have a special proneness to random measurement error and, thus, unreliability. Measurement validity cannot exceed measurement reliability. By their nonquantitative nature such observations do not lend themselves to reliability estimates. Because the participant observer often works in varying circumstances and with varying categories, we cannot assume she or he has good consistency over occasions.

Even with good reliability over time in the observations of a single researcher, qualitative data still face problems with interrater reliability and, in turn, measurement construct validity. The measuring instrument in qualitative research consists of an individual without the support of standard instruments or baseline criteria. The observer must use his or her feelings, curiosity, hunches, and intuition to explore and understand the setting. Consequently, two observers may arrive at results quite different from each other. As an example Derek Freeman (1983) came to a very different analysis of the Samoan culture than did Margaret Mead.

The qualitative observer also runs the risk of being biased by the feelings, loyalties, or antagonisms generated by the setting and the actors in it. To achieve access to the most secret behaviors and perceptions of the actors, the observer must seem trustworthy and likable. Most people would find it difficult to gain the necessary trust and friendship without returning some genuine affection. As a result of these feelings, the observer may leave the neutral role of scientist and adopt the role of committed member in the setting, a role shift called **going native**. In practice, going native poses little threat to published research since it usually terminates the study unless the observer elects to publish a propaganda piece.

Experimental construct validity has less relevance in qualitative studies since the researcher seldom tries to make experimental manipulations in the natural setting. On the other hand, the observer may welcome the chance to see the outcome of naturally occurring changes. However, the entry of observers at or near the time of a natural experiment may change the meaning of the natural event, as illustrated in *When Prophecy Fails*. Near the time that the cult was expecting a major event, the researchers brought in several new observers. Some had cover stories that raised the cult's confidence in their beliefs and social support resources. Thus, not only can the setting bias the observer but also the observer can change the setting, thereby distorting the results. A good analyst must reflect on the ways that the observers have distorted the natural setting.

Internal Validity. Qualitative research can at most approximate quasi-experimental designs, with all the threats to internal validity. More often, qualitative studies resemble correlational designs, with no manipulation of the independent variable.

In correlational designs, causal inferences depend on the association of two variables. However, an association requires that both variables take different values. Qualitative research sometimes does not meet this requirement, for example, when it describes two aspects of behavior one of which does not vary. Observing that one level of one variable and one level of another variable occur together says nothing about the variables' causal linkage. For example, suppose that an observer finds that all ten members of a cult's cell formerly belonged to the Catholic Church. Do these data imply any connection between a Catholic upbringing and cult membership? While we might make up some theory that fits such a link, these made-up data do not support such a causal claim. Neither of our two variables, former religious experience and current cult membership, shows any variability. We do not know how many noncult members come from a Catholic background. Perhaps the community had only Catholics until recently and all residents, cult and noncult alike, were reared Catholic.

Statistical Inference Validity.   More qualitative researchers are expressing their data in quantitative terms. A cult researcher could, for example, make a cross-tabulation between two variables—male/female gender versus strong/weak belief. With the data in this form, analysts can apply inferential statistics. However, most qualitative data do not lend themselves to inferential statistical analysis. As a result, we usually cannot assess the validity tested by such statistics.

This inability to make an inferential leap from a sample to a population does not trouble many qualitative researcher. Often, the qualitative researcher has little interest in generalizing to a larger population. Researchers with an ethnographic perspective want only to describe in the deepest and most detailed possible way a unique group of people. Such researchers have no desire to make any claim about people outside of the studied setting.

External Validity.   For the same reason, qualitative researchers may have even less concern about external validity—generalizing to people in other populations, places, or times. All researchers have problems in assessing external validity. We have no statistical procedure in quantitative research for checking generalizations beyond the studied samples. Thus qualitative research has no disadvantage compared to other methods in this respect.

SUMMARY

Qualitative research differs from quantitative research in its use of participant observation, semistructured interviewing, and nonstatistical methods of analysis and reporting. While quantitative research may or may not take place in the field, qualitative research necessarily takes place in the natural setting and with a minimum of disturbance.

Scientists who wish to describe everyday life from the point of view of the actors (phenomenological perspective) prefer qualitative research. Since they do not seek objective laws, they need not state any hypotheses. Qualitative research methods can also serve researchers in the positivist tradition. They may either test hypotheses that come from theory before the observations begin or make new hypotheses afterward. In the former case, qualitative research may offer the only feasible way to gather data from subjects who would otherwise avoid known researchers or react artificially to the usual methods. In the latter case, qualitative methods can help explore theory that has yet to develop clear hypotheses or operational methods for measuring constructs. These advantages come with a host of threats to construct, internal, and statistical inference validity.

Qualitative research begins with gaining entry into the target setting and defining a role in which the observer can make inquiries. Data collection consists of observing and interviewing, and those activities alternate with revising the variables and categories that guide observations. Because of its in-depth and extensive nature, qualitative data recording will usually prove lengthy. From brief note jotting to later transcribing and coding, these records become the pieces that the analyst arranges into a consistent and logical story.

EXERCISES

1. Read and critique a report of qualitative research. Short examples of qualitative literature appear in readers (for example, Golden, 1976). For critical comment on several qualitative studies, see Glazer's study (1972). Finally, for the deepest immersion, select one complete report (for example, any of those referred to in this chapter). While reading your selection, try to identify a pair of independent and dependent variables and the supposed causal link between them. What validity threats go uncontrolled and how serious do they seem? Try to design a quantitative study that might test the same hypothesis (assuming your qualitative study has or yields a hypothesis), while controlling for the major threats to the qualitative study. What advantage does the qualitative study have over your imaginary quantitative study (for example, feasibility or reactivity)?

2. Try doing a qualitative study yourself. Since a full study would take too long, plan and execute the beginning stages of a modest study. Pick a setting or group to which you do not already belong but to which you might gain entry without risking harm to yourself or others. Try to think of a causal question suitable to this setting. Try to gain entry, that is, visit, get acquainted with at least one actor, and observe and interview for a single session. While in the setting, attempt to conceptualize one or two aspects of the setting or its members around which you can organize your data. As soon as you leave the setting, write up your notes in as accurate and complete a form as possible. Then, sifting through your notes, write a brief report of your experience aimed at reaching a judgment about your hypothesis and describing the actors from their point of view. Consider in your report the ethics of observing others. Did you reveal yourself as an observer? If so, what was the effect? If not, why not, and did this pose a risk to those you observed?

KEY TERMS

Confirmatory research	**Key informant**
Entry	**Participant observation**
Ethnocentrism	**Phenomenology**
Ethnography	**Qualitative research**
Exploratory research	**Symbolic interactionism**
Field research	**Triangulation**
Going native	**Unobtrusive**
Interview guide	

↪ 14 ↩

Interpreting Research
Overview of Research Design and Review Methods

ASSESSING INDIVIDUAL STUDIES
Designs and Threats
Strategy for Appraisal

ASSESSING MANY STUDIES
Checking Facts and Resolving Conflicts
Review Methods

SUMMARY

EXERCISES

KEY TERMS

ASSESSING INDIVIDUAL STUDIES

This chapter has two main tasks. This first section reviews the key ideas from the prior chapters on validity types and their threats. Each of the earlier chapters explored only one or two validity types in the process of describing just one design type. Having met all of the validities and all of the designs, you can now see how type of threat relates to type of design. After reviewing the basic designs and their common threats, we will consider a step-by-step strategy for judging a study's overall validity.

The second section of this chapter deals with the fact that research questions often produce not just one test but rather many different reports. If all these studies agreed, knowing the results of one would tell you the results of every other study. Sadly, a **literature** (all the studies on a single question) will often reveal different findings, making it hard to decide what to conclude. The second section compares the main approaches to making sense out of many studies.

Designs and Threats

Guide to Research Designs.   This text has described a range of research designs, each with special strengths and weaknesses. What is the best design? The answer depends on the situation and subjects, the amount of control the researcher has, and the nature of the question. One design may solve a problem inherent in another design while, at the same time, risking a different type of validity threat. We gain confidence when different measures agree in their portrait of a construct. In the same way, we will have more confidence in a causal claim supported by studies using a variety of research methods (Brewer & Hunter, 1989).

Figure 14–1 presents the major types of research designs in the form of a decision tree. The first contrast separates qualitative from quantitative designs. In qualitative research, we make observations in natural settings and report our findings in everyday language, not in statistics. In quantitative research, we use standardized measures to assign numbers to observations and statistics to summarize the results.

Quantitative research divides into experimental designs and correlational designs. In experimental designs, the causal variable consists of an objective change, either a manipulation by the researcher or some unplanned event such as a natural disaster. Experiments, in turn, divide into true experiments and quasi experiments. True experiments always assign subjects randomly to differently treated groups (see design F of Table 14–2).

Quasi experiments never use random subject assignment and can take two major forms. Interrupted time series designs employ just one group (or subject) observed at several times before and after the treatment(s) as seen in design C of Table 14–2. Nonequivalent control group designs employ two or more differently treated groups as shown in design D of Table 14–2. Although not listed in Figure 14–1, a hybrid of these two types of quasi experiments combines the features of multiple groups with many pre- and postmeasures. This interrupted time series with comparison group design rivals the true experiment in internal validity (see design E of Table 14–2). Another type of experiment, called a preexperiment, does not appear in Figure 14–1 and is seldom seen in published research. Preexperiments differ from quasi experiments by their lack of some crucial

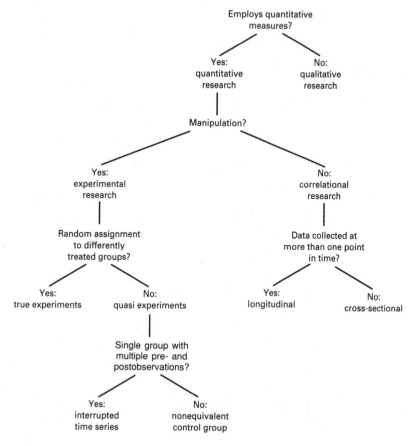

Figure 14–1   Research design typology.

observations and their resulting low internal validity (see designs A and B of Table 14–2).

Correlational designs can also take different forms. Two of these involve the time dimension. Cross-sectional designs consist of one-shot surveys. Longitudinal designs collect data at more than one time, such as panel or trend surveys.

Guide to Validity Threats.   Table 14–1 integrates the material from prior chapters on validity threats and types of research designs. Four design types extend from left to right: true experiments, quasi experiments, correlational studies, and qualitative studies. The four major types of validity appear from top to bottom: construct, internal, statistical inference, and external. Remember that the term *validity* refers to the likely truth of an assertion. Each of these validities pertains to a different aspect of a claim such as "construct *A* causes construct *B*." To judge the overall validity of such a statement, we must consider each of these four types of validity.

Table 14–1 Validity Threats and Research Designs

| | | DESIGN TYPES | | | | |
| | TRUE EXPERIMENTS | QUASI EXPERIMENTS | | CORRELATIONAL STUDIES | | QUALITATIVE STUDIES |
Validity Types		Interrupted Time Series	Nonequivalent Control Groups	Longitudinal	Cross-sectional	
1. Construct						
a. Measurement	√	√	√	√	√	*
b. Experimental	*	*	*	NA	NA	*
2. Internal						
a. Time		*		*		*
b. Group			*	*	*	*
c. Reverse causation					*	*
3. Statistical inference	√	√	√	√	√	*
4. External	*	*	*	*	*	*

52Key: √ = threat should be checked in the data.
 * = threat difficult to check.
 NA = not applicable.
 blank = validity threat probably ruled out.

Each validity type asks a simple question shown visually in Figure 14–2 and verbally as follows:

Construct validity: Does the measured or experimental variable reflect only or mainly the intended construct? A measure or treatment that reflects some other construct or nothing at all (that is, an unreliable measure) has poor construct validity.

Internal validity: Is the observed impact on the outcome due to the presumed cause or does the apparent effect stem from some other variable or causal process? Internal validity pertains to the design of studies and requires attention to a variety of threats or rival explanations.

Statistical inference validity: Does the observed connection between the variables hold for the population from which the sample was drawn, or is it so small that it probably occurred by chance (that is, by sampling error)? Inferential statistics help judge this validity.

External validity: Does the observed finding generalize to other populations, places, and times? If not, we need to limit our claims to the people or setting studied and to ask what unique factors help account for the results.

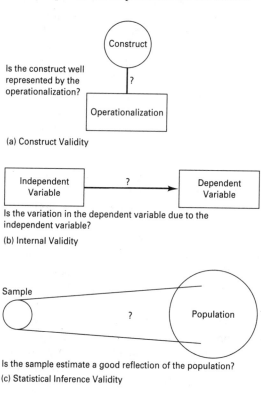

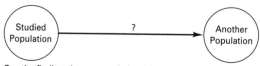

Figure 14–2 Graphic summary of validity types.

Table 14–1 notes two major subtypes of construct validity. Measurement construct validity refers to the extent that measures of observed events reflect the intended constructs. The most common threats to this validity come from poor instrument development leading to excessive random error (unreliability) or systematic error (measurement of the wrong construct). A different type of problem comes from mortality or attrition, which changes the sample on which measures are based. Sometimes counted as a problem for internal validity, mortality is treated here as a source of construct invalidity.

Experimental construct validity refers to the extent to which manipulated variables reflect their intended constructs. Experimental variables risk contamination of either the experimental group or the control group. This problem area includes demand characteristics (for example, placebo effect) and experimenter bias.

Internal validity threats also fall into subtypes, three of which appear in Table 14–1. The threat of reverse causation arises in cross-sectional correlational studies that leave us in doubt as to causal direction. Another type, time threats to single-group studies, includes such rival explanations as history, maturation, instrumentation, and pretest reactivity. Although regression toward the mean may also trouble single-group studies, this threat is best controlled by means suitable to the group threats. The time threats include causes other than the treatment variable that can affect the outcome variable measured over time. The third type, group threats, includes selection, regression toward the mean, and selection-by-time-threat interactions. These threats usually involve preexisting differences between experimental and control groups that can account for group differences in outcome or change scores. Selection also appears as a threat in correlational designs, where we refer to it as confounding or spuriousness.

Design Strengths and Weaknesses.   Research design type cannot rule out one validity threat—external validity. Whether we use a true experiment or a qualitative study, we cannot assume that the results will generalize beyond our studied population. In order to judge external validity, we might compare the subjects, setting, and time of the study to the population, location, and era to which we want to extend our claims. However, confidence about external validity requires us to replicate our study with other types of subjects, places, and times. For this reason, Table 14–1 uses the asterisk (*) in all design columns for external validity to indicate "threat difficult to check."

For all other validity types (rows) in Table 14–1, different design types (columns) have different patterns of strengths and weaknesses. For example, statistical inference validity can be assessed with some precision in any study using quantitative variables and inferential statistics. Thus the checkmark (✓) indicating "threat should be checked in the data" appear in the columns for all experimental and correlational designs. But in the column for qualitative studies, the asterisk shows that this validity problem cannot be checked by inferential statistics. A similar pattern of checks and asterisks appears in the measurement construct validity row. Quantitative studies, but not qualitative ones, permit us to compute reliability and validity coefficients.

Experimental construct validity does not apply to nonexperimental designs. Thus, the NA for "not applicable" appears for that row in the correlational columns. In the true experimental and quasi-experimental columns, asterisks appear for experimental construct validity, to indicate the difficulty in assessing this problem area.

Finally, the internal validity threats form distinctive patterns across the design types. True experiments generally prove immune to all threats to internal validity, as indicated by the blanks in the appropriate cells. Quasi-experimental and correlational studies risk some internal validity threats but not others. Spuriousness poses a special threat to correlational studies. Correlational researchers must measure the potential confounding variable in order to check this threat statistically—hence the asterisk in the group row. Depending on the temporal design, correlational studies may also risk time or reverse causation threats. Qualitative studies, with the least control, risk all of the internal validity threats.

Strategy for Appraisal

The order of validity types listed in the left-hand column of Table 14–1 provides one logical order for assessing a study's overall validity. After locating the specific design subtype, the evaluation can proceed down the appropriate design column to check each type of validity.

Categorizing the Design.   As a first step in assessing a study we must identify its design. As described in Figure 14–1, we might begin by deciding whether the design is quantitative. Quantitative designs permit precise evaluation of measurement construct validity and of statistical inference validity as noted by the checkmarks in those rows of Table 14–1. In contrast, qualitative studies make little or no provision for gauging these kinds of validity.

Quantitative studies further divide into experimental and correlational designs by the presence or absence of an experimental manipulation. Any independent variables created by intervention, whether naturally or by intention, should be assessed for experimental construct validity. The asterisks for experimental designs in the experimental construct validity row in Table 14–1 indicate that this assessment can prove difficult. We must judge whether demand characteristics (for example, placebo effects) have contaminated the treated subjects' experience or whether the design included adequate protective features (for example, placebo control group). In contrast, purely correlational designs have no manipulated variables and thus raise no concerns about experimental construct validity.

Diagramming as an Aid to Checking Designs.   Often, diagramming the design will help both to categorize it and to suggest likely validity problems. For example, internal validity threats depend on such design features as the number of differently treated groups, the use of random assignment to compose groups, and the number of data collection points before and after the intervention. You can highlight such design facets by using the notation of Xs for manipulated independent variables, Os for observations, and Rs for random assignment to groups. After diagramming the design, you can quickly spot the internal validity threats of highest risk. Table 14–2 illustrates this idea by pairing a series of design diagrams with likely threats to their internal validity. Having identified and diagrammed the design, we can review each validity type, focusing on the most likely problems.

Table 14–2 Some Design Diagrams and Internal Validity Threats

Design and Diagram	Threats
a. Single-group preexperiment *O X O*	Time threats very plausible, e.g., maturation
b. Post-only control group preexperiment *X O* *O*	Group threats very plausible, e.g., selection
c. Interrupted time series quasi experiment *OOOOXOOOO*	Time threats, e.g., history
d. Nonequivalent control group quasi experiment *O X O* *O O*	Group threats, e.g., selection-by-time interaction
e. Interrupted time series with comparison group quasi experiment *OOOOXOOOO* *OOOO OOOO*	Internal validity threats implausible

f. True experiment
 	
    O X O
R
    O   O
	Internal validity threats implausible

Construct Validity.   The first question in an overall validity assessment might be, "Do the variables in the study reflect the intended constructs?" If we answer "No," the other validity issues become irrelevant. Even if the study has high internal and external validity, the findings say nothing about the constructs of interest. Such a study may have some bearing on other questions (involving whatever constructs it measures), but it cannot address the theory at hand.

If the study uses quantitative methods, the authors might present numerical evidence on the construct validity of the measured variables. Experimental designs will fix one or more of the independent variables at different levels by intervention. The authors cannot assess the construct validity of such experimental variables by numerical validity coefficients. In these cases, the reader will have to inspect the research methods for possible contamination of the experimental or control groups.

Internal Validity.   If the variables reflect the intended constructs, you can proceed to the second question: "Are the observed effects due only to the studied causal variable(s), or could they result from other causes?" If the design consists of a true experiment or a very strong quasi experiment (for example, interrupted time series with comparison group), we need not concern ourselves about internal validity. These designs rule out the threats of time (for example, history), group (for example, selection), and reverse causation.

Weaker quasi experiments, correlational designs, and qualitative studies do not control all internal validity threats. Only a careful review of the procedures and, sometimes, statistical controls (for example, partial correlation) can help check the plausibility of such rival hypotheses. Designs with low internal validity cannot inspire great confidence in the study's results regardless of the level of the other validities. Suppose that we cannot determine the cause of an effect because of the study's weak internal validity. In this case, no test of statistical inference validity can increase our confidence in the causal link. In addition, we have no finding to generalize to other people, places, or times (external validity).

Statistical Inference Validity.   If the study's variables and design seem valid, the reader should ask the third question: "Could the results in favor of the hypothesis be due to sampling error?" Inferential statistics tell the likelihood that we would obtain the observed results in the sample when in fact no relationship exists in the population. Since these statistics depend so heavily on the sample size, they do not tell us the magnitude of the relationship. A rather small, socially trivial finding may reach statistical significance in a huge sample. On the other hand, a larger association suggesting a strong link between the variables may fail to reach significance because of a small sample size or a low-power statistical test. As a result, the interpretation of the results depends on the descriptive magnitude of the findings and the nature of the variables, not just the inferential statistic.

In quantitative studies, inferential statistics will routinely appear in the results sections. Some readers go first to the inferential statistics to see whether or not the findings have sufficient size (not due to chance) to warrant further inspection. However, narrowing our inspection to inferential statistics can be misleading because passing this validity test does not guarantee any of the other types of validity. Moreover, failure to reach statistical significance may, under certain circumstances (large sample size, reliable measures, and powerful statistics), yield an interesting finding against the hypothesis. Since most studies include numerous variables and hypotheses, we may need to inspect many different inferential statistics, one for each test. To interpret the pattern of findings, some significant and others not, we will need to appreciate other aspects of the study. For example, we need to understand the different variables (some with more construct validity than others) and the nature of the different design components (some with more internal validity than others). Thus the meaning of the inferential statistics will depend on prior judgments about the measures and design.

External Validity.   If an assertion appears valid on each of the three preceding types of validity, we can raise the fourth and final question: "Does the finding generalize to people, places, or times not sampled in this study?" If, however, a research finding appears due to chance, the product of a design with low internal validity, or based on invalid measures, we have little interest in whether it generalizes.

One can best answer the external validity question by repeating the study with different subjects, in different situations and places, and at later times. Such replications test the generalizability, not to all people, places, and times, but only to the subjects, settings, and time periods used in the replications. A claim that has great external validity should gain support in most replications. Any failure to replicate limits the external validity of a previous finding. Of course, such a failure to replicate may also raise doubts about the truth of the previous finding even for the subjects, setting, and time of the original study. Perhaps the first finding resulted from a Type I error in the inferential statistical analysis or poor construct validity of an experimental variable.

Successful replications (however many) cannot establish absolute external validity. There always remain another research method, population, place, and time combination not yet studied. However, replications that test the assertion in many different combinations of these variables can lend credence to an assertion. If the theory claims general applicability, aspects of subject, setting, and time period can be regarded as irrelevant. Such **heterogeneous irrelevancies** in replications ensure that the findings do not depend on the coincidental combination of just one type of subject in a special place at a particular time. Partial replications, those that differ from the original study on such irrelevancies, can prove both helpful and frustrating. Sometimes different studies of the same question yield different answers. The next problem in evaluating research is to make sense of the conflicting results from many studies.

ASSESSING MANY STUDIES

Checking Facts and Resolving Conflicts

Multiple studies of the same question often fail to converge on the same answer. A research area that produces conflicting findings invites a **literature review** to achieve two main goals: establishing any "facts" that *can* be agreed upon and suggesting new explanations to reconcile the conflict.

Selecting Studies for Review. As the first step in reviewing a literature, you need to define it. That is, which studies will you include in the review? Typically, the reviewer specifies the research question that the studies are to have in common. For example, does preschool enrichment provide long-term learning benefits (for a review of this literature, see McKey et al., 1985)? The reviewer then gathers all available studies that address this question. If the reviewer overlooks some studies, we cannot know if the conclusion holds for all studies or depends on a biased selection of studies.

Finding all studies may prove impossible or impractical. As a result, reviewers often limit their analysis by time (for example, all studies published after 1990) or location (say, all studies published in English-language journals). Other criteria may affect study selection as well, including some that can have major effects on the reviewer's conclusions.

One criterion for study selection involves the choice of constructs and the methods that operationalize them. For example, researchers can represent the broad construct of impact of preschool enrichment in different measures of cognitive development, emotional growth, and child health. One could review only those studies that measured students' educational achievement on standardized tests. Or, the reviewer could look at studies with all types of outcome measures, either treated together or assessed in measure-specific clusters. The last approach has the advantage of showing whether the intervention has more success with some outcomes than others.

Another type of selection criterion involves the quality of the study. One point of view holds that only the most valid studies deserve our attention. In this approach, the reviewer would evaluate and grade each study separately along the lines described in the first part of this chapter. Only the studies meeting or surpassing certain validity levels would be reviewed. Another point of view favors inclusion of all studies on the same question while taking into account type of design and level of validity. This latter approach permits testing the possibility that the quality of the study affects the likelihood of results favoring the hypothesis.

Confirming the Facts.   Perhaps the prime motive for literature reviews is to determine the most prevalent or credible findings. Because of the nature of inferential statistics, we expect some results to appear by chance. In any large set of studies, we should find a few Type I error results in which the sample data overestimate the population effect. By reviewing many studies together, we hope that the pattern of "true" findings will stand out from such chance results. Of course, Type II errors can also occur, and sample data can underestimate the true effect in the population (a problem discussed later in this chapter).

Studies also differ because of other validity problems besides statistical inference. Most studies will have some threats such as problems with internal validity (unless a true experiment) or construct validity. If all studies have the same validity threats, they are all doubtful for the same reason. But if different studies risk different threats, no single threat will cast doubt on all the findings. To reject all such studies as invalid, we would have to assume a very complex and unlikely chain of events. Thus a time threat to the internal validity of an interrupted time series design cannot threaten a nonequivalent control group test of the same issue. At the same time, the interrupted time series design checks on the selection threat to the nonequivalent control group design. Although neither study alone would convince us, together they give more confidence for the reviewer's conclusion. As a result, a consistent finding across studies with differing designs and measures will prove more persuasive than one from a literature of identical replications.

Consider an example of a review that converged on a clear outcome. Durlak (1979) studied the effectiveness of two different types of psychological helpers. He identified 42 studies that compared professionals and nonprofessionals. The majority of these studies (28) found no difference between type of helper. Of the minority of studies with a statistically significant difference, most favored the paraprofessional (12 of the 14). Durlak concluded from his review that paraprofessionals equal or surpass professionals as measured by client outcomes. He sorted the studies into five levels of research deficiency, but design quality did not seem to affect the overall conclusion (see Table 14–3).

Explaining Conflicts.   In other cases, the reviewer may not find consensus in a literature. Even after adjusting for study quality, there may remain too many sound studies on both sides of the question to settle the issue. Sometimes these differences stem

Table 14–3 Characteristics, Outcome, and Experimental Quality of Comparative Studies of Paraprofessional and Professional Helpers

Study	Experimental Quality	Paraprofessional Helpers	Client and Helper Sample Size[a]	Results Significantly Favoring
		Group 1: Individual or group psychotherapy or counseling		
Ellsworth (1968)	A	Psychiatric aides	327 psychiatric inpatients (?, ?)	Paraprofessionals
Jensen (1961)	B	Nurses and attendants	75 psychiatric inpatients[b] (?, 3)	Neither group
Karlsruher (1976)	B	College students	60 school children[b] (20, 6)	Neither group
Miles, McLean, & Maurice (1976)	B	Medical students	120 psychiatric inpatients (60, 27)	Neither group
O'Brien, Hamm, Ray, Pierce, Luborsky, & Mintz (1972)	B	Medical students	86 psychiatric outpatients (4, 12)	Neither group
Truax (1967)	B	Adult women	Over 300 vocational rehabilitation clients (4, 4)	Paraprofessionals
Truax & Lister (1970)	B	Adult women	168 vocational rehabilitation clients (4, 4)	Paraprofessionals
Weinman, Kleiner, Yu, & Tillson (1974)	B	Community volunteers	179 psychiatric outpatients (?, ?)	Neither group
Anker & Walsh (1961)	C	Occupational therapist	56 psychiatric inpatients (1, 1)	Paraprofessional
Appleby (1963)	C	Psychiatric aides	53 psychiatric inpatients[b] (?, ?)	Neither group
Colarelli & Siegel (1966)	C	Psychiatric aides	477 psychiatric inpatients (8, ?)	Neither group
Cole, Oetting, & Miskimins (1969)	C	Adult women	22 adolescent delinquents[b] (2, 2)	Neither group
Engelkes & Roberts (1970)	C	Adult counselors	1,502 vocational rehabilitation clients (142, 67)	Neither group
Mosher, Menn, & Matthews (1975)	C	Adult counselors	44 psychiatric inpatients (6, ?)	Paraprofessionals
Poser (1966)	C	College students	295 psychiatric inpatients[b] (11, 15)	Paraprofessionals
Sheldon (1964)	C	General physicians and nurses	83 psychiatric outpatients (?, ?)	Professionals better than physicians but equal to nurses
Mendel & Rapport (1963)	D	Psychiatric aides	166 psychiatric outpatients (?, ?)	Neither group
Covner (1969)	E	Community volunteers	Alcoholics[c] (?, ?)	Neither group
Magoon & Golann (1966)	E	Adult women	Psychiatric outpatients[c] (8, ?)	Neither group
		Group 2: Academic counseling or advising for college students		
Zunker & Brown (1966)	A	College students	320 college students (8, 4)	Paraprofessionals
Brown & Myers (1975)	C	College students	303 college students (?, ?)	Neither group
Zultowski & Catron (1976)	C	College students	188 college students (10, ?)	Neither group
Murray (1972)	C	College students	166 college students (20, 9)	Neither group

Group 3: Crisis intervention for adults

Study		Helper	Target problem	Classification
Knickerbocker & McGee (1973)	B	Community volunteers	92 adults and adolescents in crisis (65, 27)	Neither group
DeVol (1976)	E	Adult counselors	45 adults in crisis (4, 5)	Neither group
Getz, Fujita, & Allen (1975)	E	Community volunteers	104 adults in crisis (?, ?)	Neither group

Group 4: Interventions directed at specific target problems

Study		Helper	Target problem	Classification
Kazdin (1975)	A	College students	54 unassertive adults and college students (?, ?)[d]	Neither group
Lick & Heffler (1977)	A	College student	40 adult insomniacs[b] (1, 1)	Neither group
Moleski & Tosi (1976)	A	Speech pathologist	20 adult stutterers[b] (1, 1)	Neither group
Elliott & Denney (1975)	B	College students	45 overweight college students[b] (3, 1)	Neither group
Levenberg & Wagner (1976)	B	Public health officer	54 adult smokers (1, 1)	Neither group
Levitz & Stunkard (1974)	B	Community volunteers	234 overweight adults[b] (8, 4)	Professionals
Lindstrom, Balch, & Reese (1976)	B	College students	68 overweight college students[b] (4, 1)	Neither group
Penick, Filion, Fox, & Stunkard (1971)	B	Adult volunteers	32 overweight adults (2, 1)	Neither group
Russell & Wise (1976)	B	College students	42 speech-anxious college students[b] (3, 3)	Neither group
Ryan, Krall, & Hodges (1976)	B	College students	72 test-anxious college students[b] (1, 2)	Neither group
Werry & Cohrssen (1965)	C	Parents	70 enuretic children[b] (22, 4)	Paraprofessionals
De Leon & Mandell (1966)	D	Parents	87 enuretic children[b] (56, 4)	Paraprofessionals
Fremouw & Harmatz (1975)	D	College students	30 speech-anxious college students[b] (11, 1)	Neither group

Group 5: Other interventions

Study		Helper	Target problem	Classification
Lamb & Clack (1974)	B	College students	1,192 college students (?, 2)	Paraprofessionals
Schortinghuis & Frohman (1974)	C	Community volunteers	37 handicapped children (4, 3)	Paraprofessionals
Wolff (1969)	D	College students	88 college students[b] (4, 4)	Neither group

Note. A indicates that the design criteria were mainly satisfied; B, that one or two criteria were deficient; C, that three or four were deficient; D, that five were deficient; and E, that deficiencies were present in more than five criteria.
[a] Figures in parentheses are the number of paraprofessional and professional helpers, respectively; a ? indicates that the exact number of helpers was not specified.
[b] Includes no treatment or attention-placebo control groups.
[c] Five therapists participated but a breakdown according to helper groups was not provided.
[d] Client sample size was not indicated.
From Table 1 (pp. 82–83) of Durlak, 1979.

from the nature of inferential statistics. As mentioned earlier, Type I and Type II errors will tend to hide the pattern of findings in the literature.

But in some cases, reviewers will suspect that an unknown variable accounts for the conflict. Suppose A appears to cause B in some studies but not in others. Perhaps some variable C occurs when A causes B but not in those studies where A does not cause B. If so, we say that C interacts with A to cause B or, in other words, to condition the effect of A on B. Such an interaction goes to the heart of external validity.

A good example of the search for such a **conditioning factor** comes from research on attitude change under forced compliance. Experimenters created situations that obliged subjects to engage in behavior contrary to their own beliefs (for example, to give a speech that advocates a position opposite to their own). Under these conditions, people would often shift their attitude to become more consistent with their behavior. One explanation derived from dissonance reduction theory. This view holds that people become uncomfortable with dissonant beliefs such as holding one view while arguing for the opposite. Collins and Hoyt (1972) noticed a persistent conflict in this body of work. Some studies found that subjects given smaller rewards to engage in such behavior were more likely to change their belief, a finding thought to support the dissonance reduction theory. Subjects who received smaller rewards to argue against their beliefs should feel greater dissonance because they have less reason (that is, less pay) for suffering the conflict. However, other research cast doubt on this theory with results showing that greater attitude change followed greater incentives. Both kinds of studies appeared sound in terms of their validity.

Collins and Hoyt (1972) reviewed this literature in order to reconcile this conflict. They believed that the monetary incentive approach did not rule out other explanations (besides dissonance theory) that could account for the findings. They argued that the crucial element did not appear in these studies—namely whether subjects came to feel responsible for an important consequence of their behavior. They predicted that a low monetary reward would lead to more attitude change only under conditions of high responsibility and consequence, consistent with dissonance theory. They designed a new study based on their literature review and found support for this revised theory. Thus a careful review of many conflicting studies led to the discovery of new conditioning variables (responsibility and consequence) that affect the studied relationship.

Review Methods

We can review the results of multiple studies in more than one way. One approach requires that the reviewer obtain the data on which the various studies are based (for example, Cook & Gruder, 1978; Light & Smith, 1971). This method amounts to a reanalysis and goes beyond what we refer to here as literature review. Two main types of literature review can proceed with just the information commonly reported in research studies: the traditional (tabular) approach and the statistical (meta-analytic) approach.

Tabular Review. **Tabular review** uses tables to summarize the results from numerous studies. For example, Durlak (1979) in the review mentioned earlier, used the tabular approach. Table 14–3 presents the results of the Durlak review. Each line of the table describes one study with data about its findings and selected aspects of the design such as type and number of subjects. Subtables can help compare studies with different settings, levels of validity, or variants of the main hypothesis.

Meta-Analytic Review.   The tabular approach gives information about all of the reviewed studies in capsule form. In contrast, **meta-analytic review** combines the results of many studies into a single number. This approach has rapidly gained favor since its appearance in the late 1970s (Bangert-Drowns, 1986; Green & Hall, 1984). Rosenthal (1978) has described various ways of combining such statistics as t values, standardized or z scores, and p values. Detailed treatments of the meta-analytic approach have been offered by Glass, McGaw, and Smith (1981), by Wolf (1986), and most recently by Hunter and Schmidt (1990). For a brief guide to this method, you can consult Durlak and Lipsey (1991).

One early and influential example of this approach looked at 375 evaluations of psychotherapy outcomes (Smith & Glass, 1977). Each study contained at least one contrast between the average treated and control patients. The authors "standardized" each of these between-group differences by dividing it by the standard deviation of the control group. We call the resulting index an **effect size** and symbolize this particular effect size by d. For example, a d of 1.3 means that the treated group improved 1.3 standard deviations more than the control group. The authors averaged all of these ds across studies to produce an overall effect size. Before treatment, both treated and untreated groups had similar distributions, with some clients appearing relatively less well and others relatively better but with the average subject in each group having about the same level of symptoms. After treatment, the average effect size over all the studies showed that therapy clients surpassed controls by .68 standard deviation on the symptom measure used to reflect well being. This amount of improvement means that the average treated client appeared better at outcome than 75 percent of the control clients.

Besides the d statistic, other measures of effect size can serve in meta-analysis. For example, the correlation coefficient r served as the effect size in a review of the link between personality and certain diseases (Friedman & Booth-Kewly, 1987). Since different studies may report results using different kinds of statistics (group means, r, p, t, F, χ^2) the meta-analyst has to convert various results into a common metric, whether d, r, or some other effect size measure.

Expressing each study's results as effect sizes permits further quantitative review. An example of such analysis comes from the meta-analysis of professional and nonprofessional treatment outcomes by Hattie, Sharpley, and Rogers (1984). Using 39 of the same 42 studies reviewed by Durlak, these authors computed effect sizes for each of 154 possible tests. A study could have more than one test comparing professionals and nonprofessionals if it had more than one client outcome measure. Each effect size (d in this case) equaled the difference between the group means of the outcomes of the paraprofessionals' and the professionals' clients divided by the standard deviation of the latter group. Consistent with but more emphatic than Durlak's conclusion, the nonprofessionals' clients appeared much better off than the professionals' clients (average $d = .34$). Table 14–4 presents a summary of the further analyses of these findings.

Table 14–4 Summary Statistics and *F* Tests of Comparisons Between Professionals and Paraprofessionals

Criteria	No. of Effects	M	SD	F	p
From Durlak (1979, 1981)					
Quality of design					
Satisfactory	21	1.21	1.77		
1–2 deficiencies	61	−.08	1.14		
3–4 deficiencies	51	0.46	1.06		
5 deficiencies	19	0.43	1.00		
>5 deficiencies	2	−.10	0.13	4.90	<.01
Assigned to groups					
Random	96	0.42	1.35		
Matched	17	0.50	1.41		
Neither random nor matched	41	0.09	0.92	1.11	.34
From Nietzel & Fisher (1981)					
Therapist state confounded by differential type of treatment					
Yes	48	0.68	1.72		
No	106	0.18	0.96	5.39	.03
Contrasted only 1 paraprofessional, 1 professional					
Yes	22	0.19	0.80		
No	132	0.36	1.32	0.35	.56
Different amounts or durations of treatment					
Yes	13	−.41	1.66		
No	141	0.41	1.20	5.08	.03
Collaboration between paraprofessional & professional					
Yes	2	2.08	3.21		
No	152	0.31	1.22	3.95	.05
Validity					
Valid (15 studies)	57	0.20	0.97		
Not valid (27 studies)	97	0.42	1.40	1.01	.32
Adequacy					
Adequate (5 studies)	23	0.40	0.47		
Not adequate (37 studies)	131	0.33	1.35	0.07	.79
Crucial flaws					
Yes (24 studies)	75	0.40	1.55		
No	79	0.28	0.91	0.38	.54

From Table 1 (p. 537) of Hattie, Sharpley, & Rogers, 1984.

These follow-up analyses began by dividing all of the reports into two or more groups according to different aspects of the studies. For example, the authors compared those judged valid (15 studies) with those judged not valid (27) on the average effect sizes of these two groups. The average effect size of the 15 "valid" studies (.20) fell short of the average effect size of the 27 less valid studies (.42). Should we conclude that invalid studies produce higher effect sizes than valid studies? We cannot draw this conclusion because the inferential statistical test of this difference failed to reach significance ($F = 1.01$, $p = .32$). That is, the difference between these two effect sizes may result only from chance. Observe that the researchers condensed the information about effect size and validity into a single contrast with a clear test of the outcome. Compare this analysis with that of Durlak who graded the validity of each study (A to E) and then simply listed all of the results (Table 14–3). Clearly, the meta-analytic method permits much more precision in exploring such relations.

Selecting a Review Method. Both tabular and meta-analytic review methods have their proponents. Meta-analysis, as we have just seen, has the advantage of precision and conciseness in summarizing a host of studies in a few indices. To mimic this kind of outcome, tabular analysis might compute the percentage of studies with significant results in favor of the hypothesis. However, statistical significance depends on sample size and the vagaries of chance. Thus, this box score method may not estimate properly the support for the hypothesis.

Dealing with this problem of statistical inference gives meta-analysis a unique advantage over tabular review. Schmidt (1992) gives an example of this problem and how meta-analysis handles it. Suppose some treatment has a "true" or population effect size of .50. That is, the treatment lifts 69 percent of the treated group above the average untreated subject. If researchers conduct many tests of this treatment, they will report a variety of effect sizes because of sampling error. Some studies will draw subjects who lead us to overestimate the effect. Other studies will, by chance, tend to underestimate the effect. A few may, by chance, correctly measure the true effect size of .50. Assuming sample sizes of 15 in both the treated and control groups in each of these imaginary studies, Schmidt calculated the standard test of significance (requiring $p < .05$). He found that only studies with an effect size of .62 or greater would appear significant, that is, not due to chance. As a result most of the studies (63 percent), including those that correctly measured the actual effect size as .50, would fail to reach significance. Despite the effectiveness of the treatment (by assumption), most of the studies will portray it as useless (Type II error). A tabular analysis of 100 such studies would find that only 37 supported the hypothesis and conclude that the treatment had no effect. In contrast, meta-analysis could compute the average effect size over all of these studies, converging on the actual effect size of .50 and conclude that the treatment had value.

On the other hand, meta-analysis has limitations. We cannot use it when the literature has relatively few studies, and it cannot apply to studies that fail to report results in statistical terms. Some critics fear that boiling down results into a single measure, such as average effect size, may divert attention from the details that might explain conflicts in findings. Suppose that half of the studies found a positive relation between *A* and *B* and the other half found a negative relation. In this case, the average correlation for all studies might approach zero, indicating no relationship between *A* and *B*. However, a tabular reviewer, in a careful check of each study, might discover a conditioning variable that could explain the two different patterns of findings. Of course, meta-analytic reviewers could also divide studies into those with positive or negative effect sizes. They could then compare these two groups in terms of any measured aspect of the studies in search of this same conditioning variable.

Does Review Method Make a Difference?   To see whether different review methods yield different conclusions, a group of faculty and graduate students served as subjects in a true experiment (Cooper & Rosenthal, 1980). They reviewed the same seven research articles by either the meta-analytic or the tabular method. The meta-analytic reviewers found more support for the hypothesis and a larger effect than did the tabular reviewers. Based on this study, the authors endorsed meta-analysis as a way of reaching more rigorous and objective review conclusions.

In contrast, two other researchers compared two reviews of the same subject matter by different authors, one traditional and the other meta-analytic (Cook & Leviton, 1980). This comparison found that the differences in conclusions did not come from distortions by review method. Rather, the authors traced the disagreement to different criteria for choosing articles to review. Controlling for article selection, the different review methods would have reached the same conclusions. This study found that some alleged weaknesses of the tabular method are not inherent and that both methods, if well done, will converge on the same finding.

Meta-analysis applies only to certain kinds of quantitative reports. Therefore, the adequacy of the original reports affects the decision to include them in the review and affects the conclusions that they can support. Fields of research that rely on qualitative or case-study methods will not support meta-analysis. Where the literature on a question includes both quantitative and qualitative reports, the inclusion of only the quantitative studies in the meta-analysis may bias the review. Reporting deficiencies within studies (for example, omission of some statistics or other information about the validity of the study) may also influence the outcome of the review (Orwin & Cordray, 1985).

If the effect under review seems well accepted, meta-analysis may prove more convenient as a summarizing technique since it produces a handy average effect size. On the other hand, if the reviewers seek an unknown conditioning variable that accounts for discrepant results, neither review method will guarantee success. Only clever and persistent puzzle solving on the part of the reviewer will find the answer.

SUMMARY

This chapter has given an overview of the various threats to validity and the various research designs. It offered a strategy by which to assess any study for overall validity. The steps include identifying design type and checking the threats to each of the four major types of validity. The best support for a study's conclusions (and of the study's external validity) comes from independent replications that vary subject type, place, time, measures, and design.

Findings from many studies can be reviewed in two main ways. The tabular or traditional method briefly lists each study with its outcome. The meta-analytic method combines the results of many studies using summary numbers called effect sizes. Meta-analytic reviews are appearing with increasing frequency and may become the standard method. However, this approach only applies to literatures with sufficient numbers and types of studies. Although the two review methods possess different strengths and weaknesses, they can produce similar conclusions if both are well implemented.

EXERCISES

1. Make sure that you can categorize social research following the decision tree in Figure 14–1. First, try to make up an example of each type of design. That is, for some research question of interest to you, imagine how you could answer it using each type of design. Second, locate a published example of each design type in professional research journals and then diagram each design you collect using the X, O, and R symbols.

2. Find and read a critique of a research report along with the reply of the author(s) of the first report. Such critiques and rebuttals appear in the form of letters to the editor or commentary in many social science journals (for example, the critique by Harris, 1993, and the rejoinder by Halpern and Coren, 1993).

3. Write your own critique of a published report. Follow the strategy outlined in this chapter. Identify the study's design and assess each of the four types of validity. Draw a conclusion about the study's overall validity.

4. Find and read a literature review (for example, in *Psychological Bulletin*). Identify the type of review method used (tabular or meta-analytic). Did the review find agreement on any causal claims? Were there discrepancies in the literature that pointed to conditioning variables?

5. Try reviewing a small sample of research articles. Find a few articles (three to five) on the same question, and read them critically. Then try to draw an overall conclusion with the traditional tabular method. If you are comfortable with statistics and have access to more studies for review, try a meta-analysis of these same studies.

KEY TERMS

Conditioning factor   **Literature**
d   **Literature review**
Effect size   **Meta-analytic review**
Heterogeneous irrelevancies **Tabular review**

ᢒ 15 ᢒ

Applied Social Research

MAKING DECISIONS

Life and Death

An Arkansas court found a man named McCree guilty of murder in 1978. This court had dismissed eight potential jurors because they opposed the death penalty. Under the Sixth Amendment, defendants have a right to a jury that consists of a fair cross section of the community. However, some jurors say they would not consider the death penalty, disregarding the law of states such as Arkansas that have the death penalty. Judges may exclude such jurors from the death penalty phases of capital trials producing "death-qualified" juries.

After winning the guilty verdict, the state decided not to seek the death penalty. McCree appealed his conviction on the basis of social research and won a reversal in two lower courts. These courts based their decision on a number of studies that found that death-qualified juries would be more likely to find defendants guilty than non–death-qualified juries given the same evidence (Bersoff, 1987). If upheld, the McCree case might have required the retrial of hundreds of death row inmates on the grounds that excluded jurors might have found them not guilty.

The case went to the Supreme Court, which assessed both the value of the cited research and its relevance to the case. Reversing the lower courts, the Supreme Court held in 1986 for the states and against McCree. The majority on the Court found "flaws" in the social research evidence (for example, using simulations rather than actual juries in capital cases). Some scholars agreed with the Court that the data did not support the claim that death-qualified jurors had a significantly greater proneness to convict (Elliot, 1991). Other scholars agreed with the lower courts' view that the research supported McCree (Ellsworth, 1991). However, the Court did not disdain social science in general and, in fact, had listened to its findings in past cases (Roesch, Golding, Hans, & Reppucci, 1991).

The Court expressed its opinion in a way that took the issue out of the hands of researchers and did not ask for further evidence on the question. Instead, the Court said the Sixth Amendment required a jury that reflects the makeup of the community in terms of immutable features such as race or gender, not shared attitudes such as views on the death penalty. That is, even perfect research might not have changed the Court's judgment (W. C. Thompson, 1989).

This case makes several points. First, social science can address very serious social questions and can produce results that affect all our lives. Second, to make an impact on social choices, such research must have high quality and consistency. It must meet the scrutiny not only of fellow scholars but also of those holding opposing views (in the McCree case, the lawyers for the states). If the research in the McCree case had low validity or seemed unclear in its thrust, it would not have induced the lower courts to rule for McCree. Finally, to the chagrin of social scientists, their best findings may fail to change policy because of other reasons. Observers suspect that the Supreme Court's McCree decision reflected political concerns such as not wanting to retry hundreds of settled capital cases (W. C. Thompson, 1989). The courts tend to use research findings more when they agree with decisions arrived at on other grounds but not as the sole basis for opinions that go against the social grain.

Judging a Program

If applied research includes any study that has the potential to affect some real-world choice, it could include almost all social science. In failing to make a distinction, such a broad use of the term serves no purpose. By custom, we reserve the term *applied social research* for program evaluation, the primary focus of this chapter. However, we should not forget that other kinds of research, such as that on jury selection, can make an impact on society.

Program Evaluation Defined. Various definitions of evaluation research appear in the literature (Glass & Ellett, 1980). In this text, we will define **program evaluation** as social research used to judge a program's success.

The value of program evaluation depends on the assumption of rational social decision making. Rational institutions will support projects that prove both effective and efficient. In the private sector, profits show that firms are working well. The public sector has no such signal as profits about the success of educational, penal, health, and welfare programs. Instead, evaluation can provide feedback on nonprofit programs that meet the public's needs.

An Evaluation of Compensatory Education. Researchers have assessed a wide array of programs, including some at great expense. For example, the federal government spent millions of dollars on such projects as the Survey of Income and Program Participation and the Income Maintenance Experiments (Hunt, 1985). In this chapter we will focus on one compensatory education program in order to illustrate several subtypes of evaluation. This program worked with disadvantaged children in order to raise their later educational achievements. The poor cannot afford to "buy" such services, and many of the benefits of such projects accrue to society as a whole. Thus profit cannot serve as a measure of the program's worth.

Early efforts to offset childhood disadvantages (for example, Head Start) began with great hopes but became mired in controversy about their effectiveness (Zigler & Muenchow, 1992). Some of the disputes arose from the methods used in these studies. For example, some early Head Start reports arrived at opposing conclusions, depending on the method used to control for preexisting differences between treated and control subjects (see McDill, McDill, & Sprehe, 1972; also Chapter 11). Because of the importance of such programs and the difficulty in assessing them, researchers have produced many evaluations of them in the past two decades. One review of this literature found an overall positive effect (McKey et al., 1985).

One of these compensatory programs has reported unusual success—the Perry Preschool Project, begun in 1962 (Schweinhart & Weikart, 1980). This project derived from a theory that holds that extra stimulation of impoverished preschoolers would raise cognitive ability at school entry, expectations for success in school, commitment to schooling, and learning through high school. The authors tested these predictions on 123 of the poorest black children in a small midwestern city. These children came from five birth cohorts (1958 to 1962) of families of low socioeconomic status living in the same elementary school attendance area. All the children had IQ scores at entry in the educably retarded to low normal range of 70 to 85. The researchers divided these children into treated (preschool education) or control groups as their cohorts reached age 3 (for the 1959 to 1962 cohorts) or 4 (for the 1958 cohort). They followed both groups through high school to assess the long-term impact of the program.

A description of the children's family circumstances shows the need for this kind of program. Less than 20 percent of the parents had high school diplomas themselves. About 50 percent of the families were headed by a single person. In 40 percent of the families, no one had a job, and most of those who worked had unskilled jobs.

In the preschool years of the five cohorts, the treated subjects received 12½ hours of intervention in the classroom and, with their mothers, 1½ hours at home each week for 30 weeks per year. The classroom intervention offered a high ratio of teachers to students (4 per 20 to 25 students). The exact nature of the preschool program evolved as the teachers worked with both their students and the researchers. The resulting curriculum used a cognitive approach (as detailed in Hohmann, Banet, & Weikart, 1979). Several researchers carefully monitored the school and home visit components at all times, both to assess the project and to describe the technique for later use by others.

To avoid the conflicts raised by previous studies of compensatory programs, the evaluators designed the evaluation to have the highest possible validity. To avoid pretreatment group differences, they used a quasi-random method to assign children to groups (for a debate about this method see Spitz, 1993; Zigler & Weikart, 1993). This approach assured that the treated and control groups had no differences on initial IQ, sex ratio, and average socioeconomic status. The researchers matched children into equal IQ pairs and then exchanged them between groups to balance sex and status. Finally, the two groups were arbitrarily assigned to the experimental ($n = 58$) or control ($n = 65$) conditions. These groups had unequal numbers because of two exceptions in the assignment process. First, younger children always went to the same group as their older siblings. This rule prevented an older sibling in the preschool program from sharing the experience with a younger sibling in the control condition. Second, five children originally assigned to the experimental group could not participate because their mothers worked. As a result, they had to transfer to the control group. Except for the proportion of working female heads of family (resulting from the just noted shift of five experimental subjects), these two groups appeared similar at entry into the project.

Attrition poses a major threat to studies that extend over long periods. Fortunately, the Perry Preschool Project maintained contact with most of the subjects through age 19 (121 of 123 completed the age-19 reinterview; Berrueta-Clement, Schweinhart, Barnett, Epstein, & Weikart, 1984). Given the similarity of the groups in the beginning and the low attrition at follow-up, the posttest difference between groups should reflect accurately the program's impact. On many measures, the experimental group did better than the control group: value placed on schooling, years spent in special education, competence in skills of everyday life, likelihood of being arrested, likelihood of being employed, median income, and job satisfaction.

The Perry Preschool Project appeared to return a "social profit" in dollars of program benefits compared with the program's costs. The evaluators arrived at this favorable conclusion through a sequence of stages, as described in the following sections.

Types of Evaluation

Basic Versus Applied Research. The terms *basic* and *applied* (that is, evaluative) imply a clear distinction between two classes of research. However, this distinction does not derive from the method, site, or motive of the work. All kinds of research methods appear in the evaluation literature, from true experiments to qualitative research (see Patton, 1990, for the use of qualitative methods in applied social research). Applied research does often take place outside academe in the populations served by the projects being evaluated (Rossi, Wright, & Wright, 1978). Nevertheless, university scholars also often test their theories in the field in an effort to achieve better validity.

Perhaps the most common distinction between basic and applied research involves motives—whether to solve a social problem or to advance theory (Deutsch, 1980). Research for theory supposedly has the following characteristics: a focus on isolated variables (that is, it is analytic), a search for enduring or general truths, and exploration of curious rather than mundane events. In contrast, research for solving problems has the opposite stereotype: operation within a set of interacting, real-world variables (that is, it is synthetic), a search for pragmatic solutions to particular problems, and a pursuit of social concerns with a high ethical awareness of research implications. However, these characteristics need not conflict. Some of the best research serves both theory and practice. For example, the Perry Preschool study would qualify as problem centered, but the project derived from a theory. The resulting data served not only to judge the treatment but also to test the theory. Calling a study "program evaluation" may only imply a primary motive in problem solving, not that it disdains theory.

Ideally, theory and practice should interact in research. Theory can guide in program design and help identify the constructs for use in a sound evaluation of the treatment. In exchange, programs offer real-world contexts in which to test causal claims. For example, psychologists and economists might want basic research to test the supposed link between the security of a person's income and the desire to work. But such a study will prove expensive. We can defend its cost only if it is conducted as part of a program for solving a major policy question (as in the income maintenance experiment described by Hunt, 1985).

The desire to make public decisions in a rational way provides a common bond between basic and applied researchers. The movements for consumer rights and public sector efficiency have helped strengthen the demand for assessments of both private goods and public services. Evaluations have become required components in the budgets of some social programs. As a result, we can expect a continuing demand for social researchers with evaluation skills.

Social Impact Assessment Versus Program Evaluation. Social research methods can gauge the outcome of public policy in different ways (Finsterbusch & Motz, 1980). We will contrast two main types: social impact assessment and program evaluation research.

Both **social impact assessment (SIA)** and evaluation research (ER) estimate the effect of planned change. Athough they may appear closely related, several characteristics of SIA help distinguish it from ER. Unlike ER, SIA usually (but not always) assesses the outcome of a proposed change before it takes place. Planners rely on SIA in order to compare different options on their future costs and benefits. Whereas ER focuses mainly on whether or not a program met its stated goals, SIA attempts to measure all possible outcomes of a project. This distinction becomes blurry because good ER tries to observe important unexpected outcomes. Moreover, we cannot expect SIA (or any research for that matter) to measure all types of possible effects. Nevertheless, SIA usually draws on more disciplines than ER, using experts in each area of possible impact. Finally, SIA can apply to any project, public or private (for example, expanding or building an airport, a nuclear reactor, or a city). In contrast, ER usually focuses on more narrow interventions (for example, effects on children of a new teaching method).

Compared to ER, SIA tends to seek a broader range of data—longer range effects on the whole population in more domains. This wider breadth of interest thus points to different methodologies from ER. For example, collecting data about a whole population may require survey or archival measures. At present, we have recurring measures of economic well-being of communities (for example, monthly unemployment rate reports) by which to assess economic policies. Some have suggested a social counterpart to such economic measures, but the government does not routinely issue reports of this kind. Called **social indicators**, these monthly or quarterly reports could summarize the health and social well-being of the population. Such social accounts could serve as a report card on the success of public policies. Although the Department of Commerce had issued some reports of social indicators, Congress has yet to mandate such a social accounting act (Finsterbusch & Motz, 1980).

The legislative model for SIA comes from the National Environmental Policy Act of 1969. This law required systematic studies of the direct and indirect effects of all federal actions affecting the human environment. Later, the courts held that social effects were included in the meaning of environmental impacts and that they must appear in any **environmental impact statements**. Under this law, new projects must await the filing and airing of the necessary environmental impact statements (Meidinger & Schnaiberg, 1980).

Stages of Evaluation Research.   The rest of this chapter will focus on evaluation research, although similar issues arise in the related area of social impact assessment. Evaluation research includes different types of data collection and analysis—each related to a different stage of the evaluation process. The present discussion divides evaluation into five phases:

1. *Needs assessment*—describing people's needs in order to set program goals.
2. *Program monitoring*—checking the ongoing program to see how well it conforms to the plan.
3. *Program impact*—testing whether the intervention has the expected effect.
4. *Efficiency*—weighing the program's success by its costs.
5. *Utilization*—judging the extent to which others use the evaluation and noting the factors that affect its use.

The following sections will briefly illustrate and describe each of these five types of research. Each could warrant its own chapter. To go beyond the present introductions to these topics, see a text on evaluation (for example, Rossi & Freeman, 1993).

NEEDS ASSESSMENT

What Are the Goals?

Definition.   The **needs assessment** stage identifies goals but does not determine whether the program has met the goals. Thus, needs assessment occurs in the early, formative stages of program planning. Often based on survey or archival data, needs assessment searches for an unmet need and describes its size and location. The resulting data both justify the program (that is, help motivate the funders to provide resources) and set its goals (that is, define the service).

Needs assessment often targets the people whom the program will serve. The definition of the program's clients may include spatial boundaries (for example, school district) or social markers (for example, children under age 6). Defining people to receive some treatment should flow from data linking the degree of unmet need with the social and spatial markers (for example, nutrition problems found in poor children).

Rationale.   Ideally, programs should dispense scarce resources with priority given to those areas and populations in greatest need. The failure to conduct a needs assessment can lead to waste. For example, an existing project may expand not because of documented need but because of staff enthusiasm. As a result, scarce resources may go to people with little need or needs different from the ones best met by the program. Needs assessment can also help in the later judgment of program impact by setting clear goals against which to measure the intervention.

Targeting Scarce Resources

Examples.   Good needs assessment will assure that scarce resources go to the people with greatest need. Mistakes in matching services to people can occur because the needs assessment is poor or absent or because criteria other than need guide the allocation decision. For example, Chu and Trotter (1974) found cases in which some federal funds for mental health went to facilities serving mainly the well-to-do, while poor areas received no increased services.

The Perry Preschool Project illustrates a successful match of a new service with a population in great need. Earlier research showed that children reared in poverty had poor academic performance. Using available archival data, the Perry researchers were able to identify the poorest area in their city. They cited an earlier housing commission study that called their target area "one of the worst congested slum areas in the state" (Schweinhart & Weikart, 1980, p. 17). Records of school dropouts and criminal behavior for the area confirmed that the target area had many of the problems commonly associated with poverty and poor school performance.

Existing Records.   Many programs, as illustrated by the Perry Preschool Project, employ existing data to assess need and target services. County and city planning offices can often describe the community using the most recent census or more specialized sample surveys. Such data may give descriptions of the residents detailed down to the census tract level (for example, age, sex, ethnicity).

Other archival records can provide further information of a more specialized kind, such as court and police records on criminal deviance, school records on attendance and performance, hospital and coroner records on health and causes of death, and election records on voting and political behavior. Together, these data can help profile any section of the community on multiple dimensions. We call such a community description a **social area analysis** and employ it as a common first step in needs assessment.

Specialized Surveying.   Existing survey and archival data may not address the specific question of the needs assessor. For example, in considering whether to build a new community mental health center, we might ask the following question: How much unmet need for mental health services exists in the catchment area? Existing records can only provide data on variables thought to relate to mental disorder (for example, poverty) or to current service delivery (that is, met need). To estimate the share of the population in need of service requires a special survey. Such a survey could measure the **incidence** (number of new cases in some time period) and **prevalence** (number of existing cases at some point in time). It also could estimate the number of people who would seek service of the kind and at the location and price to be offered by the proposed new program.

Besides such "market" surveys of the client population, we might want to see surveys of other interested parties. For example, before building a new mental health center, the planners would want to consult the current providers of mental health and related services, such as psychologists in private practice, social work agencies, police, courts, and schools as well as relevant government and civic groups in the area (Weiss, 1975).

PROGRAM MONITORING

Is the Program Operating as Planned?

Definition.   **Program monitoring** studies how the intervention proceeds as distinct from its effect. Usually it involves recording the actual activities of the project. For example, an educational program might propose certain textbooks, media aids, teaching plans, number of students, teacher-to-student ratio, and number of hours per week of student contact. The project proposal may detail these aspects of the program to both justify and estimate the funding needed to carry out the work. The subsequent monitoring of this program might count the number of students attending classes, note the actual teacher-to-student ratio, and list the texts and films used. Expert judges might even visit the classes in order to rate the quality of the learning climate. We can then compare the findings of this monitoring with the proposal in order to see how well the project is being carried out.

Rationale. Program monitoring has two main purposes: managing program resources and delivering the promised intervention. For the first function, program managers must account for the revenues and costs and keep track of the clients and staff. Every business or government agency has some method for handling these accounts. **Management information systems (MIS)** give managers constant feedback on the program's operation. Such MIS methods may count contacts between clients (for example, students or patients) and staff (for example, teachers or therapists). These MIS procedures describe programs in terms that translate into budget lines (for example, salaries for staff and revenue from client payments).

For its second function, program monitoring makes sure that the project under study offers the intervention called for in the proposal. If we think of the program service as an experimental variable, this aspect of monitoring resembles experimental construct validity. As Rossi (1978) has observed, many social service programs try to conform to high theoretical and laboratory standards. In practice, however, the actual service may differ from the planned service and thus provides no test of the intended program. Checking the match of the actual to the ideal may require a more intensive assessment of quality than that provided by the standard MIS.

Assuring Program Quality

Preschool Curriculum Example. The Perry Project illustrates the monitoring of program process and quality. This project produced, among other studies, one that compared its cognitive approach with two other teaching methods—language-training and unit-based. These three curricula followed different theories with respect to the best roles of the child and the teacher (Weikart, Epstein, Schweinhart, & Bond, 1978).

To assure proper use of these methods, the researchers used several systems to observe teacher–student interactions under the different curricula. In one system, observers recorded their perceptions every 25 seconds, with 20 records for each child in the class. Observed behavior included the child–child, child–material, and child–adult interactions. The results confirmed that the three curricula produced the expected differences in classroom process. For example, the cognitive method produced less direct teaching by adults (that is, 12 percent for showing or telling) than either of the others (33 percent in the language-training and 23 percent in the unit-based curricula).

Designing Program Monitoring. No single procedure can monitor all programs. Managers will need to adapt their MIS methods to the budget needs of the program funders. For example, if a mental health program receives money for each patient–therapist session, the MIS will need to record only these contacts (for example, identities of patient and therapist plus type of service). On the other hand, if the project serves as a test of a new procedure, the measures will have to reflect the conceptually important aspects of the intervention.

Just because a program expends funds and serves clients at the expected numerical levels does not guarantee that the program operates as planned. Checking the quality of implementation may require a **program audit** by an outside evaluator. Using the program's proposal or charter as a guide, such auditors might inspect program records (including the MIS) and collect new measures. The auditors might describe the clients and services on the dimensions pertinent to the program's mission. Areas of assessment might include coverage (who is served?), service (what is the delivered service?), finances (are expenditures proper?), and the law (is the program obeying all applicable laws?).

PROGRAM IMPACT

Does the Program Have an Effect?

Definition.   Of the five stages of evaluation, **program impact** makes the most use of the causal research methods covered in earlier chapters. Unlike the largely descriptive methods of needs assessment and program monitoring, program impact evaluation tests whether the program causes the observed outcome, if any. Although the first two types of research set program goals and describe the methods actually used to achieve them, neither answers the question of whether the means achieve the ends.

Rationale.   Program impact research plays a crucial role in evaluation; it determines the success of the program. Pursuing worthy goals with the supposedly correct method does not guarantee program success. Even if the goals are achieved, the program may not deserve the credit. On the other hand, the program may have some effect but not on the intended outcome measures. Thus the impact stage of evaluation resembles hypothesis testing in more basic research and risks all of the threats to validity covered in this text.

Guarding Against Validity Threats

Perry Preschool Project.   As with the previous stages of evaluation, the Perry team also addressed impact assessment. These researchers hypothesized that the cognitive curriculum would improve school performance and commitment to schooling as measured in later years.

Since preschool students might develop academic ability and commitment to schooling for a variety of reasons over the course of their education, this design needed a control group. The control group would face the same developmental and historical influences impinging on the preschool group and would thus "control" for these time threats to internal validity. If the preschool and control children differed to begin with, however, any later differences could be due to their initial difference rather than the treatment. To rule out such group threats to internal validity, the researchers used quasi-random assignment. As a result, any difference between groups at age 16 should come only from the differential treatment and not differences already present at age 4.

The hypothesis of the Perry Preschool study received support on several outcome measures. For example, on a high school reading test, the preschool students answered about 37 percent of the items correctly, compared to just 30 percent for the control group. This difference passed the test of statistical inference validity. Such a large difference would occur by chance (that is, by sampling error when there was really no dif- ference) less than 5 percent of the time (Schweinhart & Weikart, 1980, p. 41). The measure had high reliability and seemed a valid reflection of the reading construct. As discussed earlier, the program monitoring step found high experimental construct valid- ity. In terms of external validity, the cognitive preschool program should generalize to similarly disadvantaged children assuming its application with the same high quality. In sum, the researchers judged the Perry Preschool Project a success.

Research Design Problems.   Critics can raise the same doubts about the validity of program evaluations as are raised in all social research. The same techniques that protect against validity threats in more basic social research can, in principle, serve in applied research. Doing valid research faces challenges under the best circumstances. However, program impact evaluation operates under special constraints.

Sometimes, the best design for internal validity purposes (that is, the true experi- ment) is not feasible because of the nature of the intervention. For example, consider a study that compares vehicle deaths in states with newly introduced safety laws (the ex- perimental group) against those in other states without these laws (control group). In such cases, the evaluator cannot assign states to a condition and must use a quasi ex- periment to study the effect, for example, in an interrupted time series (D. T. Campbell, 1975).

Impact assessment faces several different problems that arise more often in eval- uation than in basic research. Although some of these problems can also appear in other stages of evaluation, we note them here because they regularly trouble attempts to grade the success of programs. We will note three problems: (1) resistance and bias on the part of program participants; (2) hindrance in using random assignment to groups; and (3) difficulty measuring all the effects.

Resistance and Bias of Participants.   Program participants include staff and clients, both of whom may have psychological or financial reasons for bias about their project's evaluation. For example, although early research on Head Start found few signs of success based on test scores, parents consistently endorsed the program (Scheirer, 1978). From cognitive consistency theory, one would predict that parents sending their children to a program with high hopes for success would rather believe the program a success than a failure. Similarly, staff members become psychologically (from the same consistency theory) and materially (income from job) invested in the success of their program. The self-interest of the program participants makes difficult the objective assessment of a program's success (Scheirer, 1978). Evaluators must ex- pect such bias and adjust for it.

This bias has two major effects: one in measuring outcomes and the other in gain- ing access to the program. The participants' biases cast doubt on any measures of a sub- jective kind. A survey showing that most participants like their project will prove less persuasive than more objective measures of the project's impact. Thus self-report meas- ures, if taken at all, should be supplemented by outcome measures with less bias.

The second problem consists of resistance to the very idea of an evaluation. Staff may offer various reasons for such resistance. For example, staff might claim that any evaluation will overlook subtle but valuable effects or that it will inhibit program innovation. Behind such stated reasons may lie the staff's fear that the findings will not support continuing the program and thus lead to job loss. In either event, the staff may resist entry into the program files by the evaluators. Staff can withhold cooperation with evaluators by declining to assist in giving objective measures to their clients. In extreme cases, staff may even sabotage the assessment by changing program records. Gaining entry and cooperation is an art requiring interpersonal skills and sensitivity on the part of the evaluator. The evaluator, more than the basic researcher, must remember that research has emotional as well as scientific meanings to the participants.

Hindering Random Assignment. Random assignment maximizes the internal validity of an impact assessment. But even when possible in principle, random assignment may not prove feasible in practice. Evaluators do sometimes achieve the ideal of randomized assignment to groups. For example, the income maintenance studies randomly assigned subjects to different levels of guaranteed income and taxation rates (Robins, Spiegelman, Weiner, & Bell, 1980). In these studies, the subjects received a powerful financial incentive to participate in the experimental condition to which they were randomly assigned. Moreover, those assigned to the control condition suffered no harm by joining that group of the design. In many evaluations, in contrast, denial of the intervention to the control group seems harmful to the clientele. Sometimes, political pressure tries to extend the attractive new service to those in the control group, thus destroying the internal validity of the impact assessment. Other times, the staff of the project may compromise their own random assignment plan because they feel that the treatment should go to the most needy, whether originally assigned to the experimental group or not.

In his analysis of 12 evaluations, Conner (1977) found several keys to successful randomization. In planning the evaluation, he recommends researcher control of the assignment process, fixed randomization with no exceptions, and the blocking of clients prior to random assignment for maximum group equivalence in small samples. In the implementation phase, he advises a central control point for assigning cases, a single person to conduct the assignment, training of this person for valid randomization, and a monitoring of the success of the randomization.

Random assignment often faces less resistance when the denial of the treatment does not appear harmful or when the demand for the treatment far exceeds its supply. In the latter case, random assignment actually seems a fair way to distribute a scarce service. On ethical and public relations grounds, evaluators will want to reward the control subjects for their patience, perhaps by offering them the experimental treatment after the evaluation concludes. This delayed equity and the perception of "fair" assignment will often ease the pressure to abort the random assignment plan. Moreover, the delayed treatment control group lends itself to a multiple time series design in which the first-treated group becomes, in the second phase of the study, a control for the later-treated replication (Heath, Kendzierski, & Borgida, 1982).

Assessing Multiple Outcomes. Program evaluation has a greater concern with unhypothesized effects than does basic research. Basic researchers typically choose outcome measures to reflect just the constructs specified in the tested theory and do not routinely look for serendipitous findings (that is, those not predicted). In contrast, evaluators have come to expect unhypothesized effects and may even design their research to capture them. Practical experience has shown that programs often produce desirable and undesirable side effects besides the intended effects predicted from theory. For example, Head Start may not have produced the expected academic outcomes but almost certainly improved the nutrition and medical care of the enrolled children. Although health was not its primary goal, the Head Start program, in its early stages, revealed substantial health problems in the children from poor families. Judging the overall value of a program, therefore, requires that we account for all its pluses and minuses.

Impact assessments often conclude that the expected goal was not achieved (Chen & Rossi, 1980). Nevertheless, it seems unlikely that a major change effort should produce no effect. It follows that evaluators must employ more sensitive and more numerous outcome measures to capture the missing effects. One extreme view even proposes that we ignore the stated goals in order not to miss the actual achievement (Scriven, 1972). Such goal-free research fails to provide guidance about what to measure and needlessly ignores the most likely outcomes.

At minimum, evaluators might supplement the program's primary goals with other possible outcomes predicted from relevant theory. Chen and Rossi (1980) call this the multigoal, theory-driven approach. They point to the negative income tax (income maintenance) studies designed to test the disincentive effect of such income on work. Since work and income are linked theoretically to many other variables, the income maintenance experiments collected measures to reflect potential changes beyond work incentive—for example, distress, divorce, job satisfaction, and desire for children (see Robins et al., 1980).

EFFICIENCY ANALYSIS

Are We Getting Our Money's Worth?

Definition.   **Efficiency analysis** measures the impact of the project relative to its cost. Efficiency analysts use either of two general methods: cost–benefit analysis and cost–effectiveness analysis. **Cost–benefit analysis** measures both the benefits and the costs of the program in monetary terms and expresses their relationship as a ratio or difference.

Sometimes social service programs produce intangible benefits that do not translate easily into monetary terms. In that case, **cost–effectiveness analysis** may prove more suitable. This approach expresses outcome goals or achievements in nonmonetary units and compares different programs in terms of the monetary costs for achieving the same ends.

Rationale.   Basic research usually tests hypotheses without regard to the cost of manipulating the causal variable. In contrast, program evaluation seeks the most efficient cause for the desired effect. An intervention that achieves the desired effect but at an exorbitant cost will not get adopted elsewhere and will prove unsuccessful despite its positive impact.

Cost–benefit and cost–effectiveness analyses help guide policy decisions in choosing among competing programs. Cost–effectiveness analysis can guide choices between alternatives for achieving the same outcomes (for example, alternate screening methods for early cancer detection). However, cost–effectiveness analysis cannot guide choices between programs with different targets (for example, whether to invest in a cancer-screening program or a preschool education program). Cost–benefit analysis, which can express different outcomes in the same monetary metric, can aid in choosing between otherwise noncomparable programs.

Gauging Returns on Investments

Perry Preschool Cost–Benefit Analysis. Our continuing example of program evaluation, the Perry Preschool Project, also employed an efficiency analysis (Barnett, 1985). This cost–benefit study first determined the costs of providing the program to the treated students (that is, teachers' salaries, supplies, and overhead). For example, one year of preschool for each student cost $4,963 in 1981 dollars.

The accounting of benefits to the Perry Preschool Project illustrates some of the tasks involved in attaching monetary value to the outcomes of social programs. First, the evaluators had to identify the different effects of the program (that is, ways in which the preschool students differed from the control students). For their efficiency study, the researchers chose to include social benefits (those to the society as a whole) as well as those to the individual student. They made this choice because the costs of public preschool programs are paid by society as a whole. Several types of benefits were accounted from among the many that might have been studied:

1. Savings in child-care time of the parents of the experimental subjects
2. Savings in special education required later by the control subjects but not by the experimentals (potentially offset by added educational costs for increased college attendance by experimentals over control subjects)
3. Savings in criminal or delinquent behavior (not including estimates of pain and suffering of the victims)
4. Earning differences because of greater employment
5. Savings in welfare and economic dependency

Together, these net benefits totaled $10,077 at age 19 in 1981 dollars for each student given one year of preschool. Based on these costs and benefits, the Perry Preschool Project appears to return a net benefit of $5,114 per student through age 19. Of course, the benefits should not stop at age 19. One estimate of lifelong benefits for one year of preschool shows a net benefit of over $90,000 in 1981 dollars (Barnett, 1985, p. 87).

Before concluding that these cost–benefit results prove the value of the Perry Preschool Project, we must take into account the effects of time. Most of the benefits occur years after preschool. A dollar of benefits in 1995 may not equal a dollar of costs in 1958 for two reasons: inflation and opportunity costs. Because of inflation, a dollar in 1995 would not have the same purchasing power as a dollar in 1958. To adjust for inflation, the Perry researchers measured costs and benefits in **constant dollars**, using 1981 as the standard. That is, they expressed the estimated future benefits and the actual costs in 1981 terms. To do this, they calculated an inflation coefficient for each year relative to the criterion year. For example, if a 1995 dollar equals 50 cents in 1981, we would multiply the estimated 1995 benefits by .5 to find their value in 1981 constant dollars.

A second and more complicated matter involves **opportunity cost**, the value of the best alternative use of the project's resources. If the Perry Preschool Project did not spend $4,963 per year on each student, this money might have gone to some other project. How can we compare the return to one project against the potential return of the same resources invested elsewhere? One approach uses a **discount rate** to adjust future benefits for the rate of gain of the same investment placed in some other project. A bank could loan the money to some borrower for a constructive activity (for example, starting a business or buying a house). An investment of $100 at 5 percent interest (net of inflation) will yield $105 one year later. Conversely, $105 of program benefits promised one year from now has a **present value** (that is, discounted by 5 percent) of $100 because the $105 could have been returned on $100 placed in a bank at 5 percent.

To compare present costs with future benefits thus requires adjusting the future benefits not only for inflation but also by some discount rate. The choice of discount rate becomes crucial. Choosing a higher discount rate will make future benefits appear smaller and the program less efficient. For example, the Perry Project's reported net benefit of $5,114 at age 19 derives from a 0 percent discount rate. A discount rate of 3 percent would reduce the net benefit to $2,339, and a 7 percent rate would make the benefit nearly disappear ($40).

An alternative method of presenting cost–benefit results uses the **internal rate of return (IRR)**. The IRR represents the rate at which the investment (the cost) grows in value. For the Perry Project, the IRR for one year of preschool exceeded 11 percent based on lifelong return. But if we use the IRR method, what rate of return must a project give in order to appear successful? No objective rule exists for setting this rate. If we want to reflect the opportunity costs of diverting resources from the private to the public sector, we should use the current rate of return to private investment (say, that of long-term, secure bonds as suggested by Baumol, 1969). The higher this rate, the more we will prefer private investments over investments in social programs. Those who feel we should take a longer range view and maximize social investments will favor applying a lower **social discount rate** in judging public projects. Obviously, the time preference in selecting discount rates has a large subjective and political component.

Problems in Estimation. The costs of social programs would seem easy to determine, since a program's budget states the salaries, materials, and overhead. We can even estimate the value of unpriced costs (for example, the time of volunteer staff in a free clinic) using **shadow prices**—their value if purchased in the market place.

Accounting external effects or **externalities** can prove harder. Internal effects occur between two parties—the provider and the consumer or client. External effects occur to third parties not directly involved in the project. A coal-powered plant, for example, produces electricity, and its internal costs include the value of construction, fuel, and staff. Such internal costs all pertain to the production of electricity and must not exceed the utility bills paid by the electricity consumers. But suppose that the power plant has costly side effects on third parties—for example, the production of acid rain, which damages forests in other states or countries. From society's perspective, these external costs seem quite real, and someone must pay them. Ideally, we would bill such external costs to their source. In other words, the project should "internalize" the costs in order to judge its overall efficiency. In the same way, social programs should try to measure their external costs in their cost–benefit evaluations.

Externalities may add not only to the true costs of a project but also to its benefits. The Perry Project, for example, may have produced unaccounted benefits by lowering the school dropout rate, increasing the labor force participation rate, reducing the crime rate, reducing the participation in welfare programs, and so on. If we counted all these benefits, the preschool program might appear even more valuable.

A related problem in efficiency analysis involves intangibles—benefits with no dollar equivalent. As an example of this problem, consider the difficulty in placing a money value on human life. Just such a problem arises in the analysis of health or other projects intended to save or extend life. How much should the public spend to save a life (for example, to redesign a highway exit ramp with a high fatality record)? To answer such questions, cost–benefit analysts have considered such monetary aspects of life as the person's future earnings (if he or she survives) and the amount that others would pay for the benefits of the person's life (for example, for friendship). These considerations have produced different formulas (M. S. Thompson, 1980, chap. 8). Nevertheless, the problems (including the morality) of such valuations point us to cost–effectiveness rather than cost–benefit analysis in such cases.

In cost–effectiveness analysis, we need not attach a monetary value to the benefits of the program. Only the costs of achieving some goal vary across competing programs. Suppose we aim to save lives from accidental death. We can compare different programs for preventing accidental death on a single value: cost per life saved (Thompson & Fortess, 1980). For example, two programs advised hypertensive patients regarding factors such as diet, smoking, and stress (Bertera & Bertera, 1981). The programs used different methods (clinic versus telephone), but both achieved reductions in blood pressure (the nonmonetary outcome target). The cost–effectiveness ratio consisted of the number of patients counseled divided by the total cost of counseling them. This ratio favored the telephone method ($39) over the clinic method ($82).

UTILIZATION RESEARCH

How Can We Promote Good Programs?

Definition.   The final stage of evaluation deals with the use of program evaluations. The study of **utilization** concerns the aspects of new knowledge that influence its use. Despite its origins in the older field of social change research, utilization assessment appeared only in recent decades (Zaltman, 1979). Although the study of utilization can apply to any type of knowledge including basic research (Ganz, 1980), we will focus on evaluations of social interventions.

The term *utilization* has different meanings (Leviton & Hughes, 1981), but it differs both from *impact* and *utility*. *Utility* means that the evaluation has relevance and value regardless of whether it leads to program change. *Impact* implies that the evaluation contributes to program change, although change also depends on political and economic factors. Thus we may utilize an evaluation even when little or no impact occurs. Three meanings of utilization have appeared: instrumental, conceptual, and persuasive or symbolic (Leviton & Hughes, 1981). **Persuasive utilization** includes the use of program evaluation to influence others to accept its implications. **Conceptual utilization** presents evaluation results as an information base. Like persuasive utilization, conceptual utilization does not entail adoption. However, unlike persuasive utilization, it serves by its power to clarify rather than to compel attitude change. Finally, in **instrumental utilization**, the evaluation actually has an impact in a decision-making or program-shaping way.

Rationale.   The concern with utilization stems from the purpose of evaluation and the widespread view that it has little effect. Researchers do evaluations in order to help policy makers choose more successful projects and project managers to improve existing ones. If these decision makers do not rely on the evaluations, why continue to conduct them?

Program evaluators do not routinely check on the utilization of their findings. As a result, our sense of the utilization rate often derives from anecdotes and small samples. Reviews of utilization research present a mixed picture (Davis & Salasin, 1975; Hennigan, Flay, & Cook, 1980). Evaluation and social research generally receive some attention, and in some cases, we may find overutilization, as when policy follows poorly conducted research. But the prevailing view holds that evaluations seldom guide policy directly and specifically (instrumental utilization). More commonly, evaluations serve as general background information (conceptual utilization) or to justify decisions already made (persuasive or symbolic utilization). The fear that evaluation has too little impact has motivated efforts to find those ingredients of evaluations that increase their use.

Giving Science Away

Examples of Disseminating Evaluations.   The Perry Preschool results described in this chapter have appeared in many published reports and workshops. However, a perception exists that compensatory preschool education has little value, and the Perry team sometimes found it needed to use unorthodox methods and alliances with policy makers to disseminate its findings. After the election of Ronald Reagan in November 1980, President Carter's White House staffers feared the loss of federally funded programs for children in the next administration. An anecdote describes how one of those staff members, Peggy Pizzo, helped broadcast the Perry findings in an effort to build public support for Head Start (Zigler & Muenchow, 1992, pp. 191–192). At a conference of educators, Pizzo met Larry Schweinhart of the High Scope Educational Research Foundation, which had conducted the Perry Preschool Project.

> "I hear that High Scope has some new research data on the effectiveness of preschool," Pizzo said.
>
> "Yes, and I'm having the hardest time getting Carnegie to hold a press conference on the Perry Preschool data," he told her. The Carnegie Corporation of New York was convinced that no reporters would come to hear what had happened to a little over 100 children who had participated in a preschool program many years ago in Ypsilanti, Michigan. . . .
>
> Pizzo offered to help. As a former Carnegie grant recipient who worked in the White House, she called key executives at Carnegie on High Scope's behalf. Then she recommended that High Scope tie the Perry Preschool findings to Head Start. If the research had implications for Head Start funding, reporters would be interested.
>
> By mid-December, there were editorials all over the country about the benefits of "Head Start–like" programs.

Going beyond such anecdotes, we need systematic research on how best to give away evaluation results. A good example of such research comes from Fairweather, Sanders, and Tornatzky (1974). Fairweather and his associates had previously assessed an innovative program for treating mental patients in community dormitories or lodges (Fairweather, Sanders, Maynard, & Cressler, 1969). The very positive results from this study argued for the widespread adoption of the lodge program by mental hospitals. Fairweather and his colleagues then conducted a national experiment to get mental hospitals to try this new approach.

They studied the effects of three different persuasion techniques in 255 hospitals. Less than 10 percent of the contacted hospitals agreed to establish the lodge program. The brochure and workshop persuasion approaches had more success gaining initial entry to the hospital. However, after gaining entry, the more active in-hospital demonstration approach had more success in getting the hospital to implement the lodge. A second experiment, using 12 matched pairs of adopting hospitals, studied the effect of personal versus written consultation in aiding the adoption of the lodge. As expected, the personal consultation hospitals made better progress in lodge adoption. This massive study shows the potential for valid utilization research. With 12 percent or less of the contacted hospitals adopting the lodge in the most persuasive approach, the results pointed to a continuing need for such research.

Aids to Utilization.   Guidelines for increasing utilization range from improving the presentation of evaluation results to improving the evaluations themselves (see Rossi & Freeman, 1993). For example, extensive research has documented the spacing effect: For a given amount of study time, spaced presentations yield better learning than massed presentations (Dempster, 1988). Nevertheless, educational programs have not widely adopted this apparently important finding. Dempster, after reviewing possible hindrances to its adoption, concludes that the spacing effect remains little known among educators. To solve this problem, researchers may have to make greater efforts to transmit the finding from their laboratories to the teacher training classrooms.

In other cases, the findings of basic researchers are well known but simply not convincing to practitioners. For example, psychologists have pointed to the adverse effects of crowding in prisons, but corrections officers have remained unimpressed (Ruback & Innes, 1988). Basic researchers may have more success in getting their findings used if they change their research in order to include policy variables (those controllable by the corrections officers in this case) and dependent variables of greater relevance to practitioners.

Evaluation results and methods seldom play the most important role in making up the minds of decision makers. For example, the massive income maintenance experiments tested the hypothesis that guaranteed income would greatly reduce work motivation. The results showed relatively small reductions in work effort by primary wage earners, and Congress clearly knew of these findings. Nevertheless, Congress either ignored the study or used minor apects of it to reinforce the preexisting sentiment against the income maintenance policy (Neubeck & Roach, 1981). In short, policy makers may interpret, use, or ignore program evaluations to suit their predetermined needs.

One model suggests that policy makers will utilize an evaluation to the extent that it meets three criteria: relevance, truth, and utility (Weiss & Bucuvalas, 1980). A relevant evaluation is one that seems timely and pertinent to the user's sphere of responsibility. The criteria of truth and utility, however, appear more complicated.

In a study of the ratings of research reports by 155 decision makers, the truth and utility criteria each had two components. The truth test depended on the perceived quality of the research (that is, the various types of validity) and its conformity to the user's expectations. If the evaluation report ran counter to the user's own experience, the evaluation received more critical attention to its research quality (that is, a double standard was used).

The two aspects of the utility test included feasibility (how possible the proposed change was to make) and challenge to the status quo (whether it meant going against prevailing practice and sentiment). If the evaluation did not challenge the status quo, the feasibility component received more attention for the specific steps that might be taken. If the evaluation challenged the status quo, it might raise the conceptual interest of the decision maker, but it would not facilitate utilization.

Utilization of evaluation depends on two types of factors—those under the control of the evaluator (such as quality of the research) and those not under their control (for example, the political and economic constraints of the policy maker). When researchers produce conflicting results, the decision makers will more likely base their policies on factors other than the mixed advice from social scientists. In such cases, scientists themselves need to help clarify the situation. Ultimately, utilization may require the establishment of science courts made up of disinterested scholars who could identify the best research and evaluations for the use of decision makers (Hennigan, Flay, & Cook, 1980, pp. 135–143).

Just as researchers may produce conflicting results, so potential users of evaluations may have conflicting views. Any person or group with a stake in a program might rise to reject or accept an evaluation depending on how it affects their interests. Thus, the evaluator will need to take into account the whole range of stakeholders for a project, both in conducting and in sharing the study (Greene, 1988; Rossi & Freeman, 1993).

SUMMARY

Applied and basic research differ mainly in the degree of emphasis placed on problem solving versus theory testing. Program evaluation differs from other applied or policy-related research such as social impact assessment. Evaluation typically judges the success of an actual program in achieving its intended benefits. In contrast, social impact assessment estimates the future consequences of potential interventions, draws on more disciplines, and tries to monitor or forecast social indicators of the whole society.

Most evaluations involve one or more phases of study. Needs assessment and program monitoring both employ descriptive methods. The first defines the ends of the project, and the second verifies that the means are being implemented as planned. Program impact research employs hypothesis-testing methods to decide whether the program actually achieved the stated goals or had other unplanned side effects. Impact research risks the same validity threats as basic causal research. However, it has additional constraints beyond those encountered in basic research (for example, bias and resistance of staff or clients, problems with random assignment, and difficulties in measuring all of the intervention's effects). Efficiency analysis expresses the net impact of a program relative to the monetary cost of the intervention. Finally, utilization research asks how and why evaluations are used and helps evaluators increase the use of their findings.

EXERCISES

1. Find a report of a program evaluation from a journal such as *Evaluation Review*. Identify the type(s) of evaluation (needs assessment, program monitoring, impact assessment, efficiency analysis, or utilization research). Critique the study's validity. Then assess it from the standpoint of its feasibility, the clarity of its implications, and the extent to which they agree with current political, cultural, and economic forces. Repeat until you have found and criticized one example of each of the five types of evaluation.

2. Locate and assess a social impact assessment. You might contact your local government to see if it has a recent environmental impact assessment available for a proposed development that affects the quality of life in your own community.

3. Finally, if you can enter an ongoing project, try your hand at program evaluation. Select an appropriate type of analysis from needs assessment (if the project is just being formed) to an evaluation of utilization (if a program evaluation has already been completed and disseminated).

KEY TERMS

Conceptual utilization   Cost-effectiveness analysis
Constant dollars   Discount rate
Cost-benefit analysis   Efficiency analysis

Environmental impact statements
Externalities
Incidence
Instrumental utilization
Internal rate of return (IRR)
Management information
 systems (MIS)
Needs assessment
Opportunity cost
Persuasive utilization
Present value

Prevalence
Program audit
Program evaluation
Program impact
Program monitoring
Shadow prices
Social area analysis
Social discount rate
Social impact assessment (SIA)
Social indicators
Utilization

Appendix

INTRODUCTION

Summarizing and Clarifying

Graphic Summary.   Suppose you received a score of 16 on a 20-point quiz and your grade is to be based "on the curve." How would you go about comparing your score to your classmates' scores? If the professor listed the class's scores (and other data such as sex, practice test score, and major) alphabetically by initial, they might look something like Table A–1. But how does the score of 16 compare with the 26 quiz scores spread over the table? If your class had 200 students, you would have even more trouble making sense of the scores.

To get a clearer picture, you would need to sort the individuals by scores rather than by initials. Figure A–1a shows such a relisting of the 26 scores in Table A–1. Each set of initials stands for one student. We know that student R.D. got a score of 8 because those initials appear over the number 8. We know that only one person received a score of 8, because only those initials appear over that number. Figure A–1a gives a clearer picture than Table A–1 because it shows at a glance how many persons got each score.

Table A–1   Quiz Scores, Sex, Practice Pretest Scores, and Major, by Initials

Initials	Quiz Scores	Sex	Practice Scores	Major
B.A.	17	M	18	Yes
D.B.	11	F	10	Yes
J.B.	18	F	18	No
T.C.	9	M	7	No
R.D.	8	M	10	Yes
P.D.	16	F	16	No
F.E.	15	M	16	Yes
G.F.	14	M	13	Yes
T.F.	17	M	17	Yes
R.G.	10	F	15	Yes
C.H.	12	F	10	No
L.K.	14	F	18	Yes
T.M.	17	M	14	No
B.N.	15	M	16	Yes
S.O.	12	F	16	Yes
S.P.	20	F	19	No
J.R.	15	F	14	No
T.R.	17	M	15	Yes
N.R.	13	F	15	Yes
P.S.	16	F	12	No
D.T.	16	M	16	No
P.T.	18	M	19	Yes
K.T.	17	M	15	Yes
S.U.	15	F	14	No
A.W.	16	M	17	Yes
R.Y.	19	F	20	No

We can simplify Figure A–1a by dropping the initials, which are of less interest than the group's overall performance. Figure A–1b gives an example of a **frequency distribution**. The frequency, abbreviated **f**, tells the number of occurrences of each score as indicated on the vertical line, or axis. The horizontal axis displays the scores or categories. The frequency distribution can take different forms. Figure A–1b shows the form called a **histogram**. Figure A–1c shows another form of frequency distribution, called the **frequency polygon**. Such displays reduce or remove unnecessary information and organize and highlight the remaining information (for more information on graphic methods, see Bowen, 1992; Tukey, 1977).

Statistical Summary.   Such data reduction need not stop with visual frequency distributions. Suppose you wanted to express the effort of the whole section of 26 stu-

(a) Individuals (initials) grouped by quiz scores

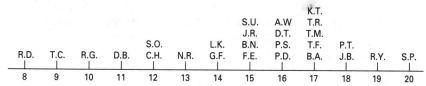

(b) Quiz score histogram

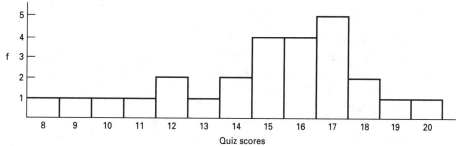

Quiz scores

(c) Quiz score frequency polygon

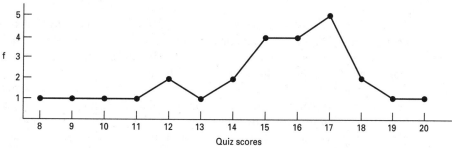

Quiz scores

Figure A–1 Frequency distributions.

dents in a single number rather than a picture. You could produce the mean by adding up all the individual scores and dividing by the number of students. Adding up all 26 quiz scores gives 387. Dividing by 26 gives the mean score of 14.88. This number serves as a **descriptive statistic** because it describes an aspect of a group. You could now assess your score of 16 as being a little more than one point above the mean of the group.

We can use different kinds of descriptive statistics to summarize different aspects of a group of scores. Some of the most commonly used descriptive statistics will appear in later sections of this chapter. You need to understand them if you are to understand reports of social research.

Levels of Measurement

Measurement and Different Types of Variables. Measurement consists of assigning values to observations in a systematic way. A characteristic that can have differing values is called a **variable**. Some variables are regarded as **qualitative variables** because observations about them are assigned to different levels or groupings. If you sorted persons according to their religion (Catholic, Jewish, Moslem), you would create a qualitative variable. Often variables have numeric values. When the levels of a qualitative variable are given numeric codes, we can think of these codes as naming devices. For example, if we code Catholic = 1, Jewish = 2, Moslem = 3 for purposes of recording our data, we do not imply that a Moslem is three times a Catholic on any dimension; the 3 is just a brief designation for Moslem.

In contrast, for **quantitative variables**, numerical values assigned to observations reflect different degrees of the measured dimension. For example, when you measure your weight you step on a set of scales, which produces a number for pounds or kilograms. A 200-pound person weighs twice as much as one weighing 100 pounds. Measuring weight also falls in another category, that of a **continuous measure**, in that a person's weight could take any value including some fraction such as 133.23 pounds. In contrast to continuous measures, a **discrete measure** can have gaps between possible values. We use discrete measurement when we count items that cannot have a partial value. To come back to our religion example, we would use a discrete quantitative scale to count the number of individuals with any particular religion, for example, 14 Catholics and 9 Jews in a particular group.

Four Levels of Measurement. You will see references to four **levels of measurement** according to the amount of information encoded in an observation. The four measurement levels ascend in order of the amount of information each level carries: from nominal through ordinal and interval to ratio.

In **nominal-level** measurement, we group observations of the same attribute together, for example, categorizing people by religion. Nominal-level measurement gives us only one kind of information, the equivalence of observations within the separate categories of the variable and their difference from observations in other categories. All of the Catholics have in common that they are Catholic and that they differ on religion from members of other religions. We also call this level of measurement the categorical level because observations are grouped in mutually exclusive categories. As indicated previously, this level involves qualitative variables.

Ordinal-level measurement goes one step beyond the nominal level in that we not only group like observations together, but we also rank them. You can remember the meaning of ordinal-level measurement because it involves ordering. Military rank illustrates this notion of order from low to high: private versus major versus general. Many social research measures ask for a level of agreement with some statement. For example, the question "Would you rate your social support as very good, satisfactory, or very poor?" asks for an ordinal judgment. Sometimes, ordinal measures use numbers for convenience in coding the answers. In the previous example, you might have to choose from the following answer options: very good (3), satisfactory (2), and very poor (1), and then write the number that matches your answer. However, you must remember that numbers for ordinal categories may serve only as handy abbreviations or labels. In that case, they, along with the nominal level, fall in the qualitative type of variable. In the preceding example, you could not conclude that someone answering with a 3 had two units more social support than someone answering with a 1, or three times as much social support as someone answering with a 1. On the other hand, some researchers use ordinal measures to approximate underlying quantitative realities and treat them much like the next level of measurement.

Interval-level measurement goes one step beyond ordinal measurement. Not only do we group equivalent observations together in ordered categories, but we also consider the intervals between adjacent categories as equal. You can remember the meaning of interval-level measurement if you think of it as "equal-interval" measurement. Equal-interval measurement has the benefit that numeric values for different categories are meaningful as numbers. Thus, simple arithmetical operations such as subtraction become appropriate. Time of day, in hours and minutes, illustrates equal-interval measurement. The numbers on the clock face such as 1 and 3 not only identify which is earlier and later but also indicate that 3 is exactly as much later than 2 as 2 is later than 1. Unlike ordinal measurement, interval measurement establishes the distance between any two levels. However, with an interval-level measure of temperature, we cannot say that 100 degrees centigrade is twice as hot as 50 degrees because that implies that 0 degrees represents no heat. On the centigrade scale, zero does not signify the absence of heat, since there is a whole range of negative temperature levels.

The highest level, **ratio-level** measurement includes all of the characteristics of the interval level plus the additional one of having a true zero point. The measures with a true zero can compare different observations by dividing one measure by another. You can remember the meaning of ratio-level measurement because division produces ratios. Weight illustrates ratio measurement. One could weigh oneself (say 150 pounds) and one's pet dog (say 25 pounds) and then express the relationship between the two as a ratio (150 is to 25 as 6 is to 1, or a ratio of 6). Interval and ratio measurements typically appear as continuous, quantitative variables.

Permissible Statistics Controversy. You may encounter the warning that only certain kinds of statistics can be used with certain levels of measurement and you should, therefore, know that a controversy surrounds this matter (see for example, Gaito,

1980; Townsend & Ashby, 1984). Typically, such guidelines state that ordinal-level data should not be analyzed using statistics (such as the *t* test) supposedly limited to interval-level or ratio-level measures. In practice, many researchers commonly apply such statistics to ordinal-level measures. A wise researcher will choose an analysis based on the assumptions of the particular statistic, the nature of the construct being measured, and the distribution of the observations (Binder, 1984; Borgatta & Bohrnstedt, 1980; Davison & Sharma, 1988; Maxwell & Delaney, 1985; Michell, 1986).

The remainder of this chapter will present some of the descriptive statistics most commonly seen in the social science literature: first, the statistics used to describe one variable; then a few measures of association between two variables; and finally, a widely used procedure for analyzing three or more variables—multiple regression. Many more statistics exist than can be covered here (for an overview, see Andrews, Klem, Davidson, O'Malley, & Rodgers, 1981).

UNIVARIATE STATISTICS

Central Tendency and Variability

Univariate statistics describe one variable. Two important aspects of a single variable include its **central tendency** (its midpoint) and its **variability** (or dispersion). We will discuss these two univariate statistics after reviewing the visual approach of the frequency distribution.

Visual Summaries of One Variable for One Group. A frequency distribution refers to a picture of the scores for a whole group of individuals. It tells the number of individuals (frequency on the vertical axis) getting each score (values along the horizontal axis). The frequency, or count of individuals getting any given score, is a quantitative measure of the type earlier defined as discrete. By using the frequency, it is possible to generate numbers even for nominal- and ordinal-level measurements (for example, 10 Methodists or 17 generals) as well as for interval- and ratio-level measurements. Thus we can derive descriptive statistics for any level of measurement.

Reviewing a frequency distribution such as the one in Figure A–1, we can notice at least four different characteristics. First we observe the central tendency of the distribution, that is, the score that is most representative of the scores of the whole group. A glance at Figure A–1 suggests that the typical person fell in the vicinity of 15 to 17. But "falling in the vicinity of" will prove too vague for precise work, and "typical" might refer to the most common, the middle, or the average. To be more exact, we will need to use one of the descriptive statistics designed to measure central tendency.

Second, we want to assess variability or dispersion. Variability refers to the distance of the values from each other. Two different measures commonly reflect the distance between observations—range and standard deviation. Since dispersion pertains to the distance of ordered values from each other, it does not apply to nominal measures.

Third, we can gauge at a glance the **symmetry** of a frequency distribution. If you folded the distribution in Figure A–1 on a vertical line down the middle, would the two sides match each other or would one side or *tail* stretch out farther than the other? If one appears longer than the other, we call the distribution skewed. **Skewness** tells the degree of departure from symmetry. Income in a general population will usually form a skewed distribution (with many low incomes but few high incomes). Just as central tendency and dispersion have precise expressions using descriptive statistics, so also we can measure skewness. The skewness statistic has a value of 0 in a perfectly symmetric distribution (skewness for the variable quiz in Table A–1 = -.64). As distributions skew to the left (a longer tail pointing to the lower values), the skewness statistic takes on increasingly large negative values. Distributions skewed to the right (a long tail trailing off to the larger values) have positive skewness statistics (see Note 3 for the calculation of the skewness statistic).

A fourth characteristic of a distribution also pertains to its shape. Does the distribution appear relatively flat and spread out or relatively tight and peaked? **Kurtosis** refers to the degree of peakedness of a distribution and can be measured precisely (see Note 3 for its computation). Often the kurtosis coefficient is adjusted so that a normal distribution has a value of 0, and such normally peaked distributions are said to be mesokurtic. Negative values of the adjusted kurtosis statistic indicate flatter distributions, called platykurtic, and positive values indicate an increasingly peaked shape called leptokurtic. For the variable quiz (Table A–1), kurtosis is −.28.

Central Tendency.   Although you will frequently encounter the mean as a measure of central tendency, other measures exist that sometimes prove more suitable. For example, you will embarrass yourself if you calculate the mean for religious preference because that expression has no meaning. The **mode** will serve better as a measure of central tendency for nominal-level variables such as religion. The mode consists of the value that is most frequently occurring. In the case of Figure A–1, the mode has the value 17, the score of the highest point of the distribution. Unfortunately, the mode fails to reflect information about the frequency of the other categories. If another score also has a high frequency, you can report two modes, and we call such a distribution bi-modal.

Another statistic can describe central tendency if the level of measurement is at least ordinal. The **median** reflects the middle value—the one that divides the distribution so that as many observations fall above as below it. In a distribution such as 4, 7, 8, 8, 9, 10, 11, 14, 22, the median is 9 because there are four observations (4, 7, 8, 8) below and four observations (10, 11, 14, 22) above. In Figure A–1 the median has a value not actually observed—one that falls between two values. The median for the data in Figure A–1 is 15.5, since 13 scores fall above and 13 scores fall below that value.[1]

We can calculate the median for ordinal- and higher level measures but not for nominal measures, since for them there is no meaning to the terms *above*, *middle*, and *below*. The median, unlike the mode, takes into account all of the observations. Unlike the mean, the median does not give any more weight to extreme scores than to more typical scores.

The **mean (*M*)** is simply the sum divided by the number of observations[2], and it is often abbreviated either M or $\overline{X}$. Just as it does not make sense to calculate the average religious preference, so it may sometimes not make sense to calculate the mean rank of an ordered variable (for example, among captain, major, and colonel).

The mean takes into account the value of each observation and thus gives greater weight to *outliers*—those extremely low or high observations that are located far away from the typical scores in a frequency distribution. As a consequence, the mean will often differ from the median and mode. Only in symmetric distributions will the mode, the median, and the mean all equal each other. In a skewed distribution, the extreme scores at the end of the longer tail "pull" the mean toward that end. For example, the mean of the four observations $10,000, $20,000, $30,000, and $500,000 comes to $140,000 (pulled far above the three lower, more typical incomes). The median does not respond to the magnitude of the extreme observations and may, therefore, provide a better central tendency measure for badly skewed variables. The mode does not respond at all to the skew since it remains at the point of the greatest concentration of observations (see Figure A–2).

Variability: Measures of Dispersion. The variability measures of range and standard deviation appear most often in social research. **Range** measures the span between the lowest and highest observations. Range and other measures of variability do

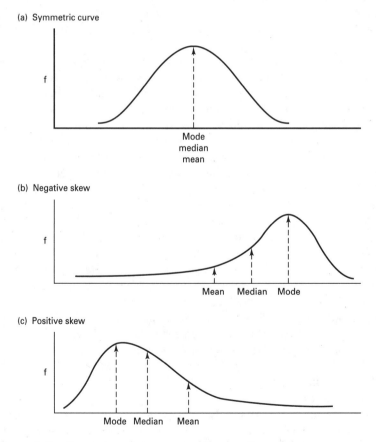

Figure A–2 Symmetry, skewness, and the location of the mean, median, and mode.

not apply to nominal measures. Since nominal measures do not have the property of order, it makes no sense to assess the distance from "lowest" to "highest." But range does apply to ordinal and higher measures. In Figure A–1, observerd scores range from 8 (the lowest score) to 20 (the highest score), or a range of 12.

The range provides a handy but rough way of describing the dispersion of a group of observations. The range can mislead when the distribution is peculiar (for example, 2, 3, 4, 5, 5, 5, 11, 39). Here the scores range from 2 to 39, but most of the observations cluster together in the lower part of this wide range (that is, 2 through 5).

The **standard deviation (SD)**, symbolized as *s* or *SD*, takes into account each observation's distance from the mean, not just the values of the two most extreme observations, as in the case of the range. You can calculate the standard deviation as follows: First, obtain the difference between each observation and the group mean. For example, a group of three observations such as 2, 4, and 6 would have a mean of 4 [that is, (2 + 4 + 6)/3 = 12/3 = 4]. Subtracting the mean from each observation yields the deviations from the mean, for example, 2 − 4 = −2 for the first observation.

How can we combine all of these deviations to yield a single measure of variability? Because the negative and positive values of the deviations cancel each other, averaging them will always produce zero, no matter how dispersed or concentrated the distribution. To avoid the offsetting of positive and negative deviations, you will need to square each deviation before averaging. For example, squaring the first deviation $(-2)^2$ produces $-2 \times -2 = 4$.

In the third step you will average the squared deviations by adding them up and dividing the sum by the number of observations. In the case of our example, the three squared deviations (4, 0, and 4) add up to 8. The sum of squared deviations (before dividing by the number) is called, naturally enough, the **sum of squares**. Dividing this sum by 3 yields the value of 2.67 for the average squared deviation. The average of the squared deviations is called the **variance**. In the fourth and final step, you would take the square root of the variance (in this case, $\sqrt{2.67}$) giving the standard deviation in this example of 1.63. When these four steps are applied to the data in Figure A–1, we obtain a standard deviation[3] of 2.99.

Standard Scores and the Normal Curve

Standard Scores. The **standard** or *z* **score** describes an individual's score relative to the group. You can standarize an individual's raw score by transforming it into a *z* score. First, you would subtract the group mean from the individual's score. Then divide this difference by the standard deviation.[4] To return to the original example from the beginning of this chapter, suppose you had a score of 16. Subtracting the group mean of 14.88, you get a difference of 1.12. Dividing by the standard deviation of 2.99, you get a *z* score of .37. You can calculate a *z* score in a similar way for any individual's quiz score.

Standard scores have several uses. First, the *z* score summarizes a score's relative position in a group. A *z* score of .37 indicates two things at a glance. The positive sign of the *z* score tells us that the raw score exceeded the mean of the group. A negative *z* score would have told us that the score fell below the mean of the group. Second, the magnitude of this z score informs us that the raw score fell only a little above the mean—in this case less than 1 standard deviation (.37 of a standard deviation to be precise). A z score of 2 would indicate that the raw score was exactly two full standard deviations above the mean, a relatively large amount.

As another benefit, z scores aid us in comparing scores from different distributions. Suppose you got the same score of 16 on a later quiz that was much more difficult than the first one. You sense that your score of 16 on the later quiz took a greater effort than the earlier 16. Z scores make it is easy to express such comparisons. Assume that on the later, harder quiz, the average student scored three fewer points (that is, the mean was 11.88). Also assume that the student scores fell closer together (for example, that the standard deviation was half its earlier value, or 1.5). In this case, your z score equals (16 - 11.88)/1.5, or 4.12/1.5, or 2.75. Now you can see that your raw score on the later quiz translates into a much larger z score, almost 3 standard deviations above the mean. Thus, z scores can help us compare scores from distributions that differ in their means, standard deviations, or both.

Another benefit of z scores appears when a whole group of scores is standardized. The new mean of the standardized scores equals 0, and the new standard deviation equals 1. When working with several groups of scores or when handling complicated statistics, it often helps to have groups share the same simple means and standard deviations.

Normal Curve.   If you were to observe many frequency distributions, you would find most approaching a similar bell shape, called the **normal curve**. Figure A–3 illustrates this symmetrical curve, one that is neither very peaked nor very flat.

So many distributions resemble this normal curve that we have come to expect social science data to be approximately normally distributed. Some inferential statistics depend on the assumption that the data have a nearly normal distribution. For this reason, we take special note of ways in which observed distributions differ from normal (for example, if they are asymmetric, too peaked, or too flat).

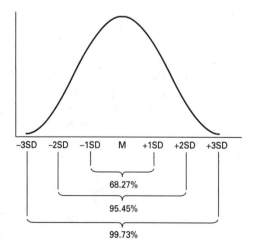

Figure A–3 Normal curve and percent of this area at 1, 2, and 3 standard deviations from the mean.

In descriptive statistics, we can make use of a special property of normal distributions—that fixed proportions of observations fall within different sections of the normal curve. For example, just over two-thirds of all scores (68.27 percent to be exact) fall between one standard deviation below and one standard deviation above the mean. Thus a z score of less than +1 but more than −1 puts that person in the company of the middle two-thirds of the group, assuming that the group's scores have a nearly normal distribution. Over 95 percent of all observations fall between +2 and −2 standard deviations, and more than 99 percent fall within ±3 standard deviations (read as "plus or minus 3"). Figure A–3 summarizes these relationships. Recalling these proportions, you can locate your standing in a group from your z score (which you can easily calculate from your raw score and the group's mean and standard deviation). For example, a z score on your test of +1 places you in the top one-sixth of the class. If your instructor grades on the curve and you know the approximate point on the curve used to distinguish each letter grade (perhaps the top 15 percent get As) you can estimate your grade.

Single Variable for More Than One Group. This chapter has focused, until this point, on the description of one variable in one group. But if you were to sample articles from a recent social science journal, you would probably not see a frequency polygon, a discussion of asymmetry, or a comment on the relative positions of the mode, median, and mean. Most social research involves many variables or multiple groups or both. Space restrictions make it impractical to print all the frequency distributions that may exist in such studies.

Consequently, most researchers summarize information about multiple groups in table or figure form. Only the most important and condensed descriptive information appears. Suppose you were interested in dividing the data of Table A–1 into four groups: male and female majors and nonmajors (that is, whether or not the student is majoring in the department giving the course). After separating the data into the four groups, you could calculate the descriptive statistics and draw the frequency polygons for each of these groups separately. Suppose you then had to select and present just the information that answers the question, "Which group did best on the quiz?" You could answer that question in a single table such as Table A–2.

In this table, ***n*** stands for number of observations (in this case, students). The mean for male majors appears in the column labeled *M* under the heading "Males" in the row labeled "Majors": 15.40. This table not only describes the scores for the four subgroups in question but also gives information about majors and nonmajors, with sexes combined, and about males and females, with majors and nonmajors combined.

Table A–2 Quiz Scores by Sex and Major

	MALES		FEMALES		TOTAL	
	n	M	n	M	n	M
Majors	10	15.40	5	12.00	15	14.27
Nonmajors	3	14.00	8	16.38	11	15.73
Total	13	15.08	13	14.69	26	14.88

Notice that the overall or grand mean appears under the vertical column heading "Total" in the row labeled "Total" and equals the value we earlier arrived at for the mean of all the students taking the quiz: 14.88. Each of the means in Table A–2 tells about a set of individual quiz scores, which could appear as a frequency distribution and for which various other descriptive statistics could be calculated. For example, we could calculate standard deviations for each of these subgroups and present them in the same table under a column heading such as "*SD*."

We could also display the information in Table A–2 in graphic form as in Figure A–4. By convention, the vertical axis displays the measure itself (in this case, average quiz scores). The horizontal axis displays the categories or groups falling along one dimension (in this case, sex). When there is a second dimension, as in this case, it can be portrayed by using different lines, as for majors and nonmajors. Further dimensions (for example, upper- and lower class standing), would require a separate figure for each level of the extra variable (for example, one for seniors, another for juniors, and so on).

BIVARIATE STATISTICS

Contingency Tables

Just as we can describe single variables both graphically and numerically, we can also describe **bivariate** (two-variable) relationships. These methods apply to situations in which each individual in a group has scores on two different variables.

Cross-Tabulation.   When both measures reflect qualitative levels or groupings (such as nominal- and some ordinal-level variables), their relationship can appear as a

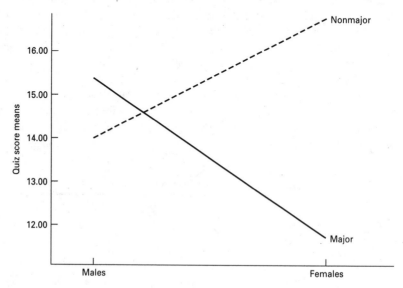

Figure A–4   Means for quiz scores by sex and major.

Table A–3   Cross-Tabulation of Students by Sex and Major

(a)	Male	Female
Major	B.A., R.D., F.E., G.F., T.F., B.N., T.R., P.T., K.T., A.W.	D.B., R.G., L.K., S.O., N.R.
Nonmajor	T.C., T.M., D.T.	J.B., P.D., C.H., S.P., J.R., P.S., S.U., R.Y.

(b)	Male	Female
Major	10	5
Nonmajor	3	8

cross-tabulation, which simply sorts individuals into the categories of both variables at the same time. For example, suppose we wanted to cross-tabulate the students from Table A–1 with respect to sex and major status. Each student is either male or female and is also either a major or a nonmajor. The cross-tabulation of students on these two dimensions requires a 2-by-2 table, as illustrated in Table A–3. We can also call this type of tabular display a **contingency table** because the sorting of individuals on one dimension (say major versus nonmajor) may be contingent on (that is dependent on) the other dimension (sex).

Each student belongs in one and only one of the four mutually exclusive cells of the fourfold table. For example, student B.A. would appear in the upper left-hand cell because he has the attributes male and major. One could assign individuals by initials, as in Table A–3a. Since the individual designations do not help our analysis, however, we need only record the number of persons in each cell as in Table A–3b.

This cross-tabulation reorganizes the sex and major data in Table A–1 to show, at a glance, the association of these two variables. In our hypothetical section, major status and being male occur together as does being female and nonmajor. Although this cross-tabulation greatly condenses the raw data about the association of sex and major, it is possible to take one more step. Certain statistics can reduce the information in Table A–3 to a single number, with the added advantage of expressing precisely the extent to which the two variables "go together." Statistics that describe association are generally called **correlation coefficients**.

Proportional Reduction of Error (PRE).   Correlation coefficients all approach one in absolute value (either +1 or −1) when the association is strong, and they approach zero when the association is weak or nonexistent. Some, but not all, correlation coefficients also tell how much knowing one variable improves the prediction of the other variable. Such prediction can measure the degree of association. If two variables have no association, knowing one tells us nothing about the other. On the other hand, if two variables have a perfect correlation, knowing the level of one variable tells the level of the other exactly.

We can express such improvement of prediction by measuring the **proportional reduction of error (PRE)**. Suppose you had to guess whether a student in our hypothetical class was a major or a nonmajor. You know only that out of 26 total students, 15 are majors and 11 are nonmajors. If you had nothing else to go on, you would guess that any particular student is a major since you would be right 15 times and wrong 11 times. If knowledge of another variable, say sex, reduces our errors in guessing majors, we say that it correlates with major–nonmajor status. By measuring the proportion of error reduced by our extra knowledge, we can state precisely how strong the association is.

The proportional reduction of error has a formula: the difference between the number of errors without knowledge of the other variable (old errors) and with that knowledge (new errors) divided by the number of errors without knowledge: (old errors − new errors)/old errors.

If knowing the other variable adds nothing to our prediction, then old errors equal new errors and error reduction equals zero (0/old errors). If knowing the other variable leads to perfect prediction, there will be no new errors and the formula equals 1 (old errors/old errors). This formula thus meets our requirement for a correlation coefficient, which approaches one as the association strengthens and zero as the association weakens.

Now let us apply this PRE notion to the information in Table A–3, using the sex of the student to reduce our errors in guessing major status. Remember that without knowing gender, we would predict that everyone in the section is a major, resulting in 11 errors (old errors). Now using the information about sex, what predictions would we make about major status and what would our error rate be? Take males first. From Table A–3 we know that of the 13 males, 10 are majors and 3 are nonmajors. If we predict that all males are majors, we will make 10 right guesses and 3 wrong ones. Next, consider females. Of the 13 females, 5 are majors and 8 are nonmajors. If we predict that each female is a nonmajor, we make just 5 errors. As a result of knowing the student's sex, we would make a total of 8 errors for the section as a whole. Applying the PRE formula: (old errors − new errors) / old errors = (11 − 8) / 11 = 3 / 11 = .27.

Using this procedure, we can estimate the association of sex and major as .27. As a PRE measure, this number says that knowledge of student's sex reduces the error in guessing major status by 27 percent. This particular coefficient has the name **lambda** (λ). Just as we earlier concentrated the information in Table A–1 into a single number such as the mean, so we have reduced the information in Table A–3 about the association of two variables to a single number.

Lambda can also be used to express the correlation among ordinal-level measures. However, other kinds of coefficients can better capitalize on the extra information contained in ordered variables. One PRE correlation coefficient often used for ordinal data is called **gamma** (γ). Gamma measures the improvement in predicting the position on one variable (high or low) from knowing the position on the other. A positive gamma indicates that the two variables have like values (both high or both low) rather than unlike values, and a negative gamma expresses the probability of observing unlike values (if high on one variable, then low on the other).

Suppose you wanted to correlate the performance of our students on the most recent quiz with their performance on the practice exam (see Table A–1). We could organize the data giving letter grades based on scores. For example let us take 11 and 17 as our dividing points. Scores up to and including 11 receive failing (F) grades. Scores

Table A–4   Cross-Tabulation of Practice Test and Quiz Scores

		PRACTICE TEST		
		Failing	*Passing*	*Honors*
	Failing	3	1	0
Quiz	Passing	1	10	2
	Honors	0	3	6

from 12 through 16 receive passing (D and C) grades. Scores of 17 and higher receive honor (B and A) grades. These categories represent ordinal-level measures because they are ranked but have unequal intervals. We can now cross-tabulate these two variables (see Table A–4).

We do not need to know the formula of gamma, but when computed for Table A–4, it yields .90. However, the lambda formula for these same data gives .46 as the result. This contrast shows that different types of coefficients can yield different estimates of association for the same data. For more information about such measures, consult a standard statistics text.

We will concentrate on the meaning of the coefficient. The positive gamma indicates that like grades (similarly high or similarly low) outnumbered unlike grades. Table A–4 indicates that most students received the same grade on the quiz as they earlier did on the practice test: three failed both, ten passed both, and six got honors on both. The opposite kind of association, where a failing practice test corresponds with honors on the quiz, is called an inverse association and would have produced a negative gamma. The gamma (.90) approaches 1.0, which is the largest possible value, thus indicating a strong association.

Unlike ordinal coefficients such as gamma, nominal coefficients such as lambda do not have negative values because nominal variables do not have the property "greater and lesser." Some coefficients such as the lambda are asymmetric, that is, the lambda for predicting major from sex can differ from the lambda calculated for predicting sex from major. In contrast, other correlation coefficients such as gamma are symmetric in that the same value occurs whether predicting quiz grades from practice test grades or vice versa. This distinction between symmetric and asymmetric correlations is unrelated to the level of measurement. You may encounter an asymmetric correlation coefficient used with ordinal data (Somer's *d*), or a symmetric lambda (a kind of average of the two possible asymmetric lambdas) used with nominal data.

Scattergrams and the Pearson Correlation Coefficient

Scattergrams.   Continuous variables can take on a large number of different values, as is common with interval- and ratio-level measures. In such cases, cross-tabulation proves very cumbersome. In the previous section, we combined the original scores of the practice exam and quiz into two 3-level variables, which were cross-tabulated in Table A–4. Suppose we had instead cross-tabulated the original raw scores. The box containing all possible combinations of these scores would have required many more cells: 13 (8 through 20 for quiz scores) by 14 (7 through 20 for practice scores) or 182 cells. If we had fractional scores, the number of possible cells could be multiplied still further.

When displaying the relationship between two interval- or ratio-level variables, we usually replace the cross-tabulation technique is usually replaced by the **scattergram**. A scattergram uses two axes, and each axis displays one of the two variables in the relationship. Figure A–5 shows the scattergram for the relationship between quiz score and practice score from Table A–1.

Each point in the scattergram represents one student in our hypothetical class. For example, student T.C. has a quiz score of 9 and a practice score of 7. His initials identify the point representing his two scores in Figure A–5. Similarly, every point locates a different student with respect to his or her two scores. Since we do not need to know the particular student associated with each point, we can drop identifying marks such as initials from scattergrams. The scattergram portrays a positive association of the two sets of scores. Students with low practice scores also tend to have low quiz scores, as appeared earlier for the association of grades based on these scores.

Pearson Correlation.   A single number can summarize the association of two variables pictured in a scattergram: the **Pearson product moment correlation coefficient**, represented by the symbol r. The Pearson r does not belong to the PRE class of coefficients. But a simple transformation—squaring r to r^2—can express something like

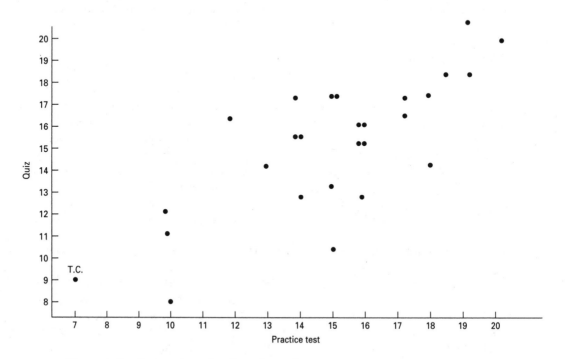

Figure A–5   Scattergram of quiz and practice test scores.

the proportional reduction of error. The value r^2 is sometimes called the **coefficient of determination**. Suppose $r = .5$. Then $r^2 = .5 \times .5 = .25$, which signifies that one variable explains 25 percent of the variability in the other.

We need not know the formula for computing r to grasp that it ranges from -1 (perfect negative correlation) to +1 (perfect positive correlation). Like gamma, r is symmetric in the sense that it has the same value regardless of the variable regarded as the predictor. For the practice score and quiz score data for Figure A–5, $r = .76$ and $r^2 = .58$.

Although research reports seldom present scattergrams of associations, you can imagine the appearance of a scattergram by using only the information from a correlation coefficient. Figure A–6 shows three examples of scattergrams corresponding to Pearson correlations of -1, 0, and $+1$, respectively. Notice that the correlation of $r = 0$ corresponds to a scattergram having no linear pattern. But the two perfect correlations ($r = +1$, $r = -1$) correspond to scattergrams in which all the points fall on a straight line. For a negative or inverse correlation ($r = -1$), the line runs from upper left to lower right, indicating that as one variable becomes smaller, the other becomes larger. For a positive correlation ($r = +1$), the points run from lower left to upper right, indicating that as one variable increases, the other also increases.

Other scattergrams would fall between these two scattergrams. For example, Figure A–5 shows a moderately strong (but not perfect) positive correlation. The points follow a linelike pattern running from lower left to upper right (marking it as positive), but many points fall away from the line (marking it as less than a perfect +1). In a smaller correlation (say .3), the points would still form a pattern from lower left to upper right, but the line would appear less distinct, with more points falling farther from the line. As a correlation becomes smaller, its scattergram increasingly resembles that of $r = 0$.

Summarizing Many Relationships.   We frequently see the analysis of many variables and their many possible relationships all in the same report. Suppose there were 10 variables that had been collected from the same group of people. Our imaginary section might have, in addition to the practice exam (variable *PE*) and the first quiz (*Q1*), three other quizzes (*Q2*, *Q3*, and *Q4*) and five homework assignments (*A*, *B*,

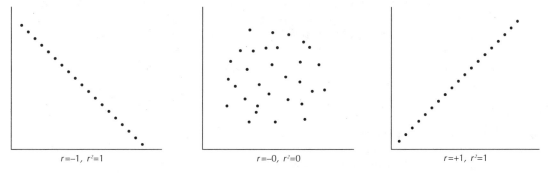

$r=-1,\ r^2=1$ $r=-0,\ r^2=0$ $r=+1,\ r^2=1$

Figure A-6   Examples of scattergrams.

Table A–5 Correlation Matrix for Tests and Homework Assignments

		PE	Q1	Q2	Q3	Q4	A	B	C	D	E
Practice Exam	PE	(1.0)	(.76)								
Quizzes	Q1	.76									
	Q2	.72	.68								
	Q3	.69	.73	.59							
	Q4	.71	.82	.70	.65						
Assignments	A	.38	.37	.30	.29	.33					
	B	.24	.25	.19	.31	.20	.82				
	C	.51	.45	.48	.39	.46	.79	.71			
	D	.09	.05	.15	.11	.10	.65	.48	.62		
	E	.40	.35	.29	.45	.31	.92	.72	.59	.64	

C, *D*, and *E*). Just as we calculated the correlation between *PE* and *Q1* ($r = .76$), we could calculate the correlations between all possible pairs of these 10 variables (for example, *PE* with *Q2*, *Q3* with *A*, and so forth). The presentation of many correlations often takes the tabular form, called a correlation **matrix** (see Table A–5).

We first note in Table A–5 that much of the space remains blank. The missing coefficients in the upper right half of the table identify this as an example of a symmetric matrix. In symmetric matrices, every coefficient (except the ones on the diagonal) could occur twice. If you folded the matrix along the diagonal from upper left to lower right, you would find that each coefficient was matched with itself. For example, the correlation of *PE* with *Q1* has already been calculated as .76 and can be located in the first column (*PE*) and second row (*Q1*). But the same correlation could also appear in the second column (*Q1*) of the first row (*PE*) as indicated by the .76 in the parentheses. To avoid duplication, we simply omit the redundant correlations from symmetric matrices.

The correlations along the diagonal each involve the correlation of a variable with itself as, for example, *PE* with *PE* in the first row, first column (indicated by the 1.0 in parentheses). Since the correlation of any variable with itself is always 1.0, all of the diagonal correlations are the same. Instead of showing all these 1s, symmetric matrices usually omit the diagonal correlations.

You will sometimes see a nonsymmetric correlation matrix with values filling all the rows and columns. This happens when one set of variables is correlated with a different set so that no variable is correlated with itself. For example, we might want a matrix consisting only of the correlations of the practice exam and quizzes (*PE* through *Q4*) with the homework assignments (*A* through *E*). These correlations would form a full rectangle as indicated by the box in the lower left of Table A–5.

MULTIVARIATE STATISTICS

Sometimes we need to study the association of two or more predictor variables with an outcome variable. Such analyses produce **multivariate statistics**, which can describe the association of two variables after adjusting for one or more others. Multivariate analyses can apply to data of any measurement level. For example, we can study nominal or ordinal variables in multiway contingency tables with as many dimensions as there are variables. Statistical procedures for such cross-classified data are now well developed (for example, loglinear analysis, see Fienberg, 1977). However, social researchers using the multivariate approach most commonly rely on regression analysis. The next section will present the logic of regression, starting with the simplest, two-variable case. The final section will illustrate how regression can handle additional variables.

Regression Analysis

Linear Assumption.   Regression analysis has a close relationship to the correlational analysis described in the prior section. Both approaches apply to ordered variables with many levels of each. In both approaches, a scattergram can visually describe the association between these variables as shown in Figure A–5. Unlike the Pearson r, which measures this association in a single number, regression describes it with the straight line, which best fits the pattern of points in the scattergram. This approach makes the **linear assumption**—that the association between the two variables resembles a straight line. If the points form a curving shape such as a U, no straight line can fit the data well.

The line that fits the scattergram's points can be uniquely defined with two numbers. The **intercept** is the value on the vertical axis where the best-fitting line crosses it. The **slope** is the angle of the line. These two values have standard abbreviations: a for the intercept (also called the constant) and b for the slope. The slope tells how much the line rises or falls, expessed in units of the vertical axis for each one unit it extends along the horizontal axis. By custom the outcome variable appears on the vertical axis with the label Y and the predictor variable on the horizontal axis with the label X. Thus each point in the scattergram has two identifiers, the y value (level on the Y axis) and the x value (level on the X axis. Because the values on the regression line are estimates, they are labeled $\hat{y}$ (estimated) to discriminate them from the actual values labeled plain y. In summary form, the regression line is defined as: $\hat{y} = a + bx$.

For any possible value of x, the corresponding estimated value of y equals the intercept (a) plus the slope (b) times x. For example, suppose we know that for each additional hour of weekly study in a course, the average student would likely get an additional five points on the exam and even without study ($x = 0$) would get at least 20 points. How many points would we estimate for the student who studied 6 hours per week? From our formula, estimated points = 20 (the intercept on the y axis where $x = 0$) plus 5 (slope) times 6 (the given value of x in this case) = 20 + 30 = 50. You can now see that the regression approach can project future y values from present x values. For example, a bank economist might regress the number of home loans customers take out (y) on the mortgage rate charged (x). Given the best-fitting line for this regression, the bankers could estimate the demand for home loans for any chosen mortgage rate.

Residual Errors and "Best" Fit.   Regression lines serve as estimates and seldom

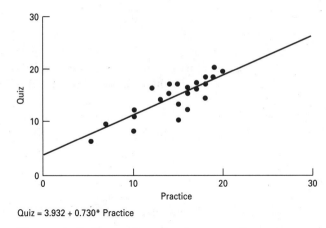

Quiz = 3.932 + 0.730* Practice

Figure A–7 Regression of quiz on practice exam.

fit perfectly with all the points in a scattergram. Other variables—besides the x that we measure—may also influence y. We can measure some of these other variables and include them in our analysis, but any study will likely omit some variables that are omitted from a study. Their omission helps explain why the regression line misses some of the points, that is, why estimated $\hat{y}$ usually differs at least a little from actual y. Such differences or deviations between actual and expected are called **residual error**, or residuals.

A regression line fits the points in a scattergram in a way that minimizes such error. One could do this visually by drawing first one line and then another to find one that appears closest to all the points. However, computer procedures will perform this function more precisely and quickly by mathematical analysis. Imagine drawing a possible regression line through the points in Figure A–5 and then measuring all of the errors. To do this, you would sum the distances between each estimated $\hat{y}$ (the value on the vertical axis of your line) and each actual y (the value on the vertical axis of the actual point) corresponding to each x). In algebric terms, you would find the difference $\hat{y}$ (estimated) − y (actual) for each x. Graphically this corresponds to measuring up or down from your line to each point of the scattergram. Since some of the points are above and some below your hypothetical regression line, these deviations will have both plus and minus values. To convert all these values to positive numbers, it is customary to square them ($\hat{y}$ estimate − y actual)^2. The sum of these squared deviations (called the sum of squares) represents all the errors for this particular regression line. By definition, the best-fitting line minimizes these errors. For this reason, we call this approach *least squares regression.*

The least squares line for the data on quiz and practice scores in Figure A–5 appears in Figure A–7. In this case, the intercept (*a*) equals 3.93 and the slope (*b*) equals .73.

Multiple Regression

Adding More Predictors.   We have learned that performance on the practice exam predicts performance on the quiz. Now suppose we were interested in the effects of other, prior variables that might predict exam scores. Perhaps women or majors perform better than men or nonmajors on such tests. To study the effects of each of these variables alone, we could regress quiz first on sex and then, in a second analysis, on major status. However, to find the effect of each controlling for the other, we must include them both in a single regression. The details of this procedure need not concern us here (for more information on regression see Berry & Feldman, 1985; Schroeder, Sjoquist, & Stephan, 1986). Just remember that the form of multiple regression analysis resembles that of bivariate regression. In addition to the constant or intercept value (a), now we will have two slopes (b_1 and b_2), one for each predictor. Each describes the increase or decrease in our dependent variable for a unit increase in the predictor. Thus our general regression formula becomes $\hat{y}$ (estimated) $= a + b_1x_1 + b_2x_2 + \ldots b_nx_n$, where there are n slope terms, one for each of n predictors.

By converting the information in Table A–1 on sex (1 for males and 0 for females) and major (1 for major and 0 for nonmajors) to numbers, these two variables can serve as predictors of quiz scores. The resulting regression gives the following results: $a = 15.42$, b_1 (sex) $= 1.12$, and b_2 (major) $= -1.90$. Of course, multiple regression can have more than two predictors. We can even include predictors made up of other predictors, such as the product of sex and major. The b for this term tests the interaction between sex and major, that is, whether one sex-by-major combination does better than another. When this term is added, we find that $a = 16.38$, b_1 (sex) $= 12.38$, b_2 (major) $= -4.38$, and b_3 (sex $\times$ major) $= 5.78$. These last results indicate that in these imaginary data the combination of sex and major does affect quiz scores. The nature of this interaction can be seen in the earlier Figure A–4, which showed that male majors and female nonmajors did best.

As we add or drop terms from an equation, we note that earlier terms may change somewhat. Different models will produce not only different coefficients but different degrees of fit. We want to find a regression model that fits as well as possible. We can judge the overall fit of a regression model by the multiple correlation coefficient R or its square R^2 (similar to the r^2 introduced earlier as the coefficient of determination). You can think of R as the correlation of the outcome variable with all of the predictors taken together. Of course with only one predictor, R equals the r between the two variables. A large R^2 (approaching 1) shows that the set of predictors chosen for the model accounts well for the outcome variable. As we compare one model with another, the change in R^2 shows how much the added predictors improve the overall fit. In the case of the model with just sex and major, the R^2 was only .09 (leaving over 90 percent of the variability in quiz scores unexplained). However when the interaction of sex and major was added, the R^2 rose to .28, a gain of 19 percent in explanatory power. Although substantially improved, this value still leaves much room for improvement and falls well below that for the model with practice scores as the predictor ($R2 = .58$).

Whether the improvement in fit from one model to another is a fluke of sampling is the concern of inferential statistics, which are treated in Chapter 8. There you will find an example of a typical presentation of multiple regression results, including tests of whether the observed effect may be due to sampling error or should be considered valid for the population from which the studied sample was drawn.

Advanced Methods

Other Approaches. Many advanced multivariate procedures have appeared, only a few of which can be mentioned in this text. For example, factor analysis (mentioned in Chapter 5) assesses tests to judge the degree to which various questions measure the same or different concepts. Multiple regression underlies path analysis (see Chapter 12). An approach called structural equation modeling combines factor analysis with path analysis. Computational packages make these procedures widely available (for example, LISREL and EQS). Another form of regression, called analysis of variance (or ANOVA), can analyze experimental designs. This approach can extend to cases in which another variable is correlated with the outcome variable (analysis of covariance, or ANCOVA) or there is more than one outcome variable (multiple analysis of variance, or MANOVA).

These techniques increase our ability to study the association of one variable with another while statistically holding constant the effects of other variables. However, these procedures carry with them added costs such as computational complexity and additional assumptions about the data. The following section uses the problem of analyzing time series data to illustrate the nature of this complexity.

Time Series Analysis: An Example. Data for the same variable(s) at numerous time points make up a **time series**, for example, the annual number of suicides for a period of years. Several different techniques have emerged to analyze time series, including regression analysis. As adapted to economic time series, for example, this approach is commonly treated under the label *econometrics* (see the standard text by Johnston, 1984). Box and Jenkins (1976) offered a different but increasingly popular alternative to time series analysis. These and other approaches tell us whether some confounding variable explains an association observed over time.

To see the potential for the influence of a third variable, consider the relationship between the number of employed persons and the number of suicides annually. For the United States, from 1900 to 1975, this correlation appears positive and quite high ($r = .83$, according to Cook, Dintzer, & Mark, 1980, p. 101). One might interpret this value as evidence that increased employment causes increased suicide because it is implausible that increased suicides raise employment. However, such an interpretation runs so counter to our intuition that we suspect the presence of a third or confounding variable.

In the case of employment and suicide, we can see the explanation in the graph of their relationship over time shown in Figure A–8a. The number of employed persons, suicides, and just about any other aspect of human activity increased steadily from 1900 to 1975 because the population increased. That is, population growth confounded the time series relationship between employment and suicide. How can we assess the relationship of employment and suicide without confounding by population growth?

We could remove the population trend from the variables by converting the data to rates. To do this, we would divide the numbers of suicides and employed by the total number of people as illustrated in Figure A–8b. When the trend is removed, the time series is said to be *detrended*. Note that the detrended series in Figure A–8b no longer has the upward trend of the series in Figure A–8a. Detrended employment and de-

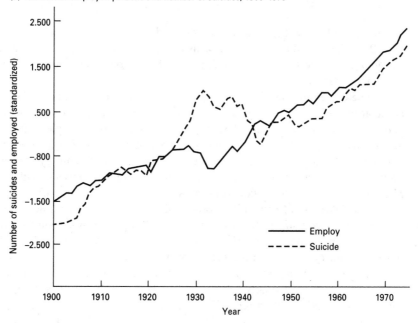

(a) Number of employed persons and number of suicides, 1900–1975

(b) Employment rate and suicide rate, 1900–1975

Figure A–8   Concomitant time series relationships with and without trend: Employment and suicide. (From Cook, Dintzer, & Mark, 1980. Copyright © 1980 by Sage Publications, Inc. Reprinted by permission of Sage Publications, Inc.)

trended suicide now correlate negatively and strongly ($r = -.59$ according to Cook et al., 1980). This finding fits better with the more intuitive hypothesis that decreases in employment cause increases in suicide and shows how attention to a third variable clarifies our understanding of two others.

The detrending in Figure A–8 worked by adjusting the data before measuring the association. In a second approach, we could measure one or more additional variables and include them in a multiple regression analysis. For example other variables, such as the share of population that is elderly, male or divorced, might contribute to the suicide rate. We can assess the unconfounded association of employment and suicide by including these age, gender, and marital variables in the analysis. A third approach applies when the potentially confounding variable cannot be identified. We may suspect some third variable of causing the observed correlation of two time series, but we may not be able to measure it. Such a variable could operate by causing similar patterns or regularities in the two time series of interest. In this case we need to remove these regularities from one or both time series even if we cannot name their source.

The Box-Jenkins (1976) method can detect and filter out regularities in a time series. Although statistically advanced, the Box-Jenkins approach relies on a simple logic. A time series with a recurring pattern contains information about itself. That is, a regularity, such as a rise in employment every November, allows us to predict what will happen in future Novembers. If we could extract information about such regularities, we could use it to make better predictions about future time points of the data series.

The Box-Jenkins approach gathers such information about regularities within a time series. The method begins with an autocorrelogram, which is the correlation of a series with lagged versions of itself. For example, a monthly series could be correlated with itself lagged one month, two months, and so on up to 12, 24, or more months. A correlation at a 12-month lag indicates an annual pattern, that is, that last year's value predicts this year's. We need not know the statistical details to understand that the method can produce best estimates of future values based on the regularities found in the autocorrelogram. Subtracting these best estimates from the actual values produces residuals with all the regularities removed. In Box-Jenkins analysis, such a time series of residuals, with all temporal patterns removed, has the name **white noise**. Suppose both the "cause" and "effect" time series are reduced to white noise. Their subsequent correlation measures their association in a way unconfounded by whatever produced the patterns in the original series. When Cook et al. (1980) "prewhitened" both employment and suicide rates, they found a strong negative association ($r = -.59$) "on time" (that is, no lead or lag).

In review, we see that a clear picture of a two-variable relationship may require complicated analysis of three or more variables. Moreover, different assumptions about the data can guide us to different methods, each with its own limits and problems.

For example, in reading reports of time series analysis, you might encounter concern with the problem of **serial correlation**. Recall that regression analysis works by fitting lines that minimize the residuals between the estimates and actual data. One assumption for the significance test of the regression coefficient holds that the residuals produced in the analysis are not themselves correlated over time. Unfortunately, time series analysis often violates this assumption of no serial correlation. As a result, time series analysts must check their work for serial correlation, for example by the Durbin-Watson test (1950, 1951). If these analysts find serial correlation, they must make adjustments for it, for example, by using generalized least squares or GLS (see Hanushek & Jackson, 1977). This example illustrates the kind of extra effort necessary for the proper use of such advanced methods (Catalano & Serxner, 1987).

SUMMARY

This chapter has emphasized reduction and clarification. Descriptive statistics make sense out of raw observations. By grouping the data or isolating certain aspects of the data, we can discover the essential amidst the irrelevant. This chapter has presented some of the many ways to summarize and present data.

The first section dealt with descriptive statistics and visual methods for summarizing single variables from single groups. A frequency distribution can portray one variable in visual form such as the histogram or the frequency polygon. Descriptive statistics usually present the central tendency (mode, median, and mean) and dispersion (range, standard deviation). Other descriptive statistics include skewness and kurtosis. The z score provides a convenient measure of one observation's relative standing.

The next section dealt with different ways of describing relationships between two variables. If the measures are nominal or ordinal, we can portray the relationship in a cross-tabulation. When the data are ordered and take on many different values, we commonly use the scattergram to picture the relationship. Coefficients of correlation condense information about association into single numbers. These numbers typically approach 1 (plus or minus) as the relationship becomes stronger and zero as the relationship becomes weaker. Some correlation coefficients derive from the idea of PRE—proportional reduction of error. PRE coefficients tell the percentage of improvement in predicting one variable that comes from knowing the other variable.

The final section presented multivariate statistics, which can study two or more predictors in relation to an outcome variable. The introduction to regression analysis began with the simple, two-variable case and followed with a multivariate example. An example of time series analysis represented more advanced statistical procedures and showed how multivariate procedures can control for confounding but at the cost of added complexity.

EXERCISES

1. Review each of the visual (frequency distribution) and statistical methods for describing a single variable. For example, use the data in Table A–1 for practice scores to make a histogram or frequency polygon as in Figure A–1. Then calculate the mode, median, and mean as well as the range and standard deviation for this variable.

2. Using the information you have generated about practice scores, compute the standardized, or z, scores for a few individuals. Assess their percentile standing on this

test, assuming the distribution is nearly normal. If your instructors provide class means and standard deviations, calculate your own z scores.

3. Review the translation of tabular data into graphic form. Calculate the means by sex and major for practice scores in Table A–1. Then create a graph such as Figure A–4 for the same data.

4. Make a scattergram (as in Figure A–5) of quiz scores and practice scores for just the majors in Table A–1, and then repeat this operation for the nonmajors. Compare these two scattergrams in terms of the direction (positive or inverse) and magnitude of the associations they portray. Try drawing a best-fitting straight line through each swarm of points based on your visual assessment, and then estimate the intercept and slope of each.

5. Find a research article with a Pearson correlation matrix (as in Table A–5) or the results of a multiple regression analysis. Select one correlation or regression coefficient from the article and name the two variables involved. Describe their relationship in ordinary language based on the sign and magnitude of the coefficient.

KEY TERMS

Bivariate statistics
Central tendency
Coefficient of determination
Contingency table
Continuous measure
Correlation coefficient
Cross-tabulation
Descriptive statistics
Discrete measure
f
Frequency distribution
Frequency polygon
Gamma
Histogram
Intercept
Interval level
Kurtosis
Lambda
Levels of measurement
Linear assumption
Matrix
Mean (M)
Median
Mode
Multivariate statistics
n

Nominal level
Normal curve
Ordinal level
Pearson product moment
    correlation coefficient (r)
Proportional reduction
    of error (PRE)
Qualitative variables
Quantitative variables
Range
Ratio level
Residual error
Scattergram
Serial correlation
Skewness
Slope
Standard deviation (SD)
Standard score (z)
Sum of squares
Symmetry
Time series
Univariate statistics
Variability
Variable
Variance
White noise

NOTES

1. When the median falls in a class of values, its calculation can be a bit complicated. For example, suppose that the distribution was 4, 7, 8, 9, 9, 10, 11, 14, 22. The value 9 is not the median since there are unequal numbers of observations above (4: 10, 11, 14, 22) and below (3: 4, 7, 8). In this case, the median falls somewhere in the range of values between 8 and 10 (that is, between 8.5 and 9.5). The formula for calculating the median in this case is as follows:

$$L + \left(\frac{\frac{T}{2} - B}{M} \right) I, \text{ where}$$

L is the lower boundary of the interval that includes the median (that is, 8.5)
I is the range of the interval that includes the median (that is, I = 9.5 - 8.5)
T is the total number of all observations in the distribution (that is, 9)
B is the number of observations below the interval that contains the median (that is, 3: 4, 7, 8)
M is the number of observations in the interval that contains the median (that is, 2: 9, 9). In this example, the median can be found by substituting into the formula:

$$8.5 + \left(\frac{\frac{9}{2} - 3}{2} \right) 1 = 8.5 + \frac{4.5 - 3}{2} = 8.5 + \frac{1.5}{2} = 8.5 + .75 = 9.25$$

2. The expression "sum divided by number" is a translation of a mathematical expression: $\Sigma\, X/N$ where N = total number of observations and Σ is the symbol for summation. $\Sigma\, X$ means that all observations or Xs are to be added together. The distribution 5, 4, 3, 2, consists of four observations. Each observation may be thought of as an X. Thus X_1 = 5, X_2 = 4, and so forth. The expression $\Sigma\, X$ means $X_1 + X_2 + X_3 + X_4$ or 5 + 4 + 3 + 2 or 14. $\Sigma\, X\, /\, N$ means 14/4 or 3.5.

3. In the form of mathematical symbols, the standard deviation is:

$$SD = \sqrt{\frac{\Sigma\, (X - M)^2}{N}}$$

Sometimes you will see a slightly different version of this formula, with $N-1$ substituted for N. The reason for this latter version is that, in small samples, it provides a better estimate of the standard deviation of the population from which the sample came. However, as sample size increases above about 30, the two versions give virtually the same result for practical purposes. Since we are not estimating population variability here, we will use the form with N in the denominator. The expression $(X - M)$ is called a deviation because it measures the distance or deviation of any observation X from the mean. The calculation of the variance requires that each deviation be squared before averaging. But lower and higher powers of this deviation could be taken. The average of the deviations is called the first moment, $\Sigma\, (X - M)\, /\, N$, which is uninteresting because it is always zero. The average of the second power of the deviations is called the second central moment (which is the variance: $\Sigma\, (X - M)^2\, /\, N$). The averages of the third and fourth powers of the deviations are called the third and fourth central moments respectively. These higher moments are the basis for calculating the statistics measuring skewness and kurtosis.

$$\text{Skewness :} \quad \frac{\dfrac{\sum (X - M)^3}{N}}{SD^3} \qquad\qquad \text{Kurtosis :} \quad \frac{\dfrac{\sum (X - M)^4}{N}}{SD^4}$$

4. In notation, $z = (X_i - M) / SD$. Here the subscript i represents any individual in the group. For example, if individual number 1 were to have his or her score standardized, i would be 1 (that is, the ith person in this case would the the first person) and $z_1 = (X_1 - M) / SD$ where X_1 is the first person's raw quiz score and Z_1 is that person's standardized score. M and SD will be the same for each person from the same group, since they describe the group of scores as a whole.

Glossary

ABAB design: Multiple-intervention design in which the experimental manipulation occurs at least twice with an intervening period in which to observe the effect of the withdrawal of the initial manipulation, also called a reversal design.

Abstract: Brief summary that appears at the beginning of most social research reports; can be retrieved by an abstracting service.

Aggregate-level data: Based on grouped data using a spatial or temporal unit of analysis.

Alpha: Probability of wrongly rejecting a null hypothesis; usually set by researcher before the study (by consensus .05 unless otherwise indicated).

Alpha problem: Difficulty of deciding whether to reject the null hypothesis when a few statistically significant results are produced by many inferential statistical tests.

Analysis of covariance: Statistical procedure for adjusting posttest scores for pretest group differences.

Archives: Ongoing records kept by institutions of society.

Attenuation: Effect of measurement error or unreliability in reducing the apparent magnitude of association of two variables.

Attrition: Loss of subjects from a study over time.

Autonomic system: Portion of human nervous system including two subsystems, the sympathetic and the parasympathetic, the former of which controls certain bodily responses indicating emotion.

Beta: Probability of wrongly failing to reject a null hypothesis.

Between-subjects design: Experimental design in which the contrast between differently treated groups measures the treatment effect.

Bias: That part of the deviation of the observed score from the true value of the construct being measured that is unchanging or tends in one direction (as distinct from randomly varying error which sums to zero over enough cases).

Bivariate association: Association between two variables.

Bivariate statistics: Descriptive statistics for the association of two variables.

Blind: Technique of avoiding experimenter expectancy by concealing assignment of subject from researcher or of avoiding demand characteristic by concealing assignment of subject from subject. When both subject and experimenter are blind to the assignment, the study is called "double blind."

Blocking: Dividing subjects into groups based on a measured independent variable.

Boolean operators: Connecting words such as *and* or *or* that can identify overlapping or nonoverlapping sets of information.

Branch: Technique that skips irrelevant questions and directs the interviewee to the next appropriate item.

Call number: Identifying code numbers and letters by which an item can be located in a library.

Canned experimenter: Standardization of experimental procedure by use of tape-recorded instructions.

Case: Unit of analysis, usually individual subject, for whom measures are collected on each variable.

Causal: Pertaining to the generation of an effect.

Census: Survey of the entire population.

Central limit theorem: Principle that the sampling distribution approaches normality as the number of samples increases.

Central tendency: In descriptive statistics, the value or score best representing a group of scores (for example, the mean).

Citation index: Database of publications searchable by the references or citations included in the articles.

Closed-ended questions: Items that can be answered from a few predetermined options.

Cluster: Sample unit consisting of a group of elements, for example, a college or city.

Codebook: Index that names the variables and specifies their location in the data set.

Coefficient alpha: Reliability coefficient of length-adjusted, inter-item, or within-test consistency appropriate for tests with items with three or more answer options (KR-20 statistic substitutes when items have two answer options).

Coefficient of determination: Transformation of r by squaring (r^2), which expresses a relationship in PRE terms, that is, percentage of the variance explained.

Cohort survey: Types of trend survey in which fresh samples are drawn and interviewed from the same subpopulation, known as a cohort and usually defined by birth year, as it ages.

Command: In the context of an online catalog search, the part of the user's instructions that tells the computer the desired action, for example FIND.

Compensatory contamination: Problem of control subjects acquiring the experimental treatment through rivalry or diffusion; has the effect of reducing the difference between experimental and control conditions.

Complete within-subjects design: Multiple-intervention design in which each subject receives all possible orders of the experimental manipulations.

Completion rate: Proportion of the sample that is successfully contacted and interviewed.

Compound item: Question that consists of two or more components.

Computer-assisted interview (CAI): Technique in which the interviewer reads questions from a computer and inputs the answers directly to the computer; either for telephone interviewing (CATI) or personal interviewing (CAPI).

Concept: Abstract aspect, attribute, or property of people, things, or events.

Conceptual utilization: Evaluation use in which the research provides background information or clarification but does not actually guide the policy choices.

Conditioning factor: Variable that affects the relationship between two other variables and may explain conflicts in literature reviews.

Confidence interval: Range of values around the sample estimate within which we can expect the population value to fall at some probability level.

Confirmatory research: Data collection and analysis aimed at testing prior hypotheses.

Confounding variable: In a case of spuriousness, the "third" variable, which actually causes the two variables and makes them appear connected.

Constant dollars: Monetary expression of costs or benefits adjusted for inflation.

Construct: Complex inferred concept.

Construct validity: Approach to measurement validity that assesses the extent to which the measure reflects the intended construct with different methods focusing on the relations among observed variables or on the fit of observed associations with theory.

Contamination: Intrasession events that cause doubt that the experimental and control groups differ only on the studied variable.

Content Analysis: Procedure for measuring the occurrences of selected lexical or vocabulary features in speech or text.

Content validity: Approach to measurement validity that judges the content of the test (for example, an achievement test) for its adequacy in representing the domain being covered.

Contingency table: Cross-tabulation among two or more variables.

Continuous measure: Type of quantitative variable that can take on any value in its possible range, for example, a person's height, which can be measured in fractions of an inch or meter.

Control group: Condition in which the experimental treatment is withheld to provide a comparison with the treated group.

Controlled vocabulary: Set of terms officially designated and recognized by a catalog or file system.

Convenience sampling: Nonprobability sampling method that depends on self-selection.

Correlation coefficient: Measure of association; can be the same (symmetric) or different (asymmetric) when predicting one variable from another or vice versa.

Correlational design: Research approach in which the independent variable is measured rather than fixed by an intervention.

Cost–benefit analysis: Approach to efficiency assessment that assigns monetary value to the benefits of a program and compares them with the monetary costs of the program.

Cost–effectiveness analysis: Approach to efficiency assessment that compares different programs producing the same type of nonmonetary benefit in terms of their respective monetary costs.

Counterbalancing: Technique for studying all possible orders of multiple interventions in incomplete within-subjects design by use of different subjects who, taken together, experience all possible orders.

Covariation: Association; level of one variable predicts the level of another.

Cover Story: False explanation for the experiment used to distract the subject from guessing the true nature of the study.

Criterion Validity: Approach to measurement validity that correlates the measure to be validated with another called a criterion, which is accepted as valid.

Critical values: Values derived from the probability distribution of an inferential statistic used to determine the statistical significance of an observed value of the statistic at any given alpha level.

Cross-level inference: Drawing a causal conclusion at one level of analysis using data from another level.

Cross-sectional correlation: Association of variables measured at the same time; also synchronous, static, or on-time correlation.

Cross-sectional survey: Survey conducted at one time.

Cross-tabulation: Tabular summary of an association in which each individual is assigned to one and only one cell, representing a combination of the levels of the variables.

Cycles: Pattern in time series marked by recurring highs and lows.

d: Commonly used effect size index consisting of the difference between the treated and untreated groups in a study divided by the standard deviation of the control group.

Data collection bias: When procedures for collecting survey data lead to a consistent distortion from the true value of the sample.

Data collection error: The random inconsistencies produced in gathering survey data.

Debriefing: Researcher's interview with the subject after the experiment to check the subject's beliefs about the study and to tell the subject about the purpose of the study.

Deduction: Drawing of specific assertions from general principles.

Degrees of freedom: In inferential statistics, amount of free information left in the data after calculating the inferential statistic.

Demand characteristics: Cues in the experimental situation that guide a subject's view of the study.

Dependent variable: In hypothesis tests, a variable that is supposed to be caused by one or more other variables, that is, it is dependent on them.

Descriptive: Characterizing something or some relationship.

Descriptive association: Observing a relationship between variables without claiming causality.

Descriptive statistics: Statistics used to characterize a group of observations (for example, central tendency or variability) or an association of two or more variables.

Deseasonalize: To remove the seasonal cycle from a time series by a statistical method.

Design: In research, the arrangement of subjects, experimental manipulation, and observation of results.

Detrend: To remove the trend from a time series by a statistical method.

Direct causal path: In a theory, a simple, one-way causal connection between two constructs.

Direct causation: Impact of one variable on another not involving another variable.

Discount rate: Interest rate used to adjust future monetary benefits for the rate of gain that could be expected by some alternative use of the same funds.

Discrete measure: Type of quantitative variable that can take on only certain values between which there are gaps; for example, counting the number of students enrolled in a class, for which fractions would be nonsensical.

Ecological fallacy: False interpretation of aggregate-level data in individual-level terms.

Ecological validity: Extent to which a research situation represents the natural social environment.

Effect size: Numerical index of the magnitude of a relationship found in a study; commonly used in meta-analysis.

Effect to variability ratio: Magnitude of an effect,

such as the effect of an experimental treatment compared to a control condition, that takes into account the dispersion of scores in the groups.

Efficiency analysis: Stage of evaluative research that weights the program's outcomes by its costs.

Element: Unit from whom survey information is collected, usually a person.

Empirical: Based on observation.

Empirical criterion approach: Measurement construction approach that selects items according to their ability to discriminate groups known to differ on the dimension to be measured.

Endogenous construct: In a theory, a construct that is caused by one or more other constructs, exogenous or endogenous, within the theory.

Entry: First step in which the researcher gains access to the social setting to be studied.

Enumeration: List of all elements in the population; usually not available.

Environmental impact statements: Social and environmental impact reports required by law to be prepared and discussed before new projects can begin.

Epistemology: Branch of philosophy dealing with the nature of knowledge and our ability to know.

Error: The deviation of observed scores from true scores, including both random errors and such nonrandom sources as bias.

Ethics: Branch of philosophy that pertains to the study of right and wrong conduct.

Ethnocentrism: Perceptual bias because of one's own cultural beliefs.

Ethnography: Field research technique originating in anthropology that emphasizes the phenomenological approach.

Evaluation apprehension: Subject's anxiety generated by being tested.

Exaggerating contamination: Problem of control subjects moving in a direction opposite to that of the experimental subjects (for example, by resentful demoralization); has the effect of increasing the difference between experimental and control conditions.

Exempt: Very low-risk category of review in which the investigator seeks clearance by an appointed administrator such as the department chair rather than the IRB.

Exogenous construct: In a theory, a construct that causes other constructs but which itself has no cause specified within the theory.

Expedited review: Category of IRB review involving low-risk research in which just one member of the IRB judges the proposal in order to hasten its assessment.

Experimental construct validity: Extent to which a manipulated independent variable reflects the intended construct.

Experimental design: Research approach in which the independent variable is fixed by a manipulation or natural occurrence.

Experimental realism: Extent to which experimental procedures produce a high level of psychological involvement and, presumably, natural behavior regardless of the degree of mundane realism.

Experimenter expectancy: Mechanism(s) by which the researcher biases the behavior of the subject to get the hypothesized results; also called self-fulfilling prophesy and Pygmalion effect.

Exploratory research: Data collection and analysis aimed at formulating hypotheses.

Ex post facto design: Experimental design in which the control group is created after the treatment has already taken place.

External validity: Generalizability of the study's findings to other populations, places, or times.

Externalities: Costs or beliefs that occur to third parties not directly involved in the project as provider or consumer; may be accounted and paid for, or "internalized," by the project.

f: Symbol for frequency.

Factor analysis: Statistical approach to measurement construction that measures the extent to which test items agree with a common underlying dimension or factor.

Factorial design: Experimental design to which each subject is assigned to one or another combination of the levels or two or more independent variables.

Faithful subject: Method for avoiding deception by asking subjects to comply with the experimental procedure and to suspend their suspicions.

Fallibilism: In epistemology, the posture of doubting our own inductions.

Falsifiability: Aspect of an assertion that makes it vulnerable to being proven false, an essential ingredient in the process of science.

Field research: Generally, any social research taking place in a natural setting; more narrowly, equivalent to qualitative research.

File drawer problem: Risk that statistically significant published findings are really Type I errors left after many statistically nonsignificant but valid research reports are left in file drawers because of the publishing bias against negative findings.

Frequency distribution: Visual summary of a group of observations in which the number of occurrences of each score (frequency) is indicated on the vertical axis and the value of the score on the horizontal axis.

Frequency polygon: Type of frequency distribution in which a line joins points representing the frequencies of the scores.

Full review: Category of IRB review in which the entire committee analyzes the research proposal.

Gamma: PRE measure of association for ordinal variables.

Generality: Theory attribute of being widely applicable, that is, being able to account for many different observations.

Generative theory: The cause produces the effect, a view of causation that requires strong tests.

Going native: Role shift in which the researcher gives up the neutral scientific perspective and becomes a committed member or proponent of the group under study.

Group threats: Internal validity threats to between-subject designs; protection against such threats is proved by random assignment to groups. (See Table 9–1 regarding the three group threats of selection, regression toward the mean, and selection-by-time threat interactions.)

Hawthorne effect: A type of demand characteristic in which the researcher's attention was supposed to increase subject's effort; not confirmed by recent research.

Heterogeneous irrelevancies: Variations across studies in method, population, place, and time that are not expected to affect the outcome of replications.

Histogram: Type of frequency distribution in which vertical bars represent the frequencies of the scores.

History: Time threat to internal validity in which some event unrelated to the experimental intervention causes the observed change.

Hypothesis: Prediction about operational variables, usually drawn by deduction from a theory.

Hypothesis test: Procedure by which a hypothesis is checked for its fit or agreement with observations.

Idiographic: Research approach that tries to understand persons or situations for their unique characteristics without trying to generalize (as opposed to nomothetic approach).

Incidence: Number of new cases of a disorder appearing in a given time period.

Incomplete within-subjects design: Multiple-intervention design in which not all possible orders of presentation of the experimental manipulations are given to each subject.

Independent variable: In hypothesis tests, a variable that is supposed to cause one or more other variables and is not caused by them, that is, it is independent of them.

Index: In the context of an online catalog search, the part of the instructions that tells the computer what type of file to search—author, title, or subject.

Indirect causation: A set of two or more causal connections by which one construct or variable causes a second indirectly via one or more intervening constructs or variables.

Individual-level data: Based on unit of analysis consisting of individuals.

Induction: Creation of general principles from specific observations.

Inferential statistics: Statistics with a known probability distribution that can be computed to determine whether an effect observed in a sample or samples is due to chance.

Informed consent: Key requirement for IRB approval in which the subject must give voluntary written consent before participating based on adequate information and ability.

Institutional review boards (IRBs): Committees established by U.S. federal regulations at each research institution to protect human subjects from abuses through prior review of research proposals.

Instrumental utilization: Evaluation use that actually affects decision making.

Integrity: In science, utter honesty in conducting research including seeking and reporting data contrary to one's own belief.

Interaction: Effect of one independent variable depends on the level of another independent variable.

Interactive causation: Direct causation of one variable by another that varies with the level of another variable.

Intercept: In regression analysis, the point on the vertical axis where it meets the regression line, that is, the estimated value of the outcome variable when the predictor variable has the value of zero; usually symbolized by the letter a.

Internal rate of return (IRR): Yield in monetary terms of a program investment expressed as an annual rate.

Internal validity: Truthfulness of the assertion that the observed effect is due to the independent variable(s) in the study.

Interrupted time series design: Single-group quasi experiment that assesses a treatment with numerous pre- and posttests.

Interval level: Type of measurement that assigns scores on a scale with equal intervals.

Intervening variable: Measured variable in a hypothesis test or a theoretical variable in a theory that is the effect of one variable and a cause of another.

Interview guide: Checklist of topics that the qualitative interviewer wants to cover.

Intrasession history: Events internal to the experimental procedure.

Kappa: Measure of interrater agreement adjusted for chance agreement.

Key informant: Member of social setting who serves as a major source of information about the setting for a qualitative researcher.

Key words: In the context of an online catalog search, the part of the instructions that tells the computer the specific term to search for—for example, the author's name or the book's title.

Kinesics: Pertaining to bodily movements, especially the study of the communicative aspects of such movements.

Kurtosis: Degree to which the frequency distribution is flat or peaked.

Lambda: PRE measure of association for nominal variables.

Latent variable: Unmeasured variable constructed statistically from two or more measured variables.

Law of large numbers: Principle that larger sample sizes make for better estimates of population values.

Levels of measurement: Categorization of measurement into four types based on the amount of information in the measure: nominal, ordinal, interval, ratio.

Linear assumption: In regression analysis, the assumption that the relationship between the studied variables is best described by a straight line.

Literature: All of the research reports on a single question.

Literature review: Analysis of all research on a topic that tries to identify consensus findings or to resolve conflicts in the work.

Longitudinal correlation: Association of variables measured at different times. One variable is said to "lead" (come before) or "lag" (come after) the other.

Longitudinal survey: Survey conducted at two or more times (for example, panel, trend, and cohort longitudinal survey designs).

Management information systems (MIS): Record-keeping procedures for a program by which managers or others can routinely monitor its operation.

Manipulation checks: Measures used to assess the effectiveness of the manipulation.

Matching: Assigning subjects to experimental and control conditions to equalize the groups on selected characteristics; can be combined with random assignment but when used alone cannot guarantee group equivalence on variables not used in the matching.

Math anxiety: Fear of math and statistics, which can result in avoidance of math-based courses or careers.

Math phobia: The fear and consequent avoidance of math-related material.

Matrix: A table of numbers such as correlations.

Maturation: Time threat to internal validity in which internal developmental processes cause the observed change.

Mean (M): Measure of central tendency consisting of the sum divided by the number of observations, symbolized by M or $\overline{X}$.

Measurement association: The correlation between observed variables that derives from their serving as measures of a latent variable.

Measurement decay: Time threat to internal validity in which changes in the measurement process cause the observed change, also called instrumentation.

Median: Measure of central tendency consisting of the score with as many observations above as below.

Meta-analytic review: Literature review approach that reduces each study to a few summary effect sizes, which can then be analyzed by statistics.

Method effects: Source of construct invalidity in which measures of different constructs using the same procedure fail to diverge.

Mixed design: Experimental design that includes both within-subjects and between-subjects features.

Mode: Measure of central tendency consisting of the most frequently occurring sources; if the distribution has two modes, the distribution is called bimodal.

Model: One possible set of causal paths that we can compare with observed data.

Modem: A device for linking computers by telephone line, an abbreviation for "modulator-demodulator."

Moderating variable: In interactive causation, the variable that determines the effect of one variable on another.

Mortality: Subject attrition from pretest to posttest, which casts doubt on the validity of the study; here conceptualized as a threat to measurement construct validity. Protection against this threat is not provided by a control group or random assignment but rather by care in defining the subjects to be measured in evaluating experimental impact.

Multiple-baseline design: Multiple-intervention design in which two or more different treatments are applied at different times and are assessed with measures of two or more different expected outcomes.

Multiple-intervention design: Within-group design in which the group or subject receives more than one experimental manipulation.

Multiple regression: One statistical procedure for conducting multivariate research.

Multivariate research: Analysis of three or more variables.

Multivariate statistics: Analytic procedures that can study three or more variables simultaneously; for example, two or more predictors in relation to an outcome variable.

Mundane realism: Extent to which a research setting resembles in physical detail a real social setting.

*n***:** Symbol for the number of individuals or observations.

Naive experimenter: Method of avoiding experimenter expectancy by concealing the hypothesis from the researcher handling the subjects.

Needs assessment: Stage of evaluative research that identifies the goals of a program.

Nominal level: Type of measurement that assigns observations to unordered categories.

Nomothetic: Pertaining to the science of general laws (as opposed to the idiographic approach).

Nonequivalent control group design: Multiple-group quasi experiment not using random assignment to compose the groups.

Nonobservation Bias: Data collection bias that occurs in the stage of contacting sampled respondents (for example, the tendency to fail to contact or get cooperation from certain types of respondents).

Nonprobability sampling: Method of sampling in which the elements have unequal chances of being selected.

Normal curve: Commonly seen, bell-shaped distribution.

Null hypothesis: Prediction of an outcome contrary to what is expected that serves as the rival hypothesis tested by inferential statistics; often symbolized by H_0.

Nuremberg Code: Statement of ethical guidelines for human research produced for the Nuremberg Military Tribunal, which judged war crimes after World War II.

*O***:** Symbol used in design diagrams to represent one or more observations collected at some time point.

Observation bias: Data collection bias that occurs in interviewing or measurement stage (for example, the tendency of respondents to give answers that are socially desirable).

Observed Score: Also called fallible score, the value obtained by the measurement procedure and assumed to contain some degree of error.

Obtrusive versus unobtrusive measurement: Dimension of measurement that separates observations known to the subject from those occurring outside the subject's awareness.

Office of Research Integrity (ORI): Institutional unit that protects against and judges cases of research misconduct such as fraud.

Online: Connected to a computer for direct interaction with the electronic database.

Online data collection: Using a computer to receive and store data directly from an experiment in progress.

Ontology: Branch of philosophy dealing with the ultimate nature of things.

Operational definition: Procedure that translates a construct into manifest or observable form.

Opportunity cost: Value of the best alternative use of the project's resources, that is, the value forgone by the decision to invest in the project.

Ordinal level: Type of measurement that assigns observations to ordered categories.

Oversample: Drawing a disproportionately large number of elements to assure an adequate number of elements from small clusters or strata.

*p***:** Symbol for probability that an observed inferential statistic occurred by chance (for example $p < .05$).

Panel: Correlational design in which a group of subjects is surveyed or measured at more than one time point; also the group itself is called a panel.

Panel survey: Longitudinal survey design involving multiple interviews with the same subjects; as a group, such subjects are known as a panel.

Paradigm: Shared framework involving common theory and data collection tools in which researchers ordinarily approach scientific problems.

Paradigm shift: The revolution in assumptions about and perception of a research problem during which one paradigm replaces another.

Paradox: Apparent contradiction between two different theories, between two different observations, or between a theory and observations.

Parsimony: Theory attribute of being simple or sparing of constructs and relationships.

Partial correlation: Measure of association between two variables after statistically controlling one or more other variables. Order of correlation is the number of variables controlled (for example, zero-order is simple correlation, first-order partial controls one variable, and so on).

Participant observation: Common qualitative research method in which the researcher enters the social setting to be studied and actively joins the subjects in their normal activities.

Path analysis: Diagram of a causal model that includes statistical estimates of relationships.

Path coefficient: Standardized regression coefficient from a multiple-regression analysis that describes the association between two variables in path analysis.

Pearson product moment correlation coefficient (r): Non-PRE measure of association best suited for interval or ratio variables.

Persuasive utilization: Evaluation use in which the research justifies decisions already made, also called symbolic utilization.

Phenomenology: Philosophical perspective that emphasizes the discovery of meaning from the point of view of the studied group or individual.

Pilot test: Small-scale research with the experimental manipulation to determine its effectiveness before using it in the main study.

Placebo: Intervention that simulates an authentic treatment but with no active ingredient.

Plagiarism: Falsely claiming credit for work authored by another.

Plausible rival hypothesis: Believable or possible alternative explanation for an observation.

Population: Collection of all elements to whom survey results are to be generalized.

Positivism: An approach to knowledge based on the assumption of an objective reality that can be discovered with observed data.

Power: The probability of a statistical test correctly rejecting a false null hypothesis (or 1 − beta).

Preexperiments: Class of experimental designs that are very vulnerable to threats to internal validity.

Prerandomization: Random assignment of subjects to treatment conditions before obtaining informed consent.

Present value: Value of future program benefits adjusted downward by some discount rate.

Pretest sensitization: Production of changes in later interviews by the experience of a prior interview.

Prevalence: Number of cases existing at some time.

Probability distribution: In inferential statistics, the likelihood of occurrence (or probability) of each level of the inferential statistic for any number of degrees of freedom.

Probability proportionate to size (PPS): Method of preserving equal probability of sampling across all elements in the population by which the number of elements drawn from each cluster is proportionate to the size of the cluster.

Probability sampling: Sampling method in which all elements have equal probability of being drawn.

Process analysis: Procedure for measuring selected grammatical or nonlexical forms in speech or text.

Program audit: Nonroutine evaluation by an outsider of a program's operation.

Program evaluation: Social research that judges a program's success, usually in one or more of the following types: needs assessment, program monitoring, program impact, efficiency analysis, or utilization.

Program impact: Stage of evaluative research that determines whether the program has an effect.

Program monitoring: Stage of evaluative research that checks whether the program's operation follows its plan.

Projective tests: Measurement procedures by which subjects respond to ambiguous stimuli; presumed to reflect significant personality characteristics.

Prompt: Blinking symbol on a computer screen showing readiness for the next step in the procedure.

Proportional reduction of error (PRE): Quality of some correlation coefficients that measure association as the degree of improvement in predicting one variable from the other.

Proxemics: Pertaining to interpersonal spacing, especially the study of communicative aspects, causes, and effects of spacing.

Pseudoeffect: Apparent treatment effect caused by contrast with noncomparable control group.

Pseudoscience: Body of assertions that appears scientific because it involves observation, but is not for lack of falsifiability, for example, astrology.

Psychometrics: Research area devoted to evaluating and improving reliability and validity of social research measures.

Purposive sampling: Nonprobability sampling method that involves choosing elements with certain characteristics.

Qualitative research: Social research based on observations made in the field and analyzed in nonstatistical ways.

Qualitative variables: Type of variable for which observations are assigned to levels rather than given precise quantitative values, for example, religious preference.

Quantitative measurement: Collecting and reporting observations numerically.

Quantitative variables: Type of variable for which observations are assigned measured values, for example, temperature.

Quasi-experimental design: Experimental approach in which the researcher does not assign subjects randomly to treatment and control conditions.

Quota sampling: Nonprobability sampling method that creates a sample matching a predetermined demographic profile.

R: Symbol used in design diagrams to represent random assignment to groups.

Random assignment: Method of placing subjects in different conditions so that each subject has an equal chance of being in any group, thus avoiding systematic subject differences between the experimental and control groups.

Random digit dialing (RDD): Method of drawing a sample of respondents for telephone interviews by composing phone numbers randomly in order to reach phone subscribers with unlisted numbers.

Random error: Random deviation, which tends to average to zero over numerous sample subjects or items.

Random sampling: Drawing a representative group from a population by a method that gives every member of the population an equal chance of being drawn.

Range: A measure of variability consisting of the span between the lowest and highest scores.

Rapport: Trusting relationship between interviewer and interviewee.

Ratio level: Type of measurement that assigns scores on a scale with equal intervals and a true zero point.

Reactivity: Extent to which a measure causes a change in the behavior of the subject.

Realism: In ontology, the view that the sources of our perceptions are real and not fictions.

Reciprocal causation: A two-way causal connection between two constructs or variables in which each causes the other.

Regression toward the mean: When the same measure is applied more than one time, the movement toward the mean of subsequent scores, to the extent that the measure is unreliable; also a group threat to internal validity caused by the tendency of extreme scores on unreliable measures to move toward the mean on subsequent tests.

Regularity theory: Causation is shown by a nonspurious association between two variables, a view of causation that requires a weak test.

Reliability: Extent to which a measure reflects systematic or dependable sources of variation rather than random error.

Reliability coefficient: Estimate of the extent to which a measure is free of random error, usually arrived at by correlating measures of the same type—for example, inter-item, interrater, parallel form, or test–retest.

Replication: Repetition of a study to see if the same results are obtained.

Residual Error: In regression analysis, the distance or deviation between the estimated value from the regression line and the actual value of the outcome variable for any value of the predictor variable; also called residuals or deviations.

Residual path: In path analysis, the causal path representing the effect on the outcome variable of all variables not specified in the study.

Response set: Tendency of a person to answer items in a way designed to produce a preferred image (for example, social desirability); can reduce construct validity.

Response style: Person's habitual manner of responding to test items that is independent of item content (for example, acquiescence); can reduce the construct validity of the measure.

Reverse causation: Threat to internal validity for an observed association in which the causal direction is opposite to that hypothesized.

Robust: Relative immunity of an inferential statistic to violation of its assumptions.

Sample: Subset of individuals selected from a larger population.

Sample bias: When numerous samples are on average unrepresentative of the population.

Sample error: Unavoidable, random deviations of different sample estimates from each other.

Sample stages: Steps at which elements or clusters are drawn as part of the sampling design.

Sampling Frame: Available list of elements from which samples can actually be drawn, usually not a complete enumeration.

Sampling unit: Either the element or grouping of elements selected at a sampling stage.

Scalar structure: Hierarchical pattern in a set of items in which harder or less frequently chosen items are chosen only if easier or more frequently chosen items are also chosen by most respondents.

Scattergram: Graphic presentation of an association in which each point indicates the two scores of an individual.

Selection: Group threat to internal validity in which differences observed between groups at the end of the study existed prior to the intervention because of the way members were sorted into groups.

Selection-by-time interaction: Group internal validity threat in which subjects with different likelihoods of experiencing time-related changes (for example, maturation or history) are placed into different groups.

Serial correlation: Assumption made in the regression analysis of a time series that the residuals or differences between estimated and actual values will be uncorrelated; such correlation is called serial correlation of the errors and requires special care in the analysis.

Setting: Experimental arrangements of the study or, more broadly, the larger social context in which the study takes place.

Shadow prices: Estimated monetary value of program resources that are otherwise unpriced (for example, volunteer time), based on estimated value in the marketplace.

Single-subject design: Also called $n = 1$ design, usually a multiple-intervention design applied to a single subject.

Skepticism: Attitude of doubting and challenging assertions.

Skewness: Degree of departure from symmetry (that is, one side or tail of the distribution is longer than the other). If the longer tail is to the right, it is called positive skew; to the left, negative skew.

Slope: In regression analysis, the angle of the best-fitting line, that is, how many units on the vertical axis the line rises or falls for each unit on the horizontal axis; commonly symbolized by the letter b.

Social area analysis: Community description usually based on archival records and used in needs assessment.

Social discount rate: Discount rate used in adjusting future returns to social programs, usually lower than the prevailing private investment rate of return.

Social impact assessment (SIA): Evaluation of all possible future costs and benefits of one or more intervention plans.

Social indicators: Regular reports on the psychological and social well-being of the population similar to what economic indicators such as unemployment rates do for economic well-being.

Social significance: In contrast to statistical significance, the societal value or importance placed on a study or its outcome.

Sociometry: Measurement approach that describes a person's social relationships from the number of "choices" of that person made by others.

Specification error: In regression analysis, omission of an important causal variable; can lead to misestimation of the relationships among variables included in the analysis.

Spontaneous remission: Apparent natural improvement of control subjects that may be due in part to compensatory contamination, that is, their acquisition of unreported treatment.

Spuriousness: Two variables associated because both are caused by another variable.

Standard deviation (SD): Measure of variability; a type of weighted average of distances from the mean of all the observations.

Standard error of the mean: Sampling variability estimate based on the standard deviation of the sample, which is divided by the square root of the sample size.

Standard score (z): Individual's score, minus the group mean, divided by the group's standard deviation.

Standardization: Arrangement of measurement procedures so that they will be identical (or nearly so) when applied to different subjects, at different times, or by different raters; also, in experimentation, the reduction of human experimenter variability in treatment of subjects by use of a fixed script.

Statistical inference validity: Type of validity tested by inferential statistics, namely, the confidence that a sample finding is not due to chance.

Statistical significance: In inferential statistics, the judgment that a finding was not due to chance.

Statistics: Numerical summaries of observations, either descriptive or inferential.

Stratification: Categorization of elements having some common characteristic. The group of all elements having such a common characteristic is called a *stratum*, for example males or females.

Suggestion: In social research, the effect on subjects of their beliefs about their situation.

Sum of squares: Sum of the squared deviations from the mean in calculations of variance or from the regression line in assessing its fit.

Symbolic interactionism: Theoretical perspective concerned with the meanings that things and events have for human beings and the production of these meanings in human interchange.

Symmetry: In a frequency distribution, the degree of similarity of shape of the left and right sides of the distribution.

Systematic sampling: Probability sampling technique in which every nth element is sampled from an existing list of available elements.

Tabular review: Traditional approach to literature review that summarizes each study by a line in one or more tables.

Test reactivity: A time threat to internal validity that occurs when the observed change over time stems from the pretest rather than the experimental variable.

Theoretical variable: Concept or construct as distinct from a variable that is measured.

Theory: Tentative or preliminary explanations of causal relationships.

Time series: Data for a variable at numerous time points, for example, the unemployment rate for each month for several years.

Time threats: Internal validity threats to within-subjects designs; protected against by control groups. (See Table 9–1 regarding the four time threats of history, maturation, instrumentation, (or measurement decay) and test reactivity.)

Total survey error: The sum of all bias and errors from sampling and data collection or the total difference between the sample survey estimate and the true or population value.

Traces: Physical records based either on wear or erosion or on leavings or accretions.

Trait: Personality characteristic or behavioral style.

Trend survey: Longitudinal survey design involving a series of cross-sectional surveys each based on a different sample.

Trends: Patterns in time series marked by long-term increases or decreases.

Triangulation: Method of comparing observations from different times and sources to arrive at a correct analysis.

True experiment: Experimental design in which suspects are randomly assigned to two or more differently treated conditions.

True score: That part of the observed score that reflects the construct of interest.

Type I error: Error of rejecting the null hypothesis when it is true.

Type II error: Error of not rejecting the null hypothesis when it is false.

Unit effect: Pattern of preexisting differences across spatial units that accounts for discrepancy between analysis over time and analysis over space.

Univariate statistics: Descriptive statistics for one variable.

Unobtrusive: With respect to qualitative research, unobtrusive observation involves disguised entry and participation without the knowledge of the subjects that they are under scientific scrutiny.

Utilitarianism: Ethical approach that seeks a rational balancing of costs and benefits of behaviors.

Utilization: Stage of evaluative research that gauges the extent to which the research report is used and provides guidance for better dissemination of evaluation results.

Validity: Extent to which a measure reflects the intended phenomenon (for example, construct, criterion, or content domain); more generally the truth value of an assertion.

Validity coefficient: Estimate of the agreement of the measure being validated with a criterion (criterion validity) or a measure thought to reflect the target construct (convergent-type construct validity).

Variability: In descriptive statistics, the dispersion of individuals' scores from each other (for example, standard deviation).

Variable: Measure or indicator thought to represent an underlying construct or concept and produced by an operational definition of the construct or concept.

Variance: Average of the squared deviations from the mean.

Verbal versus nonverbal measurement: The dimension of measurement that separates observations of verbal communication (for example, self-report or ratings of speech behavior) from observations of other kinds.

Vocational filter: Phenomenon of people removing themselves from desirable career paths due to math avoidance.

Weak Inference: Conclusion of causality based on the regularity theory of causation. Involves finding unconfounded covariation between the variables in question that is consistent with a model; equally good-fitting alternative models are not ruled out.

Weighting: Statistical adjustment that compensates for disproportionate sampling.

White noise: In time series analysis, the residuals between the estimated and actual values that have no correlation among themselves at any lag.

Within-subjects design: Experimental design in which the change in subjects from before to after the manipulation measures the treatment effect.

X: Symbol used in design diagrams to represent presence of an experimental manipulation.

References

ADAMS, J. (1978). Sequential strategies and the separation of age, cohort, and time-of-measurement contributions to developmental data. *Psychological Bulletin, 85,* 1309–1316.

AD HOC COMMITTEE ON ETHICAL STANDARDS IN PSYCHOLOGICAL RESEARCH. (1973). *Ethical principles in the conduct of research with human participants.* Washington, D.C.: American Psychological Association.

AGNEW, B. (1993, January). Special-interest science: Mounting a backlash against a science-lobbying ploy. *Journal of NIH Research, 5,* 29–30.

AMBADY, N., & ROSENTHAL, R. (1992). Thin slices of expressive behavior as predictors of interpersonal consequences: A meta-analysis. *Psychological Bulletin, 111,* 256–274.

AMERICAN PSYCHOLOGICAL ASSOCIATION. (1983). *Publication manual of the American Psychological Association* (3rd ed.). Washington, DC: Author.

_____. (1985). *Standards for educational and psychological testing.* Washington, DC: Author.

_____. (1987). *Casebook on ethical principles of psychologists.* Washington, DC: Author.

_____. (1988). *Thesaurus of psychological index terms* (5th ed.). Washington, DC: Author

_____. (1992). Ethical principles of psychologists and code of conduct. *American Psychologist, 47,* 1597–1611.

AMERICAN SOCIOLOGICAL ASSOCIATION. (1989). *Code of ethics.* Washington, DC: Author.

ANASTASI, A. (1976). *Psychological testing.* New York: Macmillan.

ANDERSEN, R., KASPER, J., FRANKEL, M., & Associates. (1979). *Total survey error.* San Francisco: Jossey-Bass.

ANDREWS, F. M., KLEM, L., DAVIDSON, T. N., O'MALLEY, P. M., & RODGERS, W. L. (1981). *A guide for selecting statistical techniques for analyzing social science data.* Ann Arbor, MI: Institute for Social Research.

ANESHENSEL, C. S., & FRERICHS, R. R. (1982). Stress, support, and depression: A longitudinal causal model. *Journal of Community Psychology, 10,* 363–376.

ARMOR, D. J. (1972). The evidence on busing. *Public Interest, 28,* 90–126.

_____. (1980). White flight and the future of school desegregation. In W. G. Stephan & J. R. Feagin (Eds.), *School desegregation: Past, present, and future.* New York: Plenum Press.

ASHER, H. B. (1976). *Causal modeling.* Beverly Hills: Sage.

ASSAEL, H., & KEON, J. (1982). Nonsampling vs. sampling errors in survey research. *Journal of Marketing, 46,* 114–123.

ATKINSON, D. R., FURLONG, M. J., & WAMPOLD, B. E. (1982). Statistical significance, reviewer evaluations, and the scientific process: Is there a (statistically) significant relationship? *Journal of Counseling Psychology, 29,* 189–194.

BABAD, E. Y., INBAR, J., & ROSENTHAL, R. (1982a). Teachers' judgment of students' potential as a function of teachers' susceptibility to biasing information. *Journal of Personality and Social Psychology, 42,* 541–547.

_____. (1982b). Pygmalion, Galatea, and the Golem: Investigations of biased and unbiased teachers. *Journal of Educational Psychology, 74,* 459–474.

BABBIE, E. R. (1973). *Survey research methods.* Belmont, CA: Wadsworth.

BAILAR, B. A. (1976). Some sources of error and their effect on census statistics. *Demography, 13,* 273–286.

BAILEY, K. D. (1988). The conceptualization of validity:

Current perspectives. *Social Science Research, 17,* 117–136.

BALES, J. (1988, November). Breuning pleads guilty in scientific fraud case. *APA Monitor,* p. 12.

BALES, R. F. (1950). *Interaction process analysis: A method for the study of small groups.* Reading, MA: Addison-Wesley.

_____. (1969). *Personality and interpersonal behavior.* New York: Holt, Rinehart and Winston.

BALTES, P. B., CORNELIUS, S. W., & NESSELROADE, J. R. (1979). Cohort effects in developmental psychology. In J. R. Nesselroade & P. B. Baltes (Eds.), *Longitudinal research in the study of behavior and development.* New York: Academic Press.

BAN ON IQ TESTING OF BLACK CHILDREN LIFTED. (1992, September 3). *Los Angeles Times,* p. A32.

BANE, M. J., & ELLWOOD, D. T. (1983). *Dynamics of dependence: The routes to self-sufficiency* (Final Report). Cambridge, MA: Urban Systems Research and Engineering. (NTIS No. PB83–258699)

BANGERT-DROWNS, R. L. (1986). Review of developments in meta-analytic method. *Psychological Bulletin, 99,* 388–399.

BARBER, B., & HIRSCH, W. (Eds.). (1962). *The sociology of science.* New York: Free Press.

BARNETT, W. S. (1985). *The Perry Preschool Program and its long-term effects: A benefit–cost analysis.* Ypsilanti, MI: High/Scope Educational Research Foundation.

BARTZ, W. R., AMATO, P. R., RASOR, R. A., & RASOR, M. O. (1981). Effects of reducing student anxiety in a statistics course. *Australian Psychologist, 16,* 347–353.

BAUMOL, W. J. (1969). On the appropriate discount rate for evaluation of public projects. In H. H. Hinrichs & G. M. Taylor (Eds.), *Program budgeting and benefit-cost analysis: Cases, text, and readings.* Pacific Palisades, CA.: Goodyear.

BAUMRIND, D. (1983). Specious causal attributions in the social sciences: The reformulated stepping-stone theory of heroin use as exemplar. *Journal of Personality and Social Psychology, 45,* 1289–1298.

_____. (1985). Research using intentional deception: Ethical issues revisited. *American Psychologist, 40,* 165–174.

BAXTER, L. R., SCHWARTZ, J. M., BERGMAN, K. S., SZUBA, M. P., GUZE, B. H., MAZZIOTTA, J. C., ALAZRAKI, A., SELIN, C. E., FERNG, H. -K., MUNFORD, P., & PHELPS, M. E. (1992). Caudate glucose metabolic rate changes with both drug and behavior therapy for obsessive-compulsive disorder. *Archives of General Psychiatry, 49,* 681–689.

BEALS, R. L. (1969). *Politics of social research.* Chicago: Aldine.

BECKER, H. S. (1958). Problems of inference and proof in participant observation. *American Sociological Review, 23,* 652–660.

BEECHER, H. K. (1970). *Research and the individual.* Boston: Little, Brown.

BEM, D. J. (1983). Constructing a theory of the triple ty-

pology: Some (second) thoughts on nomothetic and idiographic approaches to personality. *Journal of Personality, 51,* 566–577.

BENTLER, P. M. (1980). Multivariate analysis with latent variables: Causal modeling. *Annual Review of Psychology, 31,* 419–456.

_____. (1989). *EQS: Structural equations program manual.* Los Angeles: BMDP.

BENTLER, P. M., & BONETT, D. G. (1980). Significance tests and goodness of fit in the analysis of covariance structures. *Psychological Bulletin, 88,* 588–606.

BENTLER, P. M., & WOODWARD, J. A. (1978). A Head Start reevaluation: Positive effects are not yet demonstrable. *Evaluation Quarterly, 2,* 493–510.

BERELSON, B. (1952). *Content analysis in communication research.* New York: Free Press.

BERGIN, A. E., & LAMBERT, M. J. (1978). The evaluation of therapeutic outcomes. In S. L. Garfield & A. E. Bergin (Eds.), *Handbook of psychotherapy and behavior change: An empirical analysis* (pp. 239–252). New York: John Wiley.

BERKOWITZ, L., & DONNERSTEIN, E. (1982). External validity is more than skin deep: Some answers to criticisms of laboratory experiments. *American Psychologist, 37,* 245–257.

BERNARD, H. R. (1988). *Research methods in cultural anthropology.* Newbury Park, CA: Sage.

BERRUETA-CLEMENT, J. R., SCHWEINHART, L. J., BARNETT, W. S., EPSTEIN, A. S., & WEIKART, D. P. (1984). *Changed lives: The effects of the Perry Preschool Program on youths through age 19.* Ypsilanti, MI: High/Scope Educational Research Foundation.

BERRY, W. D. (1984). *Nonrecursive causal models.* Beverly Hills: Sage.

BERRY, W. D., & FELDMAN, S. (1985). *Multiple regression in practice.* Beverly Hills: Sage.

BERSOFF, D. N. (1987). Social science data and the Supreme Court: Lockhart as a case in point. *American Psychologist, 42,* 52–58.

BERTERA, E. M., & BERTERA, R. L. (1981). The cost-effectiveness of telephone vs. clinic counseling for hypertensive patients: A pilot study. *American Journal of Public Health, 71,* 626–629.

BINDER, A. (1984). Restrictions on statistics imposed by method of measurement: Some reality, much mythology. *Journal of Criminal Justice, 12,* 467–481.

BIRDWHISTELL, R. L. (1970). *Kinesics and context: Essays on body motion and communication.* Philadelphia: University of Pennsylvania Press.

BISHOP, G. F., OLDENDICK, R. W., & TUCHFARBER, A. J. (1985). The importance of replicating a failure to replicate: Order effects on abortion items. *Public Opinion Quarterly, 49,* 105–114.

BLANCK, P. D., & ROSENTHAL, R. (1984). Mediation of interpersonal expectancy effects: Counselor's tone of voice. *Journal of Educational Psychology, 76,* 418–426.

BLOOMBAUM, M. (1983). The Hawthorne experiments: A critique and reanalysis of the first statistical interpretation by Franke and Kaul. *Sociological Perspectives, 26*, 71–88.

BOOTH, A., & JOHNSON, D. R. (1985). Tracking respondents in a telephone interview panel selected by random digit dialing. *Sociological Methods and Research, 14*, 53–64.

BORGATTA, E. F., & BOHRNSTEDT, G. W. (1980). Level of measurement: Once over again. *Sociological Methods and Research, 9*, 147–160.

BOULDING, K. E. (1966). *The impact of the social sciences.* New Brunswick, NJ: Rutgers University Press.

BOWEN, R. W. (1992). *Graph it: How to make, read, and interpret graphs.* Englewood Cliffs, NJ: Prentice Hall.

BOWERS, T. G., & CLUM, G. A. (1988). Relative contributions of specific and nonspecific treatment effects: Meta-analysis of placebo-controlled behavior therapy research. *Psychological Bulletin, 103*, 315–323.

BOX, G. E. P., & JENKINS, G. M. (1976). *Time series analysis: Forecasting and control.* San Francisco: Holden-Ray.

BRADBURN, N. M., SUDMAN, S., & BLAIR, E. (1979). *Improving interview method and questionnaire design.* San Francisco: Jossey-Bass.

BRECKLER, S. J. (1990). Applications of covariance structure modeling in psychology: Cause for concern? *Psychological Bulletin, 107*, 260–273.

BREWER, M. B., & COLLINS, B. E. (Eds.). (1981). *Scientific inquiry and the social sciences.* San Francisco: Jossey-Bass.

BREWER, J., & HUNTER, A. (1989). *Multimethod research: A synthesis of styles.* Newbury Park, CA: Sage.

BROAD, W. J., & WADE, N. (1982). *Betrayers of the truth.* New York: Simon & Schuster.

BROWNE, J. (1976). Field work for fun and profit. In M. P. Golden (Ed.), *The research experience.* Itasca, IL: Peacock.

BRYSON, M. C. (1976). The Literary Digest Poll: Making of a statistical myth. *The American Statistician, 30*, 184–185.

BUFF, S. A. (1989). ASA successful in pursuing plagiarism case. *Footnotes, 17*(10), 1.

BUREAU OF LABOR STATISTICS. (1992, September). BLS handbook of methods (Bulletin 2414). Washington, DC: U.S. Government Printing Office.

BUREAU OF THE CENSUS. (1978). *The current population survey: Design and methodology. Technical Paper No. 40.* Washington, DC: U.S. Government Printing Office.

BYRNE, D. G., ROSENMAN, R. H., SCHILLER, E., & CHESNEY, M. A. (1985). Consistency and variation among instruments purporting to measure the Type A behavior pattern. *Psychosomatic Medicine, 47*, 242–261.

CACIOPPO, J. T., & PETTY, R. E. (1981). Electromyograms as measures of extent and affectivity of information processing. *American Psychologist, 36*, 441–456.

CAMPBELL, D. T. (1975). Reforms as experiments. In E. L. Struening & M. Guttentag (Eds.), *Handbook of evaluation research* (Vol 1). Beverly Hills: Sage.

CAMPBELL, D. T., & ERLEBACHER, A. (1970). How regression artifacts in quasi-experimental evaluations can mistakenly make compensatory education look harm-

ful. In J. Hellmuth (Ed.), *Disadvantaged child, Vol. 3: Compensatory education: A national debate.* New York: Bruner/Mazel.

CAMPBELL, D. T., & FISKE, D. W. (1959). Convergent and discriminant validation by the multitrait-multimethod matrix. *Psychological Bulletin, 56*, 81–105.

CAMPBELL, D. T., & STANLEY, J. C. (1963). *Experimental and quasi-experimental designs for research.* Skokie, IL: Rand McNally.

CAMPBELL, J. P. (1976). Psychometric theory. In M. D. Dunnette (Ed.)., *Handbook of industrial and organizational psychology* (pp. 185–222). Chicago: Rand McNally.

CARMELLI, D., ROSENMAN, R. H., & CHESNEY, M. A. (1987). Stability of the Type A Structured Interview and related questionnaires in a 10-year follow-up of an adult cohort of twins. *Journal of Behavioral Medicine, 10*, 513–525.

CARVER, R. P. (1978). The case against statistical significance testing. *Harvard Educational Review, 48*, 378–399.

CATALANO, R., & SERXNER, S. (1987). Time series designs of potential interest to epidemiologists. *American Journal of Epidemiology, 126*, 724–731.

CECI, S. J., PETERS, D., & PLOTKIN, J. (1985). Human subjects review, personal values, and the regulation of social science research. *American Psychologist, 40*, 994–1002.

CHAPPLE, E. D. (1949). The Interaction Chronograph: Its evolution and present application. *Personnel, 25*, 295–307.

CHARROW, R. P., & SAKS, M. J. (1992). Legal responses to allegations of scientific misconduct. In D.J. Miller & M. Hersen (Eds.), *Research fraud in the behavioral and biomedical sciences* (pp. 34–52). New York: John Wiley.

CHEN, H., & ROSSI, P. H. (1980). The multi-goal, theory-driven approach to evaluation: A model linking basic and applied social science. *Social Forces, 59*, 106–122.

CHU, F. D., & TROTTER, S. (1974). *The madness establishment: Ralph Nader's study group report on the National Institute of Mental Health.* New York: Grossman.

CICCHETTI, D. V. (1980). Reliability of reviews for the *American Psychologist:* A biostatistical assessment of the data. *American Psychologist, 35*, 300–303.

CICIRELLI, V. G. (1970). The relevance of the regression artifact problem to the Westinghouse–Ohio Evaluation of Head Start: A reply to Campbell and Erlebacher. In J. Hellmuth (Ed.), *Disadvantaged child, Vol. 3: Compensatory education: A national debate.* New York: Bruner/Mazel.

CICIRELLI, V. G., EVANS, J. W., & SCHILLER, J. S. (1970). The impact of Head Start: A reply to the report analysis. *Harvard Educational Review, 40*, 105–129.

CLEARY, T. A., HUMPHREYS, L. G., KENDRICK, S. A., & WESMAN, A. (1975). Educational uses of tests with disadvantaged students. *American Psychologist, 30*, 15–41.

CLIFFORD, F. (1987, November 27). Worrisome trend: Research funds: Not so scientific. *Los Angeles Times*, pp. 1, 3, 28.

COHEN, J. (1960). A coefficient of agreement for nominal scales. *Educational and Psychological Measurement, 20*, 37–46.

_____. (1988). *Statistical power analysis for the behavioral sciences.* Hillsdale, NJ: Lawrence Erlbaum.

___. (1992). A power primer. *Psychological Bulletin, 112*, 155–159.

COHEN, S., TYRRELL, D. A. J., & SMITH, A.P. (1991). Psychological stress and susceptibility to the common cold. *New England Journal of Medicine, 325*, 606–612.

COLE, S., COLE, J. R., & SIMON, G. A. (1981). Chance and concensus in peer review. *Science, 214*, 881–886.

COLEMAN, J. S. (1976). Correspondence: Response to Professors Pettigrew and Green. *Harvard Educational Review, 46*, 217–224.

COLEMAN, J. S., CAMPBELL, E. Q., HOBSON, C. J., MC-PARTLAND, J., MOOD, A. M., WEINFELD, F. D., & YORK, R. L. (1966). *Equality of educational opportunity.* Washington, DC: U.S. Government Printing Office.

COLLINS, B. E., & HOYT, M. F. (1972). Personal responsibility for consequences: An integration and extension of the "forced compliance" literature. *Journal of Experimental Social Psychology, 8*, 558–593.

COMSTOCK, G. W., & HELSING, K. J. (1973). Characteristics of respondents and nonrespondents to a questionnaire for estimating community mood. *American Journal of Epidemiology, 97*, 233–239.

CONNER, R. F. (1977). Selecting a control group: An analysis of the randomization process in twelve social reform programs. *Evaluation Quarterly, 1*, 195–244.

CONVERSE, J. M., & PRESSER, S. (1986). *Survey questions: Handcrafting the standardized questionnaire.* Beverly Hills: Sage.

COOK, S. W. (1985). Experimenting on social issues: The case of school desegregation. *American Psychologist, 40*, 452–460.

COOK, T. D., & CAMPBELL, D. T. (1979). *Quasi-experimentation: Design and analysis issues for field settings.* Skokie, IL: Rand McNally.

COOK, T. D., DINTZER, L., & MARK, M. M. (1980). The causal analysis of concomitant time-series. *Applied Social Psychology Annual, 1*, 93–135.

COOK, T. D., & GRUDER, C. L. (1978). Metaevaluation research. *Evaluation Quarterly, 2*, 5–51.

COOK, T. D., & LEVITON, L. C. (1980). Reviewing the literature: A comparison of traditional methods with meta-analysis. *Journal of Personality, 48*, 449–472.

COOPER, H. M., & ROSENTHAL, R. (1980). Statistical versus traditional procedures for summarizing research findings. *Psychological Bulletin, 87*, 442–449.

CORDARO, L., & ISON, J. R. (1963). Psychology of the scientist: X. Observer bias in classical conditioning of the planarian. *Psychological Reports, 13*, 787–789.

CORDES, C. (1984, January). Political pull tips NIE scale: Bank Street cries foul on award to Harvard. *APA Monitor*, pp. 1, 14, 22.

COREN, S., & HALPERN, D. F. (1991). Left-handedness: A marker for decreased survival fitness. *Psychological Bulletin, 109*, 90–106.

COUNCIL OF THE AMERICAN ANTHROPOLOGICAL ASSOCIATION. (1990). *Statement of ethics.* Washington, DC: American Anthropological Association.

COWLES, M., & DAVIS, C. (1982). On the origins of the .05 level of statistical significance. *American Psychologist, 37*, 553–558.

COZBY, P. C. (1984). *Using computers in the behavioral sciences.* Palo Alto, CA: Mayfield.

CRAIN, R. B., & MAHARD, R. E. (1983). The effect of research methodology on desegregation-achievement studies: A meta-analysis. *American Journal of Sociology, 88*, 839–854.

CRONBACH, L. J. (1975). Five decades of public controversy over mental testing. *American Psychologist, 30*, 1–14.

CRONBACH, L. J., GLESER, G. C., NANDA, H., & RAJARATNAM, N. (1972). *The dependability of behavioral measurements: Theory of generalizability for scores and profiles.* New York: John Wiley.

CRONBACH, L. J., & MEEHL, P. E. (1955). Construct validity in psychological tests. *Psychological Bulletin, 52*, 281–302.

DAVIS, H. R., & SALASIN, S. E. (1975). The utilization of evaluation. In E. L. Struening & M. Guttentag (Eds.), *Handbook of evaluation research* (Vol. 1). Beverly Hills: Sage.

DAVISON, M. L., & SHARMA, A. R. (1988). Parametric statistics and levels of measurement. *Psychological Bulletin, 104*, 137–144.

DEMPSTER, F. N. (1988). The spacing effect: A case study in the failure to apply the results of psychological research. *American Psychologist, 43*, 627–634.

DEUTSCH, M. (1980). Socially relevant research: Comments on "applied" versus "basic" research. In R. F. Kidd & M. J. Saks (Eds.), *Advances in applied social psychology* (Vol. 1). Hillsdale, NJ: Lawrence Erlbaum.

DILLMAN, D. A. (1978). *Mail and telephone surveys: The total design method.* New York: John Wiley.

DOOLEY, D., & CATALANO, R. (1980). Economic change as a cause of behavioral disorder. *Psychological Bulletin, 87*, 450–468.

___. (1986). Do economic variables generate psychological problems? Different methods, different answers. In A. J. MacFadyen & H. W. MacFadyen (Eds.), *Economic psychology: Intersection in theory and application* (pp. 503–546). Amsterdam: Elsevier Science.

DOOLEY, D., CATALANO, R., & HOUGH, R. (1992). Unemployment and alcohol disorder in 1910 and 1990: Drift versus social causation. *Journal of Occupational and Organizational Psychology, 65*, 277–290.

DOOLEY, D., CATALANO, R., MISHRA, S., & SERXNER, S. (1992). Earthquake preparedness: Predictors in a community survey. *Journal of Applied Social Psychology, 22*, 451–470.

DOOLEY, D., CATALANO, R., & ROOK, K. (1988). Personal and aggregate unemployment and psychological symptoms. *Journal of Social Issues, 44*, 107–123.

DUBIN, R. (1978). *Theory building.* New York: Free Press.

DUNCAN, G. J., & MORGAN, J. N. (1981). Persistence and change in economic status and the role of changing family composition. In M. S. Hill, D. H. Hill, & J. N. Morgan (Eds.), *Five thousand American families—patterns of progress: Volume IX. Analyses of the first twelve years of the Panel Study of Income Dynamics.* Ann Arbor, MI: Institute for Social Research.

DUNKELBERG, W. C., & DAY, G. S. (1973). Nonresponse bias and callbacks in sample surveys. *Journal of Marketing Research, 10,* 160–168.

DURANT, W., & DURANT, A. (1961). *The age of reason begins.* New York: Simon & Schuster.

DURBIN, J., & WATSON, G. (1950). Testing for serial correlation in least squares regression: Part I. *Biometrica, 37,* 409–423.

_____. (1951). Testing for serial correlation in least squares regression: Part II. *Biometrica, 38,* 159–178.

DURKHEIM, E. (1951). *Suicide: A study in sociology* (G. Simpson, Ed., J. A. Spaulding, & G. Simpson, Trans.). New York: Free Press of Glencoe. (Original work published 1897.)

DURLAK, J. A. (1979). Comparative effectiveness of paraprofessional and professional helpers. *Psychological Bulletin, 86,* 80–92.

DURLAK, J. A., & LIPSEY, M. W. (1991). A practitioner's guide to meta-analysis. *American Journal of Community Psychology, 19,* 291–332.

EKMAN, P., & FRIESEN, W. (1978). *FACS investigator's guide.* Palo Alto, CA: Consulting Psychologists Press.

ELASHOFF, J. D., & SNOW, R. E. (Eds.). (1971). *Pygmalion reconsidered.* Worthington, OH: Charles A. Jones.

ELLIOT, R. (1991). Social science data and the APA: The Lockhart brief as a case in point. *Law and Human Behavior, 15,* 59–76.

ELLSWORTH, P. C. (1991). To tell what we know or wait for Godot? *Law and Human Behavior, 15,* 77–90.

ELLSWORTH, P. C., & LUDWIG, L. M. (1972). Visual behavior in social interaction. *Journal of Communication, 22,* 375–403.

ERLEBACHER, A. (1977). Design and analysis of experiments constrasting the within- and between-subjects manipulation of the independent variable. *Psychological Bulletin, 84,* 212–219.

ERNHART, C. B., SCARR, S., & GENESON, D. F. (1993). On being a whistleblower: The Needleman case. *Ethics and Behavior, 3,* 73–93.

ERON, L. D., & WALDER, L. O. (1961). Test burning: II. *American Psychologist, 16,* 237–244.

ETHICS COMMITTEE OF THE AMERICAN PSYCHOLOGICAL ASSOCIATION. (1988). Trends in ethics cases, common pitfalls, and published resources. *American Psychologist, 43,* 564–572.

_____. (1993). Report of the Ethics Committee, 1991 and 1992. *American Psychologist, 48,* 811–820.

EYSENCK, H. J. (1973). *Eysenck on extraversion.* London: Crosby Lockwood Stapes.

FAIRWEATHER, G. W., SANDERS, D. H., MAYNARD, H., & CRESSLER, D. L. (1969). *Community life for the mentally ill.* Chicago: Aldine.

FAIRWEATHER, G. W., SANDERS, D. H., & TORNATZKY, L. G. (1974). *Creating change in mental health organizations.* Elmsford, NY: Pergamon.

FAUST, D., & ZISKIN, J. (1988). The expert witness in psychology and psychiatry. *Science, 241,* 31–35.

Federal Register. (January 26, 1981). *46* (16).

FESTINGER, L., RIECHEN, H. W., & SCHACHTER, S. (1956). *When prophecy fails: A social and psychological study of a modern group that predicted the destruction of the world.* New York: Harper & Row.

FEYNMAN, R. P. (1985). *"Surely you're joking, Mr. Feynman!": Adventures of a curious character.* New York: W. W. Norton.

FIENBERG, S. (1977). *The analysis of cross-classified categorical data.* Cambridge, MA: MIT Press.

FINSTERBUSCH, K., & MOTZ, A. B. (1980). *Social research for policy decisions.* Belmont, CA: Wadsworth.

FIREBAUGH, G. (1978). A rule for inferring individual-level relationships from aggregate data. *American Sociological Review, 43,* 557–572.

_____. (1980). Cross-national versus historical regression models: Conditions of equivalence in comparative analysis. *Comparative Social Research, 3,* 333–344.

FISKE, D. W. (1987). Construct invalidity comes from method effects. *Educational and Psychological Measurement, 47,* 285–307.

FLETCHER, R. (1991). *Science, ideology, and the media: The Cyril Burt scandal.* New Brunswick, NJ: Transaction Books.

FOSTER, S. L., & CONE, J. D. (1980). Current issues in direct observation. *Behavioral Assessment, 2,* 313–338.

FRANK, J. D., NASH, E. H., STONE, A. R., & IMBER, S. D. (1963). Immediate and long-term symptomatic course of psychiatric out-patients. *American Journal of Psychiatry, 120,* 429–439.

FRANKE, R. H., & KAUL, J. D. (1978). The Hawthorne experiments: First statistical interpretation. *American Sociological Review, 43,* 623–643.

FREEMAN, D. (1983). *Margaret Mead and Samoa: The making and unmaking of an anthropological myth.* Cambridge, MA: Harvard.

FRIEDMAN, H. J. S., & BOOTH-KEWLEY, S. (1987). The "disease-prone personality": A meta-analytic view of the construct. *American Psychologist, 42,* 539–555.

GAITO, J. (1980). Measurement scales and statistics: Resurgence of an old misconception. *Psychological Bulletin, 87,* 564–567.

GANZ, C. (1980). Linkages between knowledge creation, diffusion, and utilization. *Knowledge: Creation, Diffusion, Utilization, 1,* 591–612.

GARFIELD, E., & WELLJAMS-DOROF, A. (1990). The impact of fraudulent research on scientific literature. *Journal of the American Medical Association, 263,* 1424–1426.

GATCHEL, R. J., SCHAEFFER, M. A., & BAUM, A. (1985). A psychophysiological field study of stress at Three Mile Island. *Psychophysiology, 22,* 175–181.

GELLER, E. S. (1980). Application of behavioral analysis to litter control. In I. D. Glenwick & L. Jason (Eds.), *Behavioral community psychology: Progress and prospects.* New York: Holt, Rinehart and Winston.

GERGEN, K. J. (1985). The social constructionist movement in modern psychology. *American Psychologist, 40,* 266–275.

GHOLSON, B., & BARKER, P. (1985). Kuhn, Lakatos, and Laudan: Applications in the history of physics and psychology. *American Psychologist, 7,* 755–769.

GLASS, G. V., & ELLETT, F. S. (1980). Evaluation research. *Annual Review of Psychology, 31,* 211–228.

GLASS, G. V., MCGAW, B., & SMITH, M. L. (1981). *Meta-analysis in social research.* Beverly Hills: Sage.

GLAZER, M. (1972). *The research adventure: Promise and problems of field work.* New York: Random House.

GOLDEN, M. P. (Ed.). (1976). *The research experience.* Itasca, IL: Peacock.

GOLDMAN, R. N., & WEINBERG, J. S. (1985). *Statistics: An introduction.* Englewood Cliffs, NJ: Prentice Hall.

GORDEN, R. L. (1977). *Unidimensional scaling of social variables: Concepts and procedures.* New York: Free Press.

GOTTFREDSON, S. D. (1978). Evaluating psychological research reports: Dimensions, reliability and correlates of quality judgments. *American Psychologist, 33,* 920–929.

GREEN, B. F., & HALL, J. A. (1984). Quantitative methods for literature reviews. *Annual Review of Psychology, 35,* 37–53.

GREENE, J. G. (1988). Stakeholder participation and utilization in program evaluation. *Evaluation Review, 12,* 91–116.

GROVES, R. M. (1979). Actors and questions in telephone and personal interview surveys. *Public Opinion Quarterly, 43,* 190–205.

_____. (1983). Implications of CATI: Costs, errors, and organization of telphone survey research. *Sociological Methods and Research, 12,* 199–215.

GROVES, R. M., & FULTZ, N. H. (1985). Gender effects among telephone interviewers in a survey of economic attitudes. *Sociological Methods and Research, 14,* 31–52.

GROVES, R. M., & KAHN, R. L. (1979). *Surveys by telephone: A national comparison with personal interviews.* New York: Academic Press.

GUBA, E. G. (Ed.). (1990). *The paradigm dialog.* Newbury Park, CA: Sage.

GUENZEL, P. J., BERCKMANS, T. R., & CANNELL, C. F. (1983). *General interviewing techniques: A self-instructional workbook for telephone and personal interviewer training.* Ann Arbor, MI: Institute for Social Research.

GURIN, G., VEROFF, J., & FELD, S. (1960). *Americans view their mental health.* New York: Basic Books.

HALL, E. T. (1965). A system for the notation of proxemic behavior. *American Anthropologist, 65,* 1003–1026.

HALPERN, D. G., & COREN, S. (1993). Left-handedness and life span: A reply to Harris. *Psychological Bulletin, 114,* 235–241.

HANLEY, J. A. (1987). Standard error of the kappa statistic. *Psychological Bulletin, 102,* 315–321.

HANUSHEK, E. A., & JACKSON, J. E. (1977). *Statistical methods for social scientists.* New York: Academic Press.

HARRIS, L. J. (1993). Do left-handers die sooner than right-handers? Commentary on Coren and Halpern's (1991) "Left-handedness: A marker for decreased survival fitness." *Psychological Bulletin, 114,* 203–234.

HATTIE, J. A., SHARPLEY, C. F., & ROGERS, H. J. (1984). Comparative effectiveness of professional and paraprofessional helpers. *Psychological Bulletin, 95,* 534–541.

HEARNSHAW, L. S. (1979). *Cyril Burt: Psychologist.* London: Hodder and Stoughton.

HEATH, L., KENDZIERSKI, D., & BORGIDA, E. (1982). Evaluation of social programs: A multimethodological approach combining a delayed treatment true experiment and multiple time series. *Evaluation Review, 6,* 233–246.

HEATHER, N., & ROBERTSON, I. (1983). *Controlled drinking.* New York: Methuen.

HEISE, D. R. (1975). *Causal analysis.* New York: John Wiley.

HELMES, E., & REDDON, J. R. (1993). A perspective on developments in assessing psychopathology: A critical review of the MMPI and MMPI-2. *Psychological Bulletin, 113,* 453–471.

HENNIGAN, K. M., FLAY, B. R., & COOK, T. D. (1980). "Give me the facts": Some suggestions for using social science knowledge in national policy-making. In R. F. Kidd & M. J. Saks (Eds.), *Advances in applied social psychology* (Vol. 1). Hillsdale, NJ: Lawrence Erlbaum.

HERSHEY, N., & MILLER, R. D. (1976). *Human experimentation and the law.* Germantown, MD: Aspen Systems.

HESS, E. H. (1973). Pupillometrics: A method of studying mental, emotional and sensory processes. In N. S. Greenfield & R. A. Sternbach (Eds.), *Handbook of psychophysiology.* New York: Holt, Rinehart and Winston.

HILL, M. S., HILL, D. H., & MORGAN, J. N. (Eds.). (1981). *Five thousand American families—patterns of economic progress: Volume IX. Analyses of the first twelve years of the Panel Study of Income Dynamics.* Ann Arbor, MI: Institute for Social Research.

HOFFER, A., OSMOND, H., & SMYTHIES, J. R. (1954). Schizophrenia: A new approach. *Journal of Mental Science, 100,* 29–45.

HOHMANN, M., BANET, B., & WEIKART, D. P. (1979). *Young children in action: A manual for preschool educators.* Ypsilanti, MI: High/Scope Educational Research Foundation.

HOLDEN, R. R., MENDONCA, J. D., & SERIN, R. C. (1989). Suicide, hopelessness, and social desirability: A test of an interactive model. *Journal of Consulting and Clinical Psychology, 57,* 500–504.

HOLLANDER, M., & PROSCHAN, F. (1984). *The statistical exorcist: Dispelling math anxiety.* New York: Marcel Dekker.

HOLLINGSHEAD, A. B. (1975). *Four factor index of social status.* Privately printed. 1965 Yale Station, New Haven, CT 06520.

HOLLINGSHEAD, A. B., & REDLICH, F. C. (1958). *Social class and mental illness.* New York: John Wiley.

HOLSTI, O. R. (1969). *Content analysis for the social sciences and humanities.* Reading, MA: Addison-Wesley.

HOROWITZ, I. L. (1973). The life and death of project Camelot. In N. K. Denzin (Ed.), *The values of social science.* New Brunswick, NJ: Transaction Books.

HOSTETLER, A. J. (1987, May). Investigation: Fraud inquiry revives doubt: Can science police itself? *APA Monitor,* pp. 1, 12.

HOUSTON, P. (1993, June 28). High court relaxes curbs on expert witness testimony. *Los Angeles Times,* p. A14.

HOWE, H. L. (1981). Social factors associated with breast self-examination among high-risk women. *American Journal of Public Health, 71,* 251–255.

HUBER, P. W. (1991). *Galileo's revenge: Junk science in the courtroom.* New York: Basic Books.

HUCK, S. W., & SANDLER, H. M. (1979). *Rival hypotheses: Alternative interpretations of data based conclusions.* New York: Harper & Row.

HUGHES, J. A. (1990). *The philosophy of social research.* New York: Longman.

HUGHES, J. R., JACOBS, D. R., JR., SCHUCHER, B., CHAPMAN, D. P., MURRAY, D. M., & JOHNSON, C. A. (1983). Nonverbal behavior of the Type A individual. *Journal of Behavioral Medicine, 6,* 279–289.

HUMMEL, C. E. (1986). *The Galileo connection: Resolving conflicts between science and the Bible.* Downer's Grove, IL: Intervarsity Press.

HUMPHREYS, L. (1970). *Tearoom trade: Impersonal sex in public places.* Chicago: Aldine.

_____. (1975). *Tearoom trade*: Impersonal sex in public places (enlarged edition). Chicago: Aldine.

HUNT, M. (1985). *Profiles of social research: The scientific study of human interactions.* New York: Russell Sage.

HUNTER, J. E., & SCHMIDT, F. L. (1990). *Methods of meta-analysis: Correcting error and bias in research findings.* Newbury Park, CA: Sage.

IS THERE LEAD IN YOUR WATER? (1993, February). *Consumer Reports,* pp. 73–77.

JASON, L. A., ZOLIK, E. S., & MATESE, F. J. (1979). Prompting dog owners to pick up dog droppings. *American Journal of Community Psychology, 7,* 339–351.

JENCKS, C., & CROUSE, J. (1982). Should we relabel the SAT . . . or replace it? In W. Schrader (Ed.), *New directions for testing and measurement, guidance, and program improvement* (pp. 33–49). San Francisco: Jossey-Bass.

JENCKS, C., SMITH, M., ACLAND, H., BANE, M. J., COHEN, D., GINTIS, H., HEYNS, B., & MICHELSON, S. (1972). *Inequality: A reassessment of the effect on family and schooling in America.* New York: Harper & Row.

JENKINS, C. D., ZYZANSKI, S. J., & ROSENMAN, R. H. (1971). Progress toward validation of a computer-scored test for the Type A coronary-prone behavior pattern. *Psychosomatic Medicine, 33,* 193–202.

JENSEN, A. R. (1969). How much can we boost IQ and scholastic achievement? *Harvard Educational Review, 39,* 1–123.

_____. (1992). Scientific fraud or false accusations: The case of Cyril Burt. In D. J. Miller & M. Hersen (Eds.), *Research fraud in the behavioral and biomedical sciences* (pp. 97–124). New York: John Wiley.

JENSEN, G. (1986). *Dis-integrating integrated theory: A critical analysis of attempts to save strain theory.* Paper presented at the Annual Convention of the American Society of Criminology, Atlanta.

JOHNSON, H. H., & FOLEY, J. M. (1969). Some effects of placebo and experiment conditions in research on methods of teaching. *Journal of Educational Psychology, 60,* 6–10.

JOHNSTON, J. (1984). *Econometric methods.* New York: McGraw-Hill.

JONES, J. H. (1981). *Bad blood: The Tuskegee syphilis experiment.* New York: Free Press.

JORDAN, L. A., MARCUS, A. C., & REEDER, L. G. (1980). Response styles in telephone and household interviewing: A field experiment. *Public Opinion Quarterly, 44,* 210–222.

JORESKOG, K. G., & SORBOM, D. (1981). *LISREL V: Analysis of linear structural relationships by maximum likelihood and least squares methods.* Chicago: National Educational Resources.

JOYNSON, R. B. (1989). *The Burt affair.* London: Routledge.

JULNES, G., & MOHR, L. B. (1989). Analysis of no-difference findings in evaluation research. *Evaluation Quarterly, 13,* 628–655.

KANTROWITZ, B., & WINGERT, P. (1993, April 12). No longer a sacred cow: Head Start has become a free-fire zone. *Newsweek,* p. 57.

KASL, S. V., CHISHOLM, R. F., & ESKENAZI, B. (1981a). The impact of the accident at Three Mile Island on the behavior and well-being of nuclear workers: Part I: Perceptions and evaluations, behavioral responses, and work-related attitudes and feelings. *American Journal of Public Health, 71,* 472–483.

_____. (1981b). The impact of the accident at Three Mile Island on the behavior and well-being of nuclear workers: Part II: Job tensions, psychophysiological symptoms, and indices of distress. *American Journal of Public Health, 71,* 484–495.

KASL, S. V., & COBB, S. (1979). Some mental health consequences of plant closings. In L. Ferman & J. Gordus (Eds.), *Mental health and the economy* (pp. 255–300). Kalamazoo, MI: The Upjohn Institute.

KAZDIN, A. E. (1978). Methodological and interpretive problems of single-case experimental designs. *Journal of Consulting and Clinical Psychology, 46,* 629–642.

KIDDER, L. H. (1981). Qualitative research and quasi-experimental frameworks. In M. B. Brewer & B. E. Collins (Eds.), *Scientific inquiry and the social sciences.* San Francisco: Jossey-Bass.

KIESLER, C. A., & LOWMAN, R. P. (1980). Hutchinson versus Proxmire. *American Psychologist, 35,* 689–690.

KIESLER, D. J. (1973). *The process of psychotherapy: Empirical foundations and systems of analysis.* Chicago, IL: Aldine.

KIM, J., & MUELLER, L. W. (1978). *Introduction to factor analysis.* Beverly Hills, CA.: Sage.

KIRK, S. A., & KUTCHINS, H. (1992). *The selling of DSM: The rhetoric of science in psychiatry.* New York: Aldine de Gruyter.

KLOTZ, I. M. (1980). The N-Ray affair. *Scientific American, 242*(5), 168–175.

KOSLOSKI, K. (1986). Isolating age, period, and cohort effects in developmental research. *Research on Aging, 8,* 460–479.

KRAEMER, H. C., & THIEMANN, S. (1987). *How many subjects? Statistical power analysis in research.* Beverly Hills, CA: Sage.

KRAMER, J. J., & CONOLEY, J. C. (Eds.). (1991). *The eleventh mental measurements yearbook.* Lincoln, NE: Buros Institute of Mental Measurements.

KREISLER, S. (1993). BLS Establishment estimates revised to incorporate March 1992 benchmarks and historical corrections. *Employment and Earnings, 40*(6), 6–12.

KRITZER, H. M. (1977). Political protest and political violence: A nonrecursive causal model. *Social Forces, 55,* 630–640.

KUHN, T. S. (1970). *The structure of scientific revolutions.* Chicago: University of Chicago Press.

KURTZ, R. R., & GRUMMON, D. L. (1972). Different approaches to the measurement of therapist empathy and their relationship to therapy outcomes. *Journal of Consulting and Clinical Psychology, 39,* 106–115.

LaFOLLETTE, M. C. (1992). *Stealing into print: Fraud, plagiarism, and misconduct in scientific publishing.* Berkeley: University of California Press.

LANDY, F. J. (1986). Stamp collecting versus science: Validation as hypothesis testing. *American Psychologist, 41,* 1183–1192.

LARSEN, R. J., KASIMATIS, M., & FREY, K. (1992). Facilitating the furrowed brow: An unobtrusive test of the facial feedback hypothesis applied to unpleasant affect. *Cognition and Emotion, 6,* 321–338.

LeCOMPTE, M. D., & GOETZ, J. P. (1982). Problems of reliability and validity in ethnographic research. *Review of Educational Research, 52,* 31–60.

LEE, E. S., FORTHOFER, R. N., & LORIMOR, R. J. (1989). *Analyzing complex survey data.* Newbury Park, CA: Sage.

LEIGHTON, D. C., HARDING, J. S., MACKLIN, S. B., MACMILLAN, A. M., & LEIGHTON, A. H. (1963). *The character of danger.* New York: Basic Books.

LEVENKRON, J. C., COHEN, J. D., MUELLER, H. S., & FISHER, E. B., JR. (1983). Modifying the Type A coronary-prone behavior pattern. *Journal of Consulting and Clinical Psychology, 51,* 192–204.

LEVINE, D. W., McDONALD, P. J., O'NEAL, E. C., & GARWOOD, S. G. (1980). Classroom ecology: The effects of seating position on grades and participation. *Personality and Social Psychology Bulletin, 6,* 409–412.

LEVINE, F. J. (1993, May). ASA files amicus brief protecting confidential research information. *Footnotes, 21*(5), 2.

LEVITON, L. C., & HUGHES, E. F. X. (1981). Research on the utilization of evaluations: A review and synthesis. *Evaluation Review, 5,* 525–548.

LIBRARY OF CONGRESS, SUBJECT CATALOGUING DIVISION. (1986). *Library of Congress subject headings* (9th ed.). Washington, DC: Author.

LIEBOW, E. (1967). *Tally's corner: A study of Negro streetcorner men.* Boston: Little, Brown.

LIGHT, R. J., & SMITH, P. V. (1971). Accumulating evidence: Procedures for resolving contradictions among different research studies. *Harvard Educational Review, 41,* 429–471.

LILIENFELD, A. M. (1976). *Foundations of epidemiology.* New York: Oxford University Press.

LINEHAN, M. M., & NIELSEN, S. L. (1981). Assessment of suicide ideation and parasuicide: Hopelessness and social desirability. *Journal of Consulting and Clinical Psychology, 49,* 773–775.

LIPSEY, M. W. (1990). *Design sensitivity: Statistical power for experimental research.* Newbury Park, CA: Sage.

LITTLE, D. (1991). *Varieties of social explanation: An introduction to the philosophy of social science.* Boulder, CO: Westview.

LOCANDER, W., SUDMAN, S., & BRADBURY, W. (1976). An investigation of interview method, threat and response distribution. *Journal of the American Statistical Association, 71,* 269–275.

LOETHER, H. J., & MacTAVISH, D. G. (1980). *Descriptive and inferential statistics: An introduction.* Boston: Allyn & Bacon.

LOFLAND, J. (1966). *Doomsday cult: A study of conversion, proselytization, and maintenance of faith.* Englewood Cliffs, NJ: Prentice Hall.

_____. (1971). *Analyzing social settings: A guide to qualitative observation and analysis.* Belmont, CA: Wadsworth.

LYERLY, S. B., ROSS, S., KRUGMAN, A. D., & CLYDE, D. J. (1964). Drugs and placebos: The effects of instructions upon performance and mood under amphetamine sulphate and chloral hydrate. *Journal of Abnormal and Social Psychology, 68,* 321–327.

McCALL, G. J., & SIMMONS, J. L. (Eds.). (1969). *Issues in participant observation: A test and reader.* Reading, MA: Addison-Wesley.

McCRAE, R. R., & COSTA, P. T., JR. (1983). Social desirability scales: More substance than style. *Journal of Consulting and Clinical Psychology, 51,* 882–888.

McDILL, E. L., McDILL, M. S., & SPREHE, J. T. (1972). Evaluation in practice: Compensatory education. In P. H. Rossi & W. Williams (Eds.), *Evaluating social programs: Theory, practice, and politics.* New York: Seminar Press.

McGARVEY, B., GABRIELLI, W. F., JR., BENTLER, P. M., & MEDNICK, S. A. (1981). Rearing social class, education, and criminality: A multiple indicator model. *Journal of Abnormal Psychology, 90,* 354–364.

McGUIRE, W. J. (1969). Suspiciousness of experimenter's intent. In R. Rosenthal & R. L. Rosnow (Eds.), *Artifact in behavioral research* (pp. 13–57). New York: Academic Press.

McKEY, R. H., CONDELLI, L., GANSON, H., BARRETT, B. J., McCONKEY, C., & PLANTZ, M. C. (1985). *The impact of Head Start on children, families, and communities:*

Final report of the Head Start evaluation, synthesis, and utilization project (DHHS Publication No. OHDS 85–31193). Washington, DC: U.S. Government Printing Office.

MAGIDSON, J. (1977). Toward a causal model approach for adjusting for preexisting differences in the nonequivalent control group situation: A general alternative to ANCOVA. *Evaluation Quarterly, 1,* 399–420.

MANICAS, P. T., & SECORD, P. F. (1983). Implications for psychology of the new philosophy of science. *American Psychologist, 38,* 339–413.

MARQUIS, D. (1986). An argument that all prerandomized clinical trials are unethical. *Journal of Medicine and Philosophy, 11,* 367–383.

MARUYAMA, G., & McGARVEY, B. (1980). Evaluating causal models: An application of maximum-likelihood analysis of structural equations. *Psychological Bulletin, 87,* 502–512.

MARX, M. H. (Ed.). (1965). *Theories in contemporary psychology.* New York: Macmillan.

MATARAZZO, J. D. (1990). Psychological assessment versus psychological testing: Validation from Binet to the school, clinic, and courtroom. *American Psychologist, 45,* 999–1017.

MATARAZZO, R. G., MATARAZZO, J. D., SASLOW, G., & PHILLIPS, J. S. (1958). Psychological test and organismic correlates of interview interaction patterns. *Journal of Abnormal and Social Psychology, 56,* 329–338.

MATHEWS, K. A. (1988). Coronary heart disease and Type A behaviors: Update on and alternative to the Booth-Kewly and Friedman (1987) quantitative review. *Psychological Bulletin, 104,* 373–380.

MAUGH, T. H. II. (1988, July 27). Journal probe of lab test results sparks furor. *Los Angeles Times,* p. 3.

MAXWELL, S. E., & DELANEY, H. D. (1985). Measurement and statistics: An examination of construct validity. *Psychological Bulletin, 97,* 85–93.

MEHAN, H., & WOOD, H. (1975). *The reality of ethnomethodology.* New York: John Wiley.

MEIDINGER, E., & SCHNAIBERG, A. (1980). Social impact assessment as evaluation research: Claimants and claims. *Evaluation Review, 4,* 507–535.

MELTON, G. B., LEVINE, R. J., KOOCHER, G. P., ROSENTHAL, R., & THOMPSON, W. C. (1988). Community consultation in socially sensitive research: Lessons from clinical trials of treatments for AIDS. *American Psychologist, 43,* 573–581.

MELTZER, B. N., PETRAS, J. W., & REYNOLDS, L. T. (1975). *Symbolic interactionism: Genesis, varieties, and criticism.* London: Routledge and Kegan Paul.

MEMERING, D. (1989). *The Prentice Hall guide to research writing.* Englewood Cliffs, NJ: Prentice Hall.

MEYER, G. E. (1993). *SPSS: A minimalist approach.* Fort Worth: Harcourt Brace Jovanovich.

MICHELL, J. (1986). Measurement scales and statistics: A clash of paradigms. *Psychological Bulletin, 100,* 398–407.

MILLER, D. C. (1991). *Handbook of research design and social measurement.* Newbury Park, CA: Sage.

MILLER, D. J., & HERSEN, M. (Eds.). (1992). *Research fraud in the behavioral and biomedical sciences.* New York: John Wiley.

MILLER, N. (1980). Making school desegregation work. In W. G. Stephan & J. R. Feagin (Eds.), *School desegregation: Past, present, and future.* New York: Plenum Press.

MISHRA, S. I., DOOLEY, D., CATALANO, R., & SERXNER, S. (1993). Telephone health surveys: Potential bias from noncompletion. *American Journal of Public Health, 83,* 94–99.

MITCHELL, J. V., JR. (1985). *The ninth mental measurements yearbook.* Lincoln, NE: The Buros Institute of Mental Measurements.

MITCHELL, S. K. (1979). Interobserver agreement, reliability, and generalizability of data collected in observational studies. *Psychological Bulletin, 86,* 376–390.

MONTALBANO, W. D. (1992, November 1). Earth moves for the Vatican in Galileo case. *Los Angeles Times,* p. A8.

MOOS, R. H., & VAN DORT, B. (1979). Student physical symptoms and the social climate of college living groups. *American Journal of Community Psychology, 7,* 31–43.

MORENO, J. L. (Ed.). (1960). *The sociometry reader.* New York: Free Press.

MORRIS, R. J., & SUCKERMAN, K. R. (1974). Therapist warmth as a factor in automated systematic desensitization. *Journal of Consulting and Clinical Psychology, 42,* 244–250.

MORRISON, D. E., & HENKEL, R. E. (Eds.). (1970). *The significance test controversy: A reader.* Chicago: Aldine.

MURDOCK, G. P. (1971). *Outline of cultural materials.* New Haven: Human Relations Area Files.

NAGEL, S. S., & NEEF, M. (1977). Determining an optimum level of statistical significance. In M. Guttentag (Ed.), *Evaluation studies review annual* (Vol. 2). Beverly Hills: Sage.

NAIRN, A. (1980). *The reign of the ETS: The corporation that makes up minds.* Washington, DC: Ralph Nader.

NATIONAL COMMISSION ON EMPLOYMENT AND UNEMPLOYMENT STATISTICS. (1979). *Counting the labor force.* Washington, DC: U.S. Government Printing Office.

NEDERHOF, A. J. (1985). A comparison of European and North American response patterns in mail surveys. *Journal of the Market Research Society, 27,* 55–63.

NEEDLEMAN HEARING BOARD. (1992). *Needleman Hearing Board Final Report.* Pittsburgh: University of Pittsburgh.

NEEDLEMAN, H. L. (1992). Salem comes to the National Institutes of Health: Notes from inside the crucible of scientific integrity. *Pediatrics, 90,* 977–981.

_____. (1993a). A reply to Scarr and Ernhart. *Pediatrics, 91,* 519–521.

_____. (1993b). Reply to Ernhart, Scarr, and Geneson. *Ethics and Behavior, 3,* 95–101.

NEEDLEMAN, H. L., GUNNOE, C., LEVITON, A., REED, R., PERESIE, H., MAHER, C., & BARRETT, B. S. (1979). Deficits in psychologic and classroom performance of children with elevated dentine lead levels. *New England Journal of Medicine, 300,* 689–695.

NELKIN, D. (1979). Scientific knowledge, public policy, and democracy. *Knowledge: Creation, Diffusion, Utilization, 1,* 106–122.

NESSELROADE, J. R., STIGLER, S. M., & BALTES, P. B. (1980). Regression toward the mean and the study of change. *Psychological Bulletin, 88,* 622–637.

NETTLER, G. (1959). Test burning in Texas. *American Psychologist, 14,* 682–683.

NEUBECK, K. J., & ROACH, J. L. (1981). Income maintenance experiments, politics, and the perpetuation of poverty. *Social Problems, 28,* 308–320.

NUNNALLY, J. C. (1978). *Psychometric theory.* New York: McGraw-Hill.

O'NEIL, M. J. (1979). Estimating the nonresponse bias due to refusals in telephone surveys. *Public Opinion Quarterly, 43,* 218–232.

ORNE, M. T. (1962). On the social psychology of the psychological experiment: With particular reference to demand characteristics and their implications. *American Psychologist, 17,* 776–783.

_____. (1969). Demand characteristics and the concept of quasi-controls. In R. Rosenthal & R. L. Rosnow (Eds.), *Artifact in behavioral research* (pp. 143–179). New York: Academic Press.

ORNE, M. T., SHEEHAN, P. W., & EVANS, F. J. (1968). Occurrence of posthypnotic behavior outside the experimental setting. *Journal of Personality and Social Psychology, 9,* 189–196.

ORWIN, R. G., & CORDRAY, D. S. (1985). Effects of deficient reporting on meta-analysis: A conceptual framework and reanalysis. *Psychological Bulletin, 97,* 134–147.

OSMOND, H., & SMYTHIES, J. R. (1952). Schizophrenia: A new approach. *Journal of Mental Science, 98,* 309–315.

PALIT, C., & SHARP, H. (1983). Microcomputer-assisted telephone interviewing. *Sociological Methods and Research, 12,* 169–189.

PATTERSON, M. L. (1976). An arousal model of interpersonal intimacy. *Psychological Review, 85,* 235–245.

PATTON, M. Q. (1980). *Qualitative evaluation methods.* Beverly Hills: Sage.

_____. (1990). *Qualitative evaluation and research methods.* Newbury Park, CA: Sage.

PAYNE, J. S., MERCER, D. C., PAYNE, R. A., & DAVISON, R. G. (1973). *Head Start: A tragi-comedy with epilogue.* New York: Behavioral Publications.

PENDERY, M. L., MALTZMAN, I. M., & WEST, L. J. (1982). Controlled drinking by alcoholics? New findings and a reevaluation of a major affirmative study. *Science, 217,* 169–174.

PETTIGREW, T. F., & GREEN, R. L. (1976). School desegregation in large cities: A critique of the Coleman "white flight" thesis. *Harvard Educational Review, 46,* 1–52.

PETTIGREW, T. F., USEEM, E. L., NORMAND, C., & SMITH, M. (1973). Busing: A review of "the evidence." *Public Interest, 30,* 88–118.

PHILLIPS, D. P. (1979). Suicide, motor vehicle fatalities, and the mass media: Evidence toward a theory of suggestion. *American Journal of Sociology, 84,* 1150–1174.

PLATT, J. R. (1964). Strong inference. *Science, 146,* 36–42.

POPPER, K. (1987). Science: Conjectures and refutations. In J. A. Kourany (Ed.), *Scientific knowledge: Basic issues in the philosophy of science* (pp. 139–157). Belmont, CA: Wadsworth.

POUPARD, P. (Ed.). (1983). *Galileo Galilei: Toward a resolution of 350 years of debate—1633–1983* (I. Campbell, Trans.). Pittsburgh: Duquesne University Press.

POWELL, L. H. (1987). Issues in the measurement of the Type A Behaviour Pattern. In S. V. Kasl & C. L. Cooper (Eds.), *Stress and health: Issues in research methodology* (pp. 231–282). London: John Wiley.

RAFFEL, J. A. (1985). The impact of metropolitan school desegregation on public opinion: A longitudinal analysis. *Urban Affairs Quarterly, 21,* 245–265.

RAPPAPORT, J., CHINSKY, J. M., & COWEN, E. L. (1971). *Innovations in helping chronic patients: College students in a mental institution.* New York: Academic Press.

RAVITCH, D. (1978). The "white flight" controversy. *Public Interest, 51,* 135–149.

REDONDI, P. (1987). *Galileo heretic* (R. Rosenthal, Trans.). Princeton, NJ: Princeton University Press. (Original work published 1983.)

REED, J. G., & BAXTER, P. M. (1992). *Library use: A handbook for psychology.* Washington, DC: American Psychological Association.

REYNOLDS, P. D. (1979). *Ethical dilemmas and social science research.* San Francisco: Jossey-Bass.

_____. (1982). *Ethics and social science research.* Englewood Cliffs, NJ: Prentice-Hall.

RICH, C. L. (1977). Is random digit dialing really necessary? *Journal of Marketing Research, 14,* 300–305.

RIST, R. C. (1970). Student social class and teacher expectations: The self-fulfilling prophecy in ghetto education. *Harvard Educational Review, 40,* 411–451.

ROBINS, P. K., SPIEGELMAN, R. G., WEINER, S., & BELL, J. G. (Eds.). (1980). *A guaranteed annual income: Evidence from a social experiment.* New York: Academic Press.

ROBINSON, J. P., Athanasiou, R., & Head, K. B. (1969). *Measures of occupational attitudes and occupational characteristics.* Ann Arbor, MI: University of Michigan Press.

ROBINSON, J. P., RUSK, J. G., & HEAD, K. B. (1968). *Measures of political attitudes.* Ann Arbor, MI: University of Michigan Press.

ROBINSON, J. P., & SHAVER, P. R. (1973). *Measures of social psychological attitudes.* Ann Arbor, MI: University of Michigan Press.

ROBINSON, J. P., SHAVER, P. R., & WRIGHTSMAN, L. S. (1991). *Measures of personality and social psychological attitudes.* San Diego: Academic Press.

ROBINSON, W. S. (1950). Ecological correlations and the behavior of individuals. *American Sociological Review, 15,* 351–357.

ROESCH, R., GOLDING, S. L., HANS, V. P., & REPPUCCI,

N. D. (1991). Social science and the courts: The role of Amicus Curiae Briefs. *Law and Human Behavior, 15*, 1–11.

ROETHLISBERGER, F. J., & DICKSON, W. J. (1939). *Management and the worker*. New York: John Wiley.

ROGERS, C. R. (1957). The necessary and sufficient conditions of therapeutic personality change. *Journal of Consulting Psychology, 21*, 95–103.

ROGERS, T. F. (1976). Interviews by telephone and in person: Quality of responses and field performance. *Public Opinion Quarterly, 40*, 51–65.

RORER, L. G. (1965). The great response-style myth. *Psychological Bulletin, 63*, 129–156.

ROSENBERG, M. J. (1969). The conditions and consequences of evaluation research. In R. Rosenthal & R. L. Rosnow (Eds.), *Artifact in behavioral research* (pp. 279–349). New York: Academic Press.

ROSENTHAL, R. (1976). *Experimenter effects in behavioral research*. New York: Irvington.

_____. (1978). Combining results of independent studies. *Psychological Bulletin, 85*, 185–193.

_____. (1979). The "file drawer problem" and tolerance for null results. *Psychological Bulletin, 86*, 638–641.

ROSENTHAL, R., BLANCK, P. D., & VANNICELLI, M. (1984). Speaking to and about patients: Predicting therapists' tone of voice. *Journal of Consulting and Clinical Psychology, 52*, 679–686.

ROSENTHAL, R., & JACOBSON, L. (1968). *Pygmalion in the classroom*. New York: Holt, Rinehart and Winston.

ROSENTHAL, R., & ROSNOW, R. L. (1969). The volunteer subject. In R. Rosenthal & R. L. Rosnow (Eds.), *Artifact in behavioral research* (pp. 139–155). New York: Academic Press.

ROSENTHAL, R., & RUBIN, D. B. (1971). Pygmalion reaffirmed. In J. D. Elashoff & R. E. Snow (Eds.), *Pygmalion reconsidered* (pp. 139–155). Worthington, OH: Charles A. Jones.

_____. (1978). Interpersonal expectancy effects: The first 345 studies. *The Behavioral and Brain Sciences, 3*, 377–415.

_____. (1982). A simple, general purpose display of magnitude of experimental effect. *Journal of Educational Psychology, 74*, 166–169.

ROSNOW, R.L., & ROSENTHAL, R. (1989). Statistical procedures and the justification of knowledge in psychological science. *American Psychologist, 44*, 1276–1284.

ROSNOW, R. L., ROTHERAM-BORUS, M. J., CECI, S. J., BLANCK, P. D., & KOOCHER, G. P. (1993). The Institutional Review Board as a mirror of scientific and ethical standards. *American Psychologist, 48*, 821–826.

ROSS, S., & BUCKALEW, L. W. (1983). The placebo as an agent in behavioral manipulation: A review of problems, issues, and affected measures. *Clinical Psychology Review, 3*, 457–471.

ROSS, S., KRUGMAN, A. D., LYERLY, S. B., & CLYDE, D. J. (1962). Drugs and placebos: A model design. *Psychological Reports, 10*, 383–392.

ROSSELL, C. H. (1975–1976). School desegregation and white flight. *Political Science Quarterly, 90*, 675–695.

ROSSI, P. H. (1978). Issues in the evaluation of human service delivery. *Evaluation Quarterly, 2*, 573–599.

ROSSI, P. H., & FREEMAN, H. E. (1993). *Evaluation: A systematic approach*. Newbury Park, CA: Sage.

ROSSI, P. H., WRIGHT, J. D., & WRIGHT, S. R. (1978). The theory and practice of applied social research. *Evaluation Quarterly, 2*, 171–191.

ROTH, D. L., & HOLMES, D. S. (1985). Influence of physical fitness in determining the impact of stressful life events on physical and psychological health. *Psychosomatic Medicine, 47*, 164–173.

ROTH, P. A. (1987). *Meaning and method in the social sciences: A case for methodological pluralism*. Ithaca, NY: Cornell University Press.

ROTTER, J. (1966). Generalized expectancies for internal versus external control of reinforcement. *Psychological Monographs, 80* (1, Whole no. 609).

ROZENSKY, R. H., & HONOR, L. F. (1982). Notation systems for coding nonverbal behavior: A review. *Journal of Behavioral Assessment, 4*, 119–132.

RUBACK, R. B., & INNES, C. A. (1988). The relevance and irrelevance of psychological research: The example of prison crowding. *American Psychologist, 43*, 683–693.

RUBIN, Z. (1975). Disclosing oneself to a stranger: Reciprocity and its limits. *Journal of Experimental Social Psychology, 11*, 233–260.

RUSSELL, B. (1945). *A history of Western philosophy*. New York: Simon & Schuster.

_____. (1948). *Human knowledge: Its scope and limits*. New York: Simon & Schuster.

RUSSELL, D., PEPLAU, L. A., & CUTRONA, L. E. (1980). The revised UCLA Loneliness Scale: Concurrent and discriminant validity evidence. *Journal of Personality and Social Psychology, 39*, 472–480.

SANDERS, J. R., & KEITH-SPIEGEL, P. (1980). Formal and informal adjudication of ethics complaints about psychologists. *American Psychologist, 35*, 1096–1105.

SARASON, S. B. (1981). *Psychology misdirected*. New York: Free Press.

SCARCE RELEASED FROM JAIL. (1993), November). *Footnotes, 21*(8), 2.

SCARCE REMAINS JAILED; ASA COUNCIL ADVOCATES FOR RESEARCHER'S PRIVILEGE. (1993, October). *Footnotes, 21*(7), 1–2.

SCARR, S., & ERNHART, C. B. (1993). Of whistleblowers, investigators, and judges. *Ethics and Behavior, 3*, 199–206.

SCARR, S., & WEINBERG, R. A. (1976). IQ test performance of black children adopted by white families. *American Psychologist, 31*, 726–739.

SCHAIE, K. W. (1965). A general model for the study of developmental problems. *Psychological Bulletin, 64*, 92–107.

SCHEIRER, M. A. (1978). Program participants' positive perceptions: Psychological conflict of interest in social program evaluation. *Evaluation Quarterly, 2*, 53–70.

SCHERER, K., & EKMAN, P. (Eds.). (1982). *Handbook of methods in nonverbal behavior research*. Cambridge: Cambridge University Press.

SCHERVITZ, L., BERTON, K., & LEVENTHAL, H. (1977).

Type A assessment and interaction in the behavior pattern interview. *Psychosomatic Medicine, 39,* 229–240.

SCHMIDT, F. L. (1992). What do data really mean? Research findings, meta-analysis, and cumulative knowledge in psychology. *American Psychologist, 47,* 1173–1181.

SCHRAGER, R. H. (1986). The impact of living group social climate on student academic performance. *Research in Higher Education, 25,* 265–276.

SCHROEDER, L. D., SJOQUIST, D. L., & STEPHAN, P. E. (1986). *Understanding regression analysis: An introductory guide.* Beverly Hills: Sage.

SCHUMAN, H., PRESSER, S., & LUDWIG, J. (1981). Context effects on survey responses to questions about abortion. *Public Opinion Quarterly, 45,* 216–223.

SCHWARTZ, H., & JACOBS, J. (1979). *Qualitative sociology: A method to the madness.* New York: Free Press.

SCHWEINHART, L. J., & WEIKART, D. P. (1980). *Young children grow up: The effects of the Perry Preschool Program on youths through age 15.* Ypsilanti, MI: High/Scope Press.

SCRIVEN, M. (1972). Pros and cons about goal-free evaluation. *Evaluation Comment, 3,* 1–4.

SEDLMEIER, P., & GIGERENZER, G. (1989). Do studies of statistical power have an effect on the power of studies? *Psychological Bulletin, 105,* 309–316.

SENATE ACTION. (1991, September). *Footnotes, 19* (7), 1, 12.

SEWELL, W. H., & SHAH, V. P. (1967). Socioeconomic status, intelligence, and the attainment of higher education. *Sociology of Education, 40,* 1–23.

SHAVELSON, R. J., & WEBB, N. M. (1991). *Generalizability theory: A primer.* Newbury Park, CA: Sage.

SHOGREN, E. (1993, May 26). Sex bias in scholarship test charged. *Los Angeles Times,* pp. A3, A20.

SIEBER, J. E., & STANLEY, B. (1988). Ethical and professional dimensions of socially sensitive research. *American Psychologist, 43,* 49–55.

SIEGMAN, A. W., & FELDSTEIN, S. (1987). *Nonverbal behavior and communication.* Hillsdale, NJ: Lawrence Erlbaum.

SILVERMAN, I. (1977). *The human subject in the psychological laboratory.* Elmsford, N.Y.: Pergamon Press.

SINGER, H., GERARD, H. B., & REDFEARN, D. (1975). Achievement. In H. B. Gerard & N. Miller (Eds.), *School desegregation: A longitudinal study.* New York: Plenum Press.

SMART, B. (1976). *Sociology, phenomenology, and Marxian analysis: A critical discussion of the theory and practice of a science of society.* London: Routledge and Kegan Paul.

SMITH, M. L., & GLASS, G. V. (1977). Meta-analysis of psychotherapy outcome studies. *American Psychologist, 32,* 752–760.

SMITH, M. S., & BISSELL, J. S. (1970). Report analysis: The impact of Head Start. *Harvard Educational Review, 40,* 51–104.

SMITH, T. W. (1987). That which we call welfare by any other name would smell sweeter: An analysis of the impact of question wording on response patterns. *Public Opinion Quarterly, 51,* 75–83.

SNYDER, S. H. (1974). *Madness and the brain.* New York: McGraw-Hill.

Sociological Methods and Research. (1977, November). (Special issue) *6*(2).

SOMMER, R., & SOMMER, B. A. (1983). Mystery in Milwaukee: Early intervention, IQ, and psychology textbooks. *American Psychologist, 38,* 982–985.

SPITZ, H. H. (1993). Were children randomly assigned in the Perry Preschool Project? *American Psychologist, 48,* 915.

SROLE, L. (1975). Measurement and classification in sociopsychiatric epidemiology: Midtown Manhattan Study (1954) and Midtown Manhattan Restudy (1974). *Journal of Health and Social Behavior, 16,* 347–364.

SROLE, L., LANGNER, T. S., MICHAEL, S. T., OPLER, M. K., & RENNIE, T. A. C. (1962). *Mental health and the metropolis: The Midtown Manhattan Study* (Vol. 1). New York: McGraw-Hill.

STELZL, I. (1986). Changing a causal hypothesis without changing the fit: Some rules for generating equivalent path models. *Multivariate Behavioral Research, 21,* 309–331.

STOKOLS, D., NOVACO, R. W., STOKOLS, J., & CAMPBELL, J. (1978). Traffic congestion, Type A behavior, and stress. *Journal of Applied Psychology, 63,* 467–480.

STOUT, C. C., THORNTON, B., & RUSSELL, H. L. (1980). Effect of relaxation training on students' persistence and academic performance. *Psychological Reports, 47,* 189–190.

STOVE, D. C. (1982). *Popper and after: Four modern irrationalists.* New York: Pergamon.

SUDMAN, S. (1976). *Applied sampling.* New York: Academic Press.

———. (1983). Survey research and technological change. *Sociological Methods and Research, 12,* 217–230.

SUDMAN, S., & BRADBURN, N. M. (1982). *Asking questions: A practical guide to questionnaire design.* San Francisco: Jossey-Bass.

SUINN, R. M. (1969). The STABS, a measure of test anxiety for behavior therapy: Normative data. *Behavior Research and Therapy, 7,* 335–339.

SURVEY RESEARCH CENTER. (1976). *Interviewer's manual.* Ann Arbor, MI: Institute for Social Research.

TAUBE, G. (1993). *Bad science: The short life and weird times of cold fusion.* New York: Random House.

TAYLOR, R. (1992, December). Pitt's fuzzy verdict in Needleman case. *Journal of NIH Research, 4,* 44.

THALER, R. E. (1985, May). Fieldnotes case resolved; Scholars' rights supported. *Footnotes,* p. 1.

THOMAS, S. B., & QUINN, S. C. (1991). The Tuskegee Syphilis Study, 1932 to 1972: Implications for HIV education and AIDS risk education programs in the black community. *American Journal of Public Health, 81,* 1498–1505.

THOMPSON, J. J., CHODOSH, J., FRIED, C., GOODMAN, D. S., WAX, M. L., & WILSON, J. O. (1981). Regulations governing research on human subjects: Academic freedom and the institutional review board. *Academic, 67,* 358–370.

THOMPSON, M. S. (1980). *Benefit-cost analysis for program evaluation.* Beverly Hills: Sage.

THOMPSON, M. S., & FORTESS, E. E. (1980). Cost–effectiveness analysis in health program evaluation. *Evaluation Review, 4,* 549–568.

THOMPSON, W. C. (1989). Death qualification after *Wainwright* v. *Witt* and *Lockhart* v. *McCree. Law and Human Behavior, 13,* 185–215.

TINSLEY, H. E. A., & WEISS, D. J. (1975). Interrater reliability and agreement of subjective judgments. *Journal of Counseling Psychology, 22,* 358–376.

TOBIAS, S. (1978). *Overcoming math anxiety.* New York: W. W. Norton.

_____. (1987). *Succeed with math: Every student's guide to conquering math anxiety.* New York: College Entrance Examination Board.

TOUCHETTE, N. (1992, November). Cowering inferno: Clearing the smoke on violence research. *Journal of NIH Research, 4,* 31–33.

TOWNSEND, J. T., & ASHBY, F. G. (1984). Measurement scales and statistics: The misconception misconceived. *Psychological Bulletin, 96,* 394–401.

TRICE, A. D. (1987). Informed consent: IV. The effects of the timing of giving consent on experimental performance. *Journal of General Psychology, 114,* 125–128.

TROLDAHL, V. G., & CARTER, R. E. (1964). Random selection of respondents within households in phone surveys. *Journal of Marketing Research, 1,* 71– 76.

TUCHFARBER, A. J., & KLECKA, W. R. (1976). *Random digit dialing: Lowering the cost of victimization surveys.* Cincinnati: Police Foundation.

TUKEY, J. W. (1977). *Exploratory data analysis.* Reading, MA: Addison-Wesley.

TULL, D. S., & ALBAUM, G. S. (1977). Bias in random digit dialed surveys. *Public Opinion Quarterly, 41,* 389–395.

TURNER, C. W., & SIMONS, L. A. (1974). Effects of subject sophistication and evaluation apprehension on aggressive responses to weapons. *Journal of Personality and Social Psychology, 30,* 341–348.

VAN DER VEN, A. H. G. S., (1980). *Introduction to scaling.* New York: John Wiley.

VEATCH, R. M. (1981). Protecting human subjects: The federal government steps back. *The Hasting Center Report, 11,* 9–12.

VEROFF, J., DOUVAN, E., & KULKA, R. A. (1981). *The inner American: A self portrait from 1957 to 1976.* New York: Basic Books.

Vine, I. (1971). Judgment of direction of gaze: An interpretation of discrepant results. *British Journal of Social and Clinical Psychology, 10,* 320–331.

VOSS, H. L. (1966). Pitfalls in social research: A case study. *The American Sociologist, 1,* 136–140.

WATANABE, T. (1992, October 29). No doomsday "rapture" lifts S. Korean sect. *Los Angeles Times,* pp. A3, 10.

WEBB, E. J., CAMPBELL, D. T., SCHWARTZ, R. D., & SECHREST, L. (1966). *Unobtrusive measures: Nonreactive research in the social sciences.* Skokie, IL: Rand McNally.

WEBER, R. P. (1985). *Basic content analysis.* Beverly Hills, CA: Sage.

WEEKS, M. F., JONES, B. L., FOLSOM, R. E., JR., & BENRUD, C. H. (1980). Optimal times to contact sample households. *Public Opinion Quarterly, 44,* 101–114.

WEIGEL, R. H., & PAPPAS, J. J. (1981). Social science and the press: A case study and its implications. *American Psychologist, 36,* 480–487.

WEIKART, D. P., EPSTEIN, A. S., SCHWEINHART, L., & BOND, J. T. (1978). *The Ypsilanti Preschool Curriculum Demonstration Project: Preschool years and longitudinal results.* Ypsilanti, MI: High/Scope Press.

WEISS, A. T. (1975). The consumer model of assessing community health needs. *Evaluation, 2,* 71–73.

WEISS, C. H., & BUCUVALAS, M. J. (1980). Truth tests and utility tests: Decision-makers' frames of reference for social science research. *American Sociological Review, 45,* 302–313.

WELCH, F. (1987). A reconsideration of the impact of school desegregation programs on public school enrollment of white students, 1968–76. *Sociology of Education, 60,* 215–221.

WERNER, O., & SCHOEPFLE, G. M. (1987a). *Systematic fieldwork, Vol. 1: Foundations of ethnography and interviewing.* Beverly Hills: Sage.

_____. (1987b). *Systematic fieldwork, Vol. 2: Ethnographic analysis and data management.* Beverly Hills: Sage.

WENGER, N. S., GREENBERG, J. M., HILBORNE, L. H., KUSELING, F., MANGOTICH, M., & SHAPIRO, M. F. (1992). Effect of HIV antibody testing and AIDS education on communication about HIV risk and sexual behavior: A randomized, controlled trial in college students. *Annals of Internal Medicine, 117,* 905–911.

WESTINGHOUSE LEARNING CORPORATION & OHIO STATE UNIVERSITY. (1969). *The impact of Head Start: An evaluation of the effects of Head Start on children's cognitive and affective development* (Vols. I and II). Clearinghouse for Federal Scientific and Technical Information, U.S. Department of Commerce, Springfield, Virginia, Order No. PB 184329.

WHEATON, B. (1980). The sociogenesis of psychological disorder. *Journal of Health and Social Behavior, 21,* 100–124.

WILLIAMS, B. (1978). *A sampler on sampling.* New York: John Wiley.

WILLIAMS, W., & EVANS, J. W. (1972). The politics of evaluation: The case of Head Start. In P. H. Rossi & W. Williams (Eds.), *Evaluating social programs: Theory, practice, and politics.* New York: Seminar Press.

WILSON, F. D. (1985). The impact of school desegregation programs on white public-school enrollment, 1968–1976. *Sociology of Education, 58,* 137–153.

_____. (1987). A reply to Finis Welch. *Sociology of Education, 60,* 222–223.

WILSON, W. J. (1987). *The truly disadvantaged: The inner city, the underclass, and public policy.* Chicago: University of Chicago Press.

WOLF, F. M. (1986). *Meta-analysis: Quantitative methods for research synthesis.* Beverly Hills: Sage.

WORD, C. O., ZANNA, M. P., & COOPER, J. (1974). The nonverbal mediation of self-fulfilling prophecies in interracial interaction. *Journal of Experimental Social Psychology, 10,* 109–120.

WYLIE, R. C. (1974). *The self-concept: A review of methodological considerations and measuring instruments.* Lincoln, NE: University of Nebraska Press.

YARNOLD, P. R., & BRYANT, F. B. (1988). A note on measurement issues in Type A research: Let's not throw out the baby with the bath water. *Journal of Personality Assessment, 52,* 410–419.

ZALTMAN, G. (1979). Knowledge utilization as planned social change. *Knowledge: Creation, Diffusion, Utilization, 1,* 82–105.

ZIGLER, E., & MUENCHOW, S. (1992). *Head Start: The inside story of America's most successful educational experiment.* New York: Basic Books.

ZIGLER, E., & WEIKART, D. P. (1993). Reply to Spitz's comments. *American Psychologist, 48,* 915–916.

ZIMBARDO, P. G. (1975). Transforming experimental research into advocacy for social change. In M. Deutsch & H. A. Hornstein (Eds.), *Applying social psychology: Implications for research, practice, and training* (pp. 33–66). Hillsdale, NJ: Lawrence Erlbaum.

ZIMBARDO, P. G., HANEY, C., BANKS, W. C., & JAFFE, D. (1975). The psychology of imprisonment: Privation, power, and pathology. In D. Rosehan & P. London (Eds.), *Theory and research in abnormal psychology.* New York: Holt, Rinehart, and Winston.

Name Index

Adams, J., 127
Agnew, B., 34
Albaum, G. S., 128
Amato, P. R., 183
Ambady, N., 112
Anastasi, A., 103
Andersen, R., 132
Andrews, F. M., 161, 320
Aneshensel, C. S., 242–43, 250
Armor, D. J., 221, 227–30
Ashby, F. G., 319
Asher, H. B., 248
Assael, H., 139
Athanasiou, R., 108
Atkinson, D. R., 162

Babad, E. Y., 197
Babbie, E. R., 134
Bailar, B. A., 133
Bailey, K. D., 93
Bales, J., 32
Bales, R. J., 110
Baltes, P. B., 84, 127
Bane, M. J., 126
Banet, B., 297
Bangert-Drowns, R. L., 289
Banks, W. C., 216
Barber, B., 34
Barker, P., 7
Barnes, S., 30–31
Barnett, W. S., 297, 307
Barrett, B. S., 2

Bartz, W. R., 183
Baum, A., 173
Baumol, W. J., 308
Baumrind, D., 28, 185, 248
Baxter, L. R., 115
Baxter, P. M., 43, 108, 118
Beals, R. L., 35
Becker, H. S., 260, 266–67, 271
Beecher, H. K., 19, 21
Bell, J. G., 305
Bem, D. J., 65
Benrud, C. H., 140
Bentler, P. M., 213, 215, 245, 250
Benveniste, J., 77
Berckmans, T. R., 141
Berelson, B., 111
Bergin, A. E., 202
Berkowitz, L., 208
Bernard, H. R., 268–71
Berrueta-Clement, J. R., 297
Berry, W. D., 244, 335
Bersoff, D. N., 295
Bertera, E. M., 309
Bertera, R. L., 309
Berton, K., 110
Binder, A., 320
Binet, A., 105
Birdwhistell, R. L., 112
Bishop, G. F., 143
Bissell, J. S., 213
Blackmun, H., 10
Blair, E., 141
Blanck, P. D., 30, 197

369

Subject Index

ABAB design, 230
Abstract, 43–47, 55
Abstracting services, 43–47
Accretion trace measures, 115
Achievement tests, 105–6
Adjacencies of ratings, 87
Aggregate-level data, 251–53
Alpha (Type I error in inferential statistics), 155
Alpha coefficient (inter-item reliability measure), 85
Alpha problem, 161
American Anthropological Association ethical principles, 23, 25
American Psychological Association ethical principles, 24–25
American Sociological Association, ethical principles, 26, 35
Analysis of covariance (ANCOVA), 215, 336
Analysis of variance (ANOVA), 336
Applied versus basic research, 296, 298
Aptitude tests, 105–6
Archival records, 116–17
Attenuation, 84
Attrition, 125, 297 (*see also* Mortality)
Authority in causal inference, 4–5
Autocorrelogram, 338
Autonomic system measures, 113–14

Bales Interaction Recorder, 110
Beta (Type II error in inferential statistics), 158
Beta (standardized regression coefficient), 165

Between-subjects design, 172, 183
Bias
  measurement, 79–80
  program impact evaluation, 304–5
  sampling, 123, 131, 134–36
  survey data collection, 123, 132, 140–43
Bivariate association, 245, 326
Black box, 245
Blind design, 197, 200–201
Blocking, 183
Boolean operators, 41, 45–46
Box-Jenkins time series method, 336, 338
Branching questionnaire items, 144
Buffer, 246

Call numbers, 43
Canned experimenter method, 198
Case, 119
Categorical-level variable (*see* Nominal-level variable)
Causal inference
  authority, 4–5
  rules of evidence, 8–9
Causal relationships, 240–41
  descriptive, 240
  direct, 62, 239–40
  indirect, 63, 241, 244–45, 247–48
  interactive, 205, 241, 245–46
  measurement association, 240, 242
  reciprocal, 62, 241, 244
  reverse, 174, 178, 236, 240, 242–43
  spurious (confounded), 236–40, 243–44, 247–48